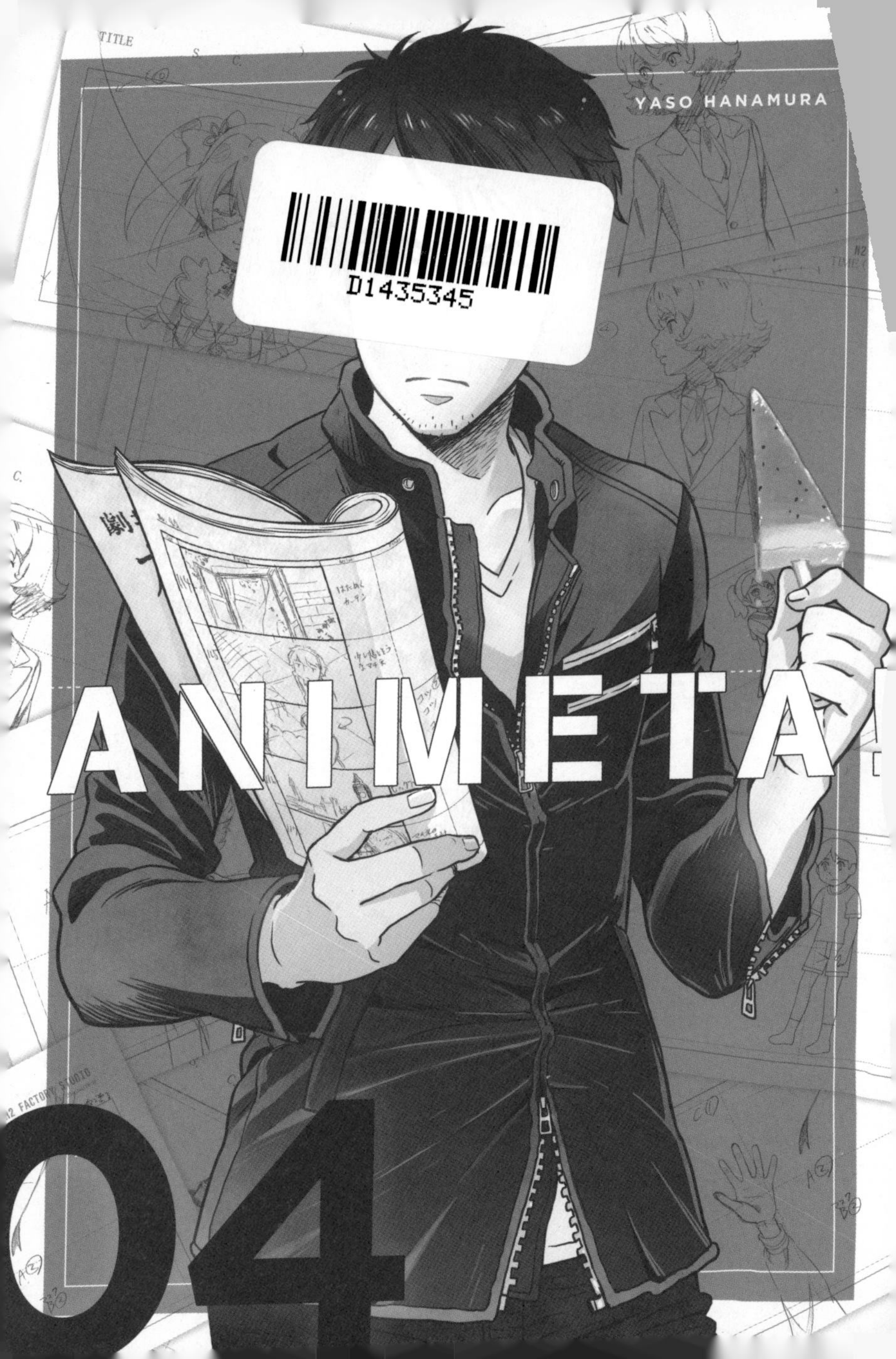
YASO HANAMURA
ANIMETA!
04

ANIMETA!

YASO HANAMURA **04**

CHAPTER 16: IT'S SAD, BUT THAT'S HOW IT IS

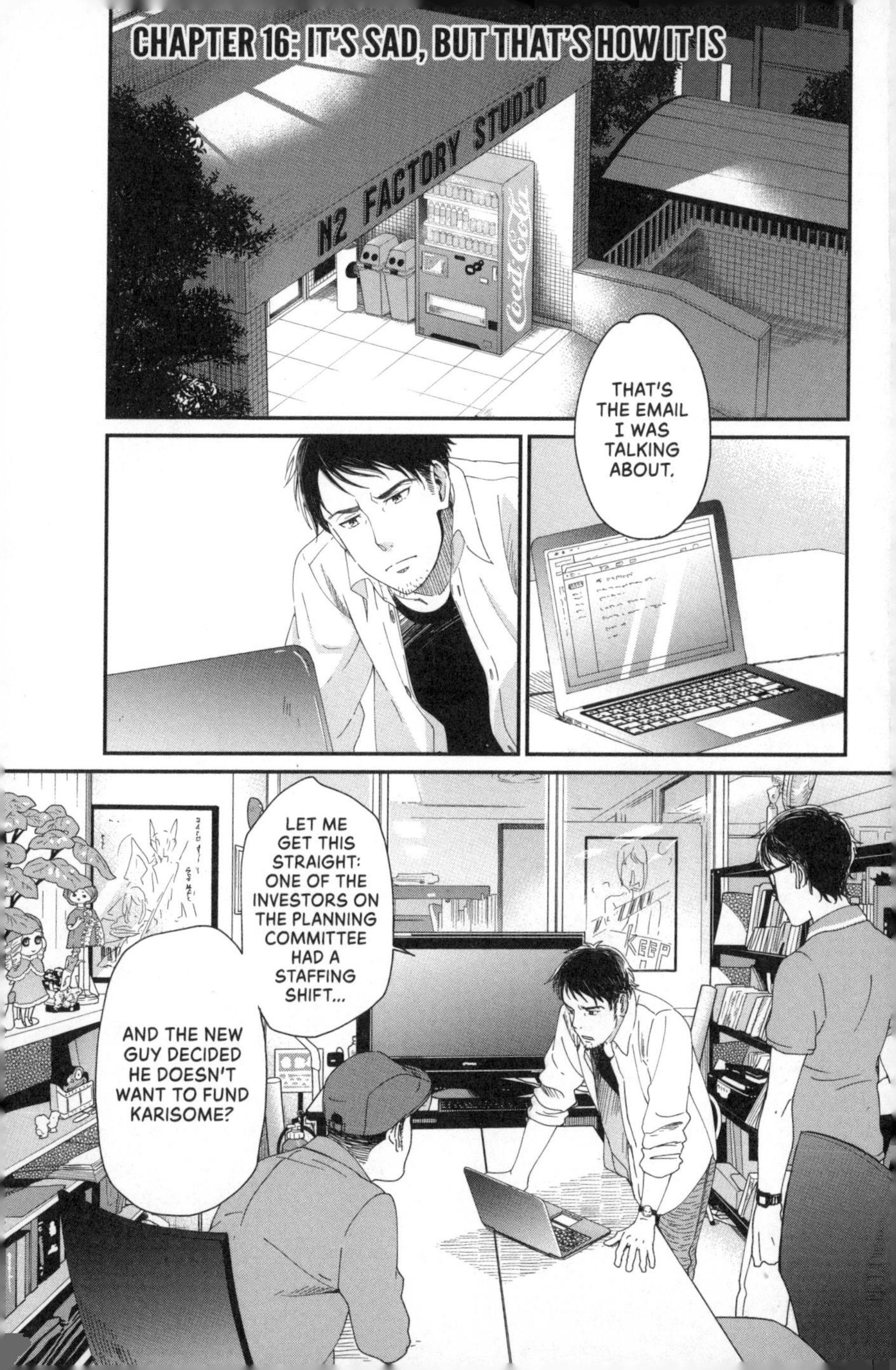
N2 FACTORY STUDIO
Coca-Cola
THAT'S THE EMAIL I WAS TALKING ABOUT.
LET ME GET THIS STRAIGHT: ONE OF THE INVESTORS ON THE PLANNING COMMITTEE HAD A STAFFING SHIFT...
AND THE NEW GUY DECIDED HE DOESN'T WANT TO FUND KARISOME?
KEEP

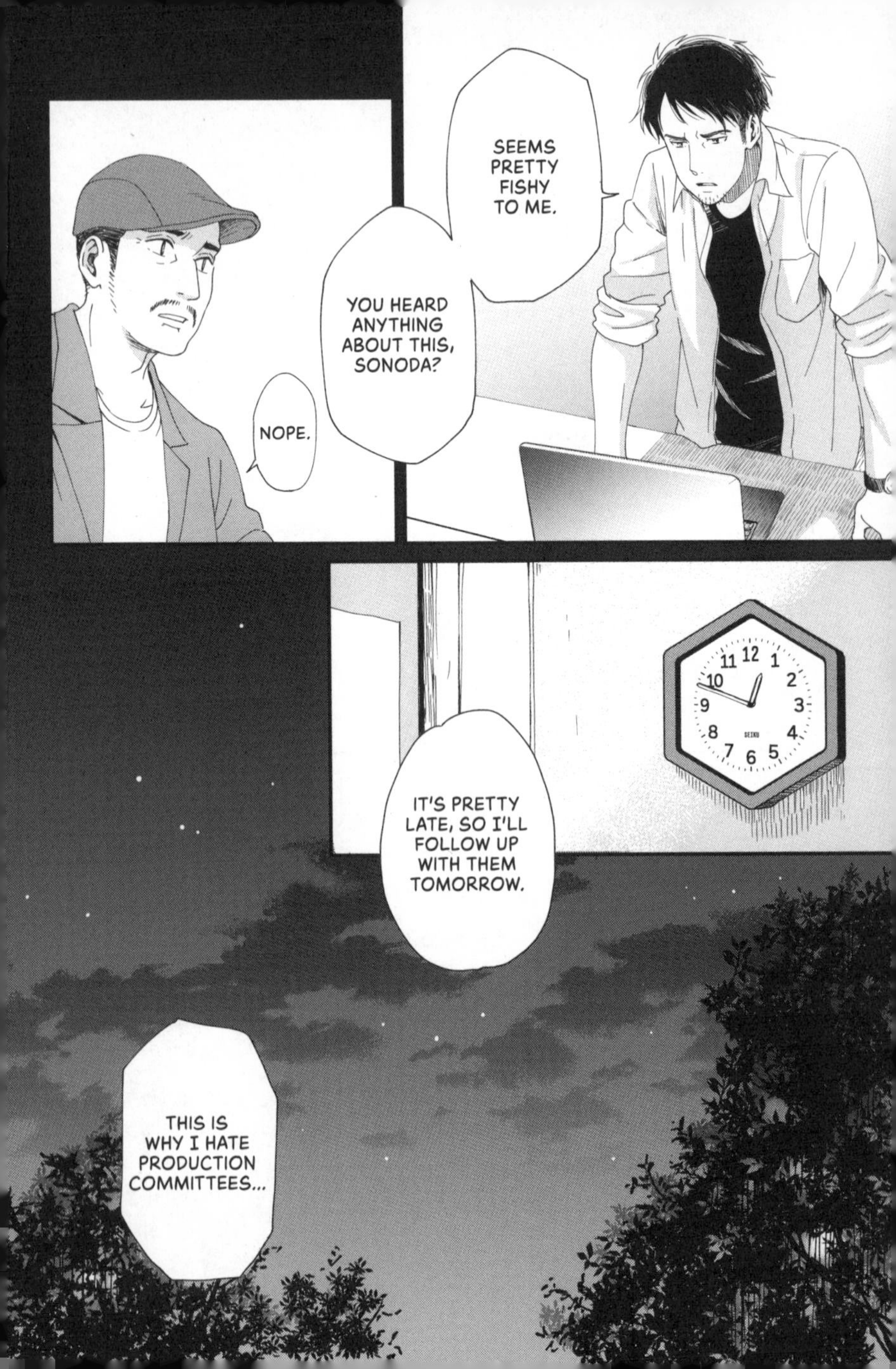
SEEMS PRETTY FISHY TO ME.
YOU HEARD ANYTHING ABOUT THIS, SONODA?
NOPE.
IT'S PRETTY LATE, SO I'LL FOLLOW UP WITH THEM TOMORROW.
THIS IS WHY I HATE PRODUCTION COMMITTEES...

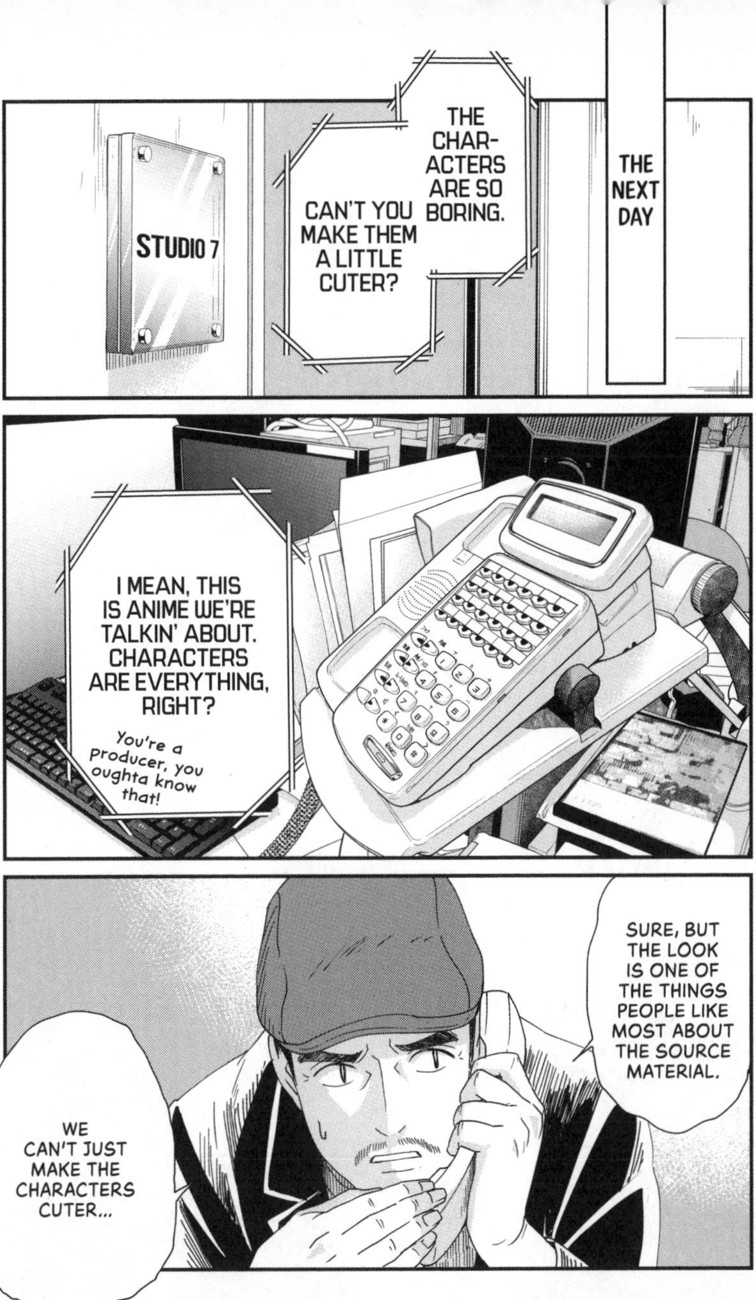
THE NEXT DAY
THE CHAR-ACTERS ARE SO BORING.
CAN'T YOU MAKE THEM A LITTLE CUTER?
STUDIO 7
I MEAN, THIS IS ANIME WE'RE TALKIN' ABOUT. CHARACTERS ARE EVERYTHING, RIGHT?
You're a producer, you oughta know that!
SURE, BUT THE LOOK IS ONE OF THE THINGS PEOPLE LIKE MOST ABOUT THE SOURCE MATERIAL.
WE CAN'T JUST MAKE THE CHARACTERS CUTER...

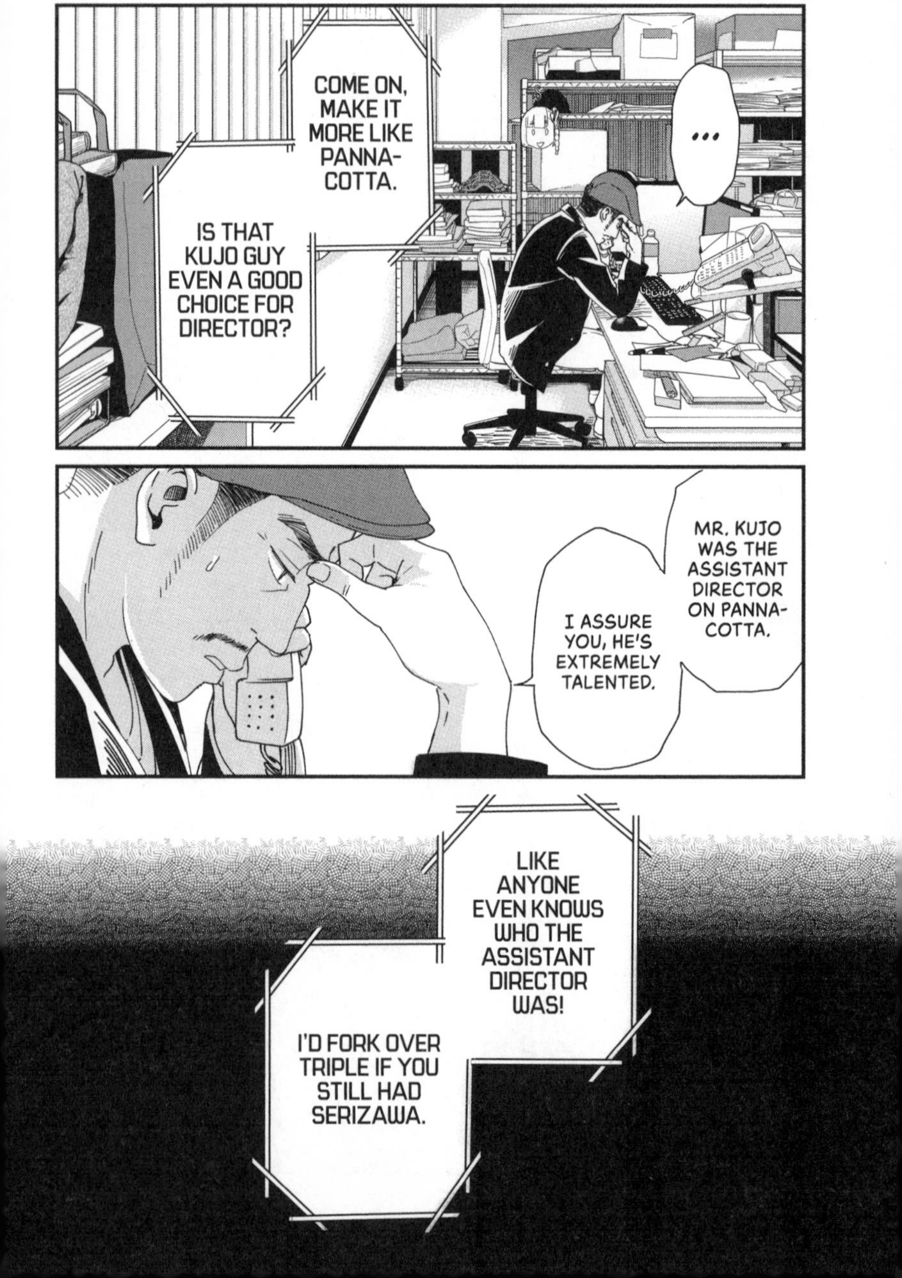
...
COME ON, MAKE IT MORE LIKE PANNA-COTTA.
IS THAT KUJO GUY EVEN A GOOD CHOICE FOR DIRECTOR?
MR. KUJO WAS THE ASSISTANT DIRECTOR ON PANNA-COTTA.
I ASSURE YOU, HE'S EXTREMELY TALENTED.
LIKE ANYONE EVEN KNOWS WHO THE ASSISTANT DIRECTOR WAS!
I'D FORK OVER TRIPLE IF YOU STILL HAD SERIZAWA.

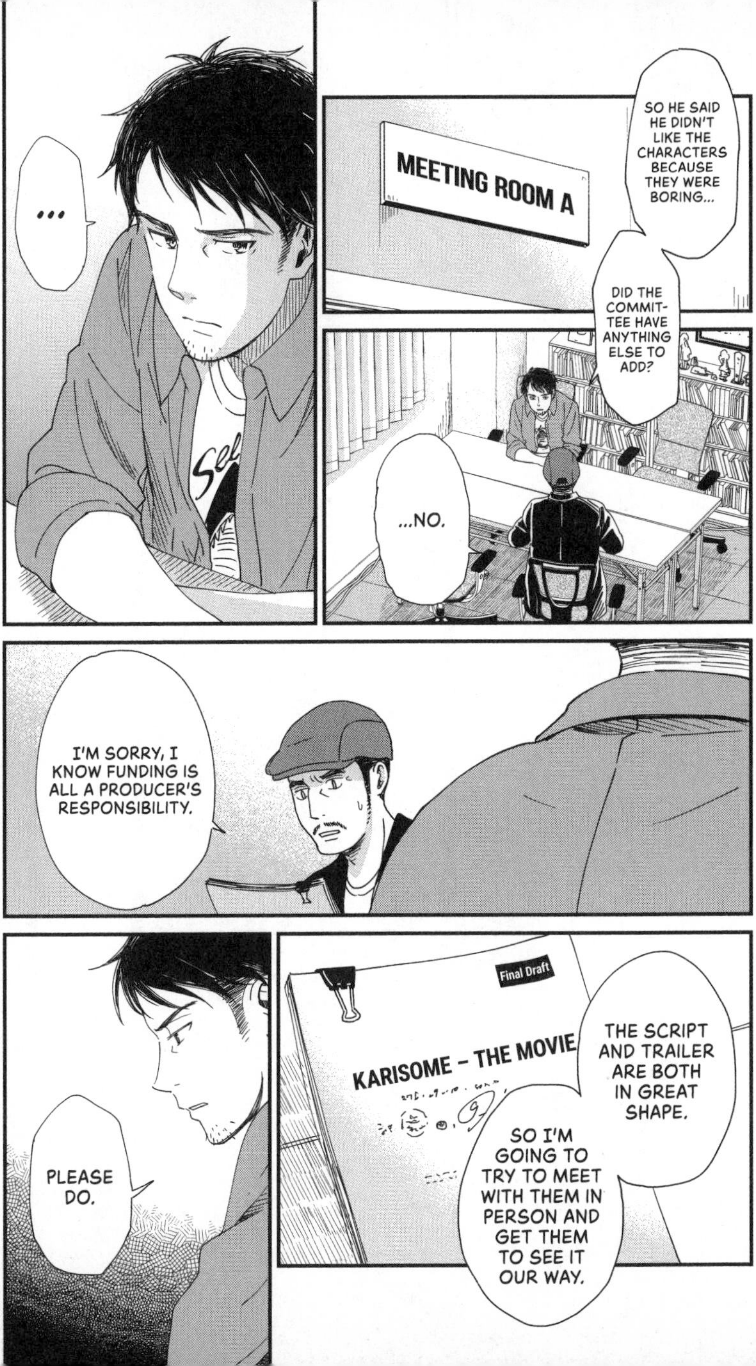
MEETING ROOM A
SO HE SAID HE DIDN'T LIKE THE CHARACTERS BECAUSE THEY WERE BORING...
DID THE COMMIT-TEE HAVE ANYTHING ELSE TO ADD?
...NO.
...
I'M SORRY, I KNOW FUNDING IS ALL A PRODUCER'S RESPONSIBILITY.
Final Draft
KARISOME – THE MOVIE
THE SCRIPT AND TRAILER ARE BOTH IN GREAT SHAPE.
SO I'M GOING TO TRY TO MEET WITH THEM IN PERSON AND GET THEM TO SEE IT OUR WAY.
PLEASE DO.

Production Staff: Encompassing a variety of specific roles, production staff connect the various departments and companies involved in a given production. Responsibilities typically involve things like managing the project's schedule and budget, collecting completed work, and assigning and managing staff.

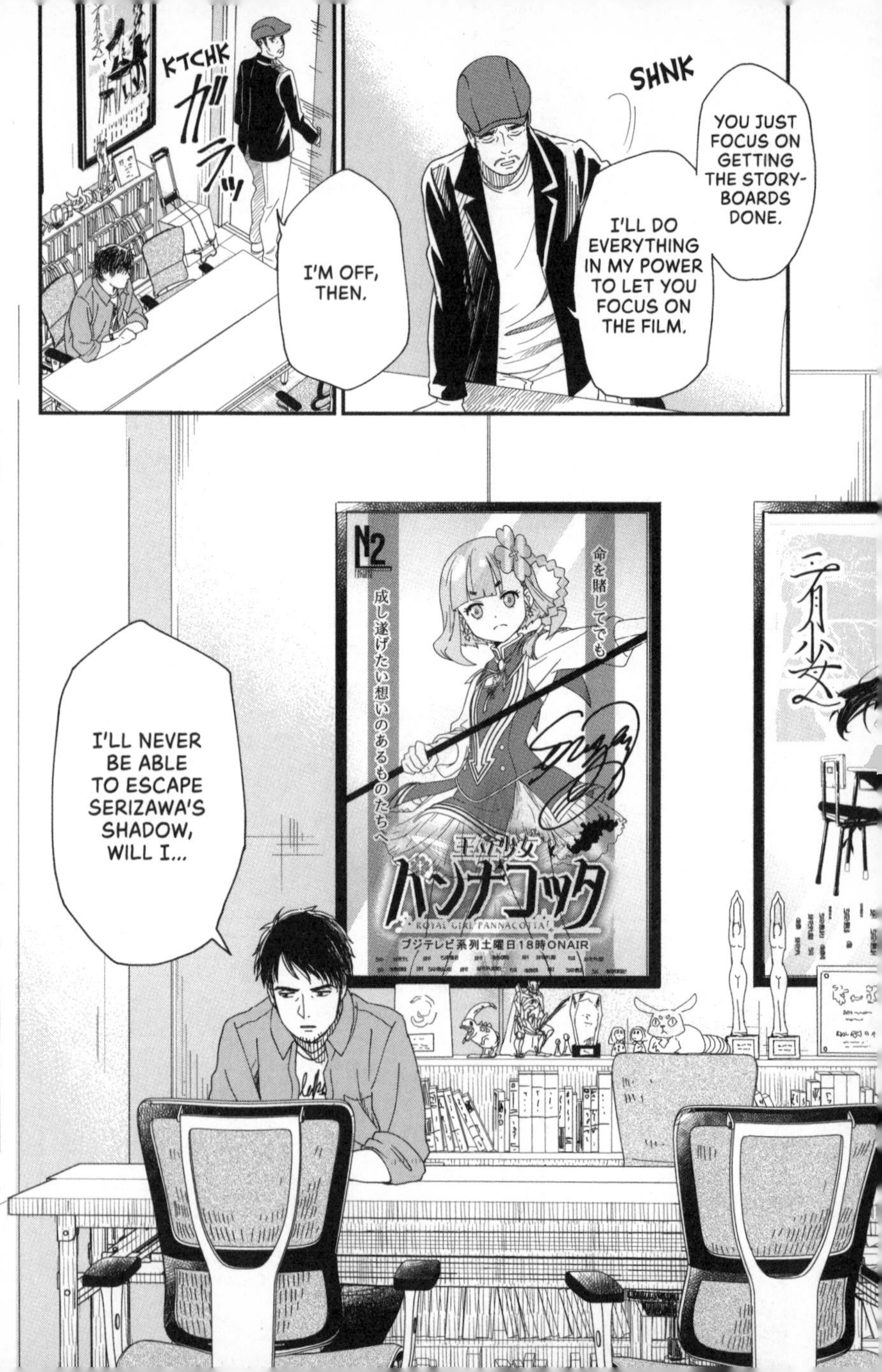
SHNK
YOU JUST FOCUS ON GETTING THE STORY-BOARDS DONE.
I'LL DO EVERYTHING IN MY POWER TO LET YOU FOCUS ON THE FILM.
I'M OFF, THEN.
KTCHK
ガラッ
命を賭してでも
成し遂げたい想いのあるものたちへ
パンナコッタ
ROYAL GIRL PANNACOTTA
ブジテレビ系列土曜日18時ONAIR
I'LL NEVER BE ABLE TO ESCAPE SERIZAWA'S SHADOW, WILL I...

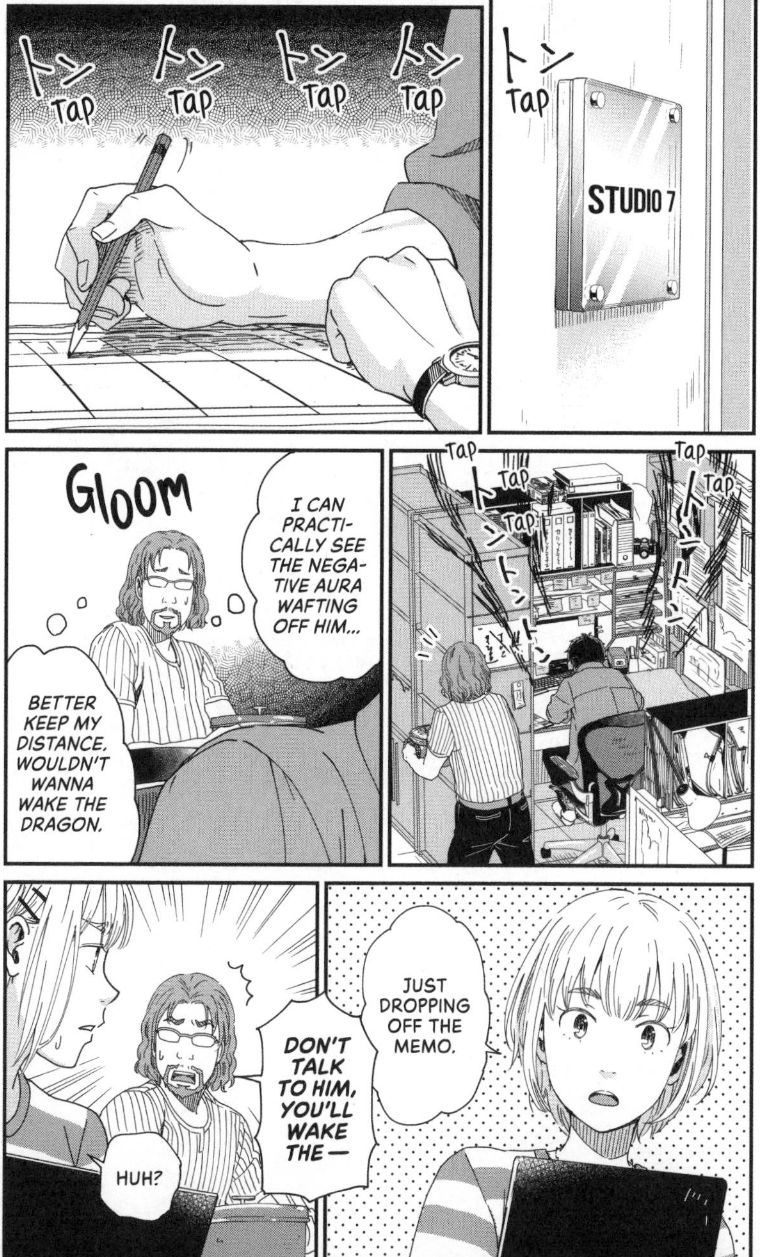
トン
Tap
STUDIO 7
トン
Tap
トン
Tap
トン
Tap
トン
Tap
Tap
Tap
Tap
Tap
Tap
I CAN PRACTICALLY SEE THE NEGATIVE AURA WAFTING OFF HIM...
GLOOM
BETTER KEEP MY DISTANCE. WOULDN'T WANNA WAKE THE DRAGON.
JUST DROPPING OFF THE MEMO.
DON'T TALK TO HIM, YOU'LL WAKE THE—
HUH?

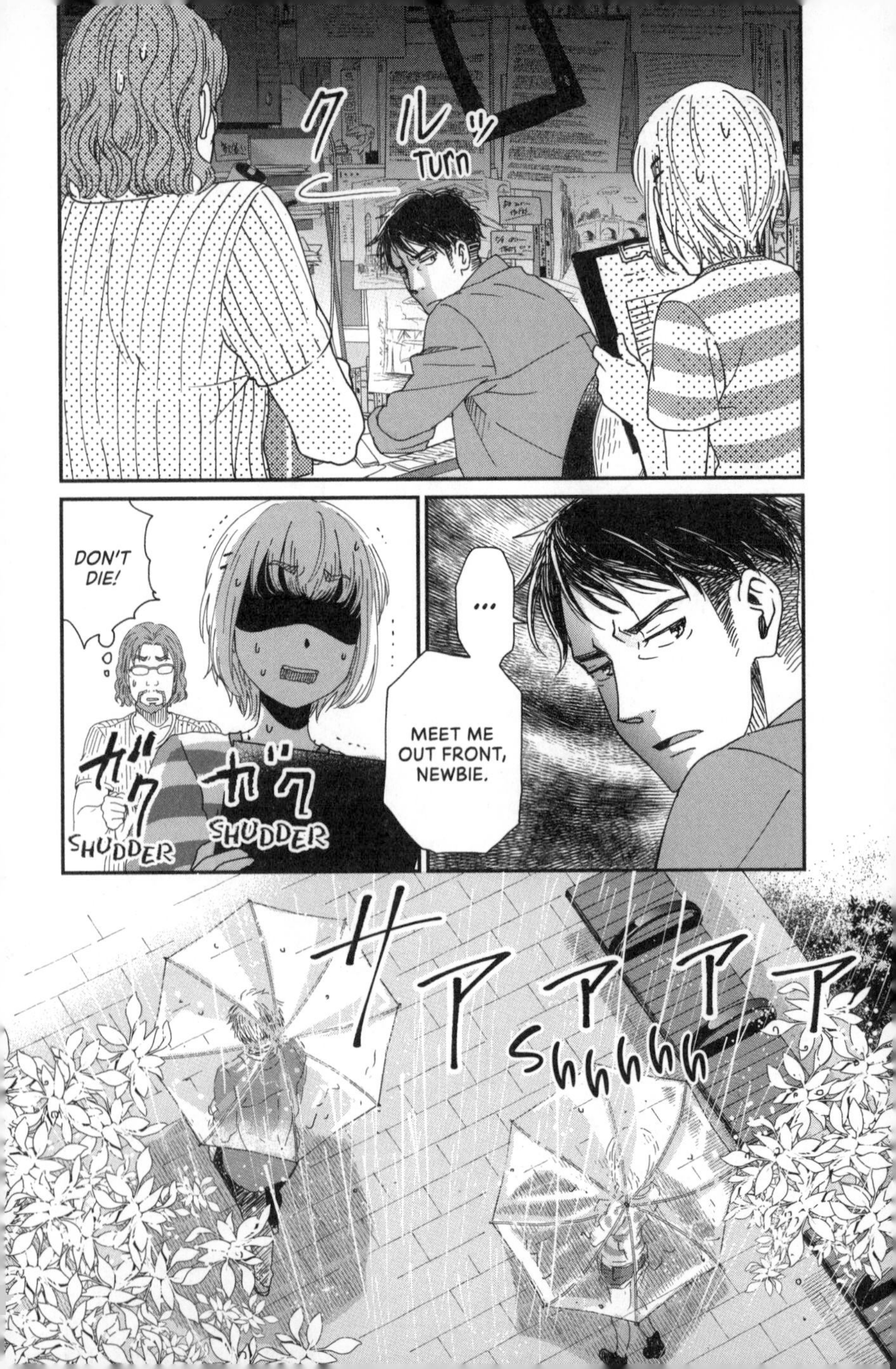
クルッ
Turn
...
MEET ME OUT FRONT, NEWBIE.
DON'T DIE!
ガク
SHUDDER
ガク
SHUDDER
サアアア
Shhhhh

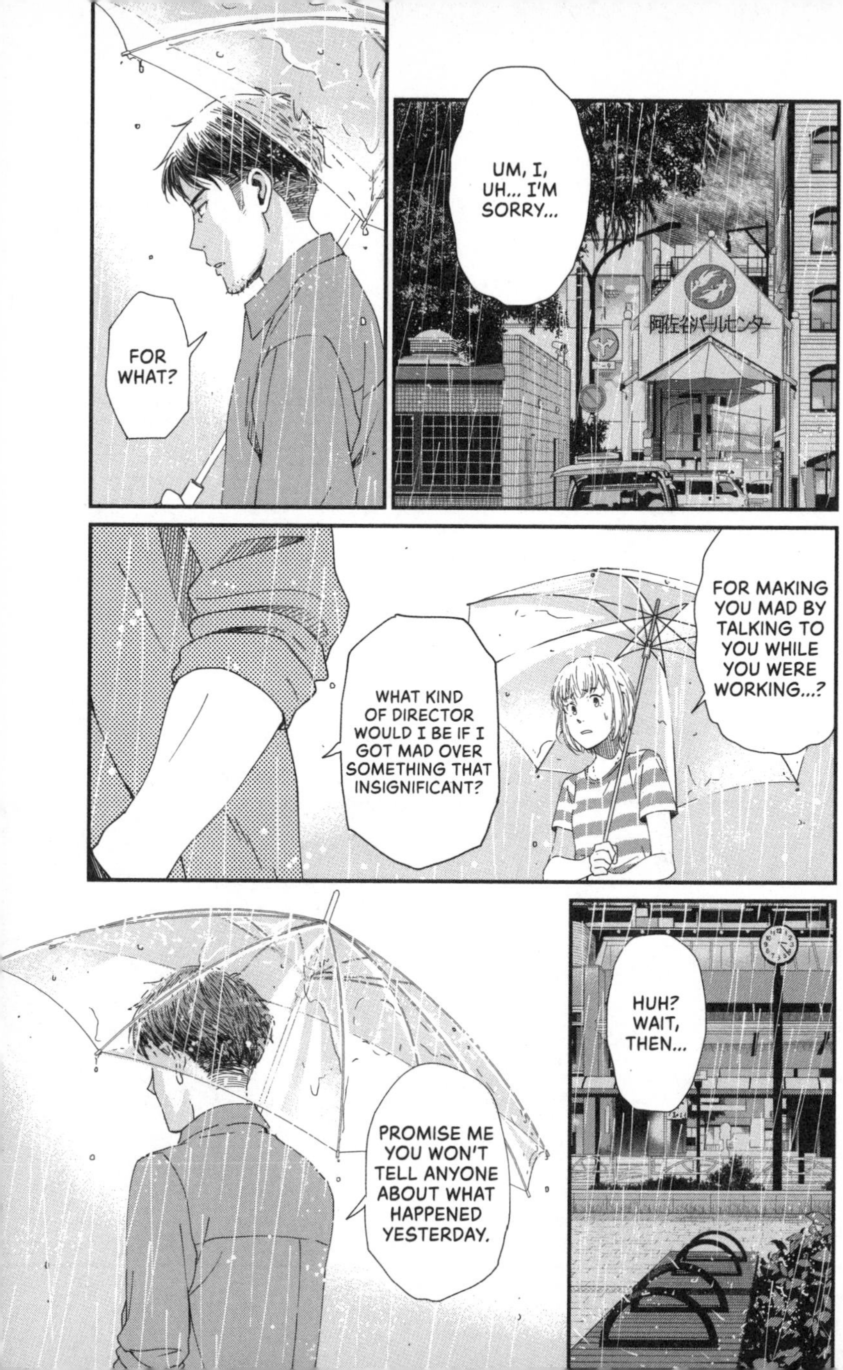
UM, I, UH... I'M SORRY...
阿佐谷パールセンター
FOR WHAT?
FOR MAKING YOU MAD BY TALKING TO YOU WHILE YOU WERE WORKING...?
WHAT KIND OF DIRECTOR WOULD I BE IF I GOT MAD OVER SOMETHING THAT INSIGNIFICANT?
HUH? WAIT, THEN...
PROMISE ME YOU WON'T TELL ANYONE ABOUT WHAT HAPPENED YESTERDAY.

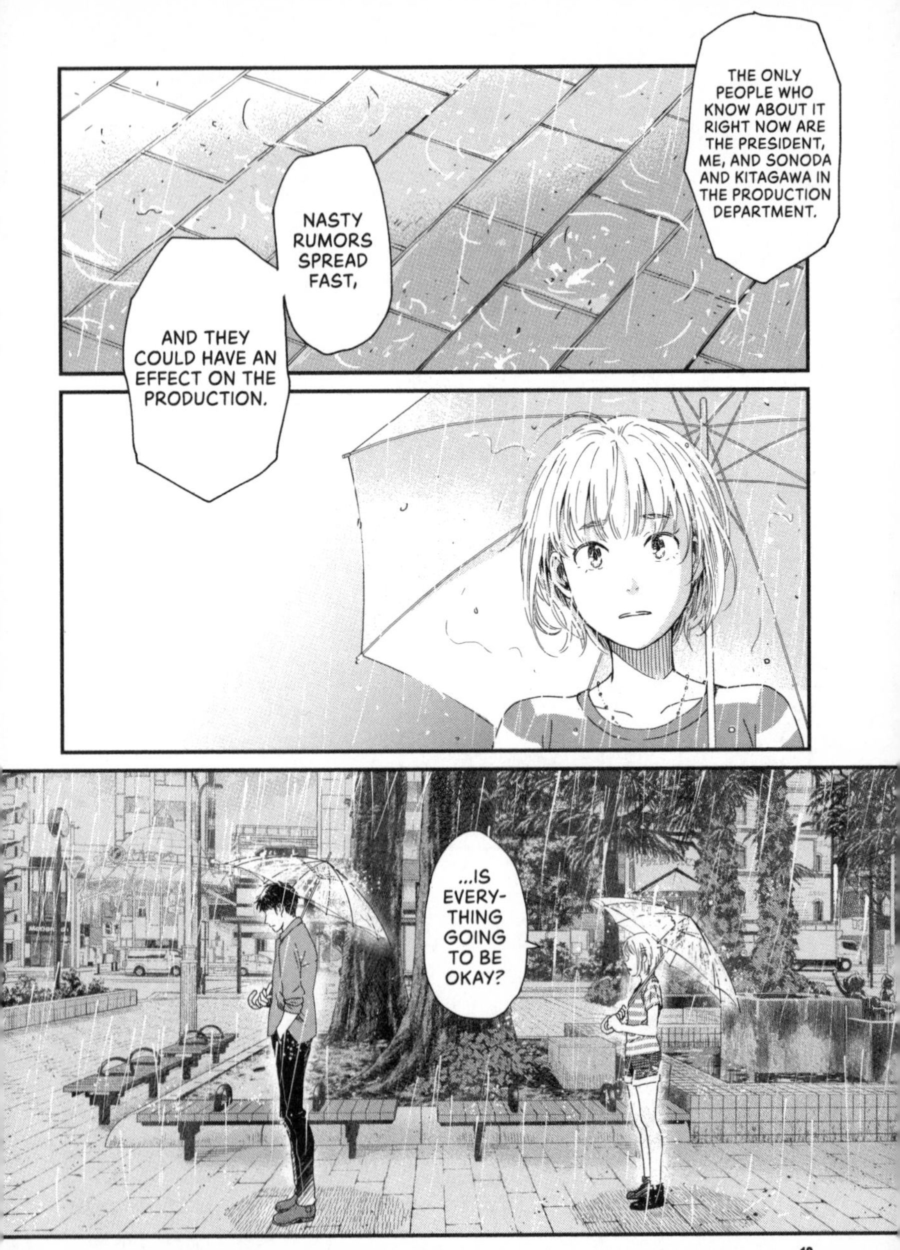
THE ONLY PEOPLE WHO KNOW ABOUT IT RIGHT NOW ARE THE PRESIDENT, ME, AND SONODA AND KITAGAWA IN THE PRODUCTION DEPARTMENT.
NASTY RUMORS SPREAD FAST,
AND THEY COULD HAVE AN EFFECT ON THE PRODUCTION.
...IS EVERY-THING GOING TO BE OKAY?

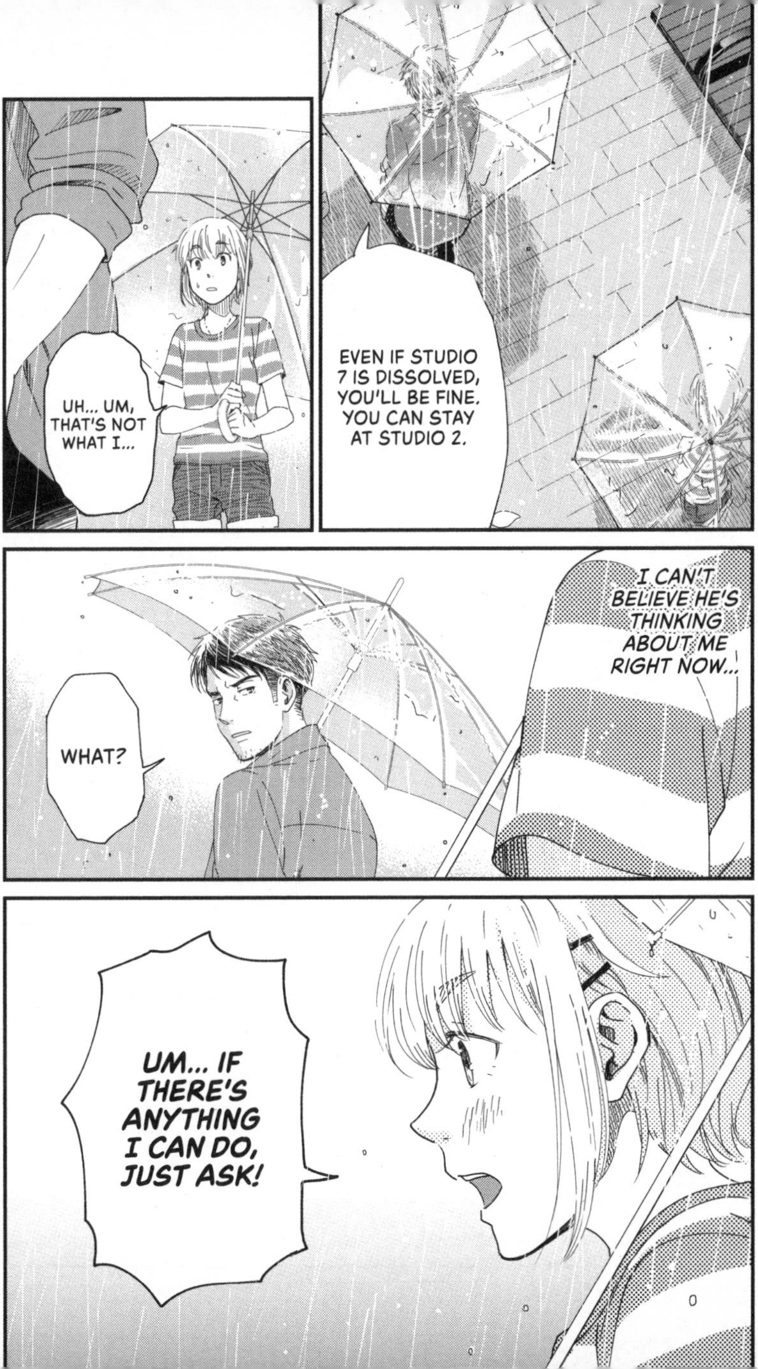
EVEN IF STUDIO 7 IS DISSOLVED, YOU'LL BE FINE. YOU CAN STAY AT STUDIO 2.
UH... UM, THAT'S NOT WHAT I...
I CAN'T BELIEVE HE'S THINKING ABOUT ME RIGHT NOW...
WHAT?
UM... IF THERE'S ANYTHING I CAN DO, JUST ASK!

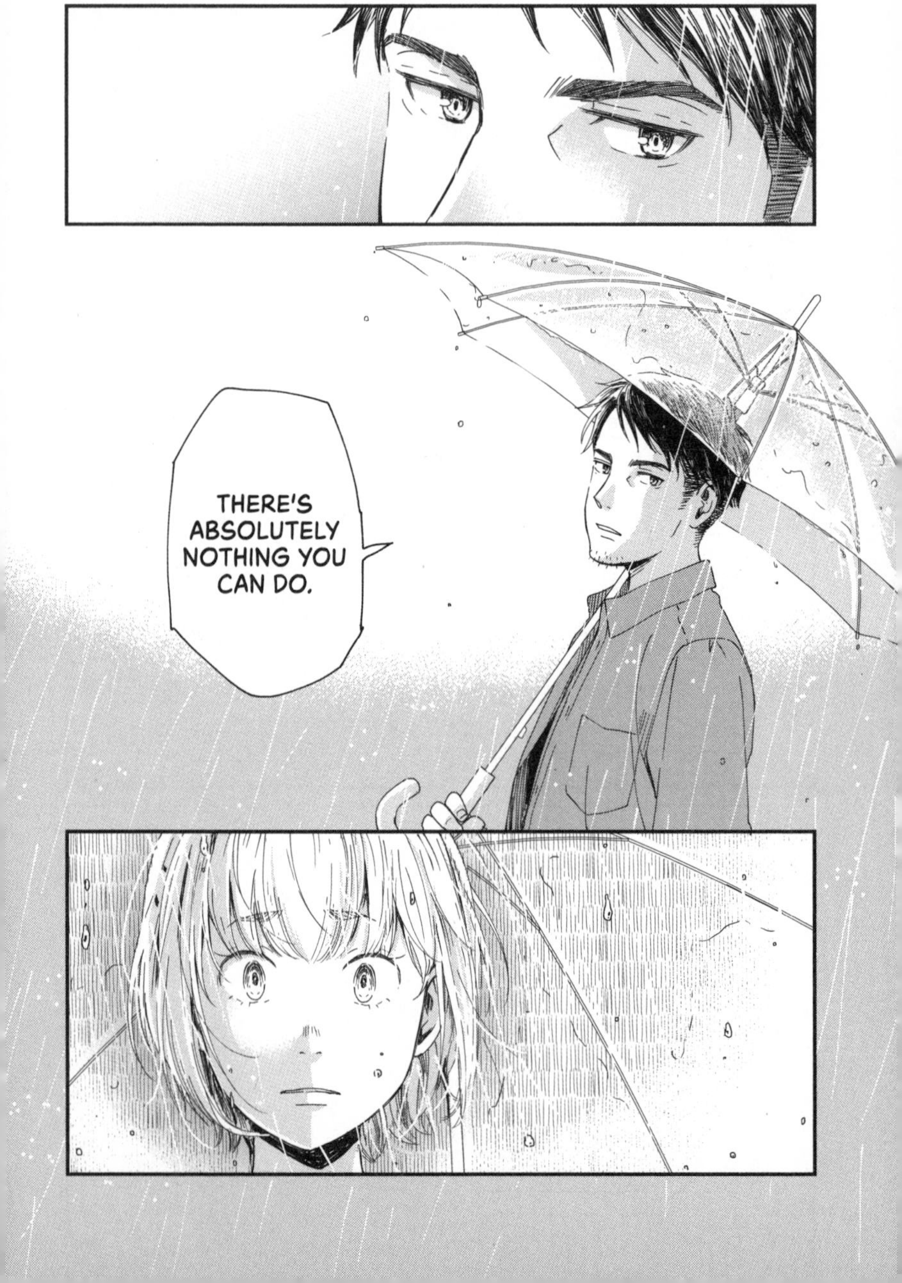
THERE'S ABSOLUTELY NOTHING YOU CAN DO.

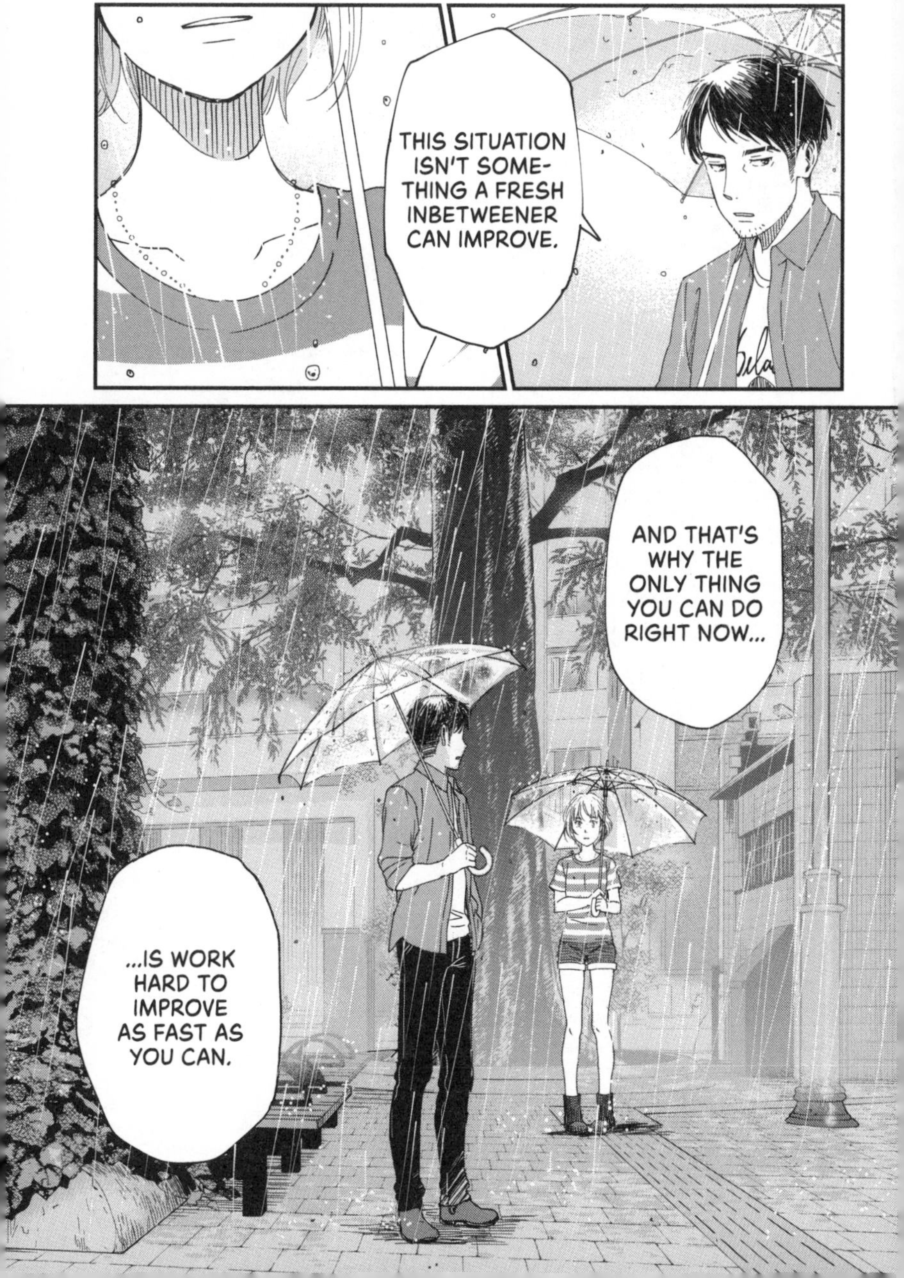
THIS SITUATION ISN'T SOME-THING A FRESH INBETWEENER CAN IMPROVE.
AND THAT'S WHY THE ONLY THING YOU CAN DO RIGHT NOW...
...IS WORK HARD TO IMPROVE AS FAST AS YOU CAN.

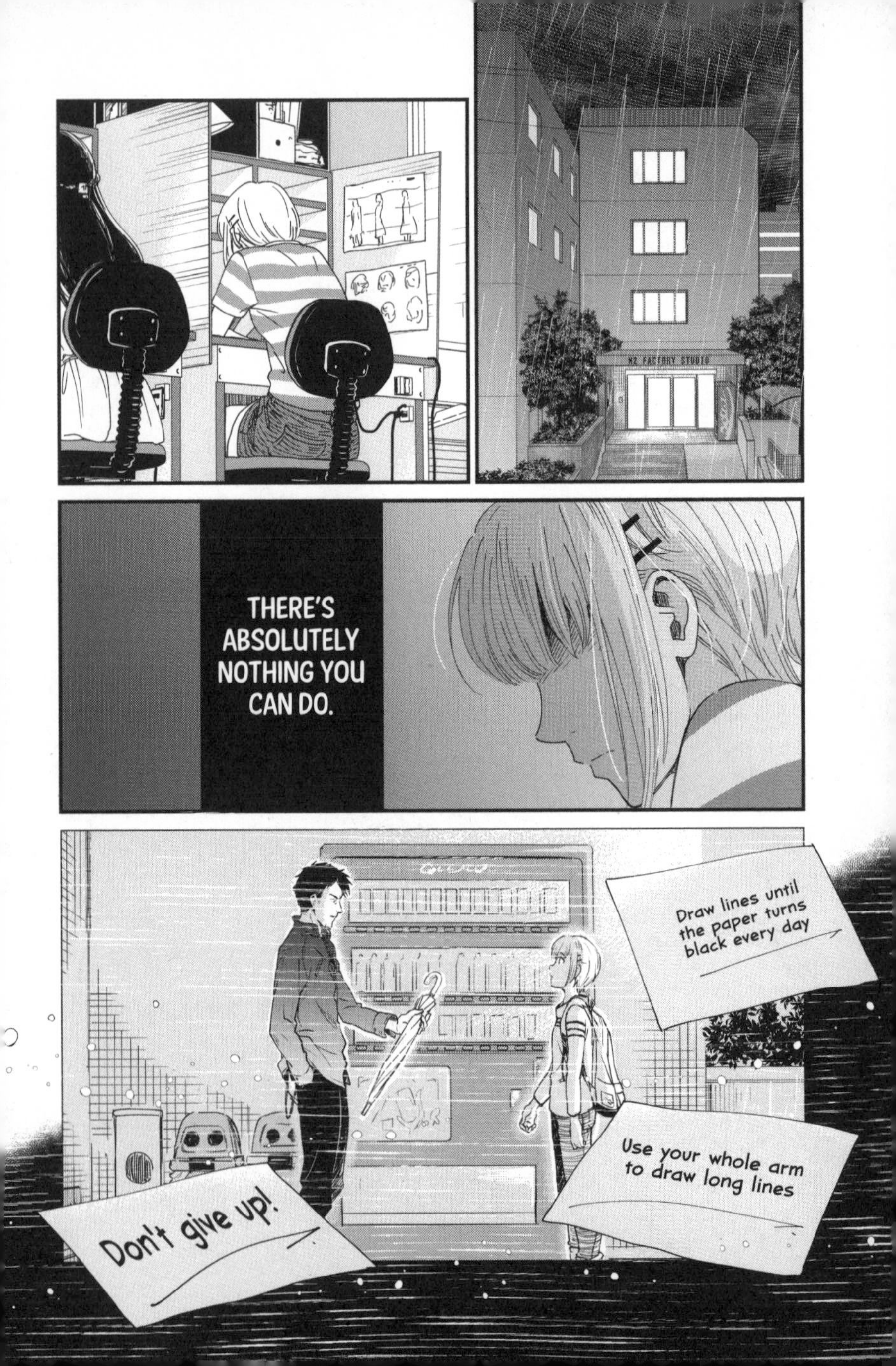
N2 FACTORY STUDIO
THERE'S ABSOLUTELY NOTHING YOU CAN DO.
Draw lines until the paper turns black every day
Use your whole arm to draw long lines
Don't give up!

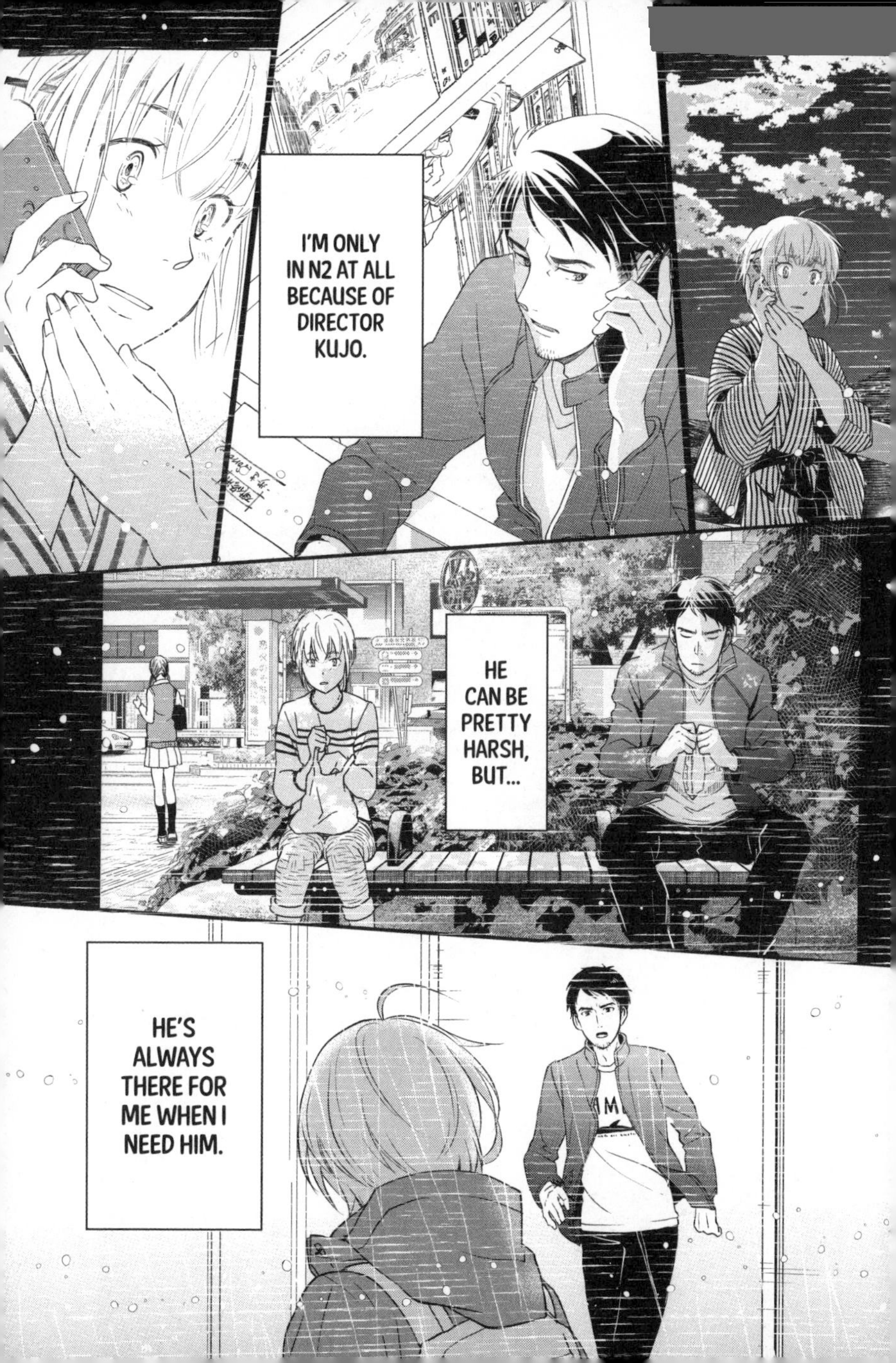
I'M ONLY IN N2 AT ALL BECAUSE OF DIRECTOR KUJO.
HE CAN BE PRETTY HARSH, BUT...
HE'S ALWAYS THERE FOR ME WHEN I NEED HIM.

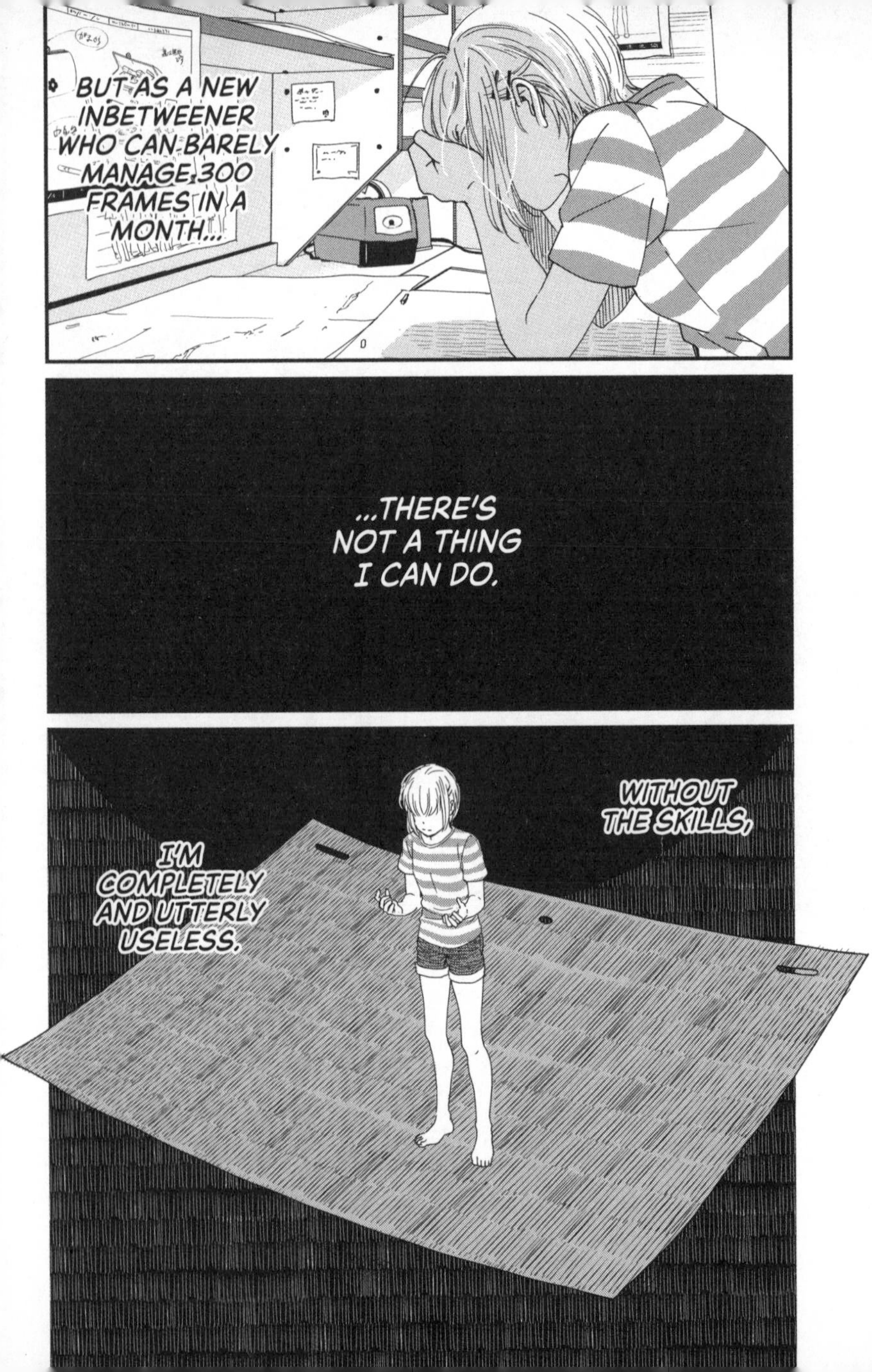
BUT AS A NEW INBETWEENER WHO CAN BARELY MANAGE 300 FRAMES IN A MONTH...
...THERE'S NOT A THING I CAN DO.
WITHOUT THE SKILLS,
I'M COMPLETELY AND UTTERLY USELESS.

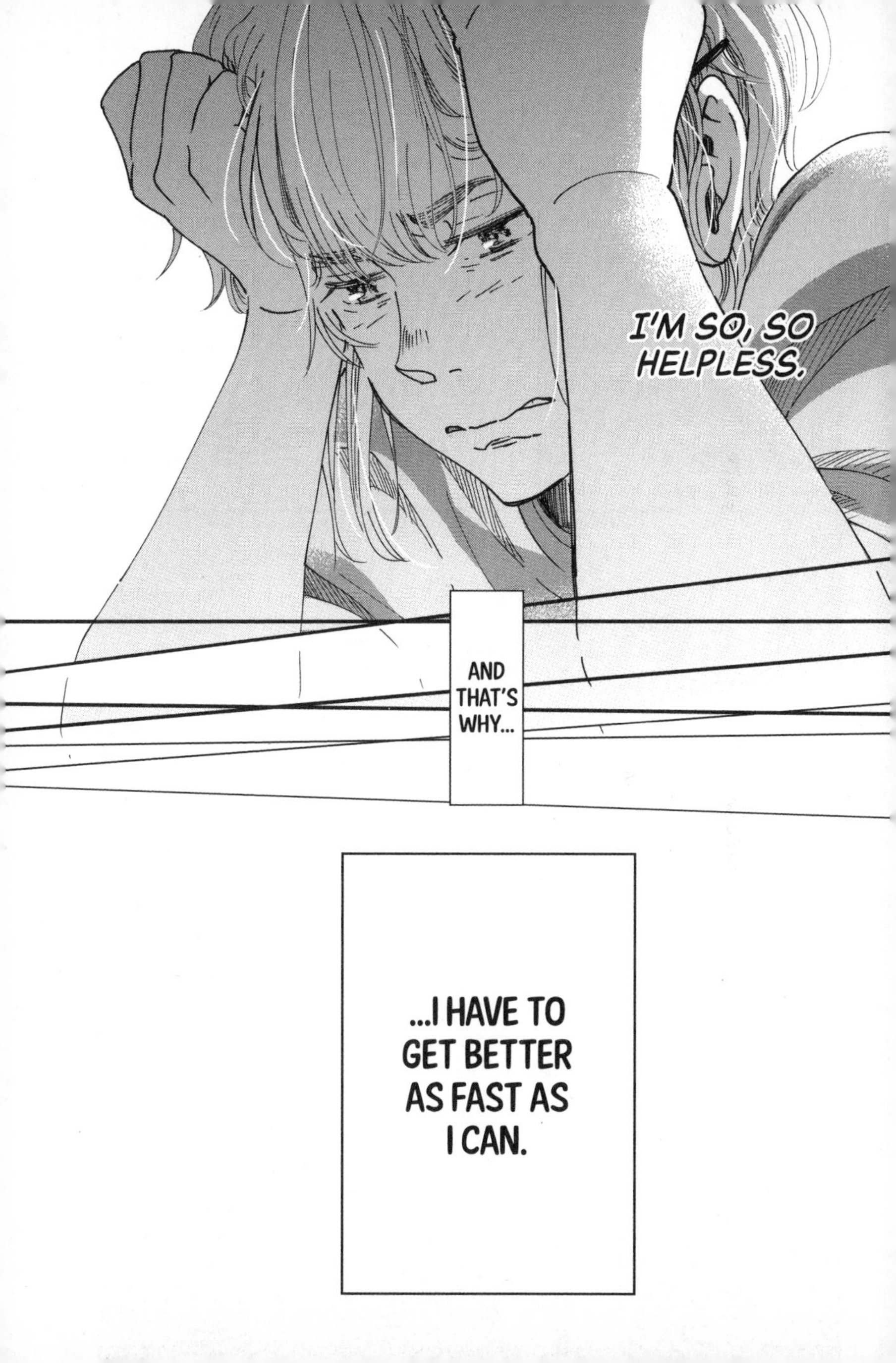
I'M SO, SO HELPLESS.
AND THAT'S WHY...
...I HAVE TO GET BETTER AS FAST AS I CAN.

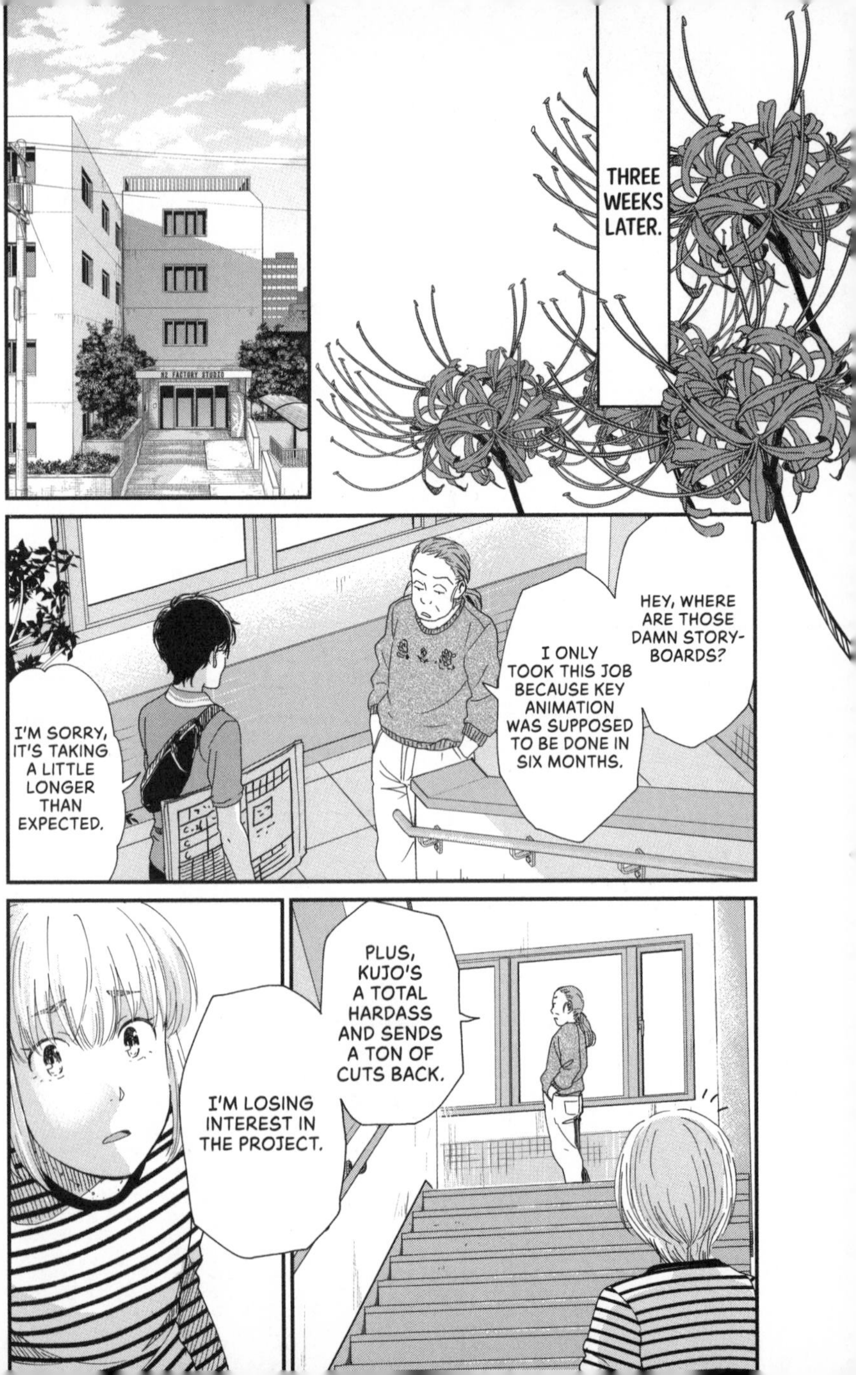
THREE WEEKS LATER.
HEY, WHERE ARE THOSE DAMN STORY-BOARDS?
I ONLY TOOK THIS JOB BECAUSE KEY ANIMATION WAS SUPPOSED TO BE DONE IN SIX MONTHS.
I'M SORRY, IT'S TAKING A LITTLE LONGER THAN EXPECTED.
PLUS, KUJO'S A TOTAL HARDASS AND SENDS A TON OF CUTS BACK.
I'M LOSING INTEREST IN THE PROJECT.

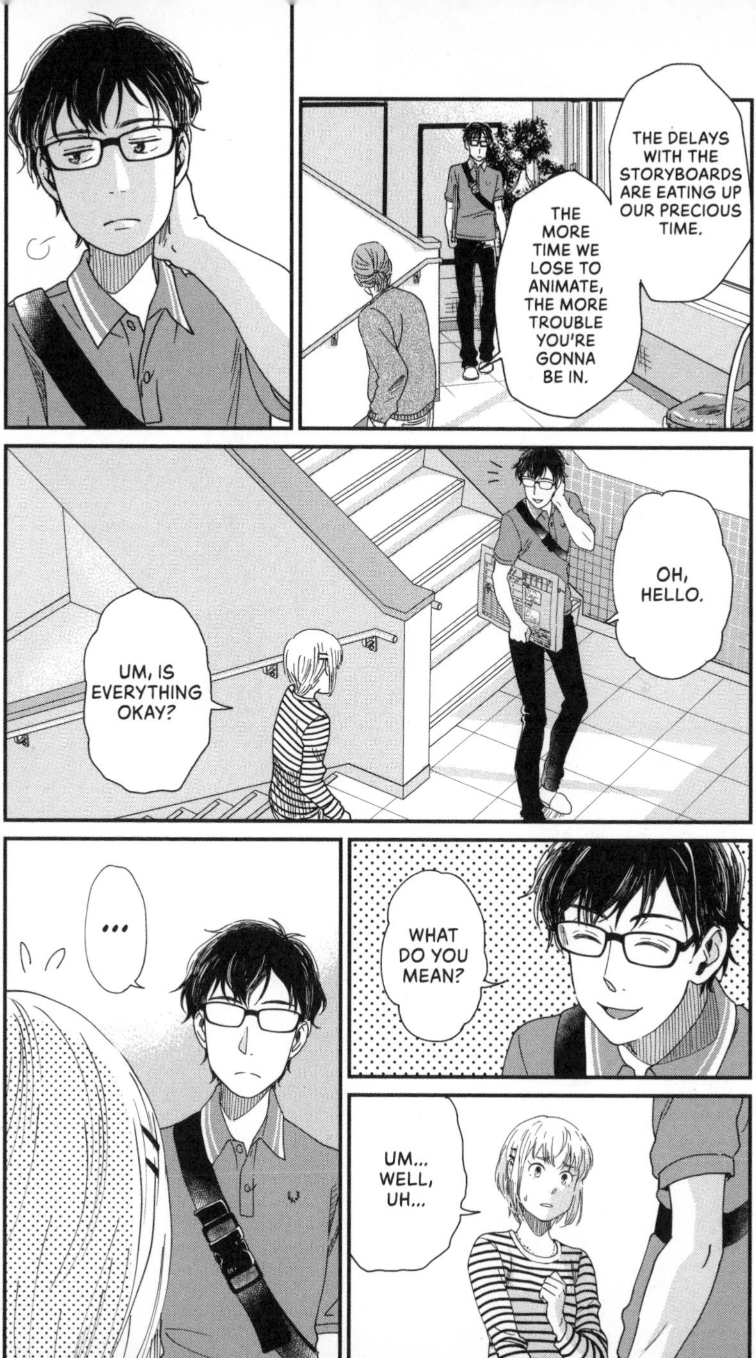
THE DELAYS WITH THE STORYBOARDS ARE EATING UP OUR PRECIOUS TIME.
THE MORE TIME WE LOSE TO ANIMATE, THE MORE TROUBLE YOU'RE GONNA BE IN.
OH, HELLO.
UM, IS EVERYTHING OKAY?
WHAT DO YOU MEAN?
UM... WELL, UH...
...

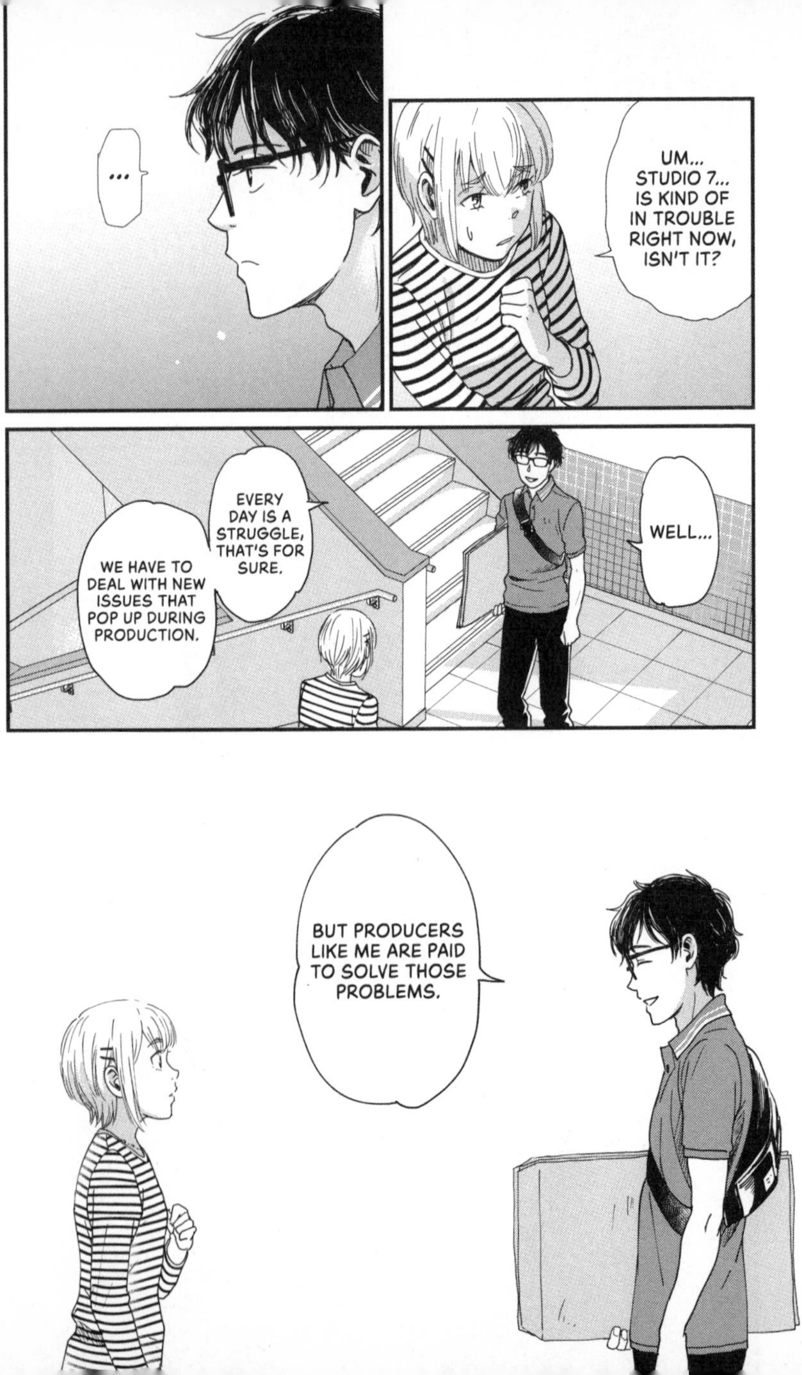
UM... STUDIO 7... IS KIND OF IN TROUBLE RIGHT NOW, ISN'T IT?
...
WELL...
EVERY DAY IS A STRUGGLE, THAT'S FOR SURE.
WE HAVE TO DEAL WITH NEW ISSUES THAT POP UP DURING PRODUCTION.
BUT PRODUCERS LIKE ME ARE PAID TO SOLVE THOSE PROBLEMS.

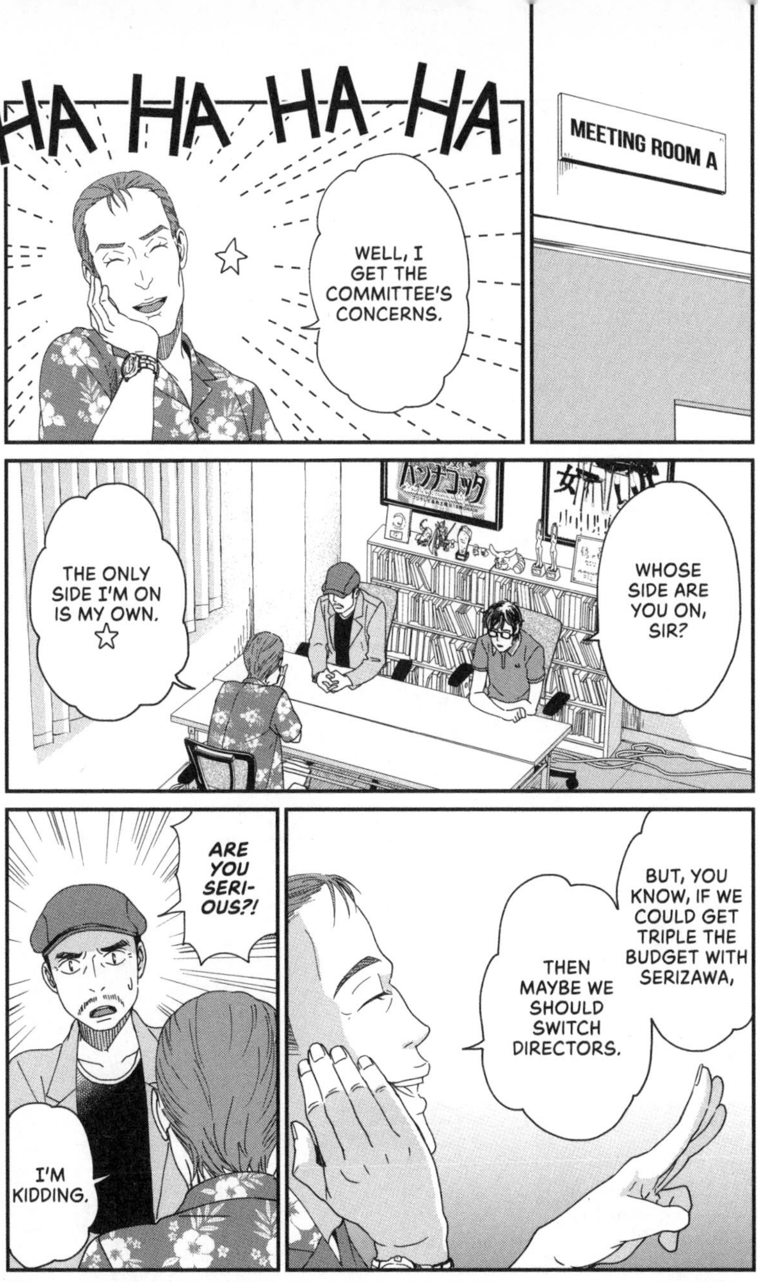
MEETING ROOM A
HA HA HA HA
WELL, I GET THE COMMITTEE'S CONCERNS.
WHOSE SIDE ARE YOU ON, SIR?
THE ONLY SIDE I'M ON IS MY OWN. ☆
BUT, YOU KNOW, IF WE COULD GET TRIPLE THE BUDGET WITH SERIZAWA,
THEN MAYBE WE SHOULD SWITCH DIRECTORS.
ARE YOU SERIOUS?!
I'M KIDDING.

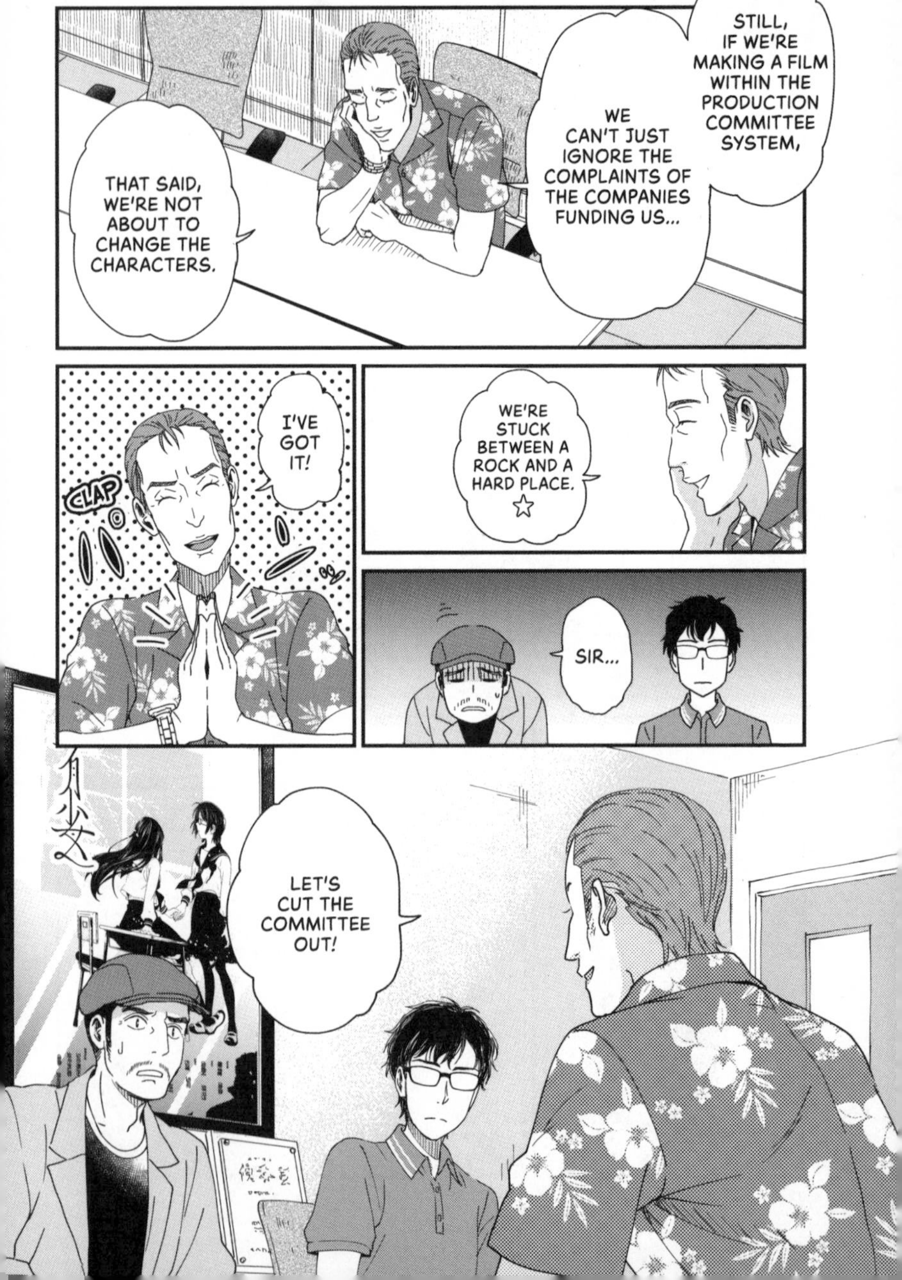
STILL, IF WE'RE MAKING A FILM WITHIN THE PRODUCTION COMMITTEE SYSTEM,
WE CAN'T JUST IGNORE THE COMPLAINTS OF THE COMPANIES FUNDING US...
THAT SAID, WE'RE NOT ABOUT TO CHANGE THE CHARACTERS.
WE'RE STUCK BETWEEN A ROCK AND A HARD PLACE. ☆
SIR...
I'VE GOT IT!
CLAP
LET'S CUT THE COMMITTEE OUT!

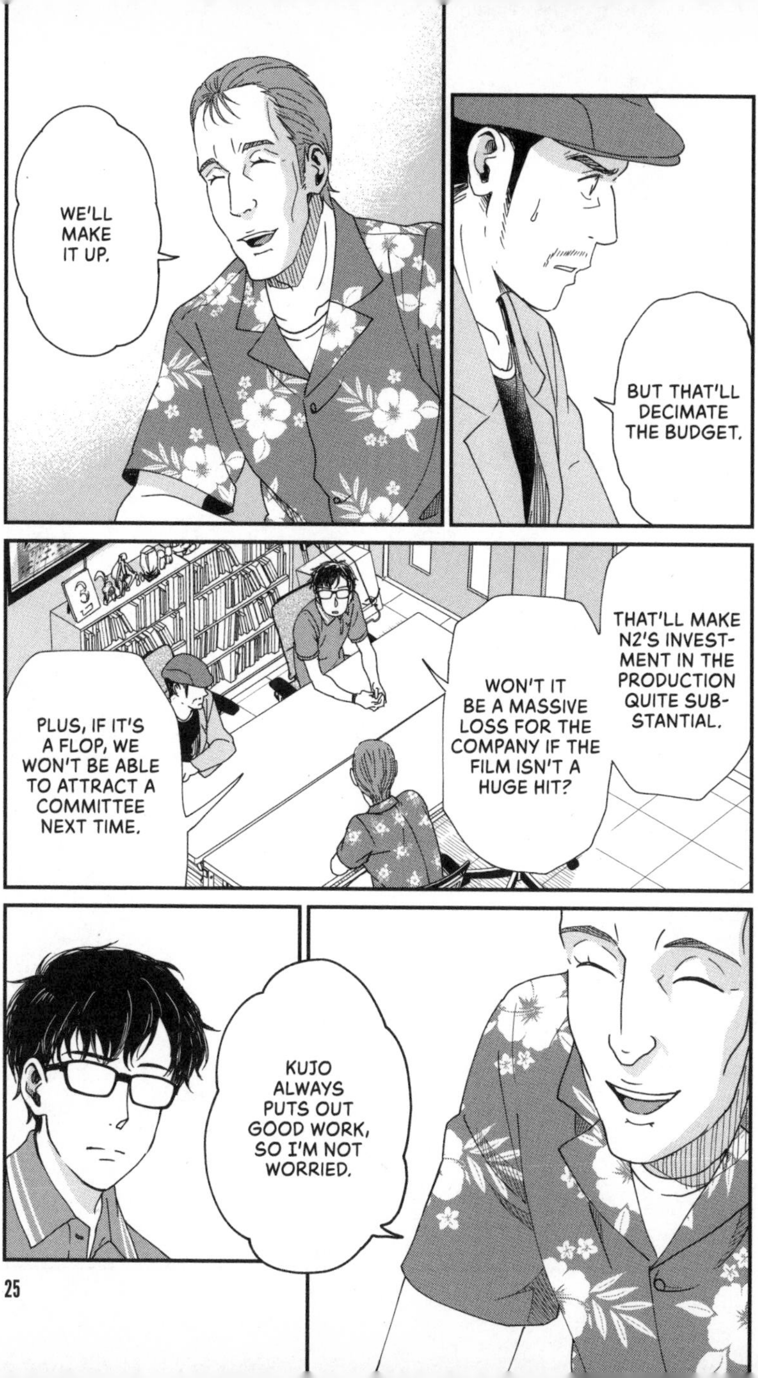
BUT THAT'LL DECIMATE THE BUDGET.
WE'LL MAKE IT UP.
THAT'LL MAKE N2'S INVEST-MENT IN THE PRODUCTION QUITE SUB-STANTIAL.
WON'T IT BE A MASSIVE LOSS FOR THE COMPANY IF THE FILM ISN'T A HUGE HIT?
PLUS, IF IT'S A FLOP, WE WON'T BE ABLE TO ATTRACT A COMMITTEE NEXT TIME.
KUJO ALWAYS PUTS OUT GOOD WORK, SO I'M NOT WORRIED.

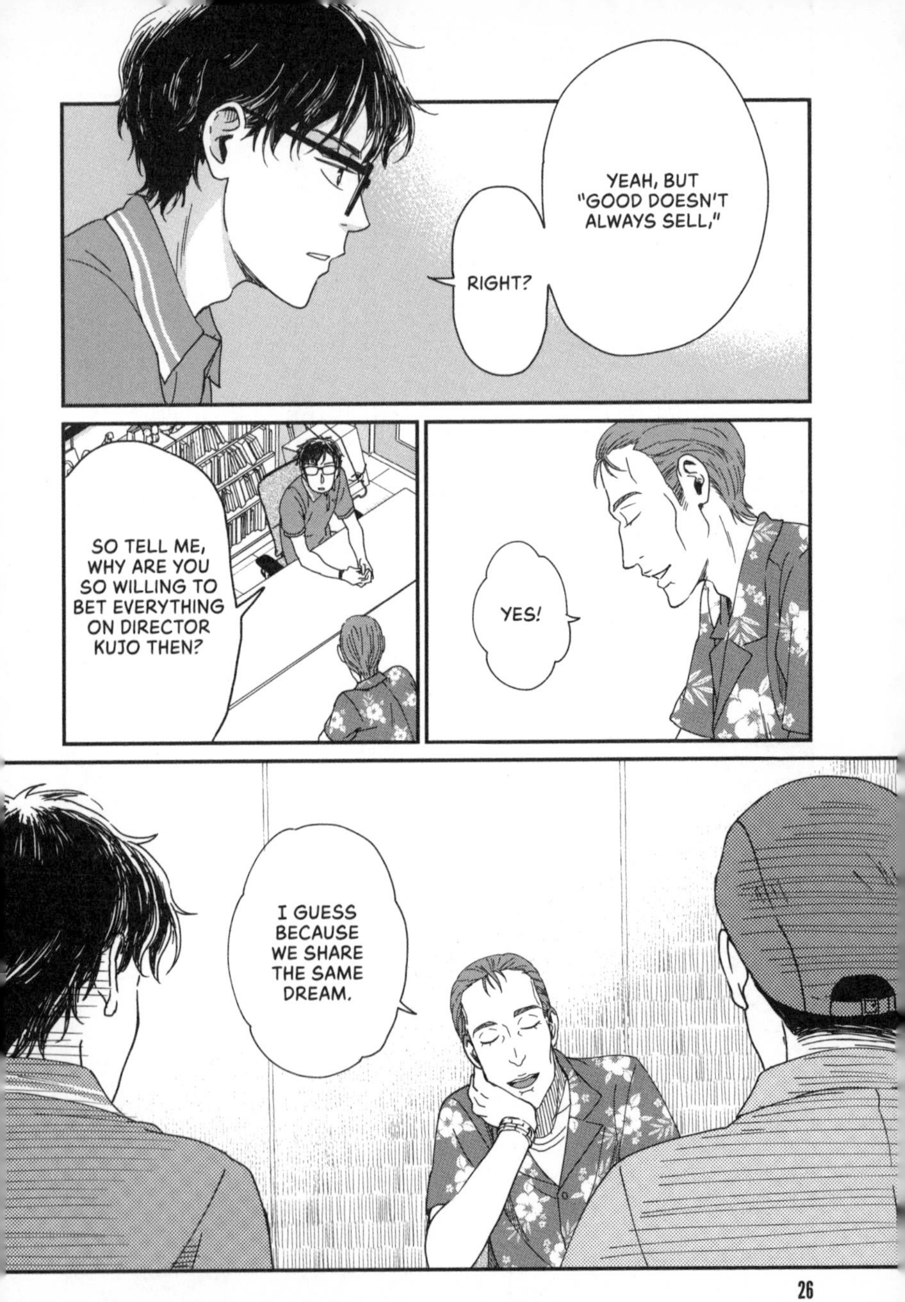
YEAH, BUT "GOOD DOESN'T ALWAYS SELL,"
RIGHT?
YES!
SO TELL ME, WHY ARE YOU SO WILLING TO BET EVERYTHING ON DIRECTOR KUJO THEN?
I GUESS BECAUSE WE SHARE THE SAME DREAM.

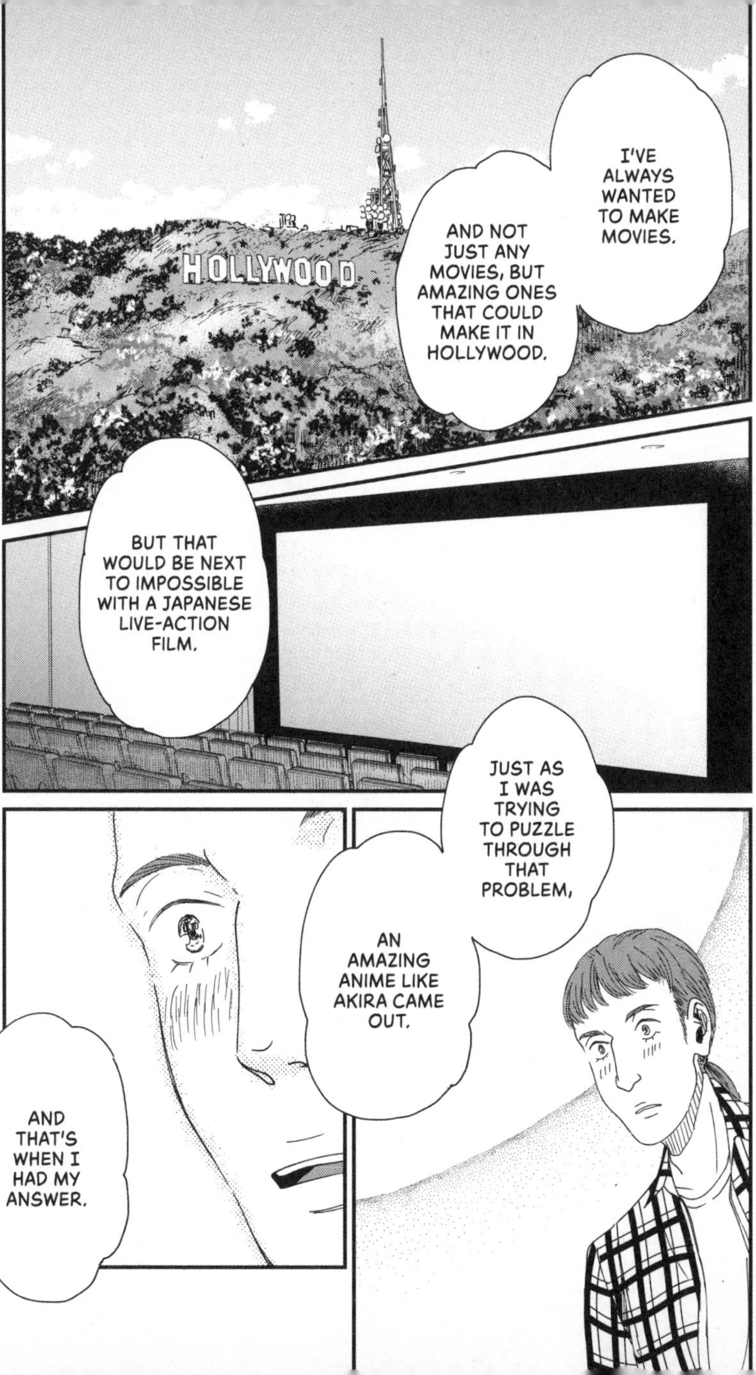
I'VE ALWAYS WANTED TO MAKE MOVIES.
AND NOT JUST ANY MOVIES, BUT AMAZING ONES THAT COULD MAKE IT IN HOLLYWOOD.
HOLLYWOOD
BUT THAT WOULD BE NEXT TO IMPOSSIBLE WITH A JAPANESE LIVE-ACTION FILM.
JUST AS I WAS TRYING TO PUZZLE THROUGH THAT PROBLEM,
AN AMAZING ANIME LIKE AKIRA CAME OUT.
AND THAT'S WHEN I HAD MY ANSWER.

I COULD COMPETE ON THE WORLD'S STAGE WITH ANIME.

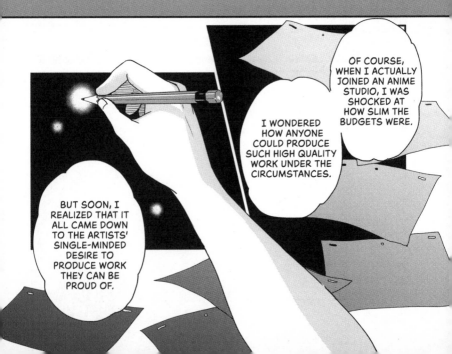

OF COURSE, WHEN I ACTUALLY JOINED AN ANIME STUDIO, I WAS SHOCKED AT HOW SLIM THE BUDGETS WERE.

I WONDERED HOW ANYONE COULD PRODUCE SUCH HIGH QUALITY WORK UNDER THE CIRCUMSTANCES.

BUT SOON, I REALIZED THAT IT ALL CAME DOWN TO THE ARTISTS' SINGLE-MINDED DESIRE TO PRODUCE WORK THEY CAN BE PROUD OF.

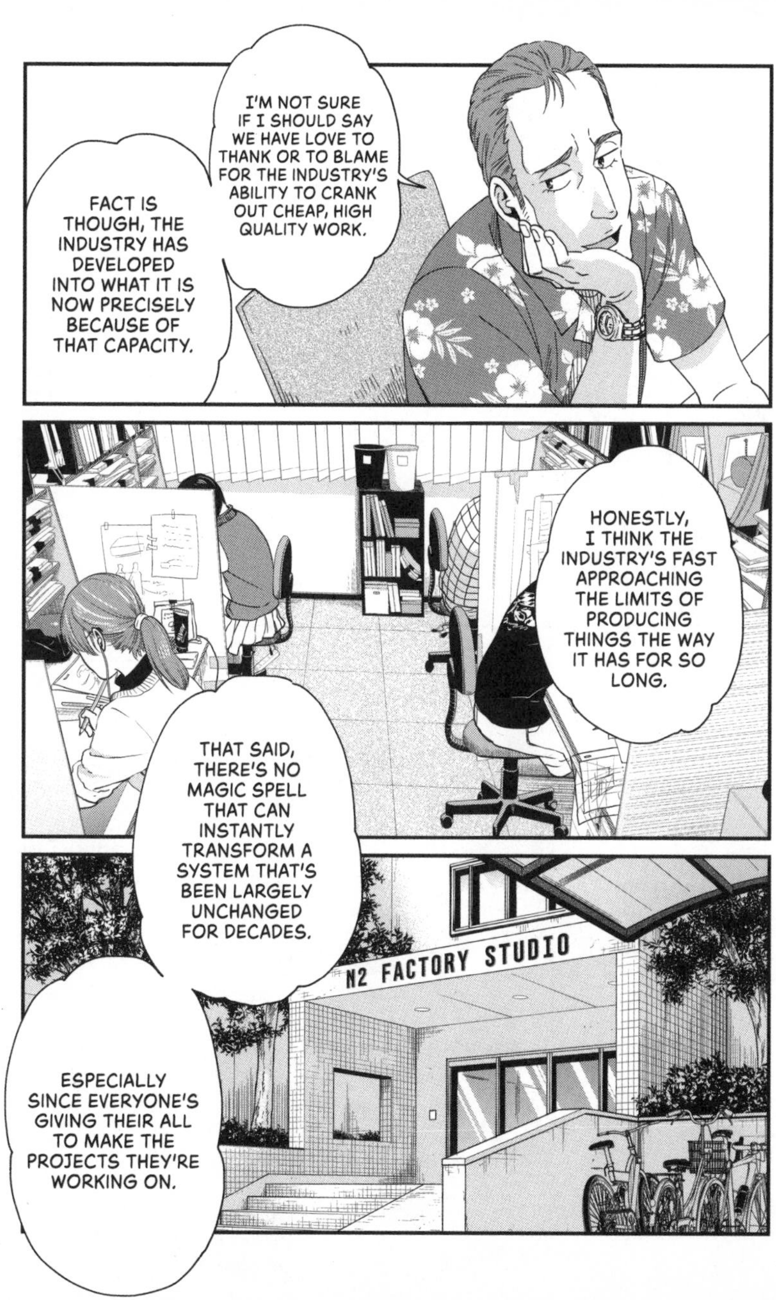
I'M NOT SURE IF I SHOULD SAY WE HAVE LOVE TO THANK OR TO BLAME FOR THE INDUSTRY'S ABILITY TO CRANK OUT CHEAP, HIGH QUALITY WORK.
FACT IS THOUGH, THE INDUSTRY HAS DEVELOPED INTO WHAT IT IS NOW PRECISELY BECAUSE OF THAT CAPACITY.
HONESTLY, I THINK THE INDUSTRY'S FAST APPROACHING THE LIMITS OF PRODUCING THINGS THE WAY IT HAS FOR SO LONG.
THAT SAID, THERE'S NO MAGIC SPELL THAT CAN INSTANTLY TRANSFORM A SYSTEM THAT'S BEEN LARGELY UNCHANGED FOR DECADES.
N2 FACTORY STUDIO
ESPECIALLY SINCE EVERYONE'S GIVING THEIR ALL TO MAKE THE PROJECTS THEY'RE WORKING ON.

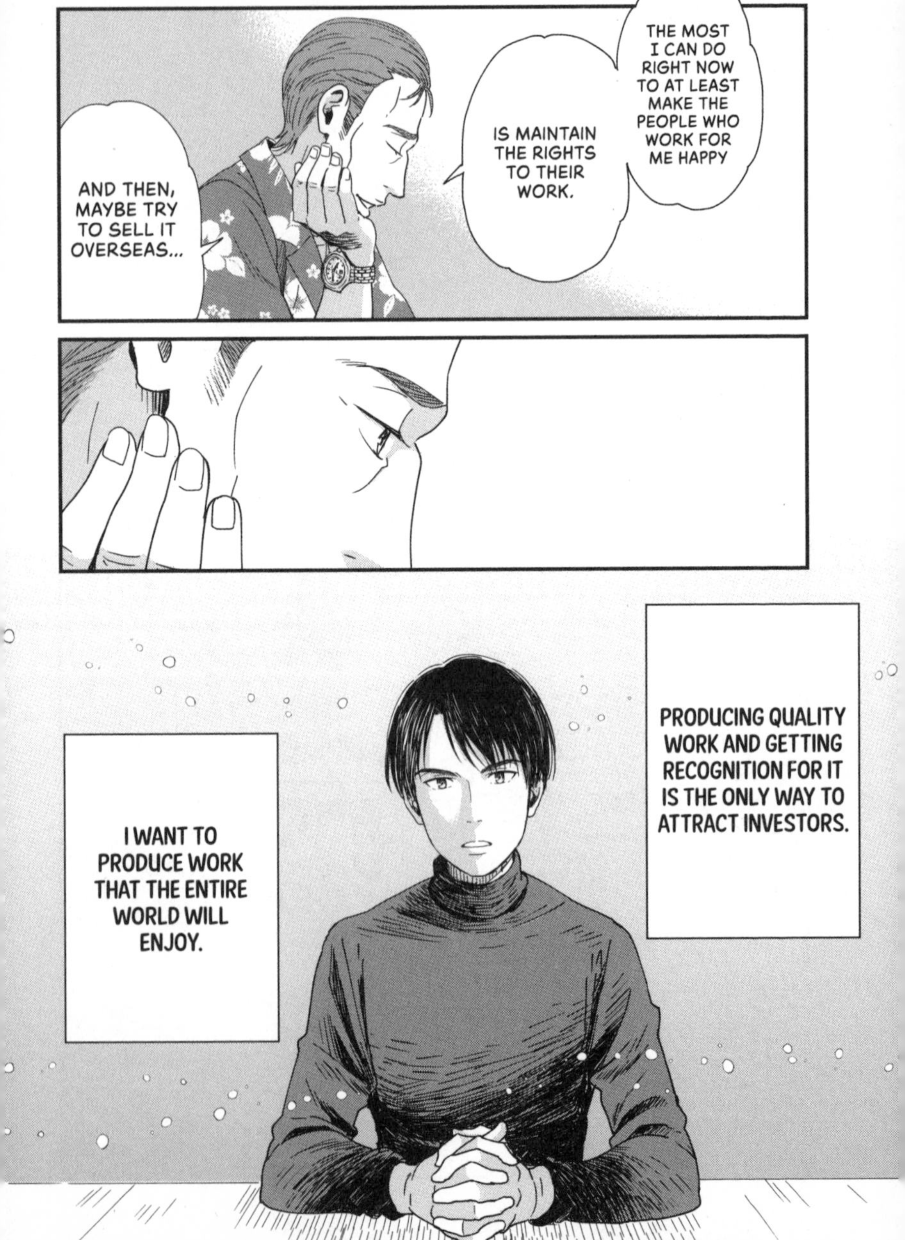
THE MOST I CAN DO RIGHT NOW TO AT LEAST MAKE THE PEOPLE WHO WORK FOR ME HAPPY
IS MAINTAIN THE RIGHTS TO THEIR WORK.
AND THEN, MAYBE TRY TO SELL IT OVERSEAS...
PRODUCING QUALITY WORK AND GETTING RECOGNITION FOR IT IS THE ONLY WAY TO ATTRACT INVESTORS.
I WANT TO PRODUCE WORK THAT THE ENTIRE WORLD WILL ENJOY.

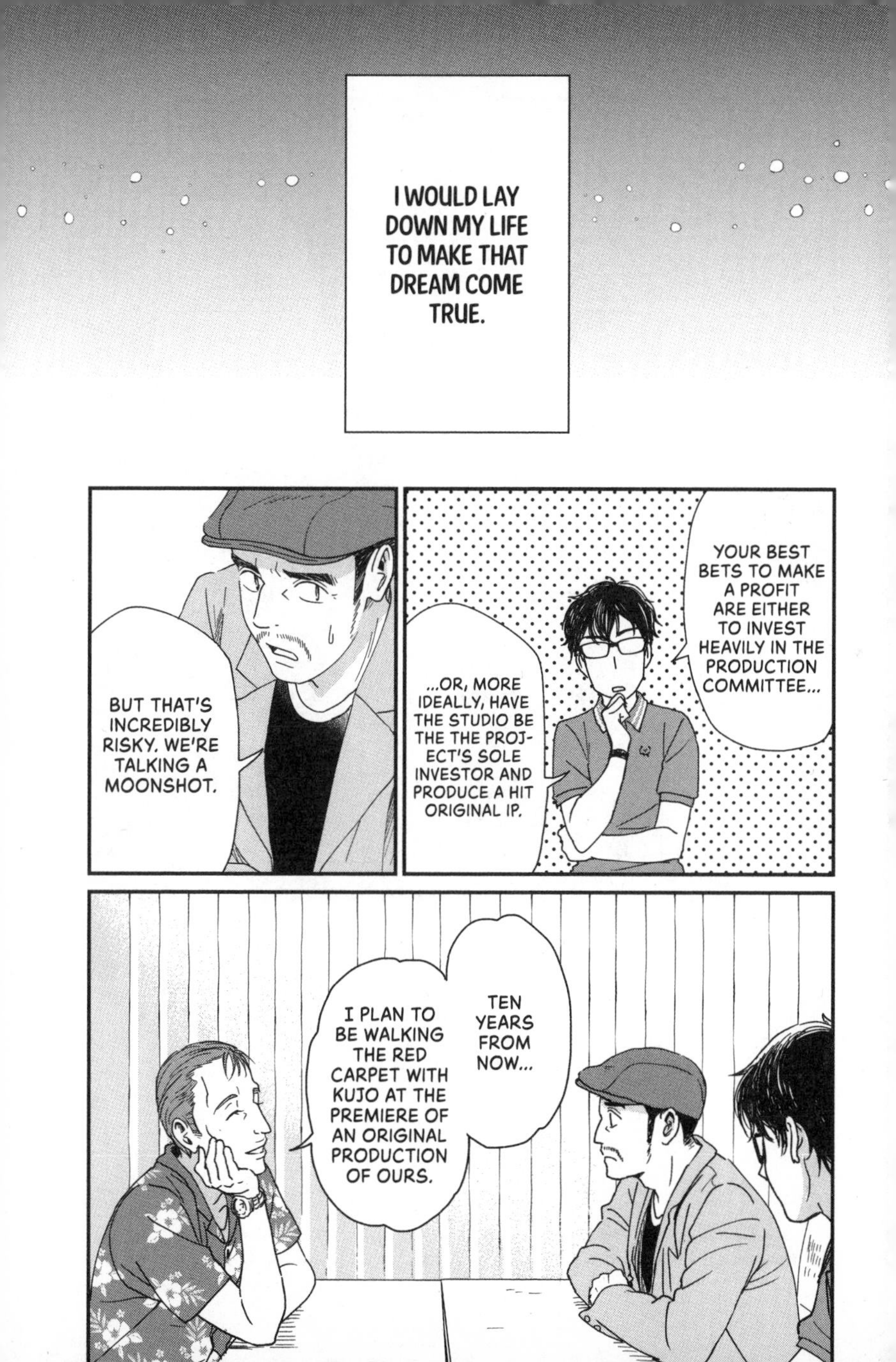
I WOULD LAY DOWN MY LIFE TO MAKE THAT DREAM COME TRUE.
YOUR BEST BETS TO MAKE A PROFIT ARE EITHER TO INVEST HEAVILY IN THE PRODUCTION COMMITTEE...
...OR, MORE IDEALLY, HAVE THE STUDIO BE THE THE PROJ-ECT'S SOLE INVESTOR AND PRODUCE A HIT ORIGINAL IP.
BUT THAT'S INCREDIBLY RISKY. WE'RE TALKING A MOONSHOT.
TEN YEARS FROM NOW...
I PLAN TO BE WALKING THE RED CARPET WITH KUJO AT THE PREMIERE OF AN ORIGINAL PRODUCTION OF OURS.

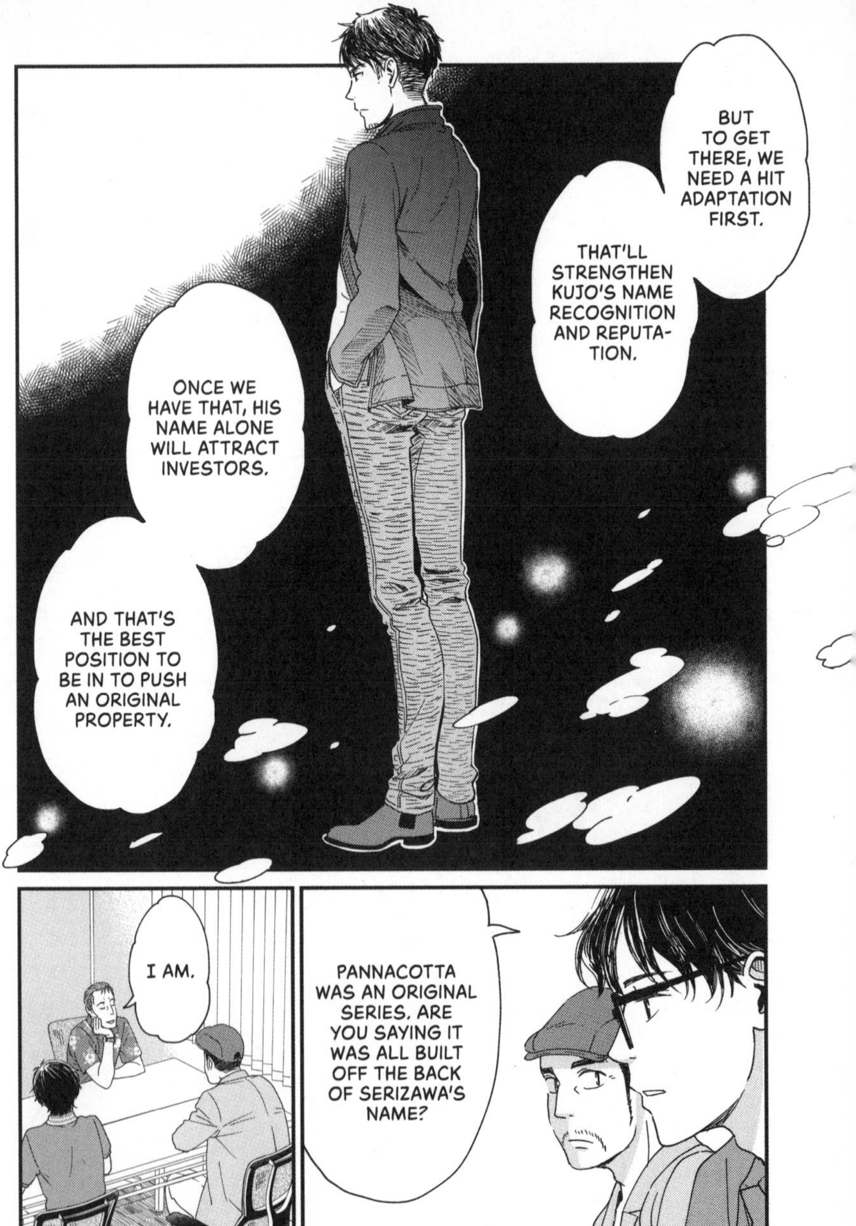
BUT TO GET THERE, WE NEED A HIT ADAPTATION FIRST.
THAT'LL STRENGTHEN KUJO'S NAME RECOGNITION AND REPUTA-TION.
ONCE WE HAVE THAT, HIS NAME ALONE WILL ATTRACT INVESTORS.
AND THAT'S THE BEST POSITION TO BE IN TO PUSH AN ORIGINAL PROPERTY.
PANNACOTTA WAS AN ORIGINAL SERIES. ARE YOU SAYING IT WAS ALL BUILT OFF THE BACK OF SERIZAWA'S NAME?
I AM.

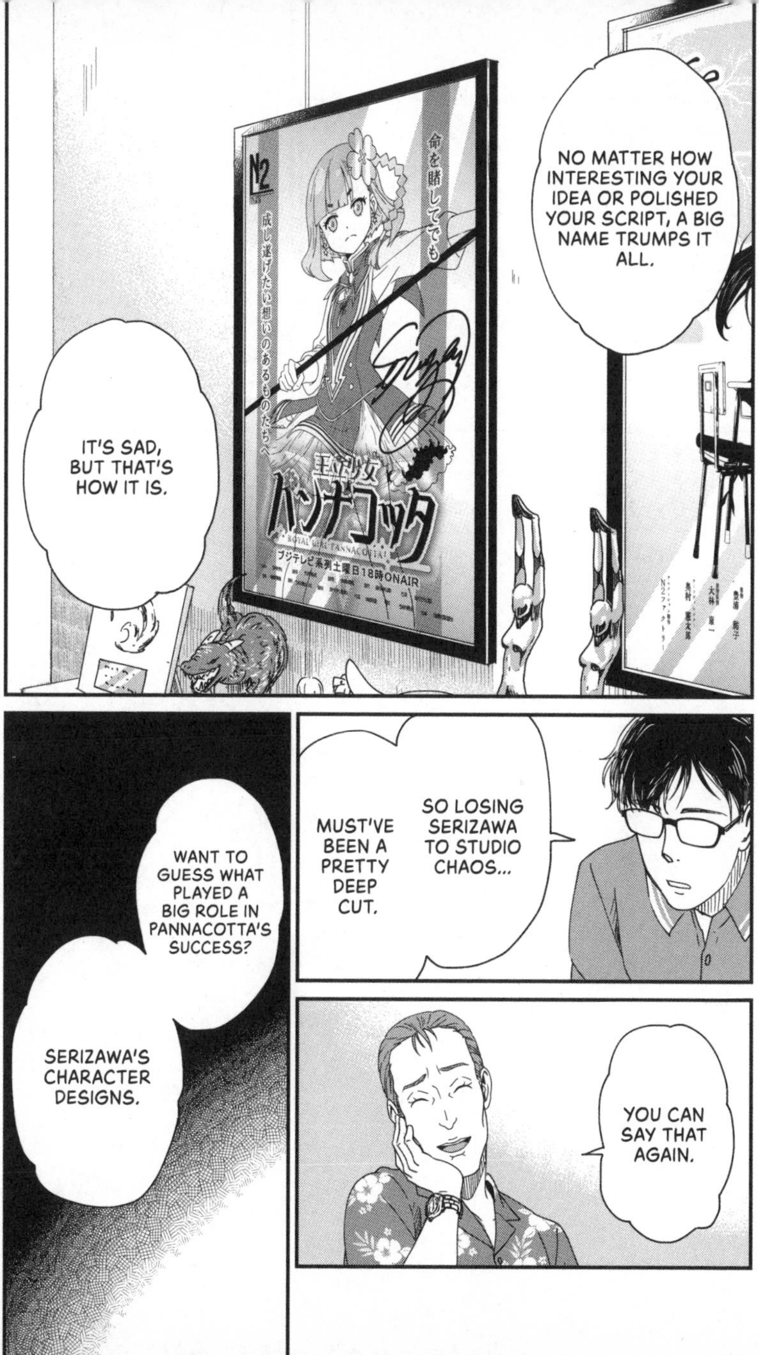
NO MATTER HOW INTERESTING YOUR IDEA OR POLISHED YOUR SCRIPT, A BIG NAME TRUMPS IT ALL.
命を賭してでも
成し遂げたい想いのあるものたちへ
パンナコッタ
フジテレビ系列土曜日18時ONAIR
IT'S SAD, BUT THAT'S HOW IT IS.
SO LOSING SERIZAWA TO STUDIO CHAOS...
MUST'VE BEEN A PRETTY DEEP CUT.
YOU CAN SAY THAT AGAIN.
WANT TO GUESS WHAT PLAYED A BIG ROLE IN PANNACOTTA'S SUCCESS?
SERIZAWA'S CHARACTER DESIGNS.

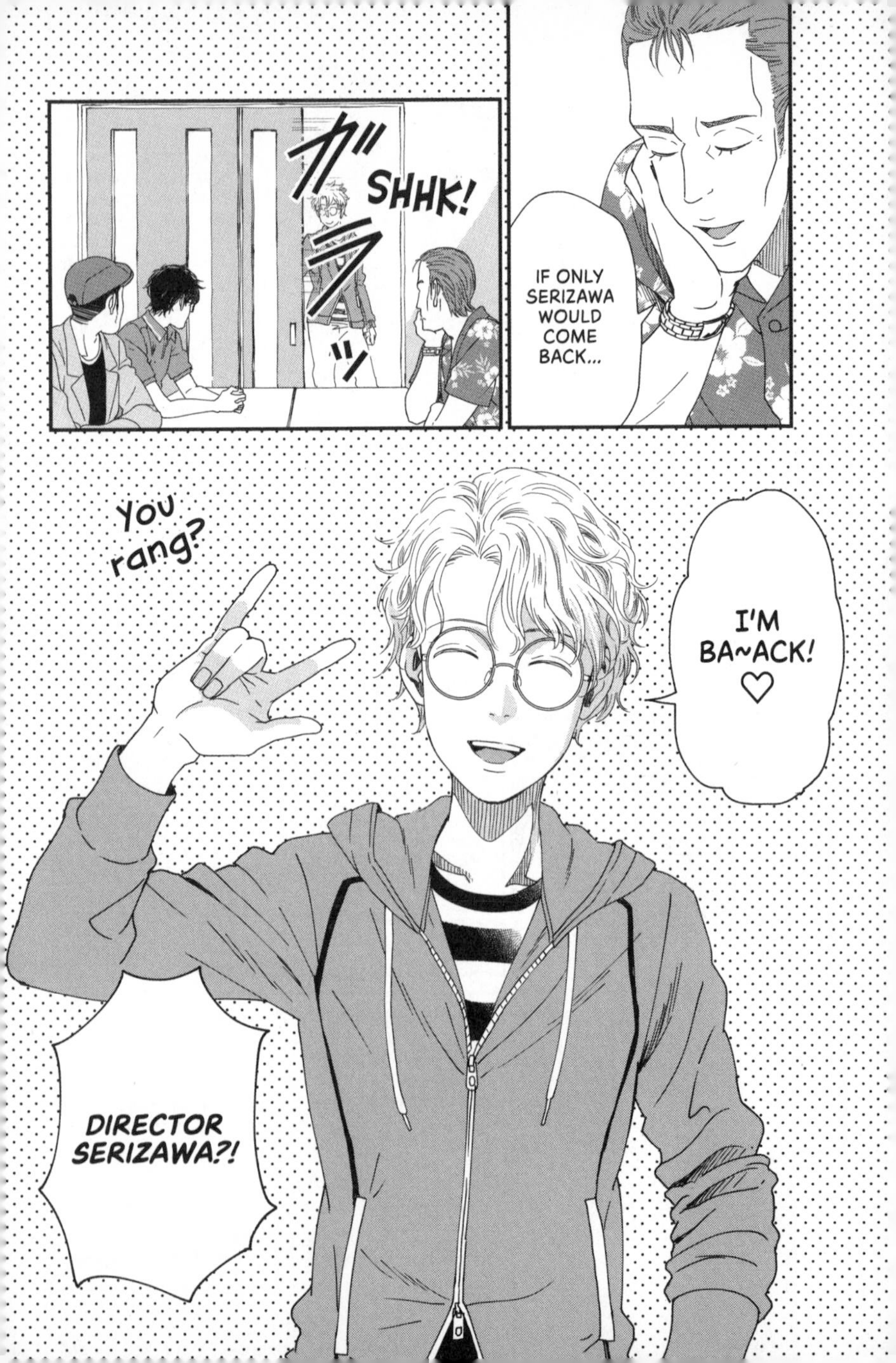
IF ONLY SERIZAWA WOULD COME BACK...
SHHK!
I'M BA~ACK! ♡
You rang?
DIRECTOR SERIZAWA?!

Explaining Anime Production Committees
Sponsors Investors
• TV Stations
• Publishers
• Advertising Agencies
• Entertainment Companies
• Game Companies
• Film Distributors
• Toy Companies
...
Etc.
Production Committee
N2 IS PART OF THIS.
¥
Pro-duc-tion Funds
¥
Main Production Studio
Sub-contracted Studio
Subcontracted Studio
BY THE WAY, IF THE STUDIO IS ONE OF THE INVESTORS, IT MAKES MONEY WHEN THE PROPERTY IS A SUCCESS. HOWEVER, ON THE FLIP SIDE, IF THE PROPERTY IS A FLOP, THE STUDIO COULD BE IN SERIOUS TROUBLE.
IF THE STUDIO IS THE SOLE INVESTOR, ALL OF THE MONEY COMES BACK TO THE STUDIO, BUT IT CAN BE EXTREMELY RISKY IF THINGS GO SOUTH. ON THE OTHER HAND, THE MORE INVESTORS, THE MORE PEOPLE YOU HAVE TO PLEASE. BUT THAT'S JUST THE WAY THINGS ARE, UNFORTUNATELY...

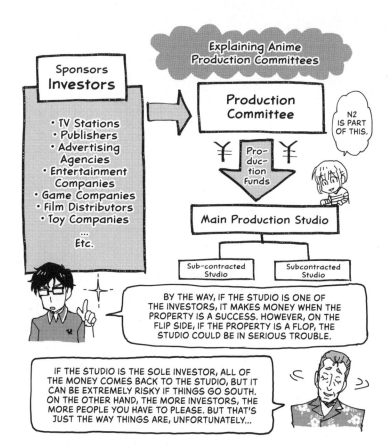

It's probably fair to say that these days, you won't see the credits of an anime without the words "— Production Committee" in them. But what exactly is a production committee? The short answer is that it's a group of companies which invested in the anime production in question. TV stations, publishers, advertising agencies, and other companies contribute money to the production of an anime and then they receive profits from that property proportional to their initial investment. For example, if a company invested 30% of an anime's total production costs, that company would receive 30% of its subsequent profits (obviously, the specific figures will vary depending on the details of the contract).

Currently, the overwhelming majority of anime is produced using this system, but with the increasing number of parties involved in committees comes more administrative complexity and more problems, so there's plenty of potential for change in the future.

nimeta! Volume 4 Release Celebration Project

llustration from Kyoji Asano!!

Head Animation Director and Character
esigner of Attack on Titan)

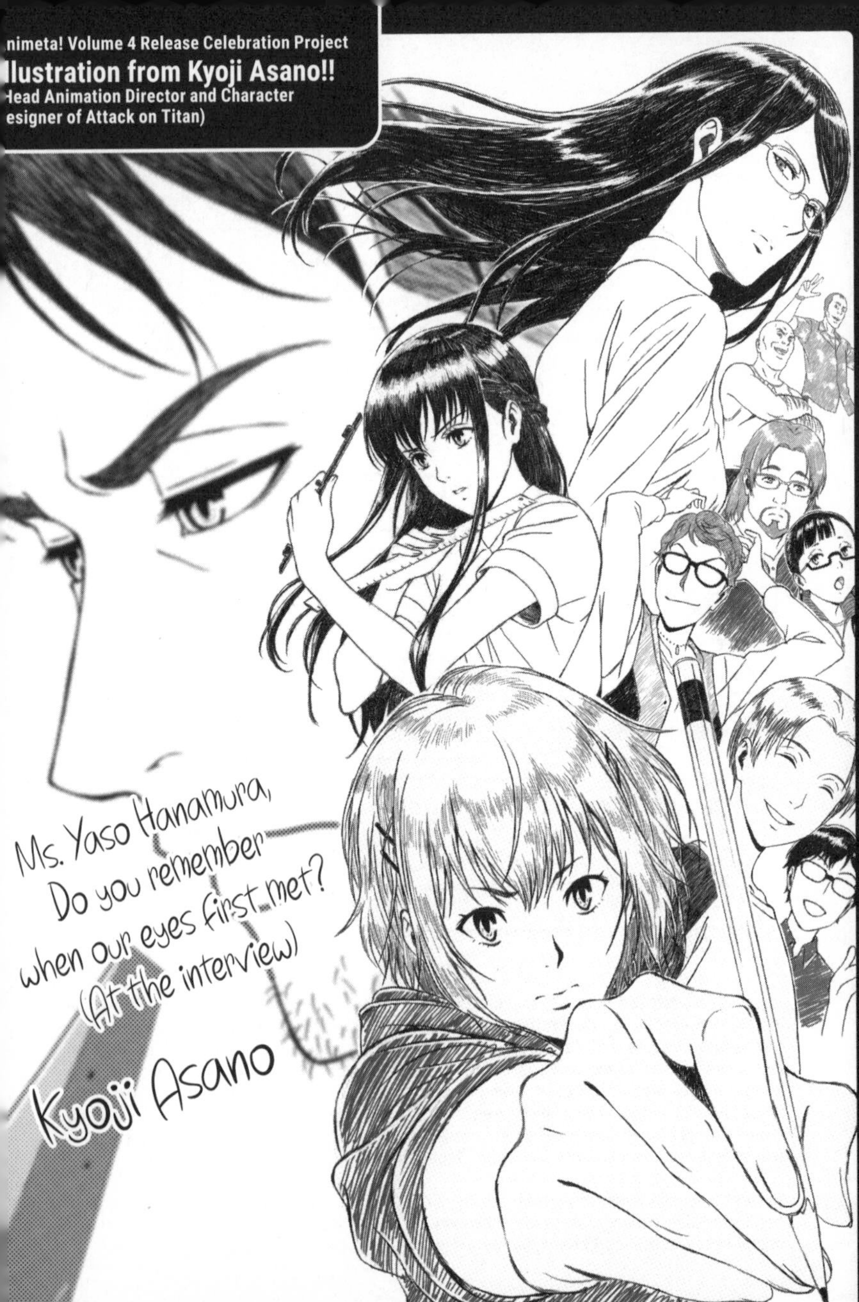
Ms. Yaso Hanamura,
Do you remember
when our eyes first met?
(At the interview)
Kyoji Asano

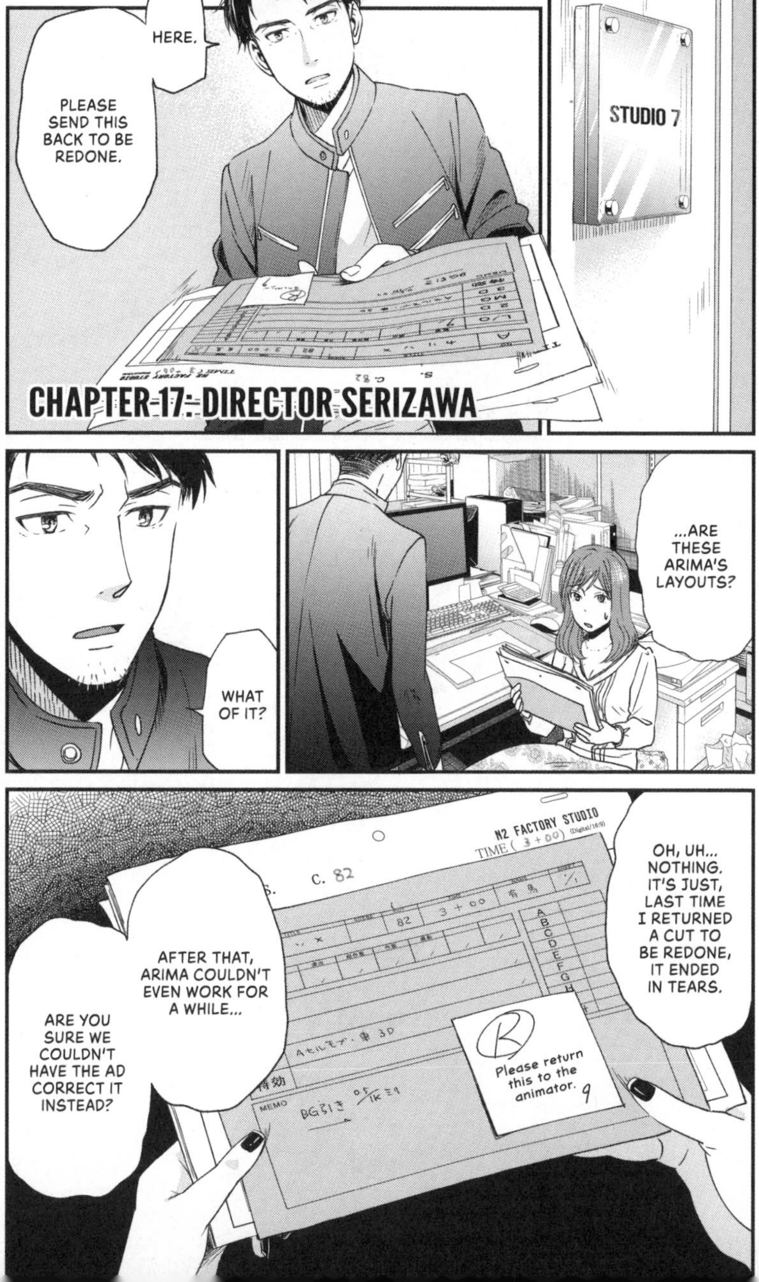
STUDIO 7
HERE.
PLEASE SEND THIS BACK TO BE REDONE.
CHAPTER 17: DIRECTOR SERIZAWA
...ARE THESE ARIMA'S LAYOUTS?
WHAT OF IT?
M2 FACTORY STUDIO
TIME (3+00)
C. 82
OH, UH... NOTHING. IT'S JUST, LAST TIME I RETURNED A CUT TO BE REDONE, IT ENDED IN TEARS.
AFTER THAT, ARIMA COULDN'T EVEN WORK FOR A WHILE...
ARE YOU SURE WE COULDN'T HAVE THE AD CORRECT IT INSTEAD?
Please return this to the animator.
MEMO

AD Corrections: Corrections to keyframes made by the animation director (AD).

Key Animation (Genga): The process of drawing the images that become the *key* moments of motion. The term used in the Japanese industry to describe keyframes, genga, literally means "original drawings" because the "original" drawings of the key animators are ultimately traced and cleaned by the inbetweeners, becoming douga, before they are filmed.

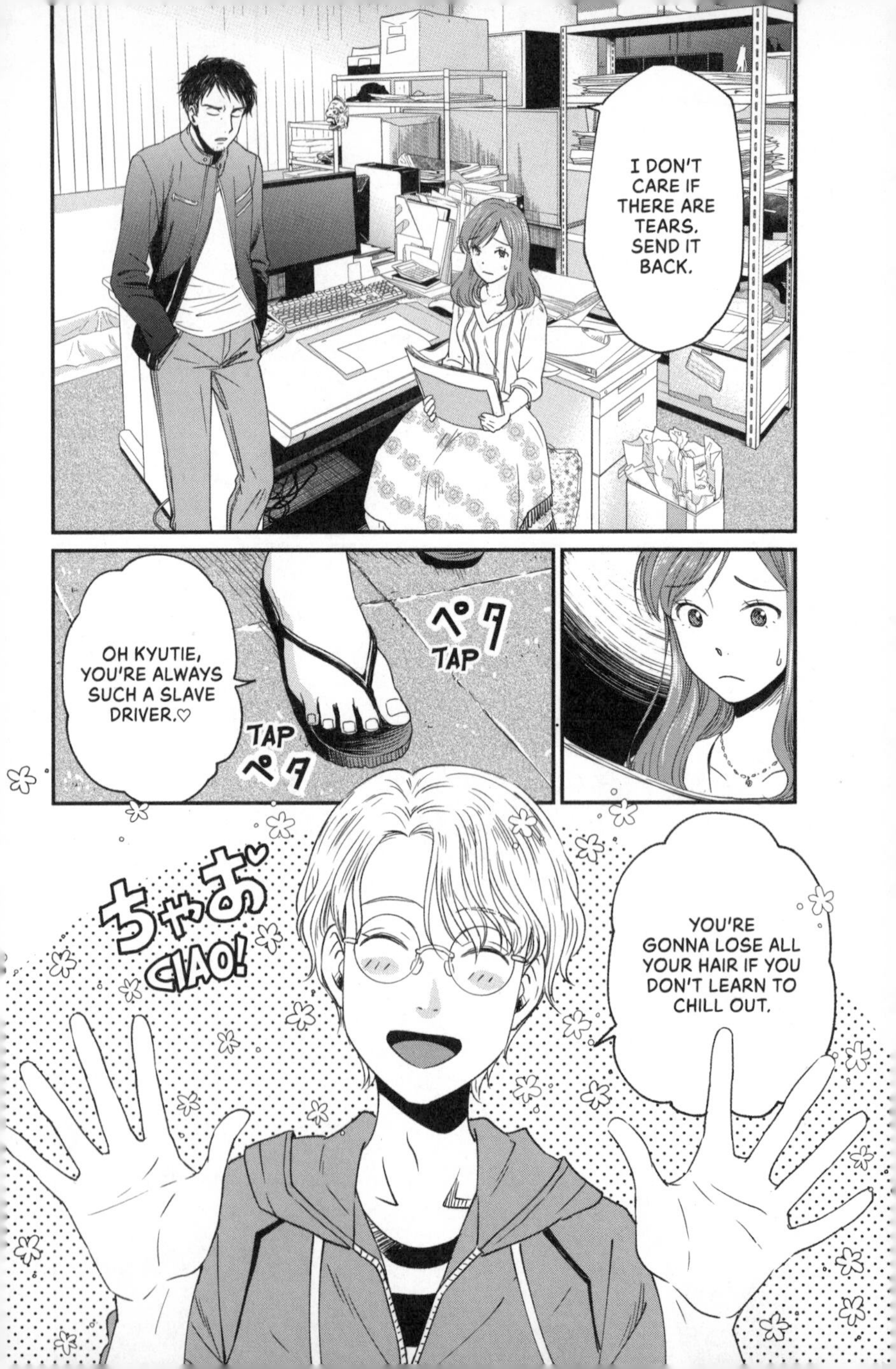
I DON'T CARE IF THERE ARE TEARS. SEND IT BACK.
ペタ TAP
OH KYUTIE, YOU'RE ALWAYS SUCH A SLAVE DRIVER.♡
TAP ペタ
YOU'RE GONNA LOSE ALL YOUR HAIR IF YOU DON'T LEARN TO CHILL OUT.
ちゃお♡ CIAO!

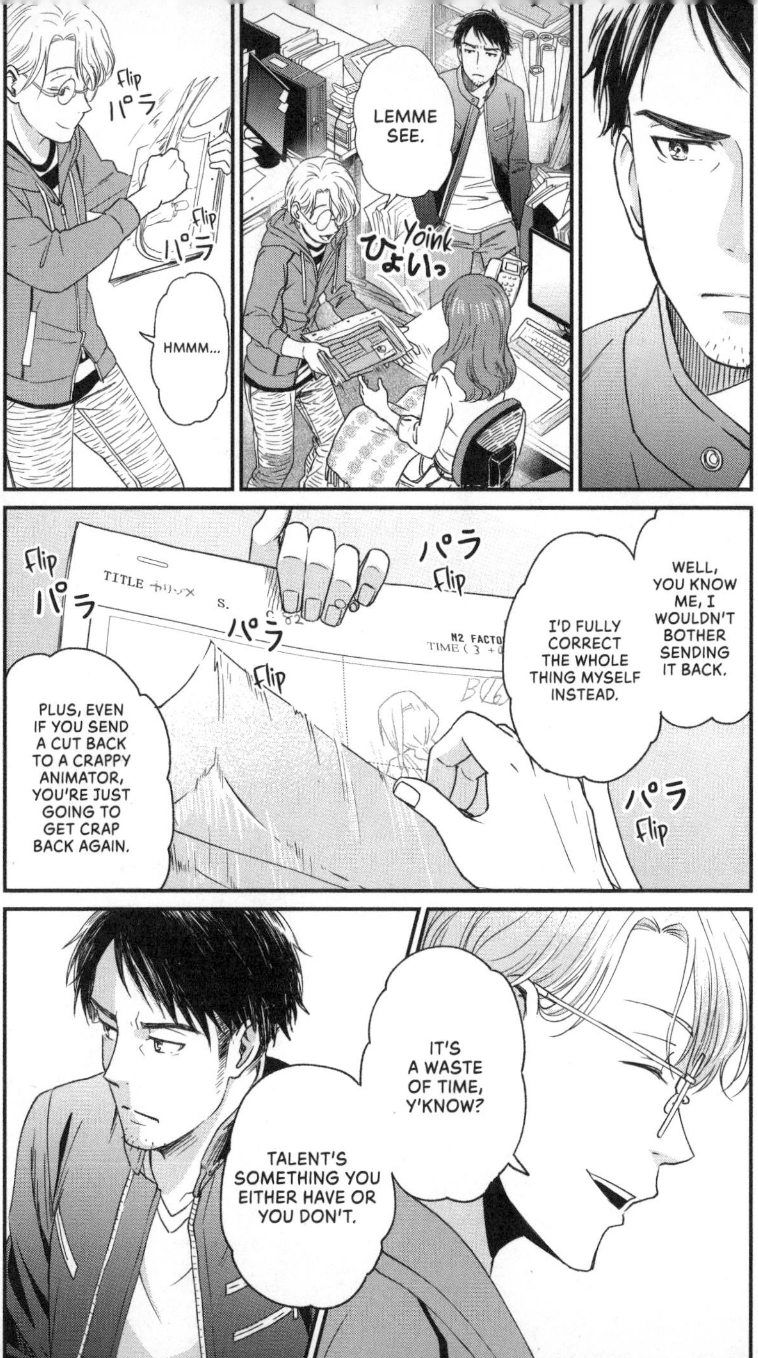
LEMME SEE.
Yoink ひょいっ
Flip パラ
Flip パラ
HMMM...
WELL, YOU KNOW ME, I WOULDN'T BOTHER SENDING IT BACK.
I'D FULLY CORRECT THE WHOLE THING MYSELF INSTEAD.
パラ Flip
Flip パラ
パラ Flip
PLUS, EVEN IF YOU SEND A CUT BACK TO A CRAPPY ANIMATOR, YOU'RE JUST GOING TO GET CRAP BACK AGAIN.
パラ Flip
IT'S A WASTE OF TIME, Y'KNOW?
TALENT'S SOMETHING YOU EITHER HAVE OR YOU DON'T.

Fully Corrected (Zenshu): When someone in a supervisory role (animation director, inbetween checker, etc) redraws work from scratch rather than correcting individual frames.

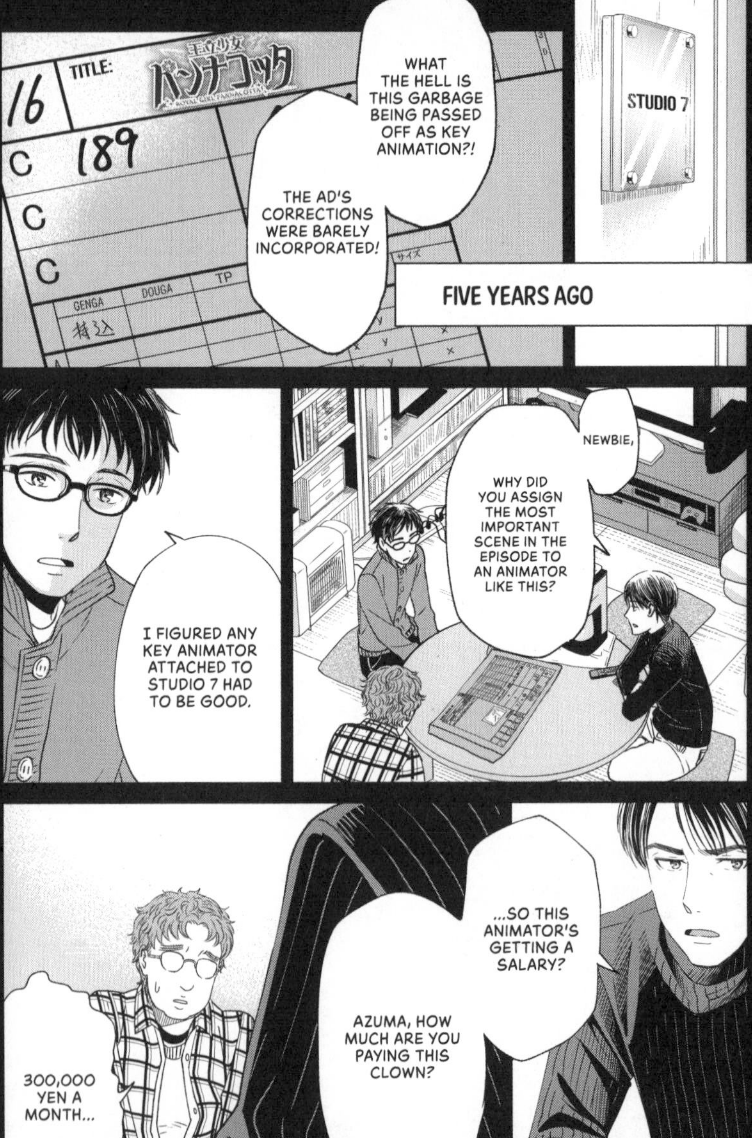
STUDIO 7
FIVE YEARS AGO
16
TITLE:
C 189
GENGA
DOUGA
TP
WHAT THE HELL IS THIS GARBAGE BEING PASSED OFF AS KEY ANIMATION?!
THE AD'S CORRECTIONS WERE BARELY INCORPORATED!
NEWBIE,
WHY DID YOU ASSIGN THE MOST IMPORTANT SCENE IN THE EPISODE TO AN ANIMATOR LIKE THIS?
I FIGURED ANY KEY ANIMATOR ATTACHED TO STUDIO 7 HAD TO BE GOOD.
...SO THIS ANIMATOR'S GETTING A SALARY?
AZUMA, HOW MUCH ARE YOU PAYING THIS CLOWN?
300,000 YEN A MONTH...

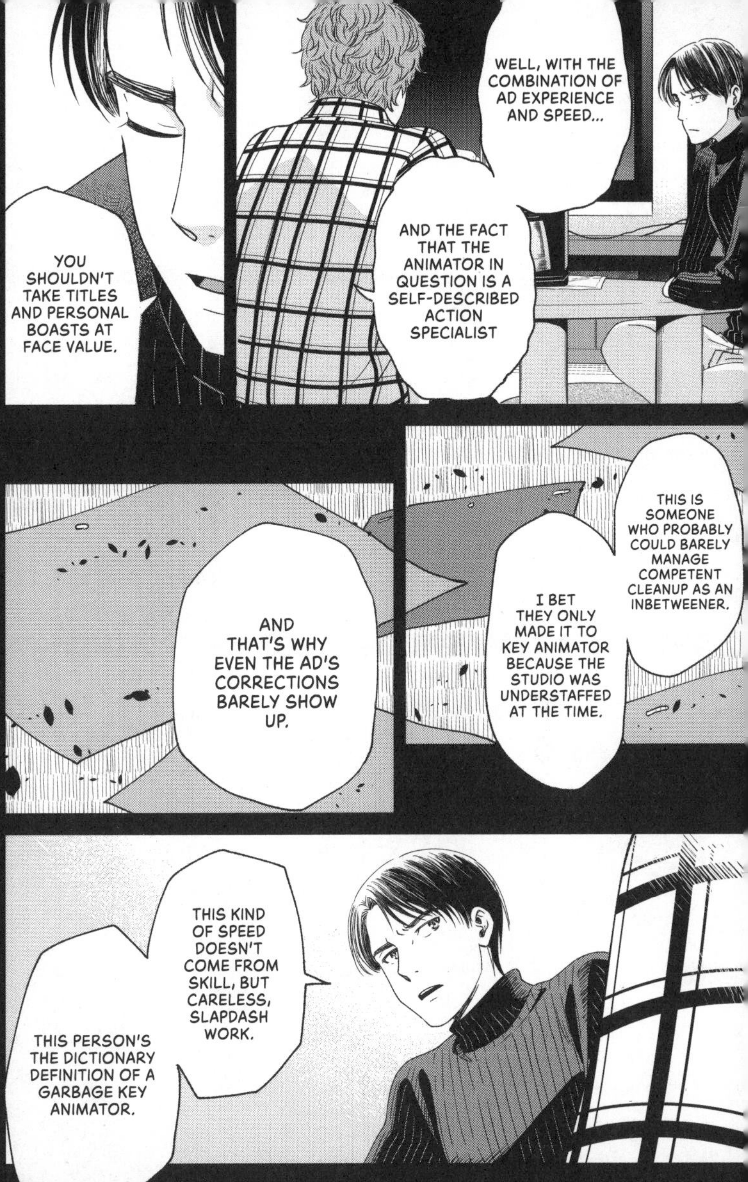
WELL, WITH THE COMBINATION OF AD EXPERIENCE AND SPEED...
AND THE FACT THAT THE ANIMATOR IN QUESTION IS A SELF-DESCRIBED ACTION SPECIALIST
YOU SHOULDN'T TAKE TITLES AND PERSONAL BOASTS AT FACE VALUE.
THIS IS SOMEONE WHO PROBABLY COULD BARELY MANAGE COMPETENT CLEANUP AS AN INBETWEENER.
I BET THEY ONLY MADE IT TO KEY ANIMATOR BECAUSE THE STUDIO WAS UNDERSTAFFED AT THE TIME.
AND THAT'S WHY EVEN THE AD'S CORRECTIONS BARELY SHOW UP.
THIS KIND OF SPEED DOESN'T COME FROM SKILL, BUT CARELESS, SLAPDASH WORK.
THIS PERSON'S THE DICTIONARY DEFINITION OF A GARBAGE KEY ANIMATOR.

Cleanup: Tracing and applying corrections to raw keyframes (genga)

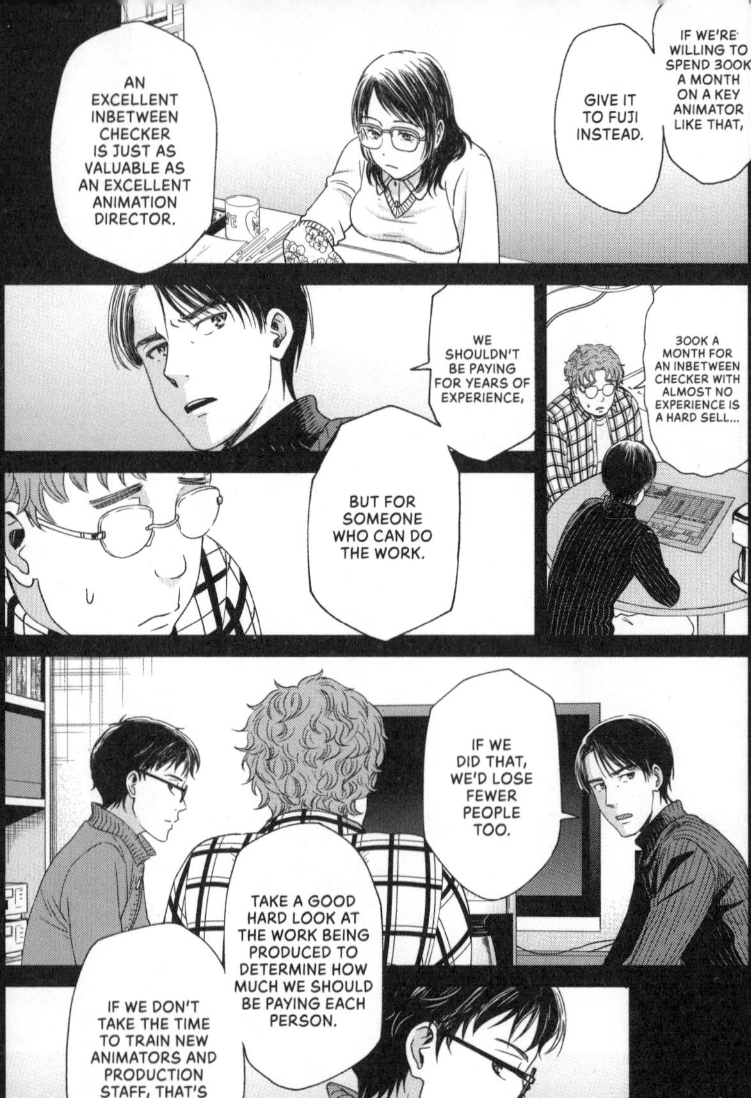
IF WE'RE WILLING TO SPEND 300K A MONTH ON A KEY ANIMATOR LIKE THAT,
GIVE IT TO FUJI INSTEAD.
AN EXCELLENT INBETWEEN CHECKER IS JUST AS VALUABLE AS AN EXCELLENT ANIMATION DIRECTOR.
300K A MONTH FOR AN INBETWEEN CHECKER WITH ALMOST NO EXPERIENCE IS A HARD SELL...
WE SHOULDN'T BE PAYING FOR YEARS OF EXPERIENCE,
BUT FOR SOMEONE WHO CAN DO THE WORK.
IF WE DID THAT, WE'D LOSE FEWER PEOPLE TOO.
TAKE A GOOD HARD LOOK AT THE WORK BEING PRODUCED TO DETERMINE HOW MUCH WE SHOULD BE PAYING EACH PERSON.
IF WE DON'T TAKE THE TIME TO TRAIN NEW ANIMATORS AND PRODUCTION STAFF, THAT'S IT FOR THIS INDUSTRY.

the inbetweens are neat and the motion smooth. Similar to the job of the Animation Director (sakuga kantoku) but for inbetweens and cleanup rather than key animation.

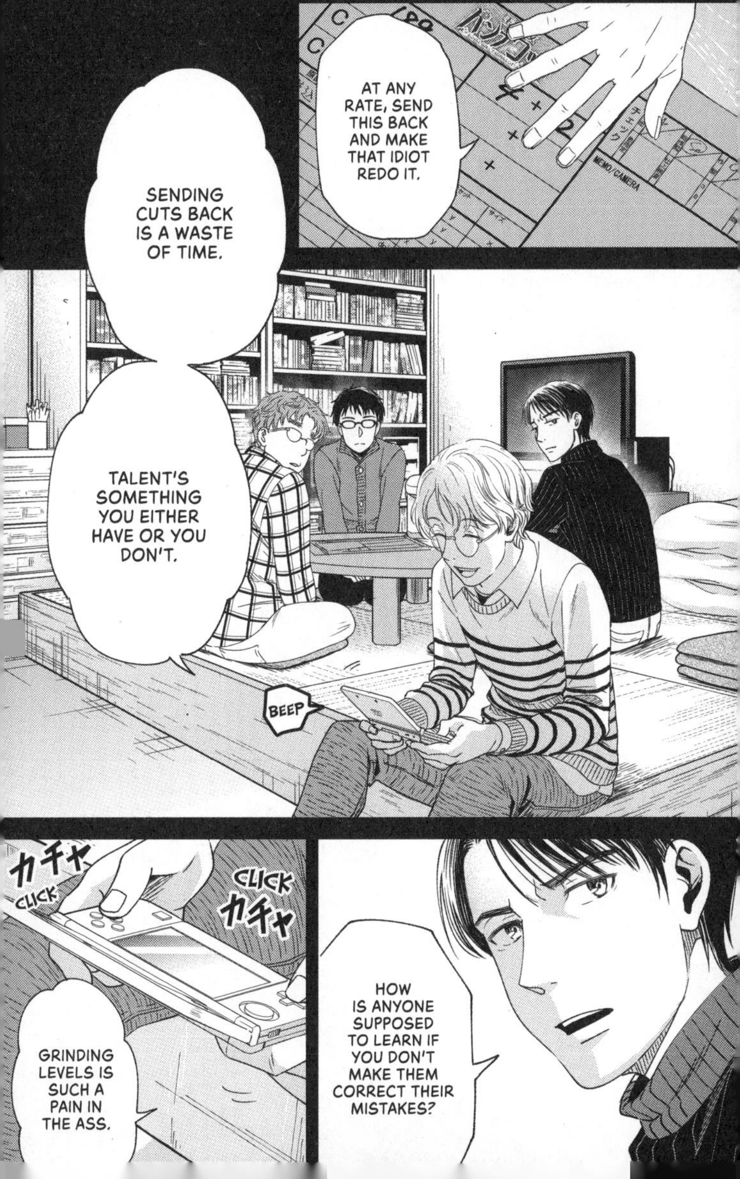
AT ANY RATE, SEND THIS BACK AND MAKE THAT IDIOT REDO IT.
SENDING CUTS BACK IS A WASTE OF TIME.
TALENT'S SOMETHING YOU EITHER HAVE OR YOU DON'T.
BEEP
HOW IS ANYONE SUPPOSED TO LEARN IF YOU DON'T MAKE THEM CORRECT THEIR MISTAKES?
カチャ
CLICK
カチャ
CLICK
GRINDING LEVELS IS SUCH A PAIN IN THE ASS.

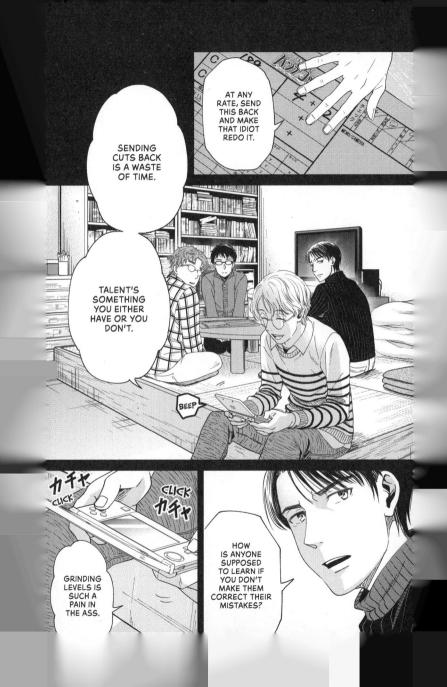

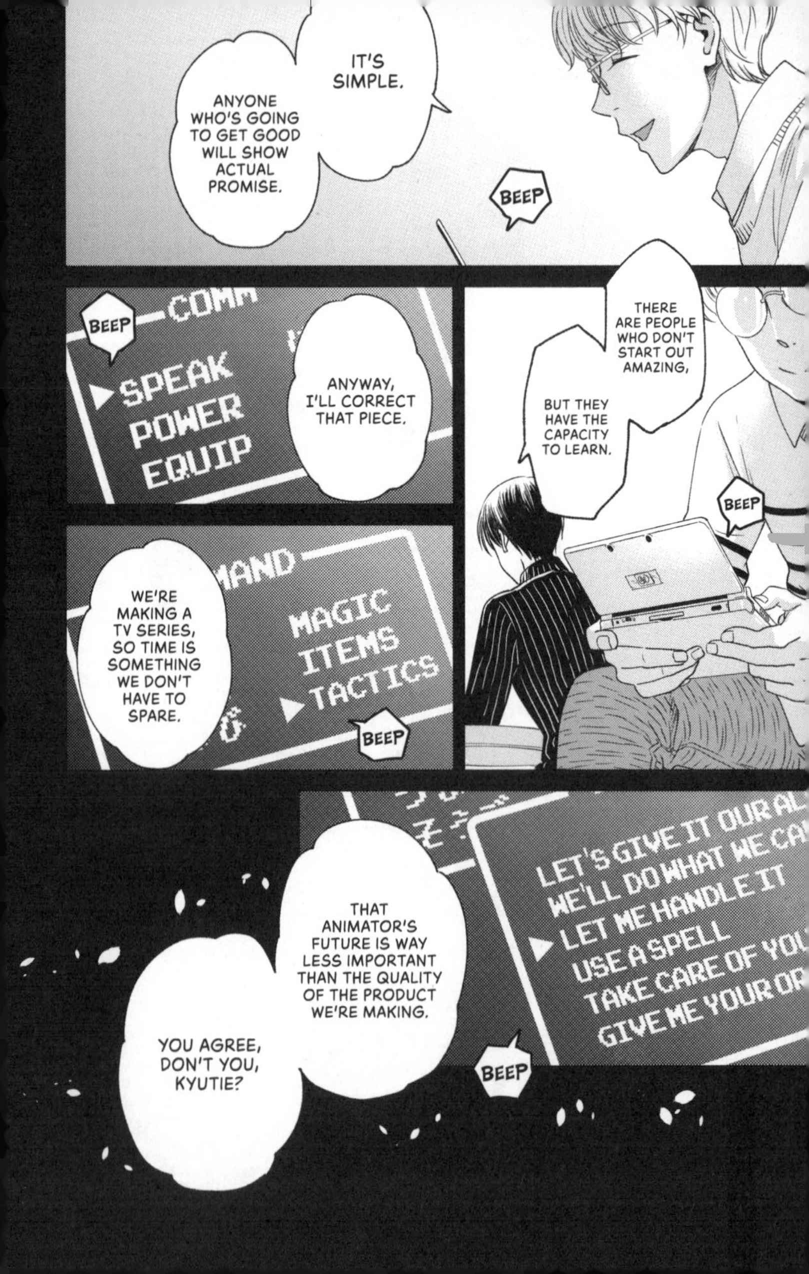
IT'S SIMPLE.
ANYONE WHO'S GOING TO GET GOOD WILL SHOW ACTUAL PROMISE.
BEEP
THERE ARE PEOPLE WHO DON'T START OUT AMAZING,
BUT THEY HAVE THE CAPACITY TO LEARN.
BEEP
ANYWAY, I'LL CORRECT THAT PIECE.
BEEP
COMM
SPEAK
POWER
EQUIP
MAND
WE'RE MAKING A TV SERIES, SO TIME IS SOMETHING WE DON'T HAVE TO SPARE.
MAGIC
ITEMS
TACTICS
BEEP
LET'S GIVE IT OUR AL
WE'LL DO WHAT WE CA
LET ME HANDLE IT
USE A SPELL
TAKE CARE OF YOU
GIVE ME YOUR OR
THAT ANIMATOR'S FUTURE IS WAY LESS IMPORTANT THAN THE QUALITY OF THE PRODUCT WE'RE MAKING.
YOU AGREE, DON'T YOU, KYUTIE?
BEEP

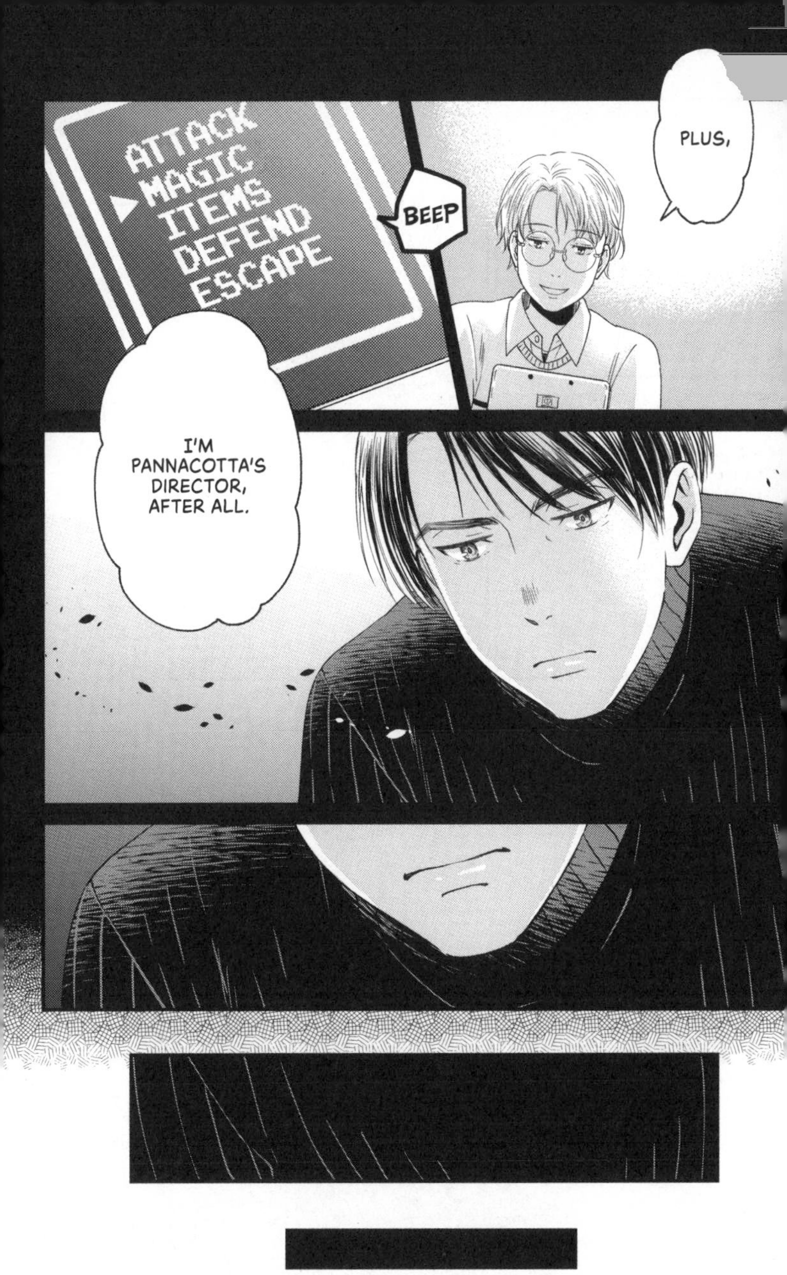
PLUS,
BEEP
ATTACK
MAGIC
▶ITEMS
DEFEND
ESCAPE
I'M PANNACOTTA'S DIRECTOR, AFTER ALL.

[redacted]

[redacted]

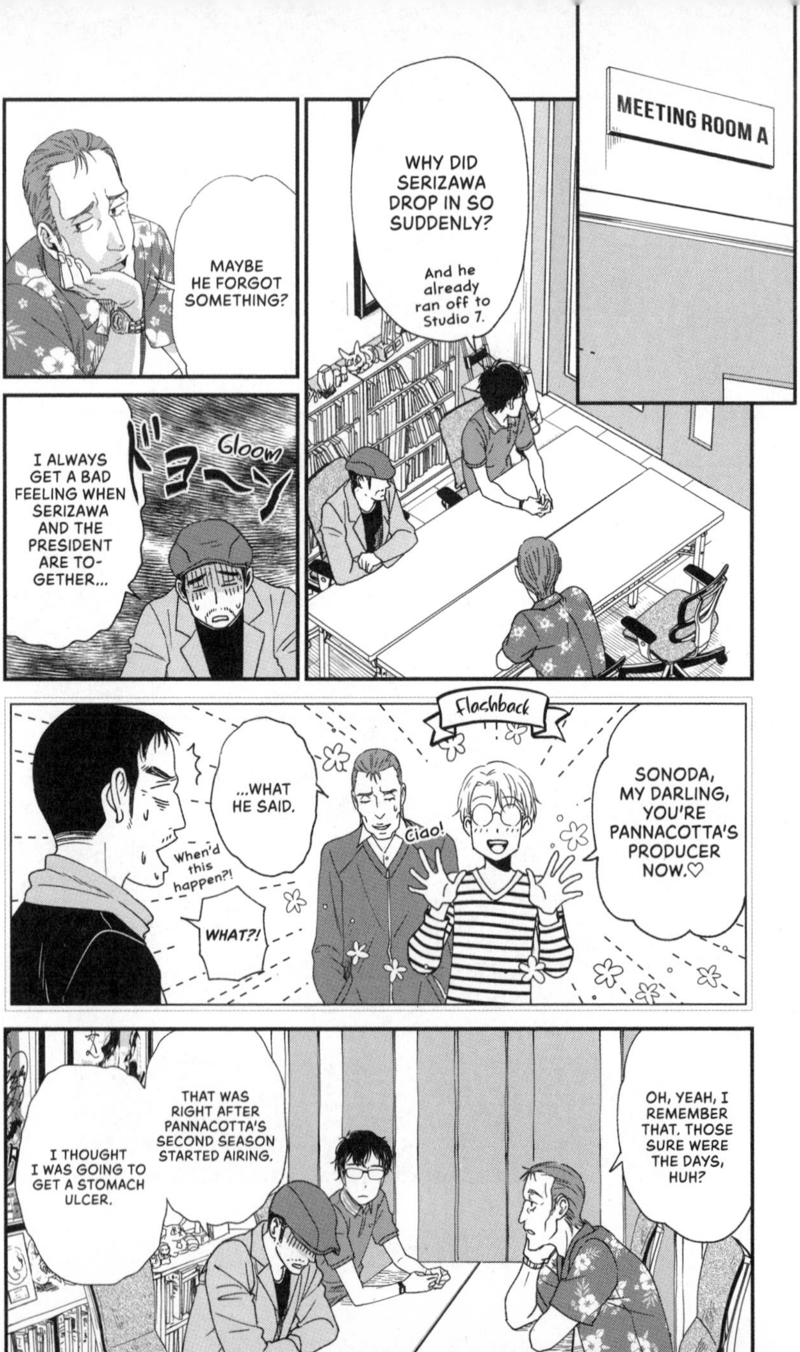
MEETING ROOM A
WHY DID SERIZAWA DROP IN SO SUDDENLY?
And he already ran off to Studio 7.
MAYBE HE FORGOT SOMETHING?
I ALWAYS GET A BAD FEELING WHEN SERIZAWA AND THE PRESIDENT ARE TO-GETHER...
Gloom
Flashback
SONODA, MY DARLING, YOU'RE PANNACOTTA'S PRODUCER NOW.♡
Ciao!
...WHAT HE SAID.
When'd this happen?!
WHAT?!
OH, YEAH, I REMEMBER THAT. THOSE SURE WERE THE DAYS, HUH?
THAT WAS RIGHT AFTER PANNACOTTA'S SECOND SEASON STARTED AIRING.
I THOUGHT I WAS GOING TO GET A STOMACH ULCER.

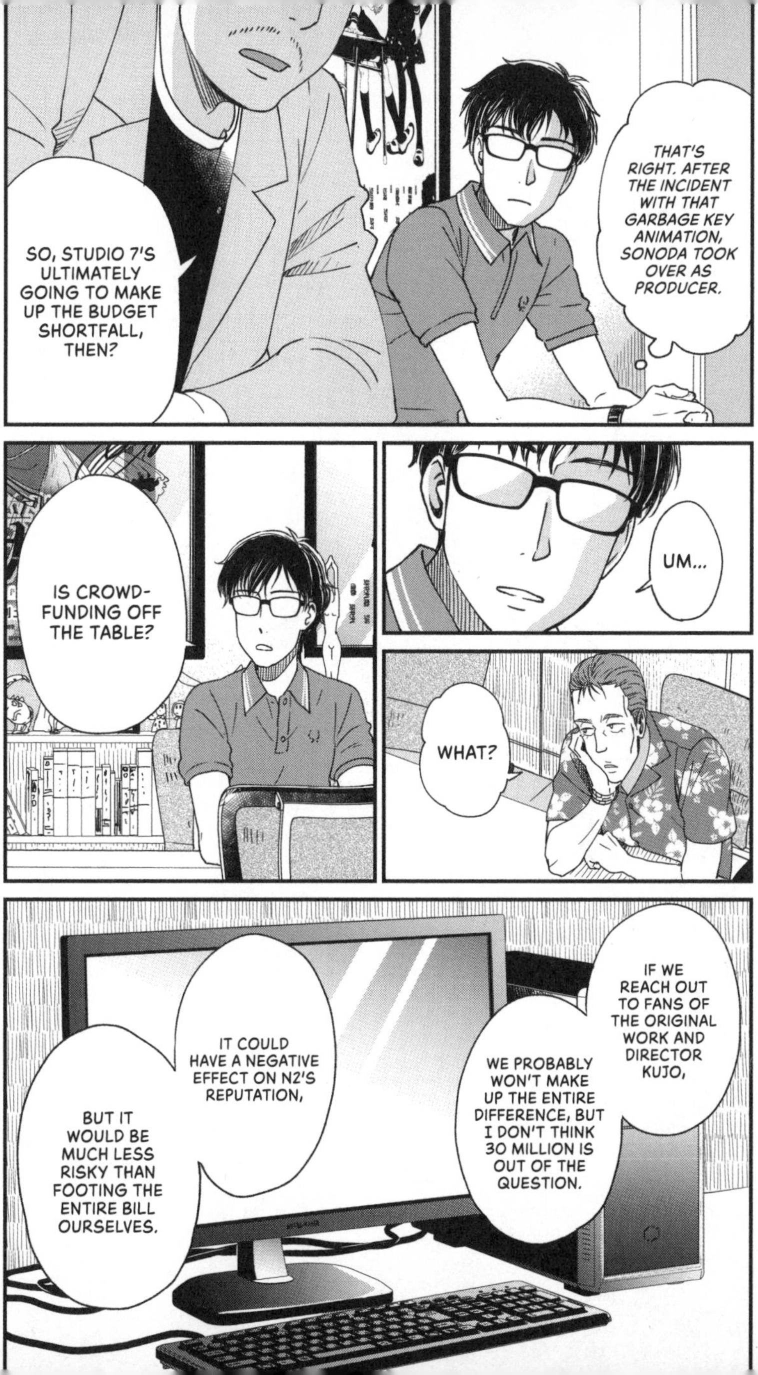
THAT'S RIGHT. AFTER THE INCIDENT WITH THAT GARBAGE KEY ANIMATION, SONODA TOOK OVER AS PRODUCER.
SO, STUDIO 7'S ULTIMATELY GOING TO MAKE UP THE BUDGET SHORTFALL, THEN?
UM...
WHAT?
IS CROWD-FUNDING OFF THE TABLE?
IF WE REACH OUT TO FANS OF THE ORIGINAL WORK AND DIRECTOR KUJO,
WE PROBABLY WON'T MAKE UP THE ENTIRE DIFFERENCE, BUT I DON'T THINK 30 MILLION IS OUT OF THE QUESTION.
IT COULD HAVE A NEGATIVE EFFECT ON N2'S REPUTATION,
BUT IT WOULD BE MUCH LESS RISKY THAN FOOTING THE ENTIRE BILL OURSELVES.

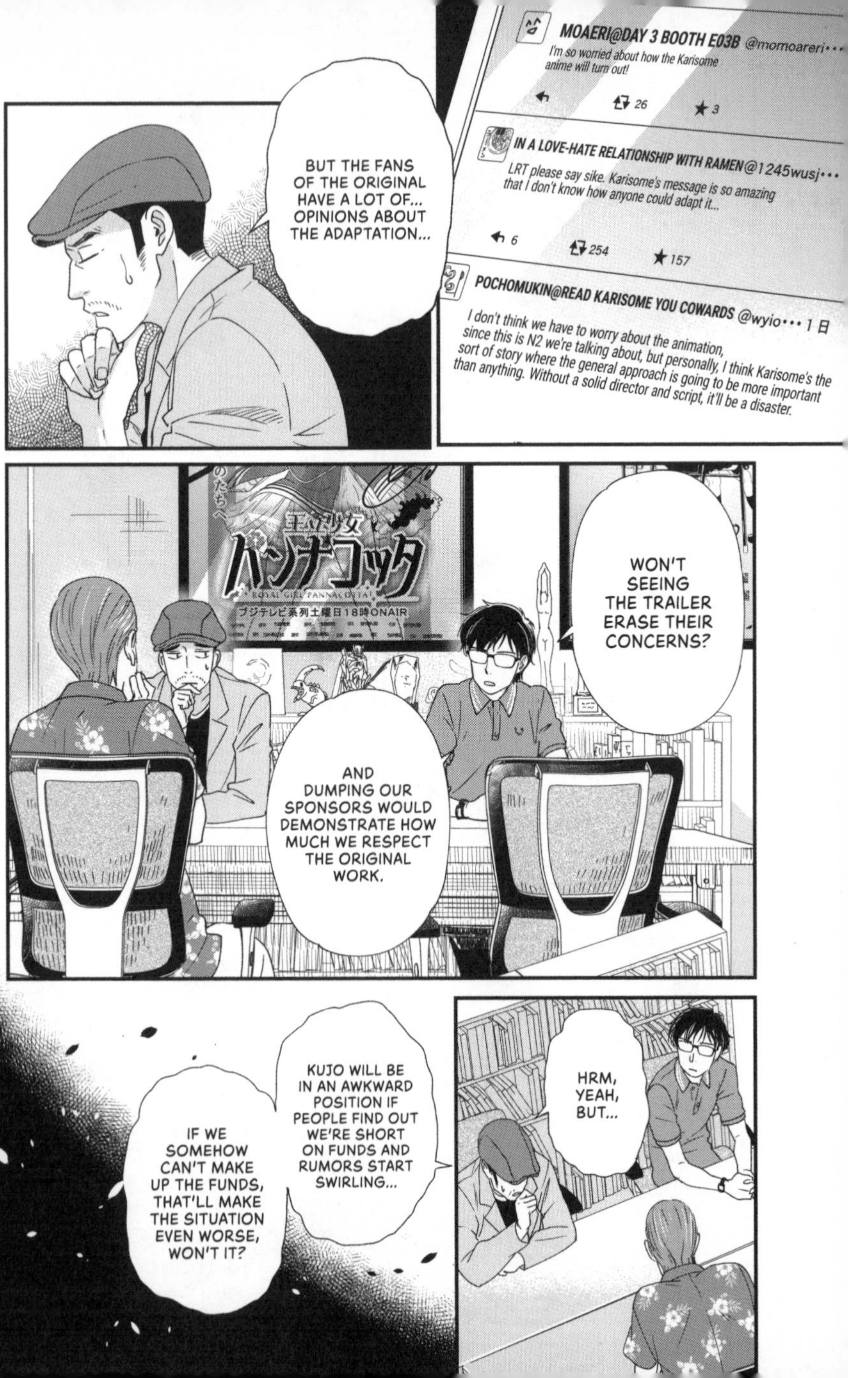
MOAERI@DAY 3 BOOTH E03B @momoareri・・・
I'm so worried about how the Karisome anime will turn out!
26
3
IN A LOVE-HATE RELATIONSHIP WITH RAMEN@1245wusj・・・
LRT please say sike. Karisome's message is so amazing that I don't know how anyone could adapt it...
6
254
157
POCHOMUKIN@READ KARISOME YOU COWARDS @wyio・・・1日
I don't think we have to worry about the animation, since this is N2 we're talking about, but personally, I think Karisome's the sort of story where the general approach is going to be more important than anything. Without a solid director and script, it'll be a disaster.
BUT THE FANS OF THE ORIGINAL HAVE A LOT OF... OPINIONS ABOUT THE ADAPTATION...
王立少女
パンナコッタ
ROYAL GIRL PANNACOTTA
フジテレビ系列土曜日18時ONAIR
WON'T SEEING THE TRAILER ERASE THEIR CONCERNS?
AND DUMPING OUR SPONSORS WOULD DEMONSTRATE HOW MUCH WE RESPECT THE ORIGINAL WORK.
HRM, YEAH, BUT...
KUJO WILL BE IN AN AWKWARD POSITION IF PEOPLE FIND OUT WE'RE SHORT ON FUNDS AND RUMORS START SWIRLING...
IF WE SOMEHOW CAN'T MAKE UP THE FUNDS, THAT'LL MAKE THE SITUATION EVEN WORSE, WON'T IT?

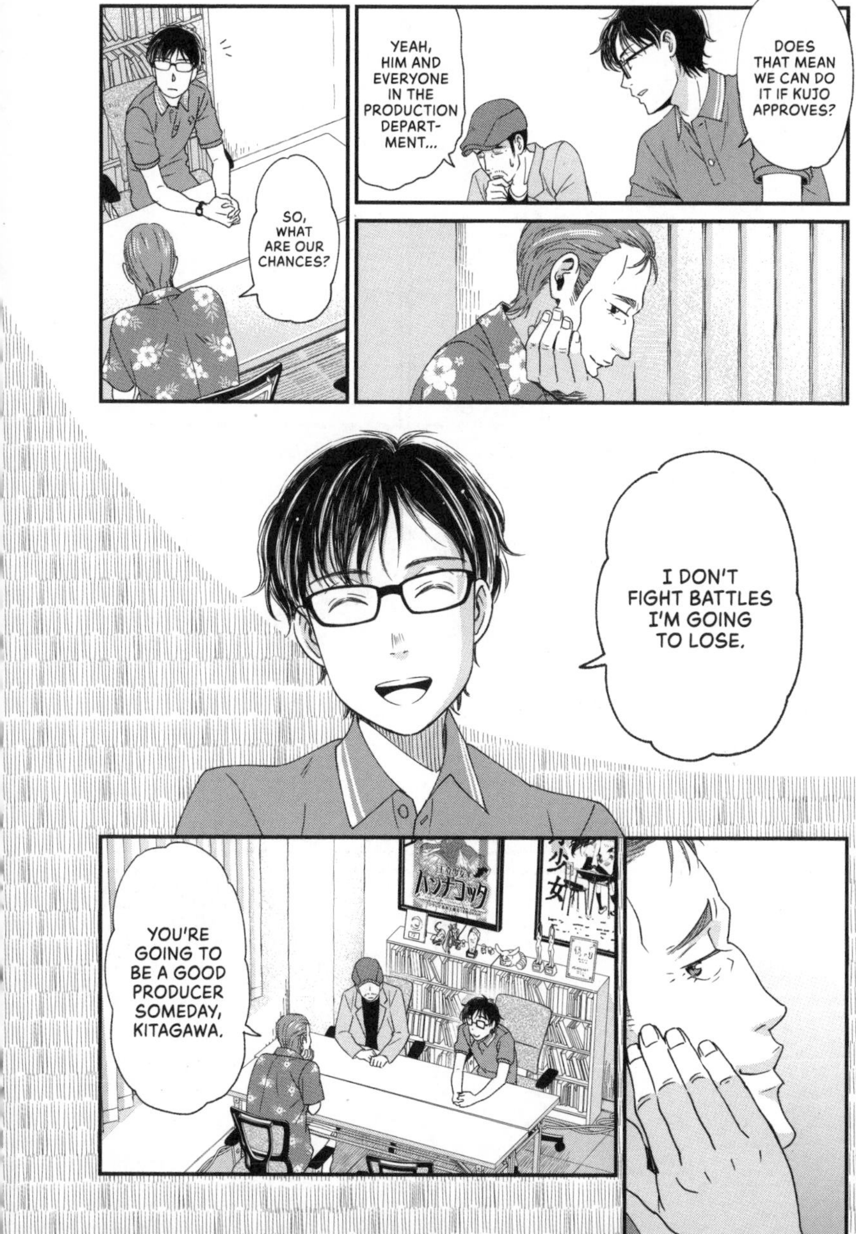
DOES THAT MEAN WE CAN DO IT IF KUJO APPROVES?
YEAH, HIM AND EVERYONE IN THE PRODUCTION DEPART-MENT...
SO, WHAT ARE OUR CHANCES?
I DON'T FIGHT BATTLES I'M GOING TO LOSE.
YOU'RE GOING TO BE A GOOD PRODUCER SOMEDAY, KITAGAWA.

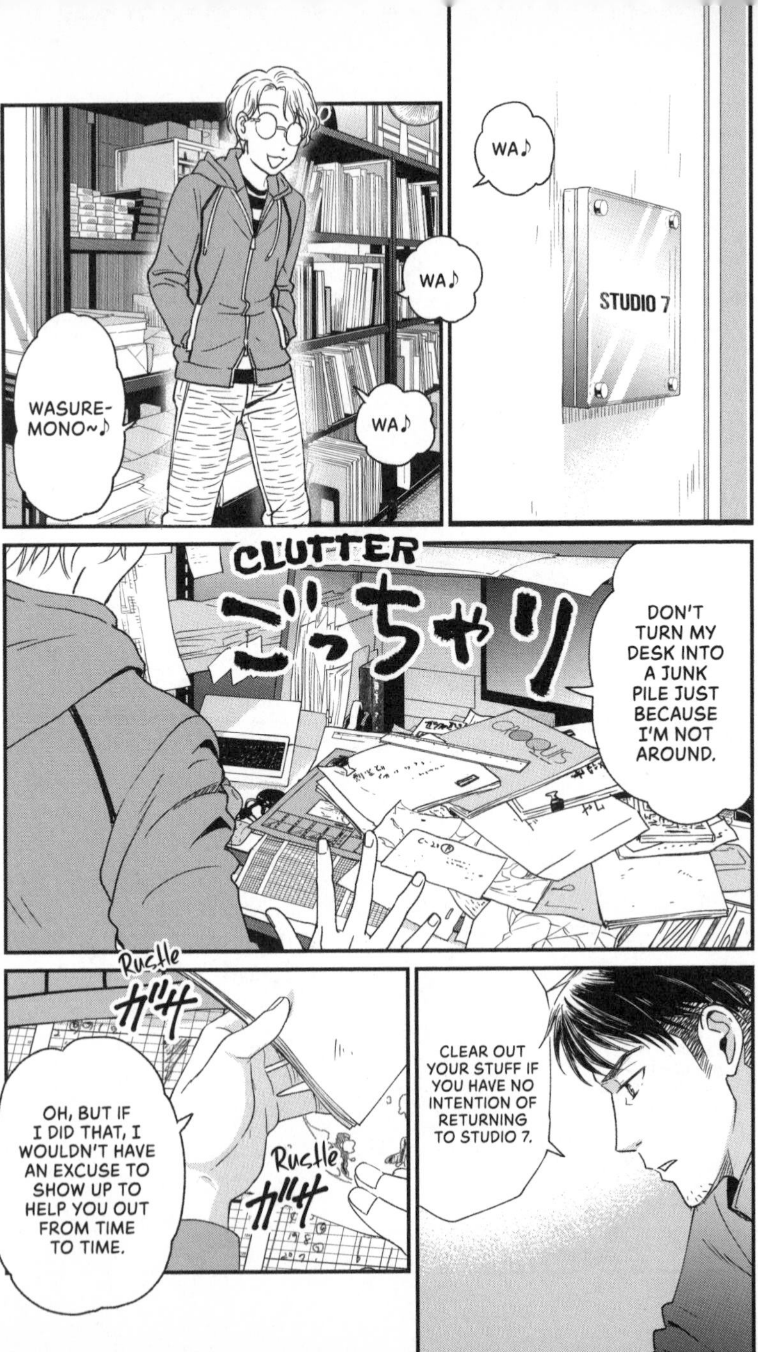
WA♪
STUDIO 7
WA♪
WA♪
WASURE-MONO~♪
CLUTTER
ごっちゃり
DON'T TURN MY DESK INTO A JUNK PILE JUST BECAUSE I'M NOT AROUND.
CLEAR OUT YOUR STUFF IF YOU HAVE NO INTENTION OF RETURNING TO STUDIO 7.
Rustle
ガサ
OH, BUT IF I DID THAT, I WOULDN'T HAVE AN EXCUSE TO SHOW UP TO HELP YOU OUT FROM TIME TO TIME.
Rustle
ガサ

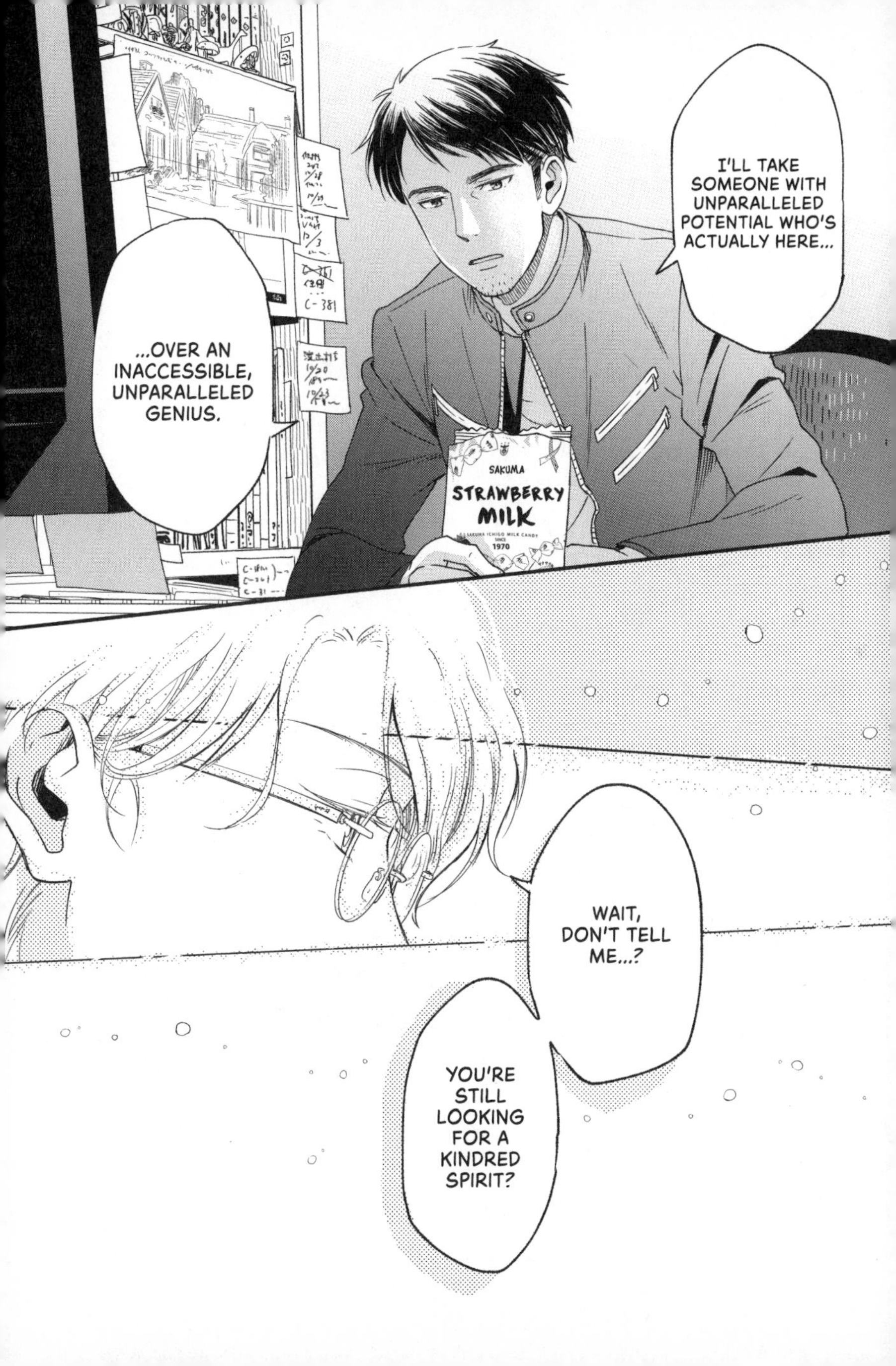
I'LL TAKE SOMEONE WITH UNPARALLELED POTENTIAL WHO'S ACTUALLY HERE...
...OVER AN INACCESSIBLE, UNPARALLELED GENIUS.
SAKUMA
STRAWBERRY MILK
SINCE 1970
WAIT, DON'T TELL ME...?
YOU'RE STILL LOOKING FOR A KINDRED SPIRIT?

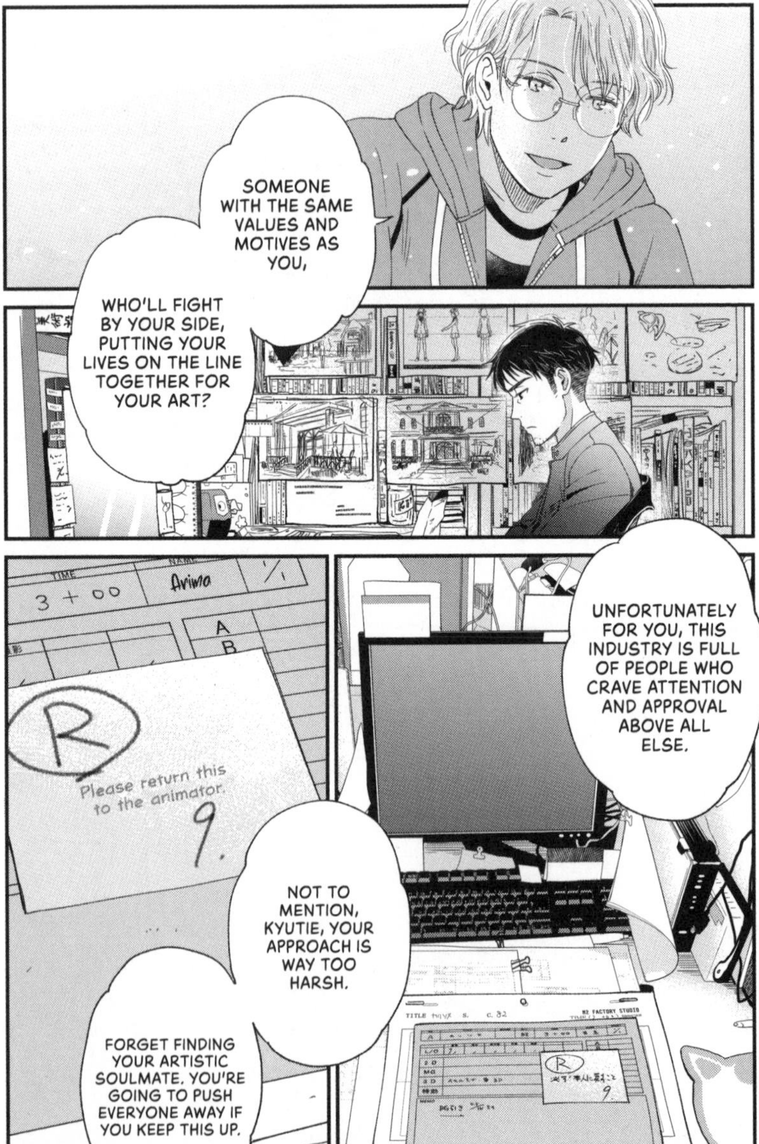
SOMEONE WITH THE SAME VALUES AND MOTIVES AS YOU,
WHO'LL FIGHT BY YOUR SIDE, PUTTING YOUR LIVES ON THE LINE TOGETHER FOR YOUR ART?
UNFORTUNATELY FOR YOU, THIS INDUSTRY IS FULL OF PEOPLE WHO CRAVE ATTENTION AND APPROVAL ABOVE ALL ELSE.
NOT TO MENTION, KYUTIE, YOUR APPROACH IS WAY TOO HARSH.
FORGET FINDING YOUR ARTISTIC SOULMATE. YOU'RE GOING TO PUSH EVERYONE AWAY IF YOU KEEP THIS UP.
Please return this to the animator.

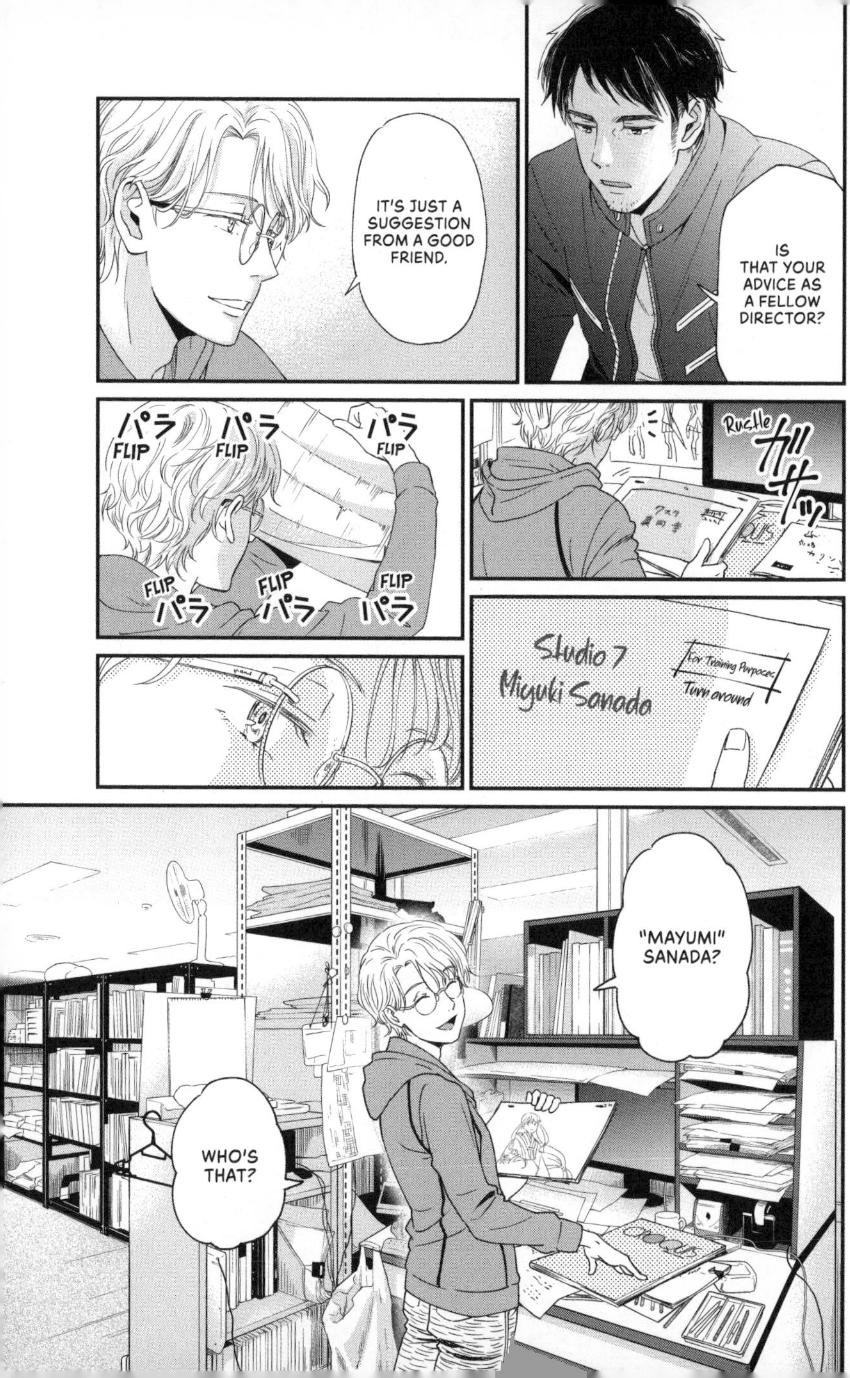
IS THAT YOUR ADVICE AS A FELLOW DIRECTOR?
IT'S JUST A SUGGESTION FROM A GOOD FRIEND.
Rustle ガサッ
パラ FLIP
パラ FLIP
パラ FLIP
FLIP パラ
FLIP パラ
FLIP パラ
Studio 7
Miyuki Sanada
For Training Purposes
Turn around
"MAYUMI" SANADA?
WHO'S THAT?

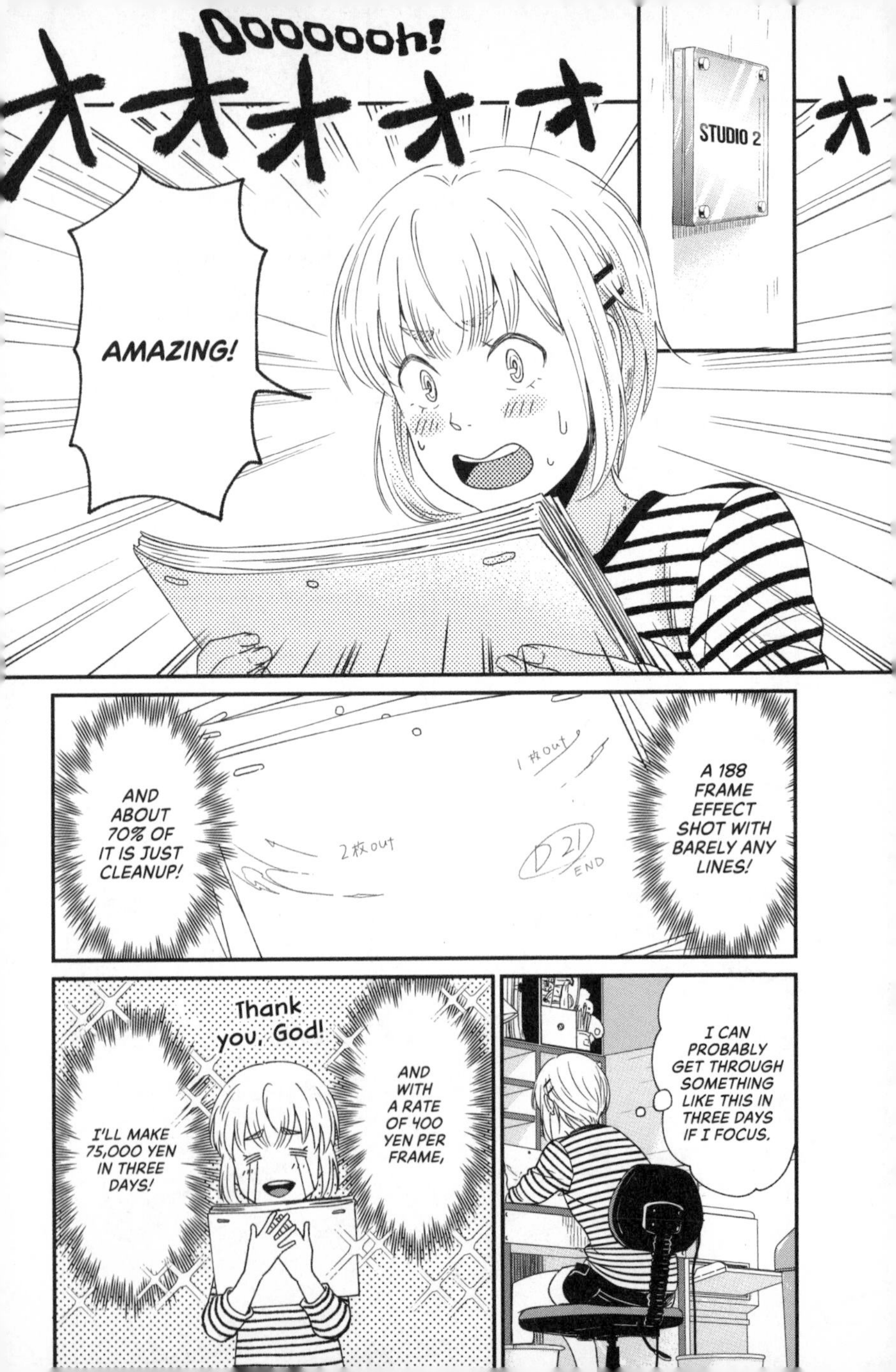

Oooooh!
オオオオオオ
STUDIO 2
AMAZING!
A 188 FRAME EFFECT SHOT WITH BARELY ANY LINES!
1枚out
D21 END
2枚out
AND ABOUT 70% OF IT IS JUST CLEANUP!
I CAN PROBABLY GET THROUGH SOMETHING LIKE THIS IN THREE DAYS IF I FOCUS.
AND WITH A RATE OF 400 YEN PER FRAME,
I'LL MAKE 75,000 YEN IN THREE DAYS!
Thank you, God!

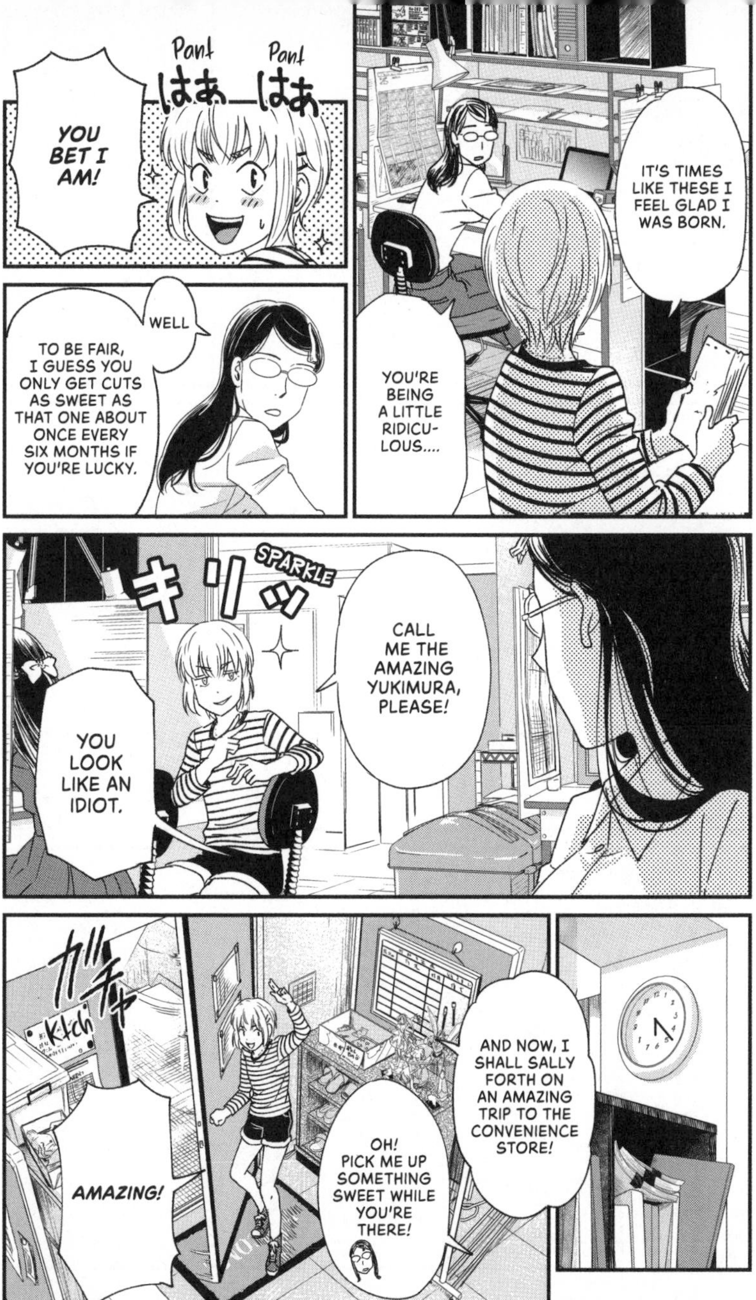
IT'S TIMES LIKE THESE I FEEL GLAD I WAS BORN.
YOU'RE BEING A LITTLE RIDICULOUS....
Pant はあ Pant はあ
YOU BET I AM!
WELL
TO BE FAIR, I GUESS YOU ONLY GET CUTS AS SWEET AS THAT ONE ABOUT ONCE EVERY SIX MONTHS IF YOU'RE LUCKY.
SPARKLE キリッ
CALL ME THE AMAZING YUKIMURA, PLEASE!
YOU LOOK LIKE AN IDIOT.
AND NOW, I SHALL SALLY FORTH ON AN AMAZING TRIP TO THE CONVENIENCE STORE!
OH! PICK ME UP SOMETHING SWEET WHILE YOU'RE THERE!
ガチャ Ktch
AMAZING!

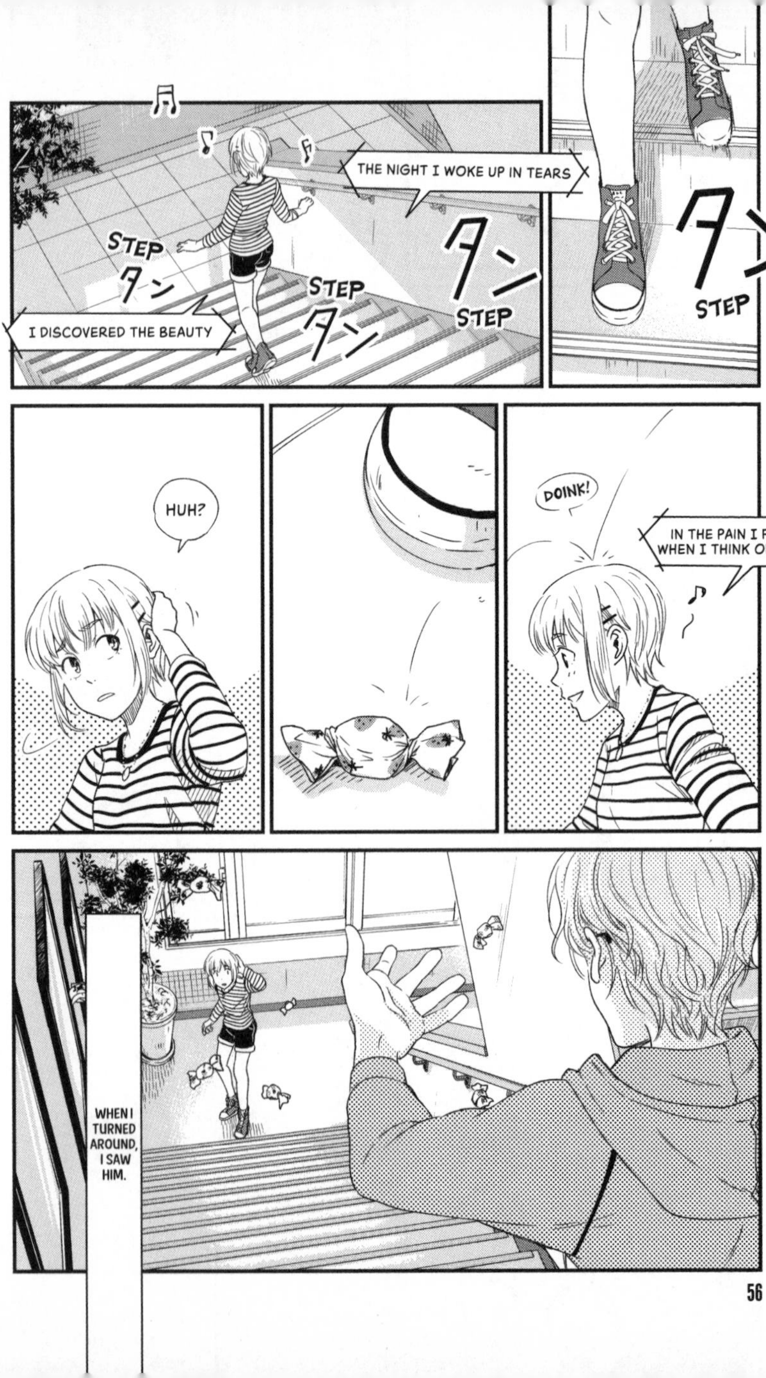
タン
STEP
THE NIGHT I WOKE UP IN TEARS
タン
STEP
STEP
タン
STEP
タン
I DISCOVERED THE BEAUTY
DOINK!
IN THE PAIN I FEEL WHEN I THINK OF YO...
HUH?
WHEN I TURNED AROUND, I SAW HIM.

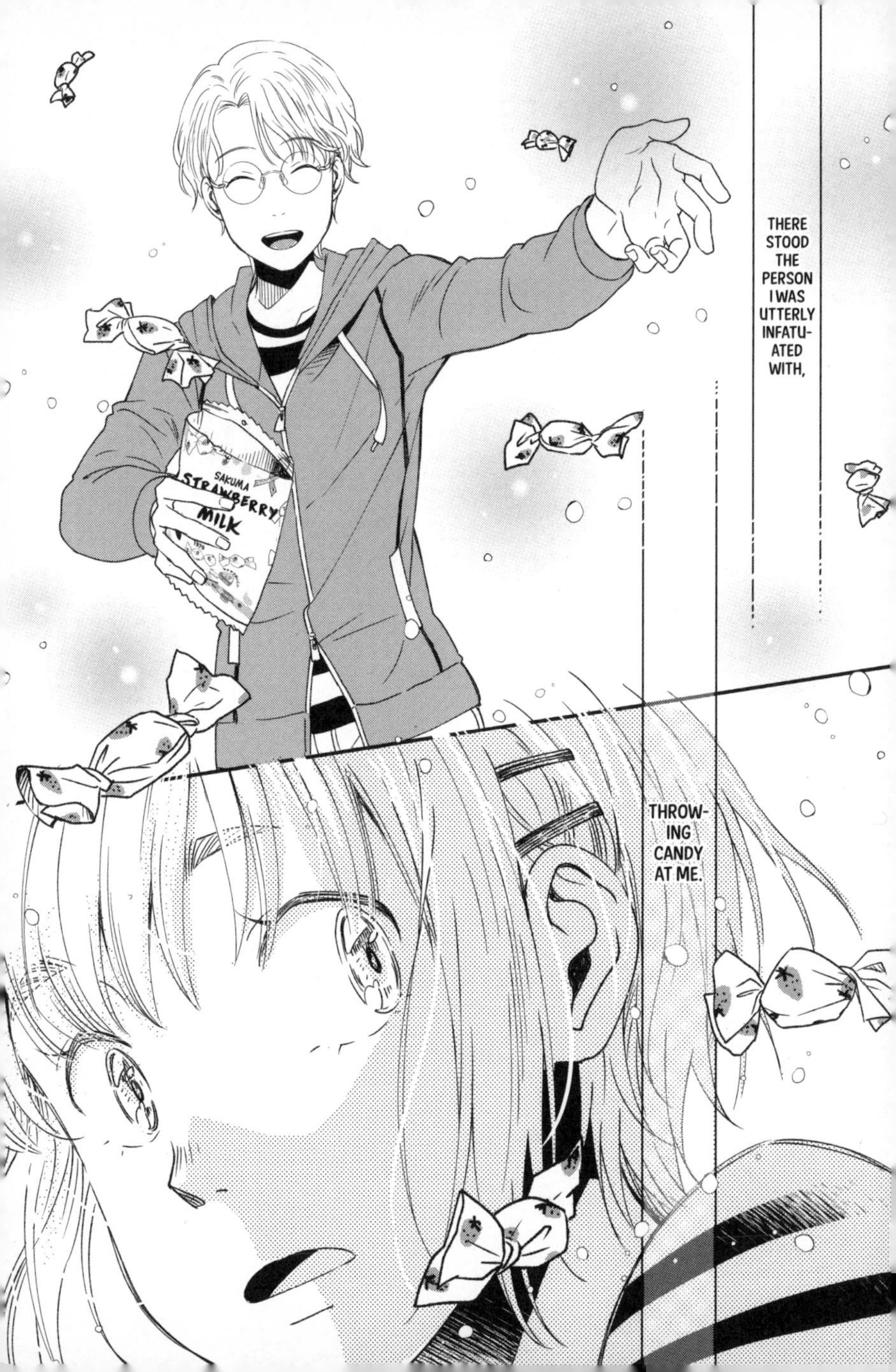
THERE STOOD THE PERSON I WAS UTTERLY INFATUATED WITH,
SAKUMA STRAWBERRY MILK
THROWING CANDY AT ME.

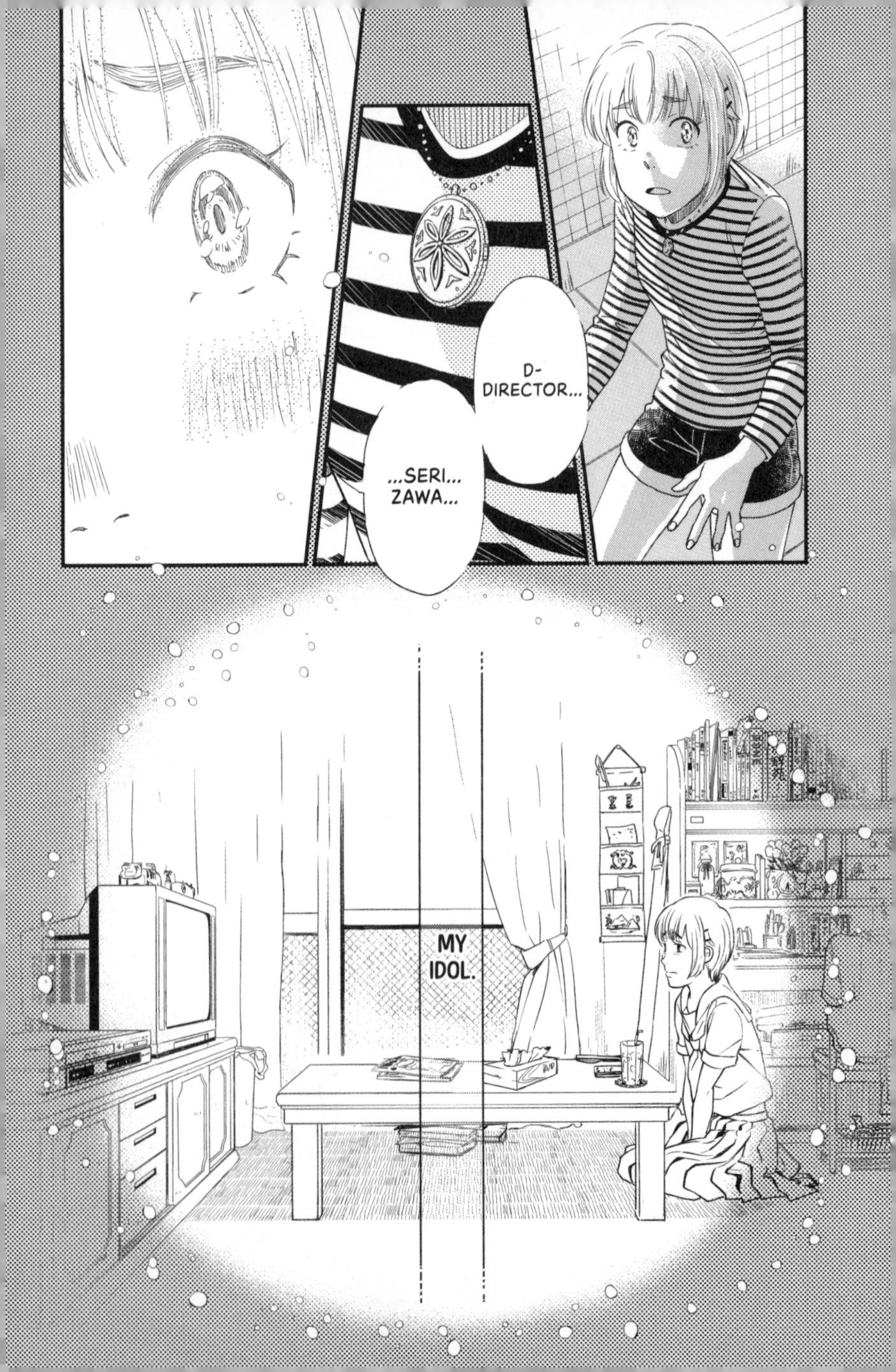
D-DIRECTOR...
...SERI... ZAWA...
MY IDOL.

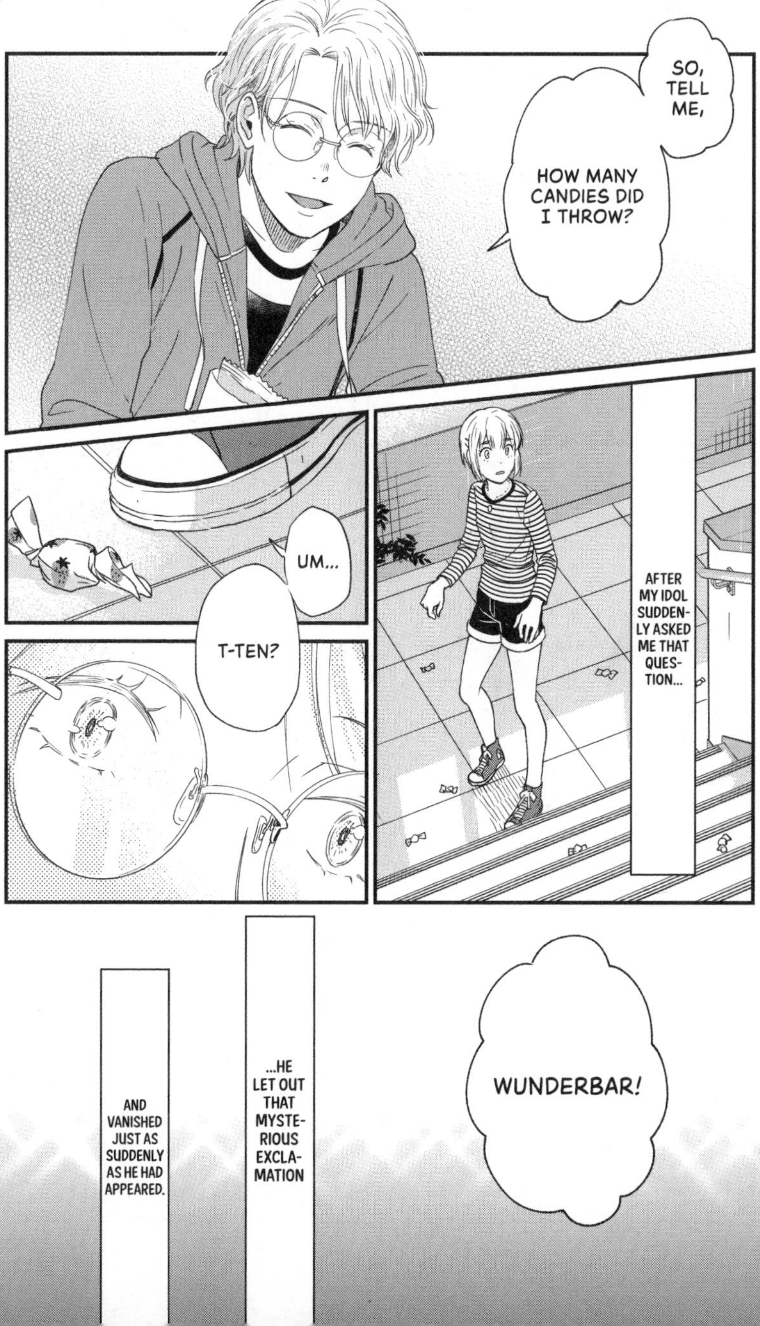
SO, TELL ME,
HOW MANY CANDIES DID I THROW?
AFTER MY IDOL SUDDENLY ASKED ME THAT QUESTION...
UM...
T-TEN?
WUNDERBAR!
...HE LET OUT THAT MYSTERIOUS EXCLAMATION
AND VANISHED JUST AS SUDDENLY AS HE HAD APPEARED.

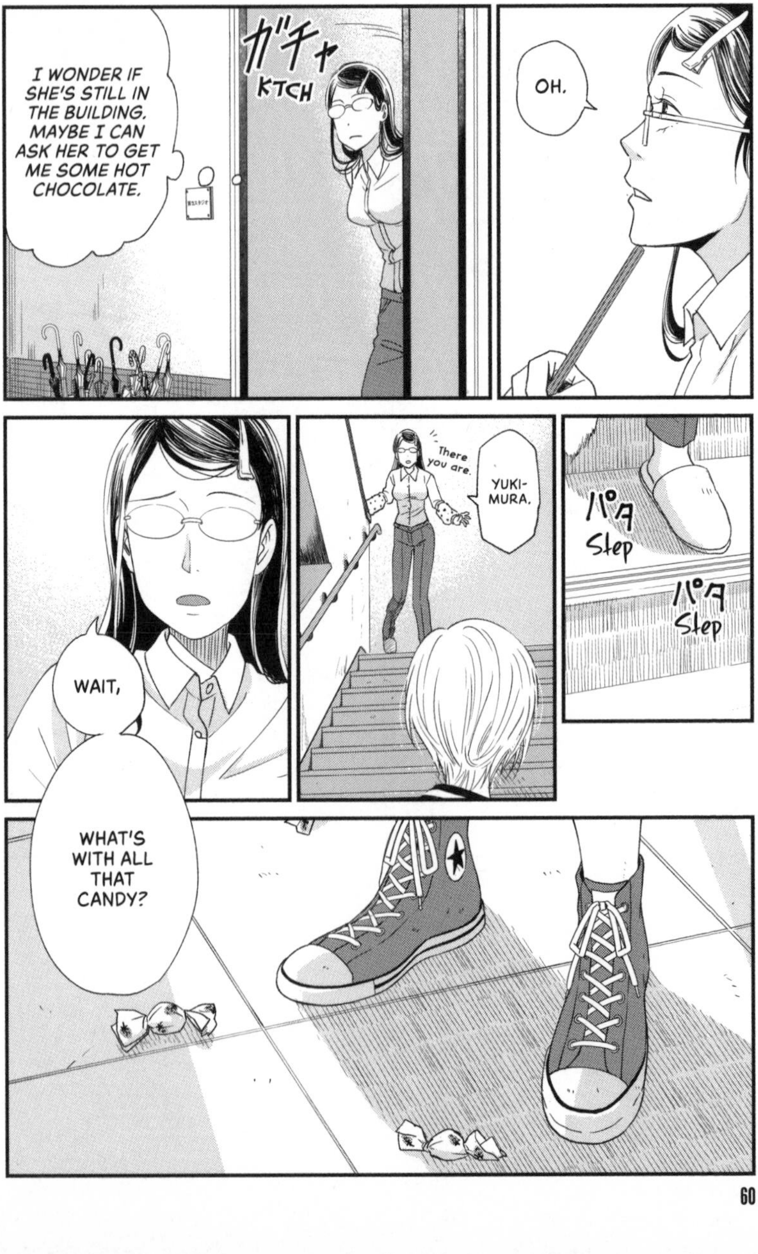
OH.
ガチャ
KTCH
I WONDER IF SHE'S STILL IN THE BUILDING. MAYBE I CAN ASK HER TO GET ME SOME HOT CHOCOLATE.
パタ
Step
パタ
Step
YUKI-MURA,
There you are.
WAIT,
WHAT'S WITH ALL THAT CANDY?

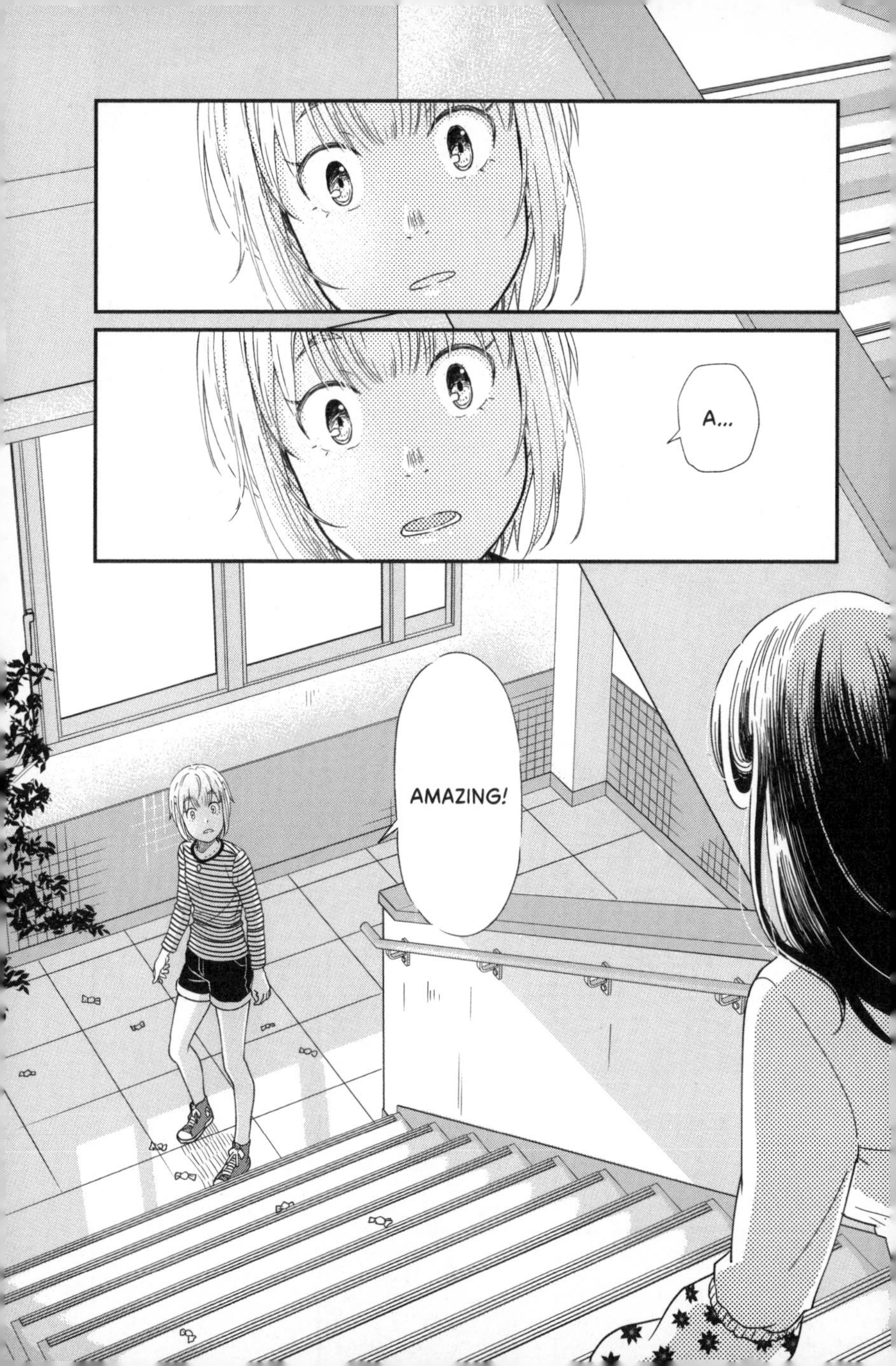
A...
AMAZING!

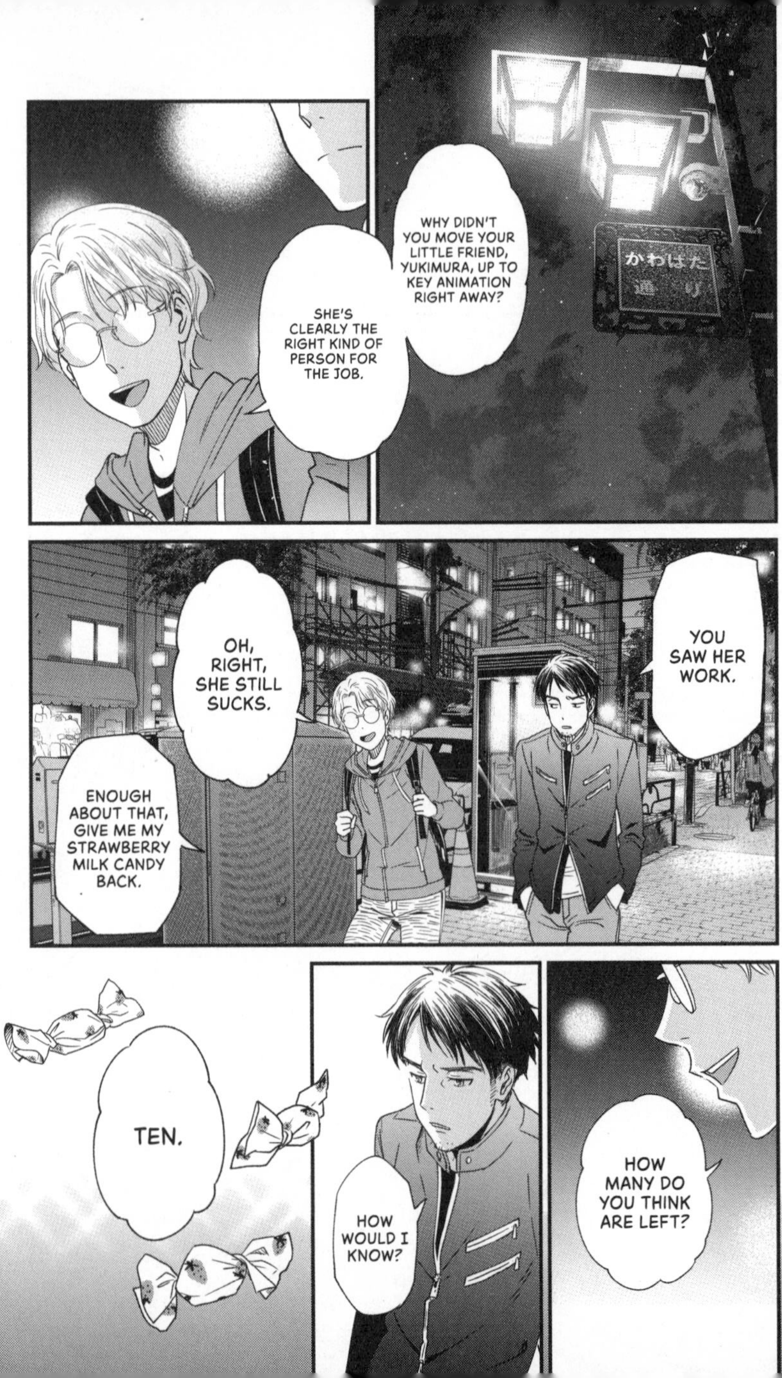
かわはた
通り
WHY DIDN'T YOU MOVE YOUR LITTLE FRIEND, YUKIMURA, UP TO KEY ANIMATION RIGHT AWAY?
SHE'S CLEARLY THE RIGHT KIND OF PERSON FOR THE JOB.
YOU SAW HER WORK.
OH, RIGHT, SHE STILL SUCKS.
ENOUGH ABOUT THAT, GIVE ME MY STRAWBERRY MILK CANDY BACK.
HOW MANY DO YOU THINK ARE LEFT?
HOW WOULD I KNOW?
TEN.

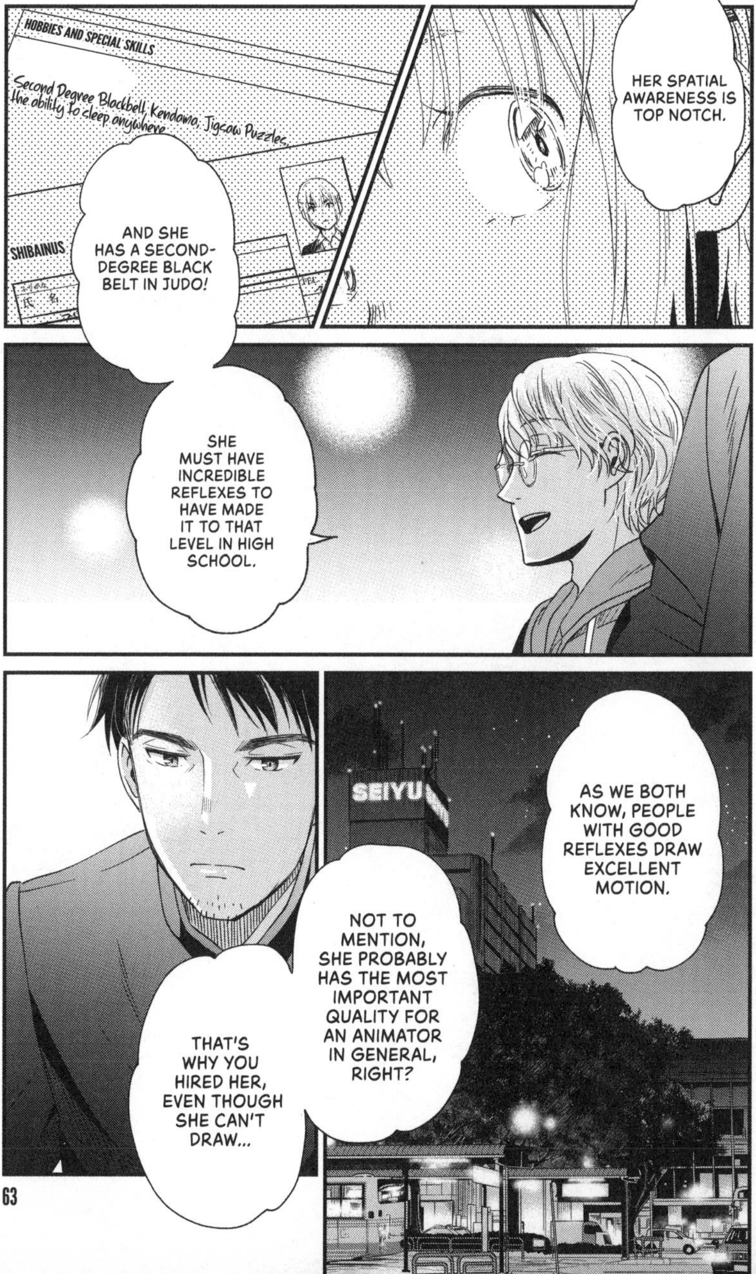
HER SPATIAL AWARENESS IS TOP NOTCH.
HOBBIES AND SPECIAL SKILLS
Second Degree Blackbell, Kendama, Jigsaw Puzzles, the ability to sleep anywhere
SHIBAINUS
AND SHE HAS A SECOND-DEGREE BLACK BELT IN JUDO!
SHE MUST HAVE INCREDIBLE REFLEXES TO HAVE MADE IT TO THAT LEVEL IN HIGH SCHOOL.
SEIYU
AS WE BOTH KNOW, PEOPLE WITH GOOD REFLEXES DRAW EXCELLENT MOTION.
NOT TO MENTION, SHE PROBABLY HAS THE MOST IMPORTANT QUALITY FOR AN ANIMATOR IN GENERAL, RIGHT?
THAT'S WHY YOU HIRED HER, EVEN THOUGH SHE CAN'T DRAW...

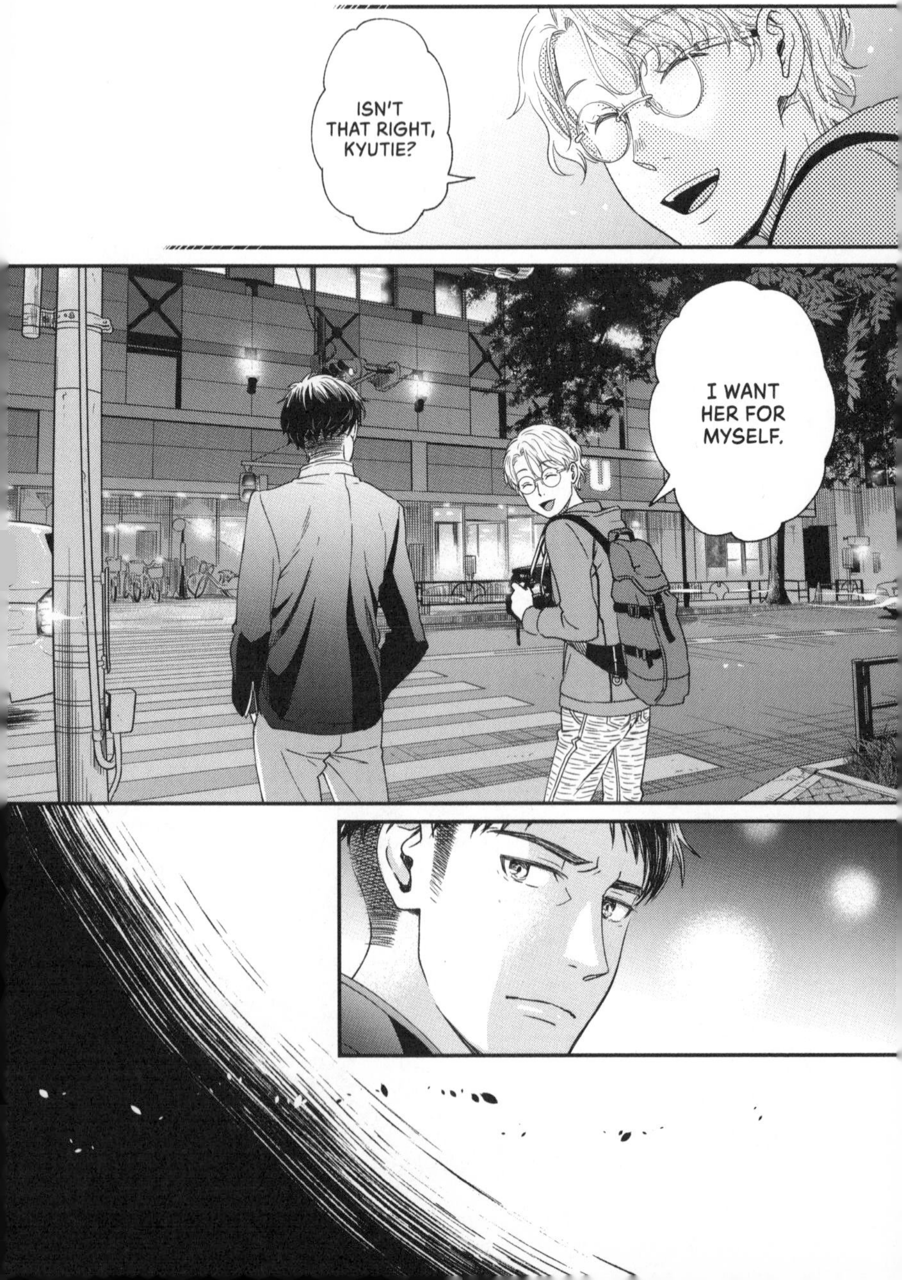
ISN'T THAT RIGHT, KYUTIE?
I WANT HER FOR MYSELF.

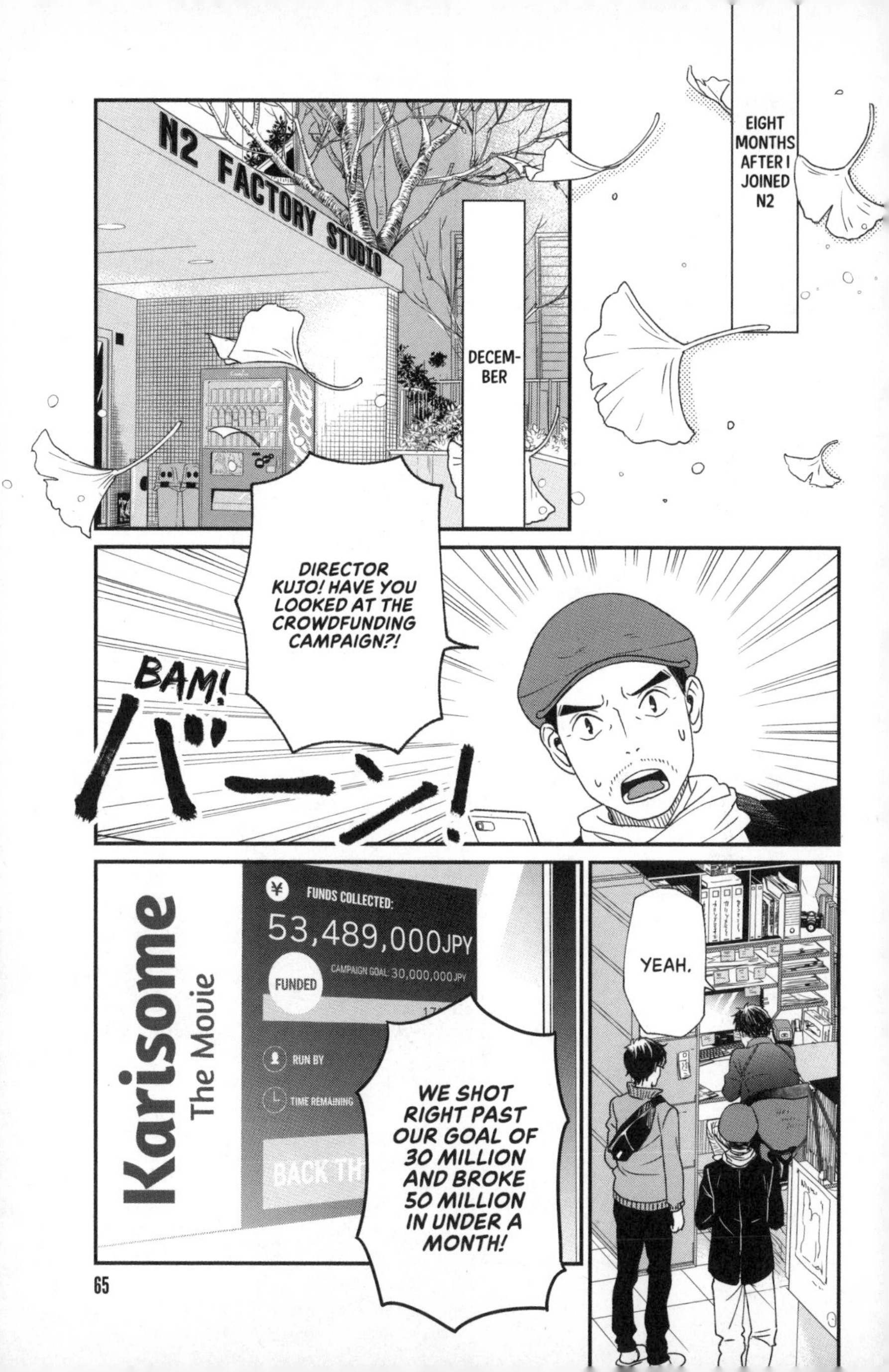
EIGHT MONTHS AFTER I JOINED N2
N2 FACTORY STUDIO
DECEMBER
DIRECTOR KUJO! HAVE YOU LOOKED AT THE CROWDFUNDING CAMPAIGN?!
BAM!
YEAH.
WE SHOT RIGHT PAST OUR GOAL OF 30 MILLION AND BROKE 50 MILLION IN UNDER A MONTH!
Karisome The Movie
FUNDS COLLECTED:
53,489,000JPY
FUNDED
CAMPAIGN GOAL: 30,000,000JPY
RUN BY
TIME REMAINING

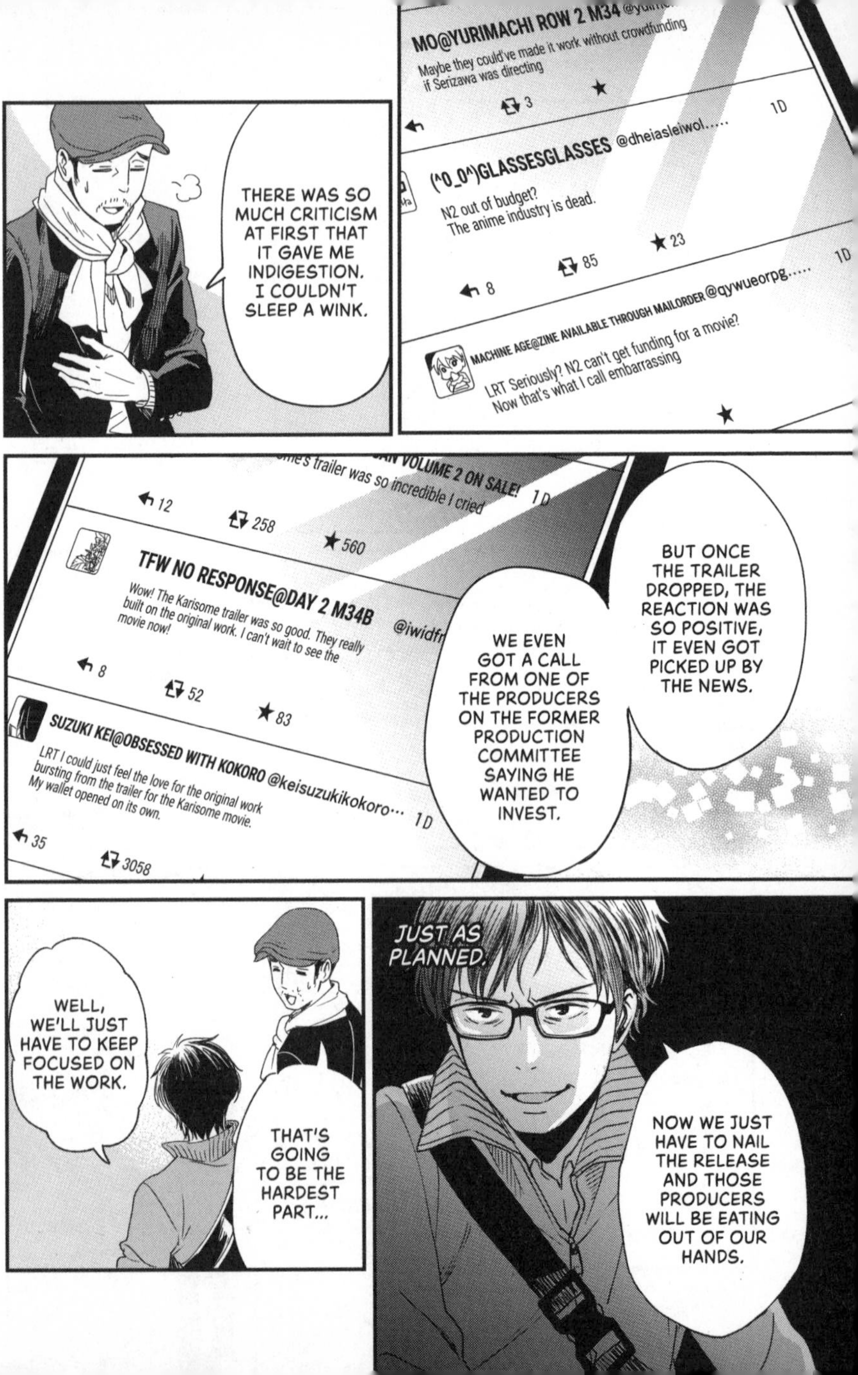

MO@YURIMACHI ROW 2 M34
Maybe they could've made it work without crowdfunding if Serizawa was directing
3
1D
(^0_0^)GLASSESGLASSES @dheiasleiwol.....
N2 out of budget? The anime industry is dead.
8
85
23
1D
MACHINE AGE@ZINE AVAILABLE THROUGH MAILORDER @qywueorpg.....
LRT Seriously? N2 can't get funding for a movie? Now that's what I call embarrassing
THERE WAS SO MUCH CRITICISM AT FIRST THAT IT GAVE ME INDIGESTION. I COULDN'T SLEEP A WINK.
VOLUME 2 ON SALE!
trailer was so incredible I cried
1D
12
258
560
TFW NO RESPONSE@DAY 2 M34B
Wow! The Karisome trailer was so good. They really built on the original work. I can't wait to see the movie now!
8
52
83
SUZUKI KEI@OBSESSED WITH KOKORO @keisuzukikokoro···
LRT I could just feel the love for the original work bursting from the trailer for the Karisome movie. My wallet opened on its own.
1D
35
3058
BUT ONCE THE TRAILER DROPPED, THE REACTION WAS SO POSITIVE, IT EVEN GOT PICKED UP BY THE NEWS.
WE EVEN GOT A CALL FROM ONE OF THE PRODUCERS ON THE FORMER PRODUCTION COMMITTEE SAYING HE WANTED TO INVEST.
JUST AS PLANNED.
NOW WE JUST HAVE TO NAIL THE RELEASE AND THOSE PRODUCERS WILL BE EATING OUT OF OUR HANDS.
WELL, WE'LL JUST HAVE TO KEEP FOCUSED ON THE WORK.
THAT'S GOING TO BE THE HARDEST PART...

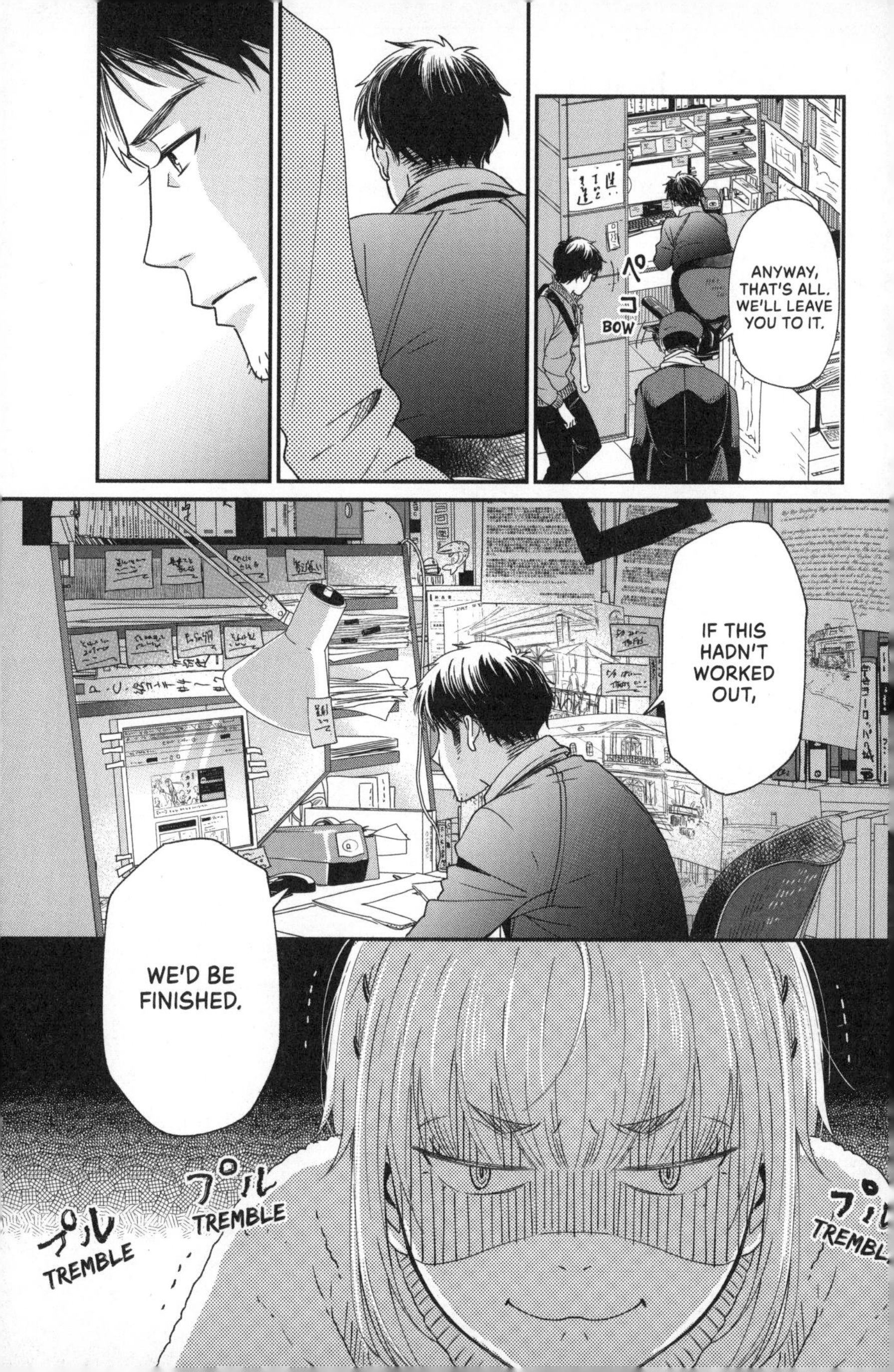

ANYWAY, THAT'S ALL. WE'LL LEAVE YOU TO IT.
ペコ BOW
IF THIS HADN'T WORKED OUT,
WE'D BE FINISHED.
プル TREMBL
プル TREMBLE
プル TREMBLE

TOTAL FRAMES FOR 11/1 - 11/30

AZUMA							425
MAKIMURA							381
YUNOSHIMA							~~445~~

I DID 518 FRAMES IN OCTOBER, 286 IN NOVEMBER AND FOR DECEMBER, IF I DON'T GET ANOTHER CAKEWALK OF A CUT LIKE THAT, I'LL ONLY BE AT ABOUT 350...

299
378
505
286

I ABSOLUTELY HAVE TO DRAW 500 FRAMES EACH MONTH.

January 500 Frames

February 500 Frames

March 500 Frames

WHICH MEANS IN THE NEXT THREE MONTHS,

IF SHE DOESN'T PASS THE KEY ANIMATION EXAM WITHIN A YEAR, SHE'S FIRED.

EVEN IF STUDIO 7'S OUT OF THE FIRE, I'M SURE NOT!

WHICH REALLY MEANS IF I DON'T DRAW 500 FRAMES NEXT MONTH, I'M OUT?!

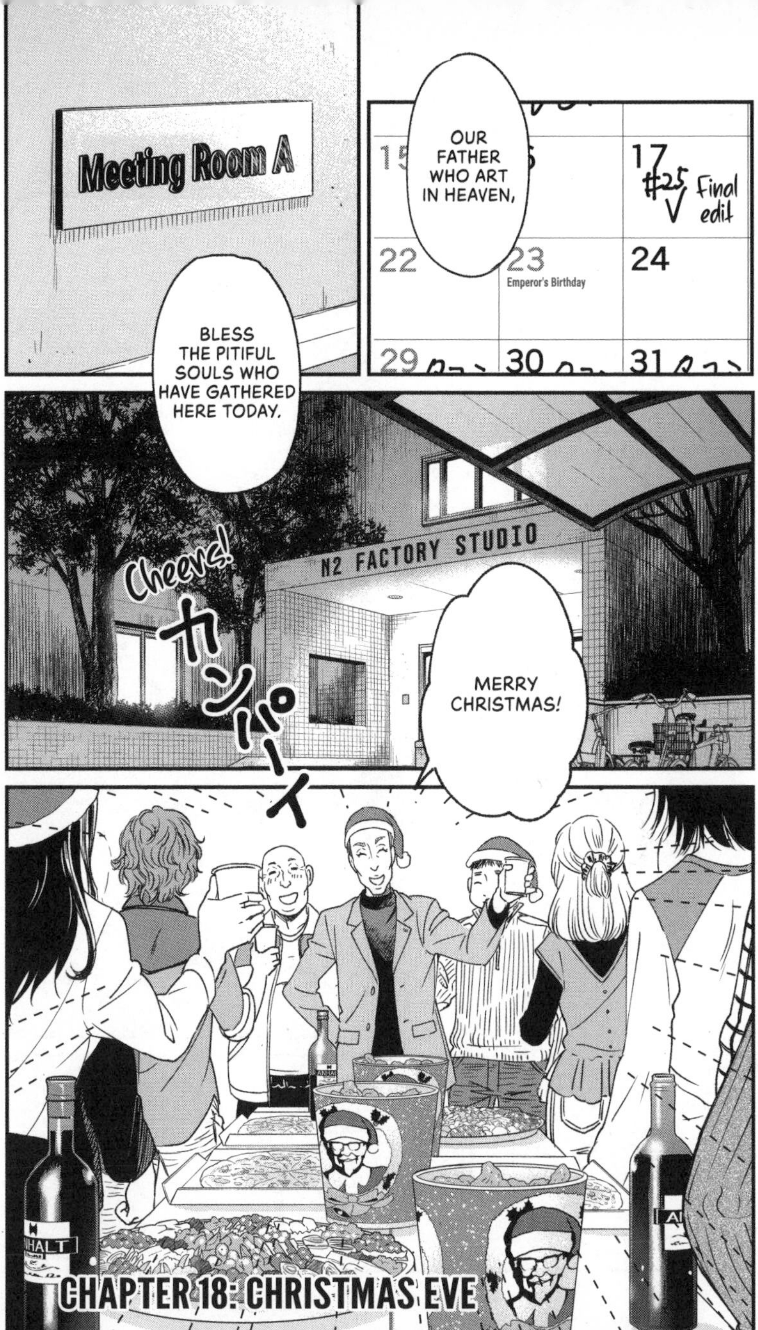
OUR FATHER WHO ART IN HEAVEN,
17 #25 V Final edit
22
23 Emperor's Birthday
24
29
30
31
Meeting Room A
BLESS THE PITIFUL SOULS WHO HAVE GATHERED HERE TODAY.
N2 FACTORY STUDIO
MERRY CHRISTMAS!
Cheers!
カンパーイ
CHAPTER 18: CHRISTMAS EVE

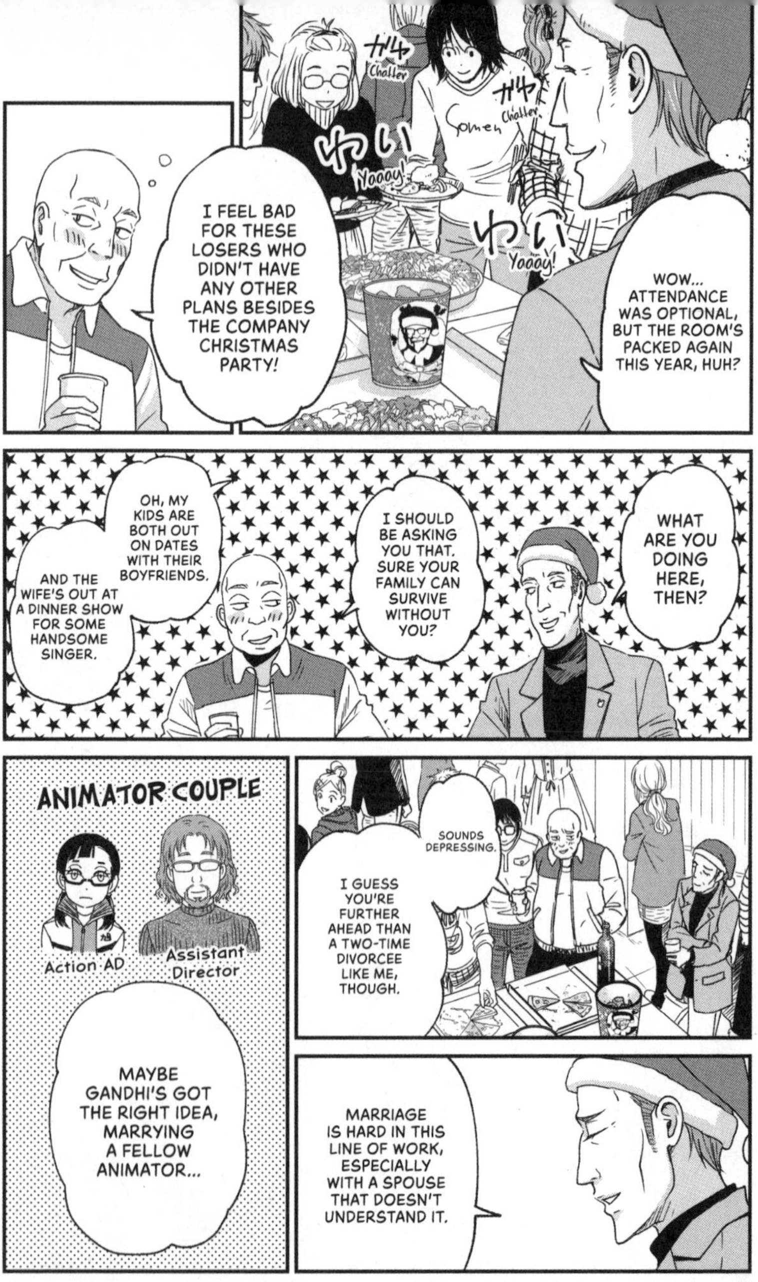

ガヤ Chatter
ガヤ Chatter
わい Yaaay!
わい Yaaay!
WOW... ATTENDANCE WAS OPTIONAL, BUT THE ROOM'S PACKED AGAIN THIS YEAR, HUH?
I FEEL BAD FOR THESE LOSERS WHO DIDN'T HAVE ANY OTHER PLANS BESIDES THE COMPANY CHRISTMAS PARTY!
WHAT ARE YOU DOING HERE, THEN?
I SHOULD BE ASKING YOU THAT. SURE YOUR FAMILY CAN SURVIVE WITHOUT YOU?
OH, MY KIDS ARE BOTH OUT ON DATES WITH THEIR BOYFRIENDS.
AND THE WIFE'S OUT AT A DINNER SHOW FOR SOME HANDSOME SINGER.
SOUNDS DEPRESSING.
I GUESS YOU'RE FURTHER AHEAD THAN A TWO-TIME DIVORCEE LIKE ME, THOUGH.
MARRIAGE IS HARD IN THIS LINE OF WORK, ESPECIALLY WITH A SPOUSE THAT DOESN'T UNDERSTAND IT.
ANIMATOR COUPLE
Action AD
Assistant Director
MAYBE GANDHI'S GOT THE RIGHT IDEA, MARRYING A FELLOW ANIMATOR...

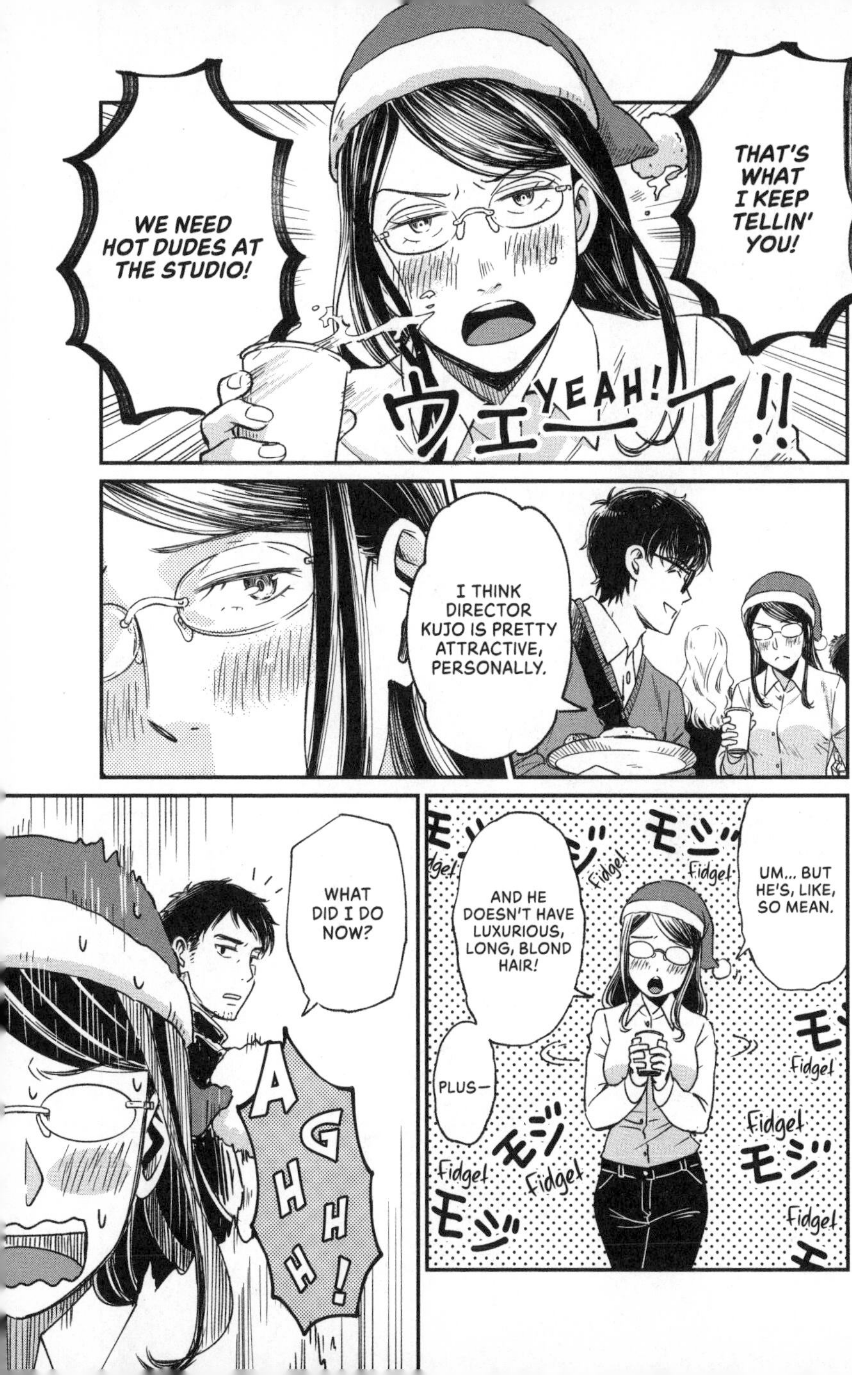
THAT'S WHAT I KEEP TELLIN' YOU!
WE NEED HOT DUDES AT THE STUDIO!
ウェーイ!!
YEAH!
I THINK DIRECTOR KUJO IS PRETTY ATTRACTIVE, PERSONALLY.
UM... BUT HE'S, LIKE, SO MEAN.
AND HE DOESN'T HAVE LUXURIOUS, LONG, BLOND HAIR!
PLUS—
モジ モジ
Fidget Fidget
WHAT DID I DO NOW?
AGHHH!

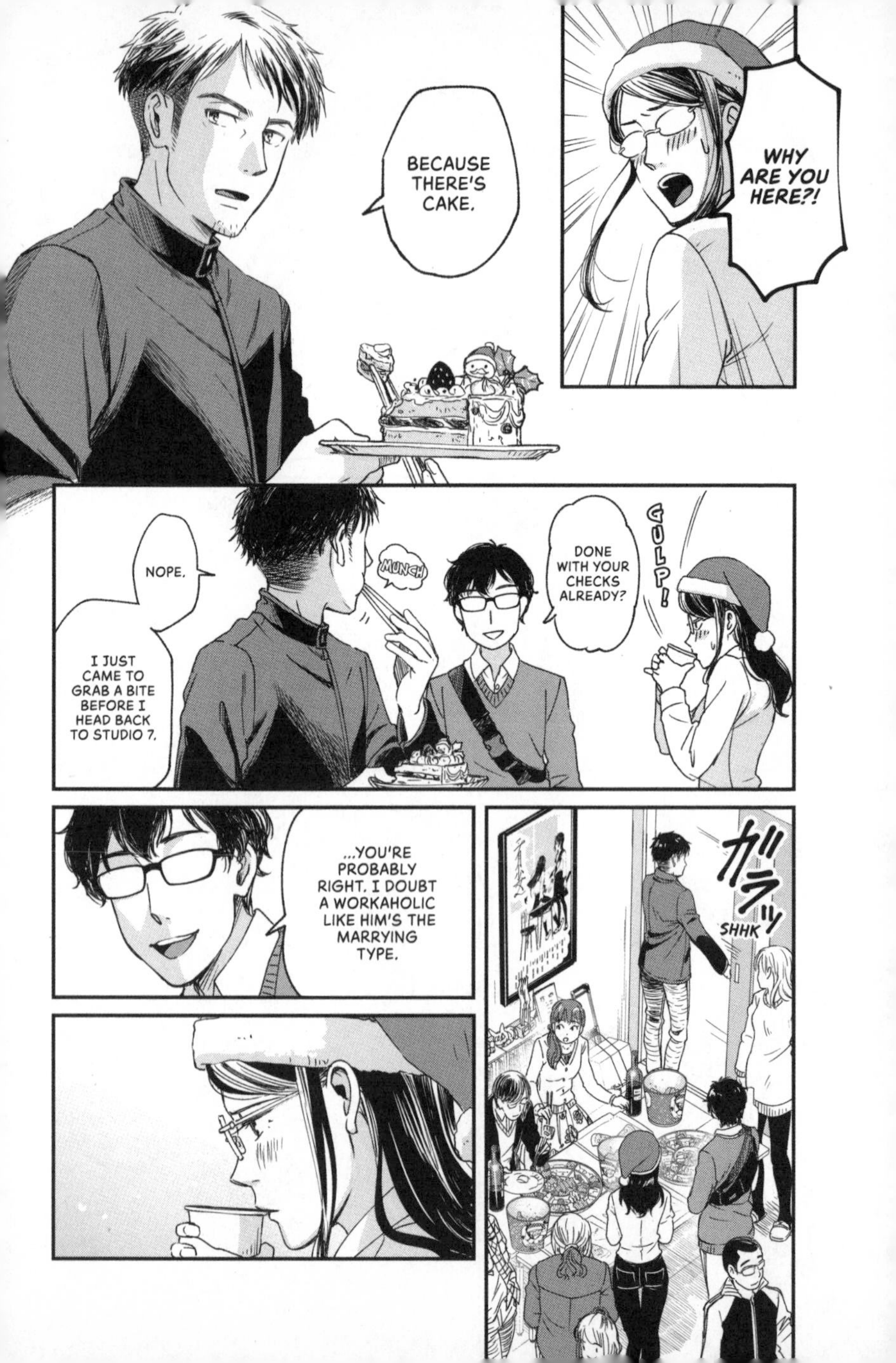
WHY ARE YOU HERE?!
BECAUSE THERE'S CAKE.
GULP!
DONE WITH YOUR CHECKS ALREADY?
MUNCH
NOPE.
I JUST CAME TO GRAB A BITE BEFORE I HEAD BACK TO STUDIO 7.
ガラッ
SHHK
...YOU'RE PROBABLY RIGHT. I DOUBT A WORKAHOLIC LIKE HIM'S THE MARRYING TYPE.
...

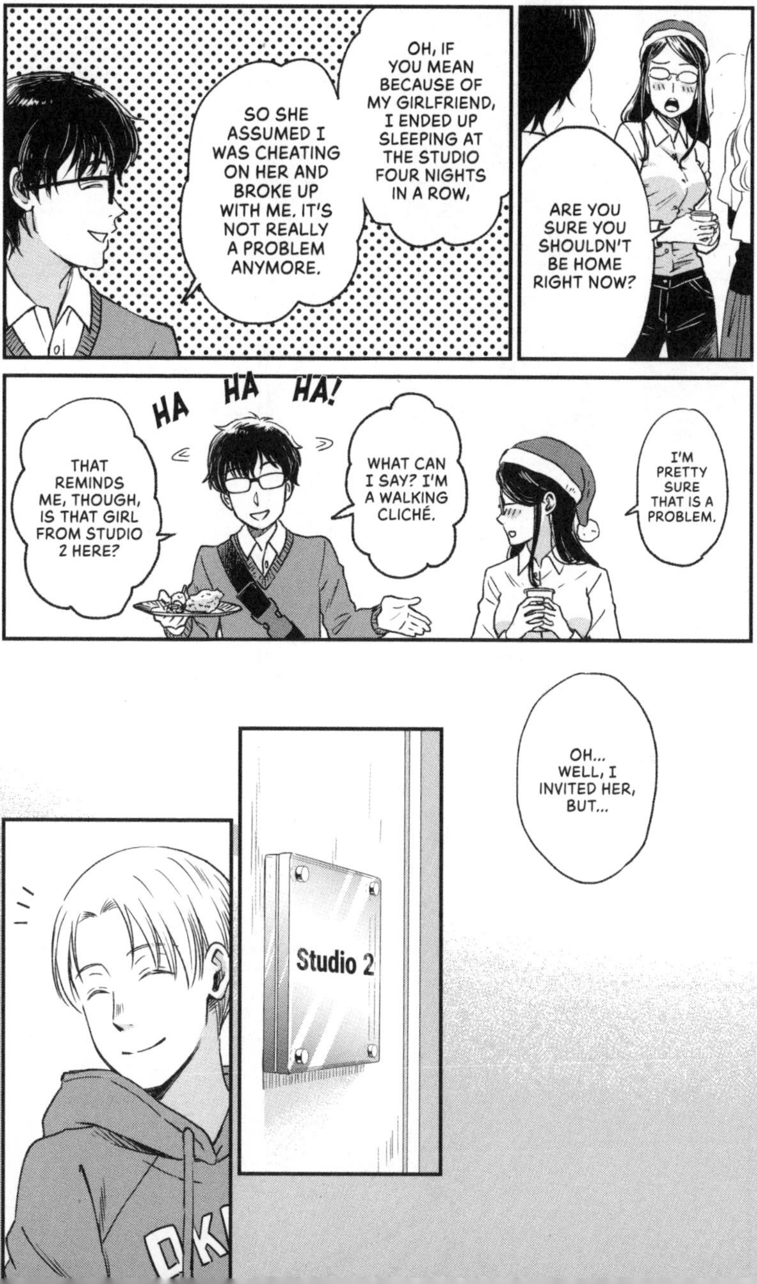
ARE YOU SURE YOU SHOULDN'T BE HOME RIGHT NOW?
OH, IF YOU MEAN BECAUSE OF MY GIRLFRIEND, I ENDED UP SLEEPING AT THE STUDIO FOUR NIGHTS IN A ROW,
SO SHE ASSUMED I WAS CHEATING ON HER AND BROKE UP WITH ME. IT'S NOT REALLY A PROBLEM ANYMORE.
I'M PRETTY SURE THAT IS A PROBLEM.
HA HA HA!
WHAT CAN I SAY? I'M A WALKING CLICHÉ.
THAT REMINDS ME, THOUGH, IS THAT GIRL FROM STUDIO 2 HERE?
OH... WELL, I INVITED HER, BUT...
Studio 2

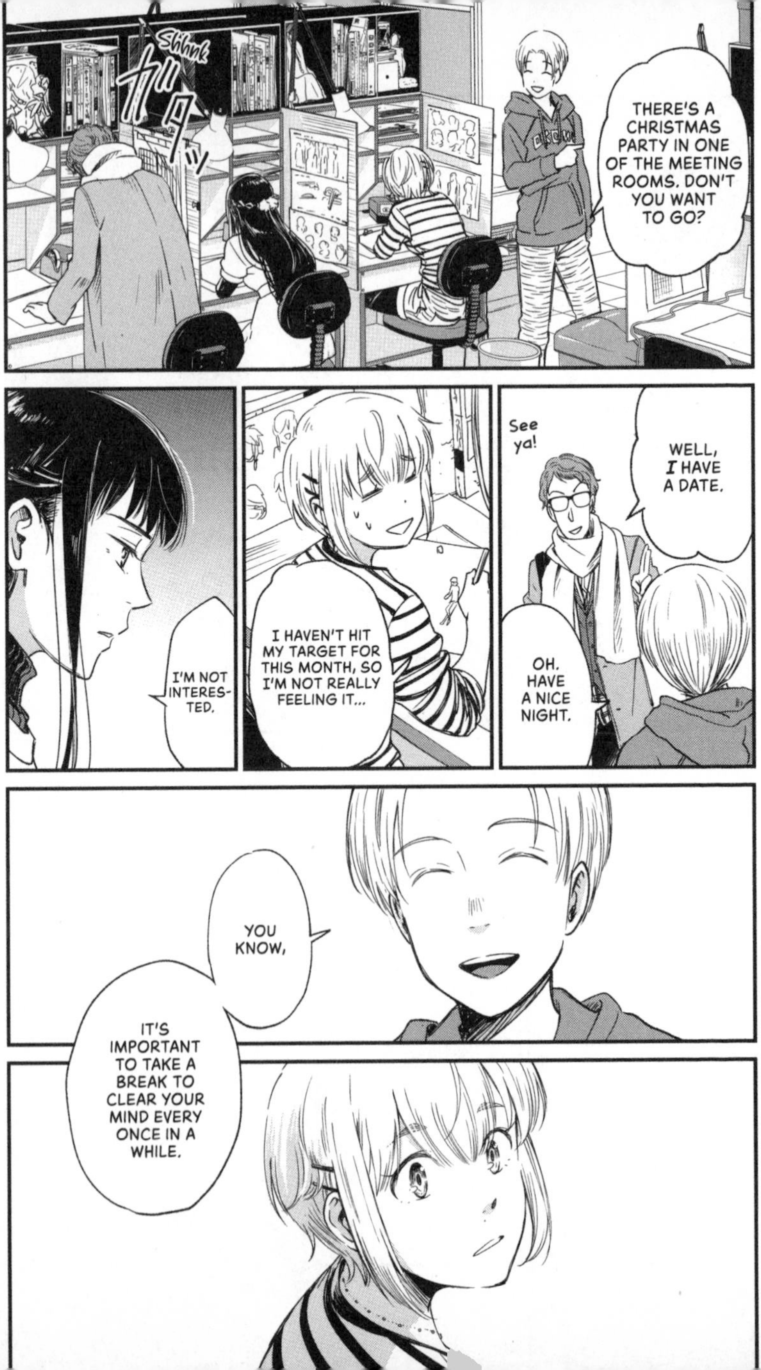
Shhnk
カリタッ
THERE'S A CHRISTMAS PARTY IN ONE OF THE MEETING ROOMS. DON'T YOU WANT TO GO?
WELL, *I* HAVE A DATE.
See ya!
OH. HAVE A NICE NIGHT.
I HAVEN'T HIT MY TARGET FOR THIS MONTH, SO I'M NOT REALLY FEELING IT...
I'M NOT INTERES-TED.
YOU KNOW,
IT'S IMPORTANT TO TAKE A BREAK TO CLEAR YOUR MIND EVERY ONCE IN A WHILE.

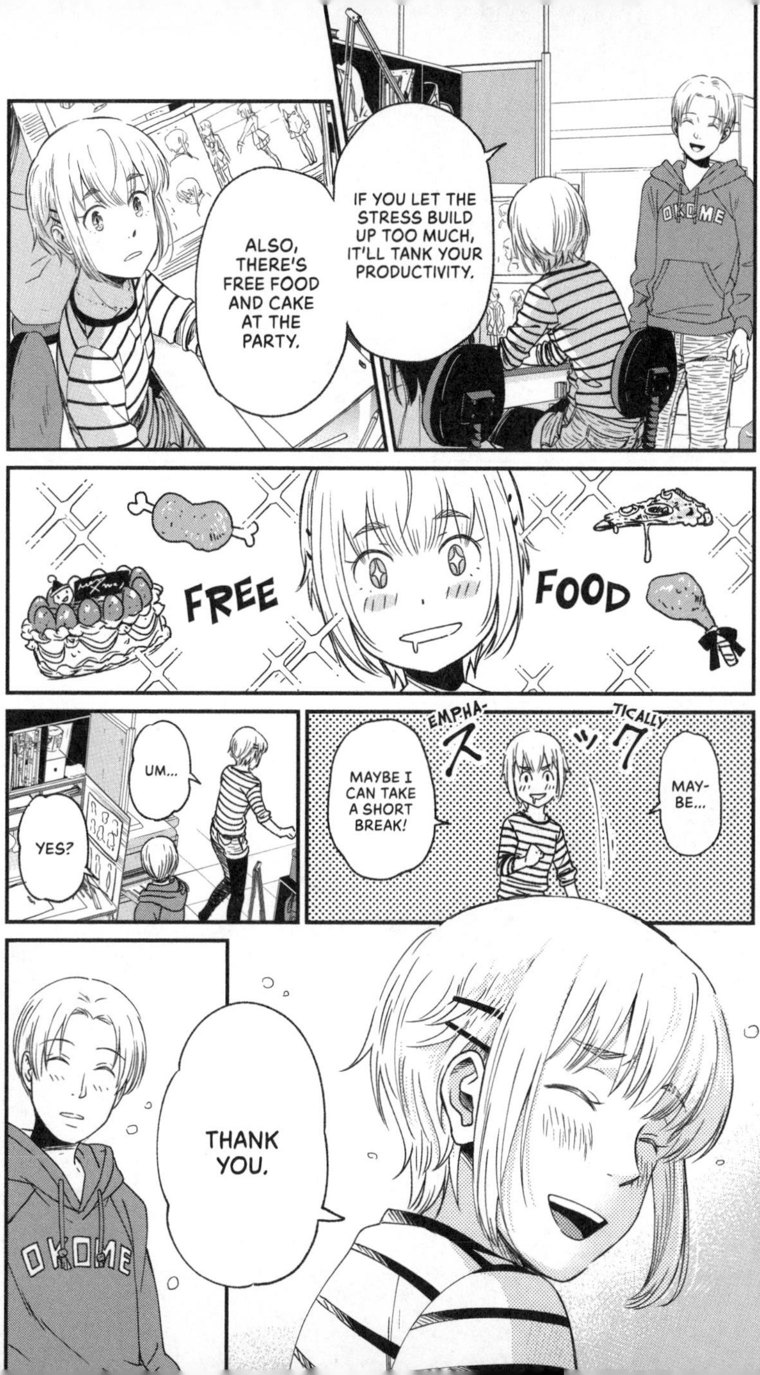
IF YOU LET THE STRESS BUILD UP TOO MUCH, IT'LL TANK YOUR PRODUCTIVITY.
ALSO, THERE'S FREE FOOD AND CAKE AT THE PARTY.
FREE FOOD
MAY-BE...
スック
EMPHA-TICALLY
MAYBE I CAN TAKE A SHORT BREAK!
UM...
YES?
THANK YOU.

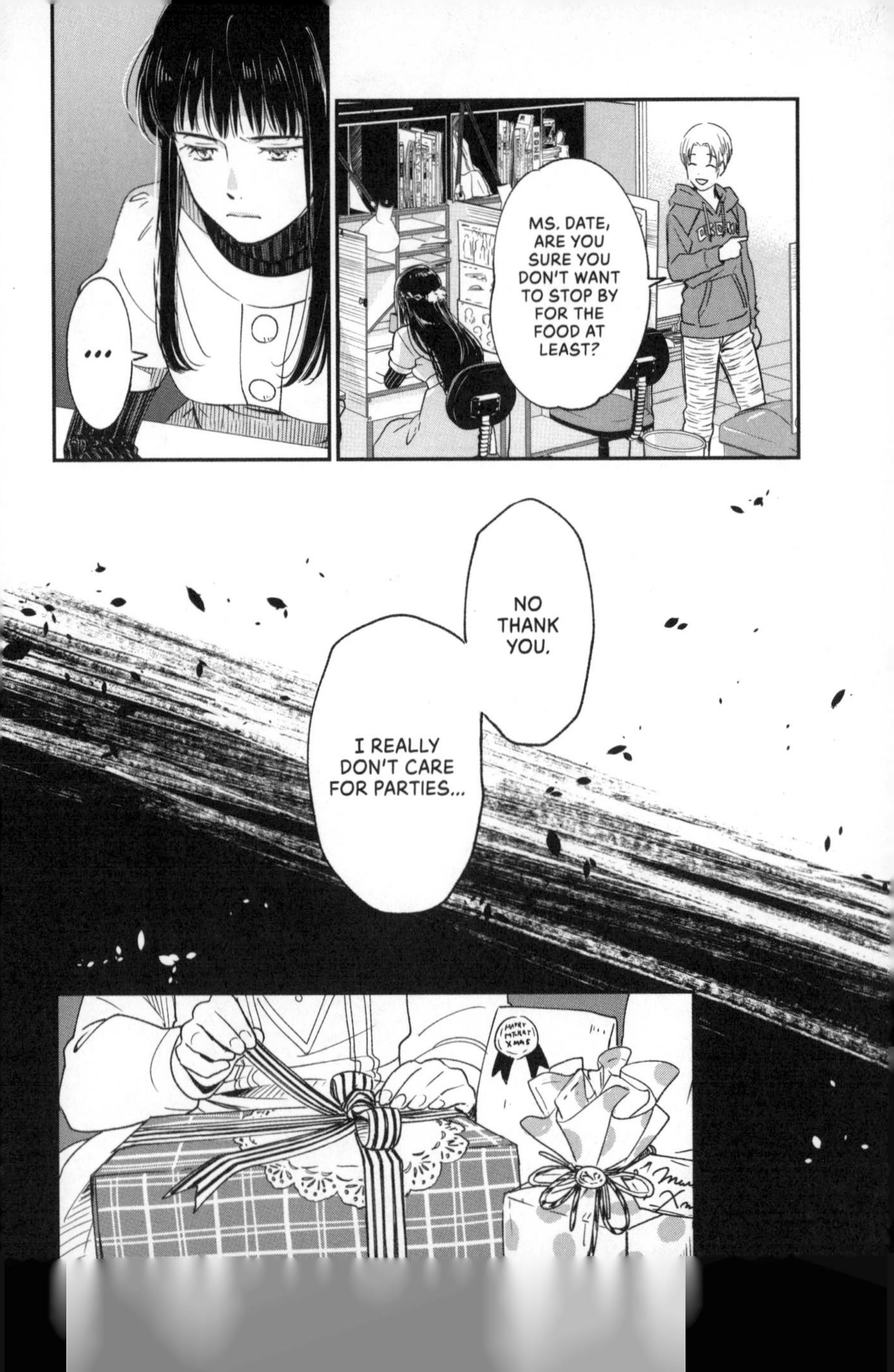
MS. DATE, ARE YOU SURE YOU DON'T WANT TO STOP BY FOR THE FOOD AT LEAST?
...
NO THANK YOU.
I REALLY DON'T CARE FOR PARTIES...

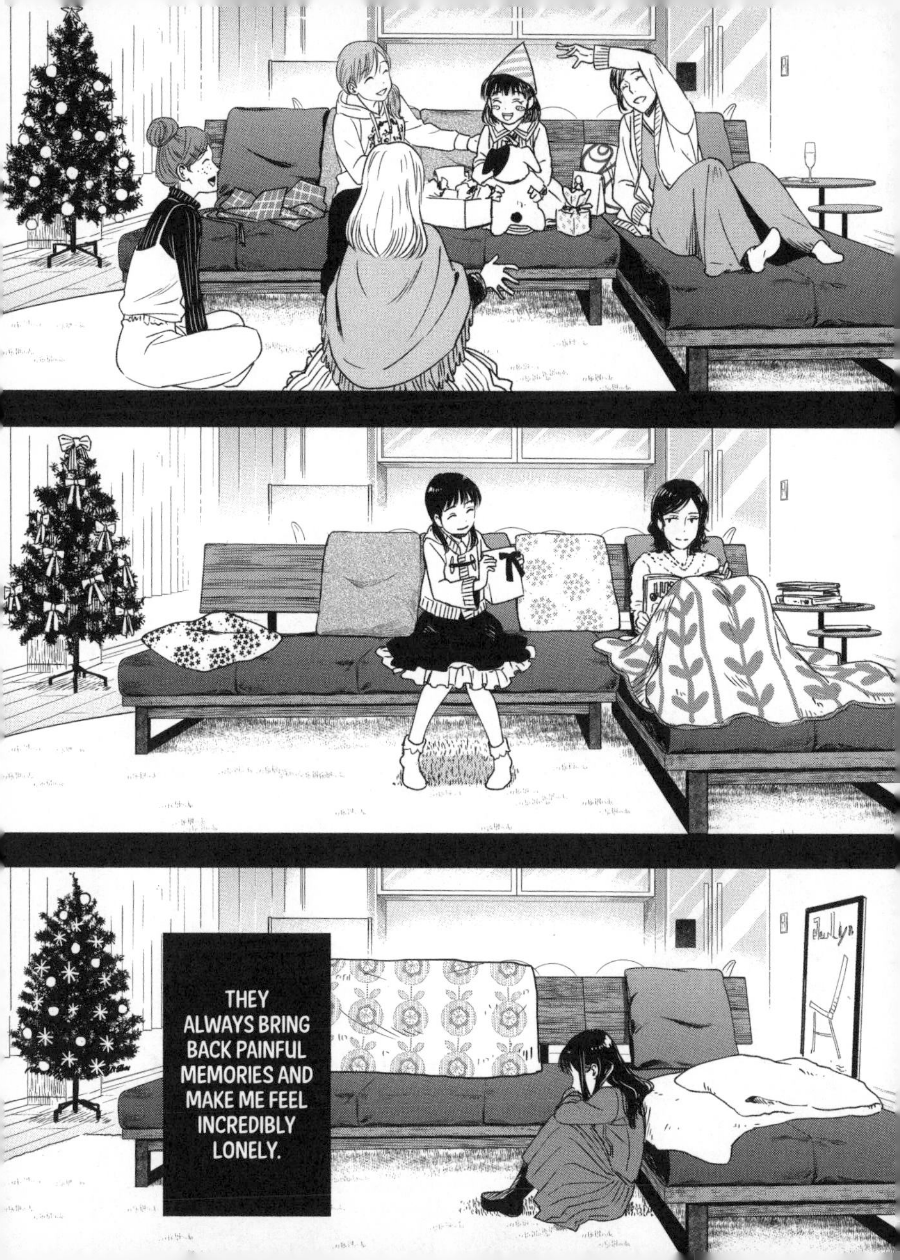

THEY ALWAYS BRING BACK PAINFUL MEMORIES AND MAKE ME FEEL INCREDIBLY LONELY.

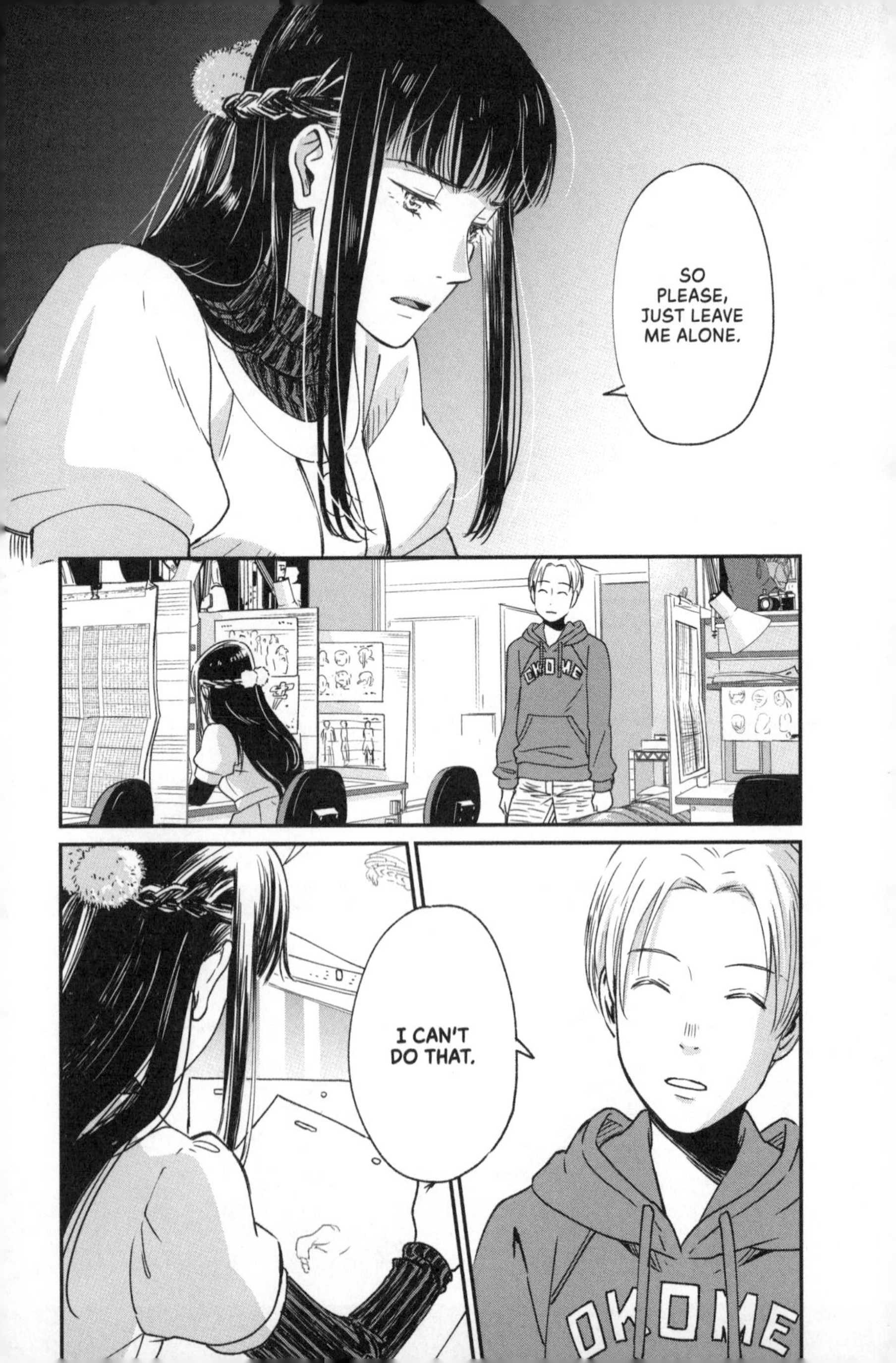
SO PLEASE, JUST LEAVE ME ALONE.
OKOME
I CAN'T DO THAT.
OKOME

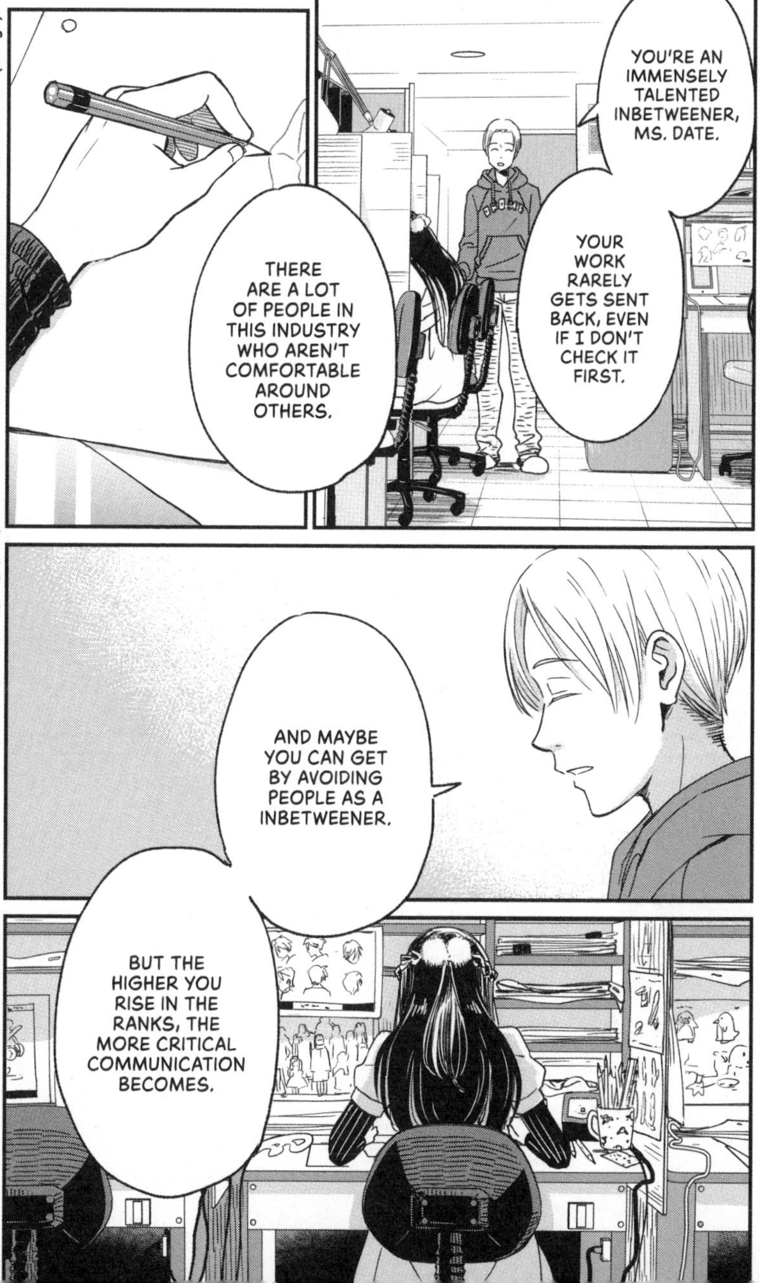
YOU'RE AN IMMENSELY TALENTED INBETWEENER, MS. DATE.
YOUR WORK RARELY GETS SENT BACK, EVEN IF I DON'T CHECK IT FIRST.
THERE ARE A LOT OF PEOPLE IN THIS INDUSTRY WHO AREN'T COMFORTABLE AROUND OTHERS.
AND MAYBE YOU CAN GET BY AVOIDING PEOPLE AS A INBETWEENER.
BUT THE HIGHER YOU RISE IN THE RANKS, THE MORE CRITICAL COMMUNICATION BECOMES.

Inbetweening (Douga): The motion in animation would be choppy if we only saw keyframes, so the job of an inbetweener is to add additional frames *between* keyframes to make the motion more fluid. In the Japanese animation industry, inbetweeners are responsible for both inbetweening and the cleaning and application of corrections to the raw keyframes (genga) to produce the finished frames of animation we see on screen (douga).

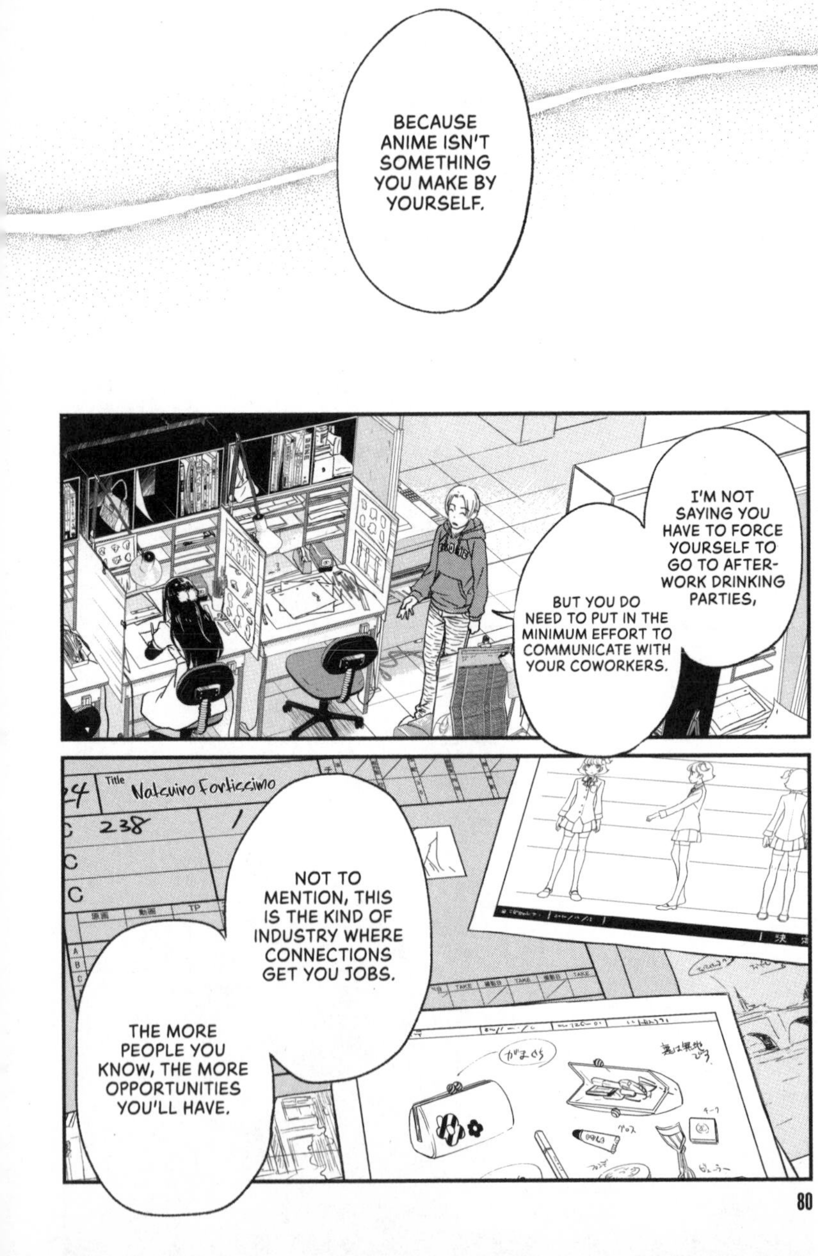
BECAUSE ANIME ISN'T SOMETHING YOU MAKE BY YOURSELF.
I'M NOT SAYING YOU HAVE TO FORCE YOURSELF TO GO TO AFTER-WORK DRINKING PARTIES,
BUT YOU DO NEED TO PUT IN THE MINIMUM EFFORT TO COMMUNICATE WITH YOUR COWORKERS.
Title Natsuiro Fortissimo
NOT TO MENTION, THIS IS THE KIND OF INDUSTRY WHERE CONNECTIONS GET YOU JOBS.
THE MORE PEOPLE YOU KNOW, THE MORE OPPORTUNITIES YOU'LL HAVE.

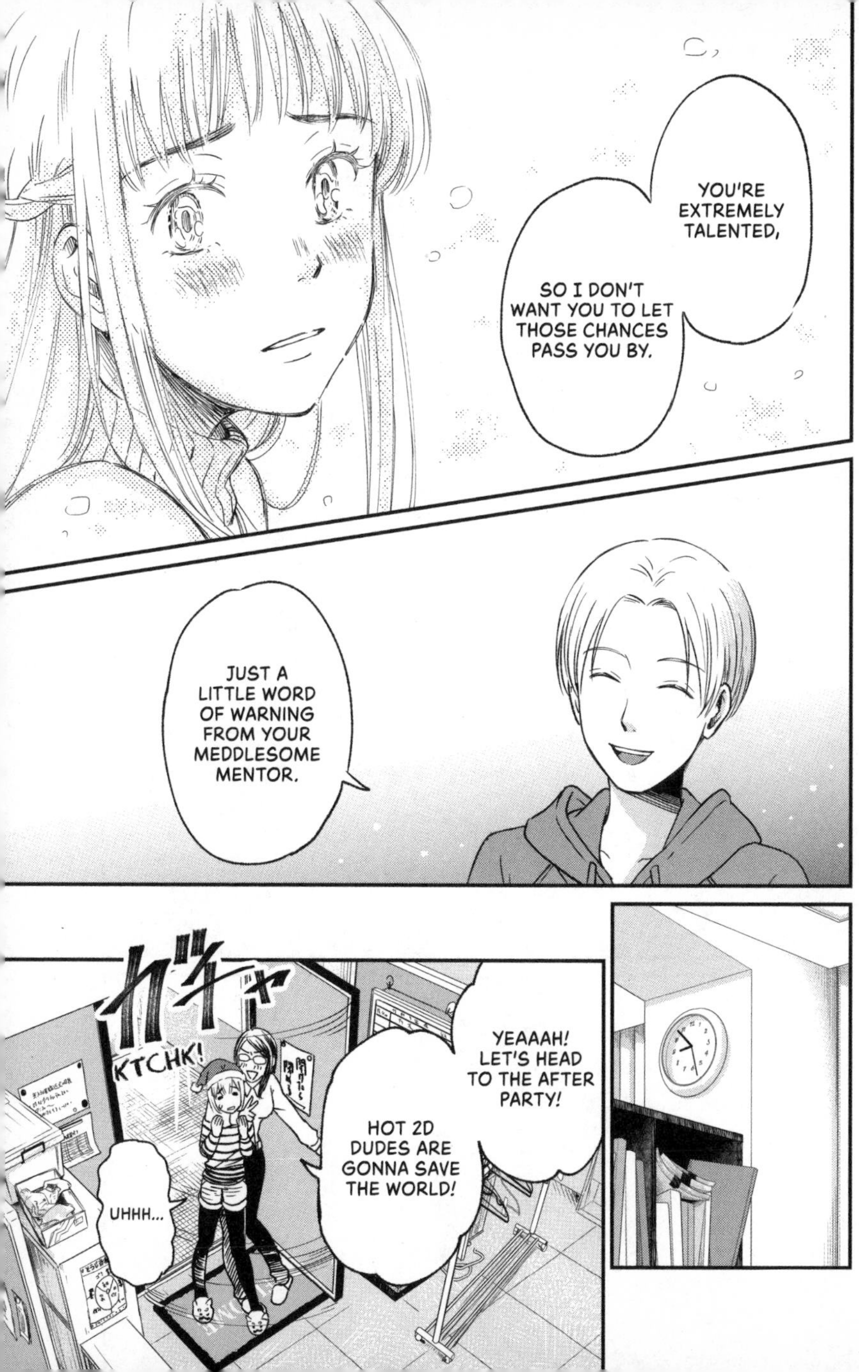
YOU'RE EXTREMELY TALENTED,
SO I DON'T WANT YOU TO LET THOSE CHANCES PASS YOU BY.
JUST A LITTLE WORD OF WARNING FROM YOUR MEDDLESOME MENTOR.
ガチャ
KTCHK!
YEAAAH! LET'S HEAD TO THE AFTER PARTY!
HOT 2D DUDES ARE GONNA SAVE THE WORLD!
UHHH...

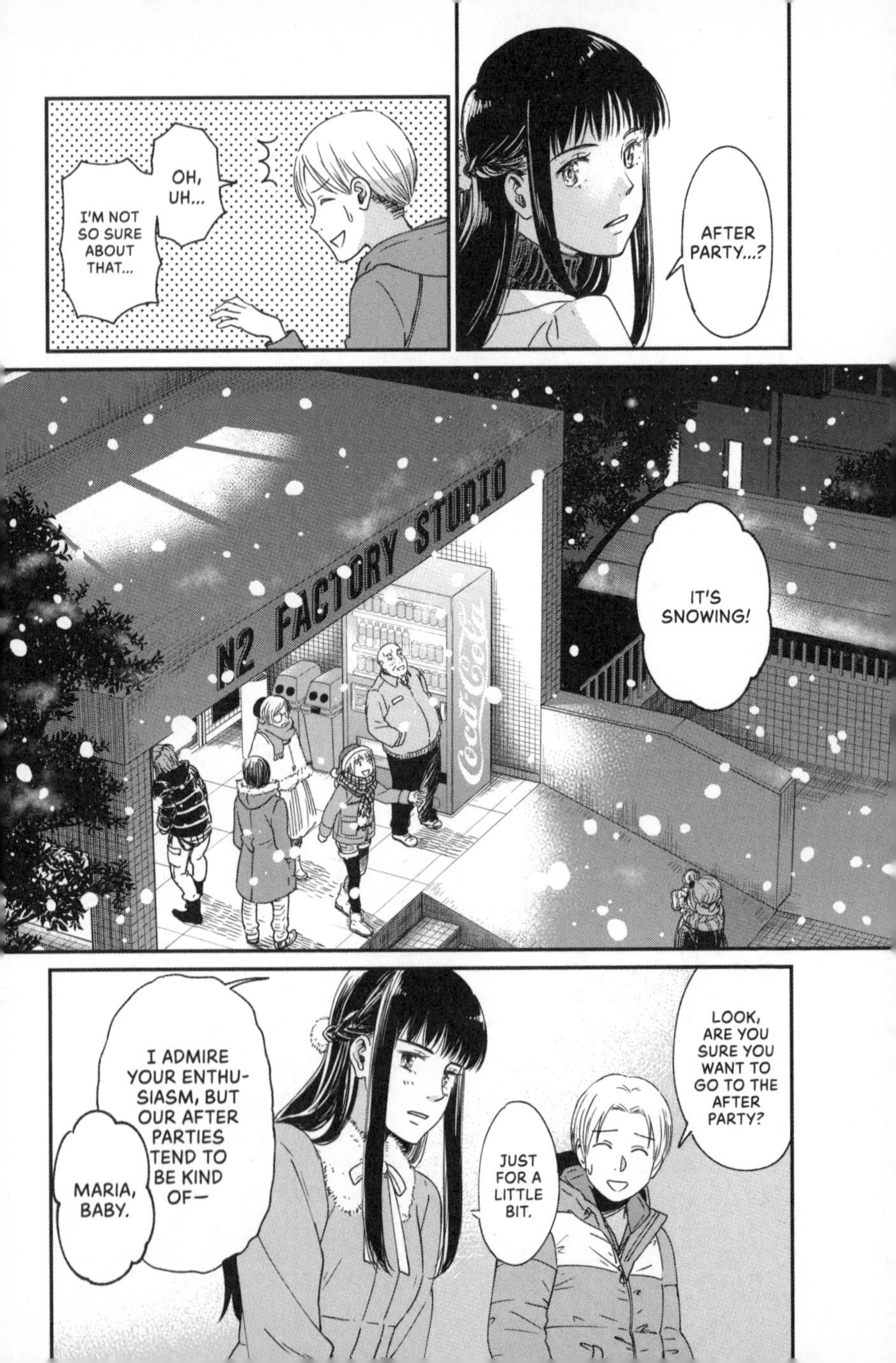
AFTER PARTY...?
OH, UH...
I'M NOT SO SURE ABOUT THAT...
N2 FACTORY STUDIO
Coca-Cola
IT'S SNOWING!
LOOK, ARE YOU SURE YOU WANT TO GO TO THE AFTER PARTY?
JUST FOR A LITTLE BIT.
I ADMIRE YOUR ENTHU-SIASM, BUT OUR AFTER PARTIES TEND TO BE KIND OF—
MARIA, BABY.

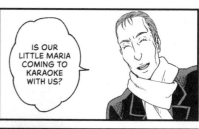

IS OUR LITTLE MARIA COMING TO KARAOKE WITH US?
WHAT...?
K-KARAOKE...
YEAH... THAT'S WHAT I WAS TRYING TO TELL YOU. YOU DON'T HAVE TO FORCE YOURSELF.
SOME-TIMES THINGS GET PRETTY CRAZY, TOO...
...
OH, BY THE WAY, MARIA.
YOU MADE IT TO THE FINAL ROUND OF THE CHARACTER DESIGN COMPETITION.

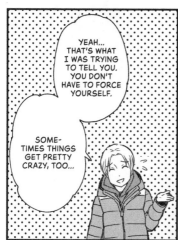

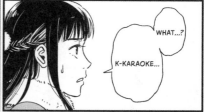

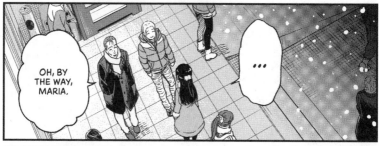

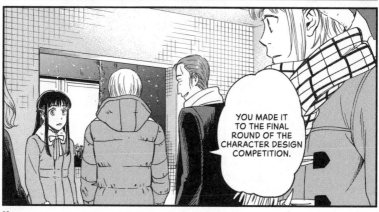

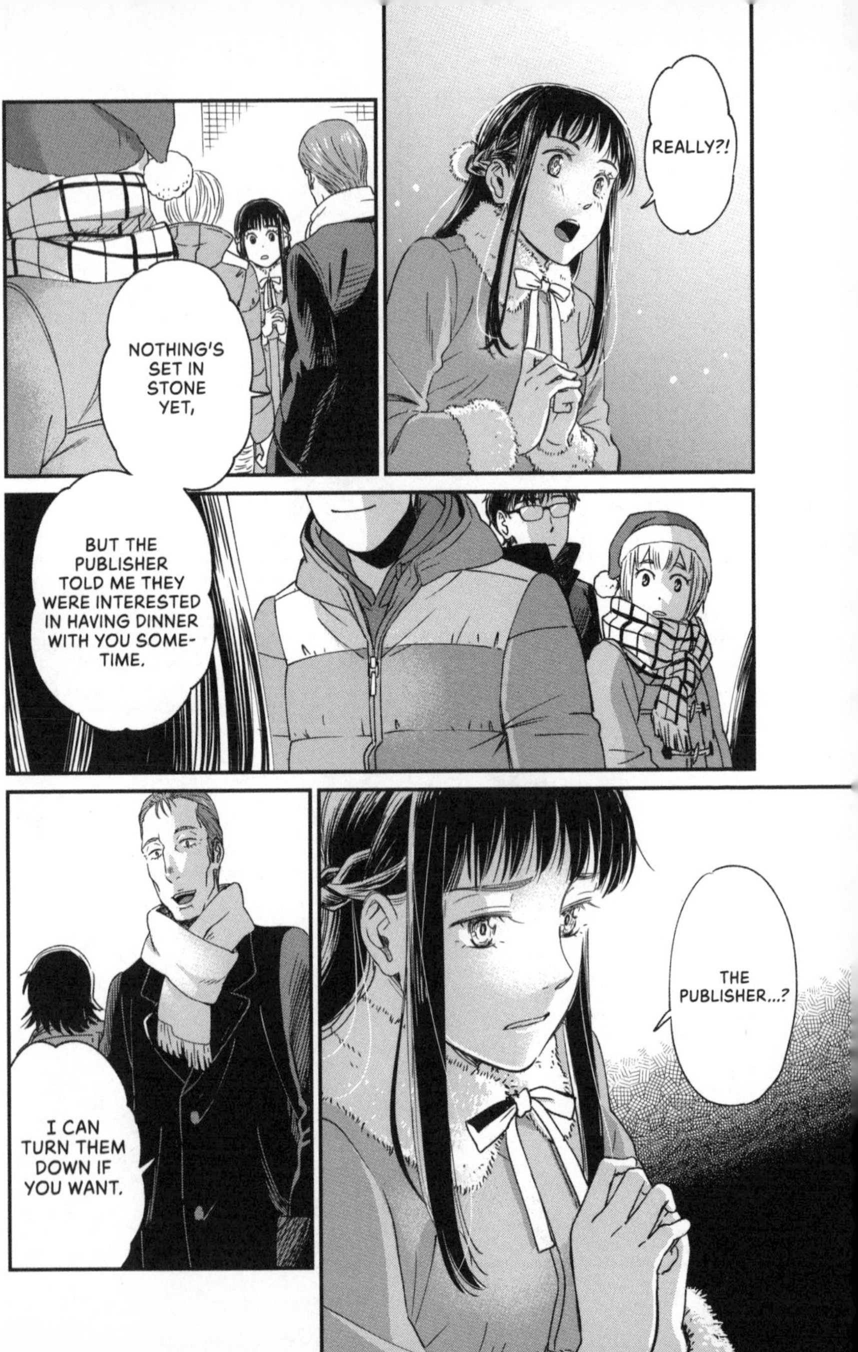
REALLY?!
NOTHING'S SET IN STONE YET,
BUT THE PUBLISHER TOLD ME THEY WERE INTERESTED IN HAVING DINNER WITH YOU SOME-TIME.
THE PUBLISHER...?
I CAN TURN THEM DOWN IF YOU WANT.

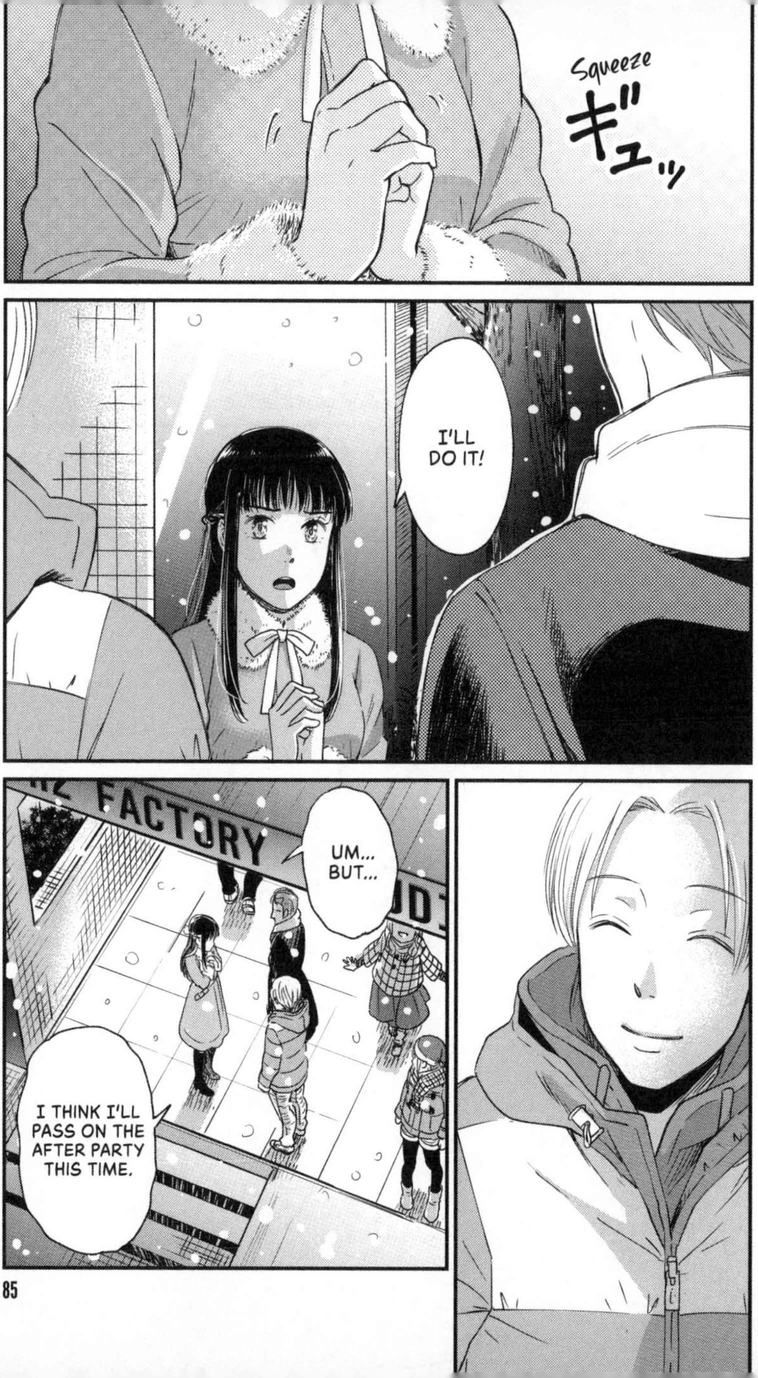
Squeeze
ギュッ
I'LL DO IT!
UM... BUT...
FACTORY
I THINK I'LL PASS ON THE AFTER PARTY THIS TIME.

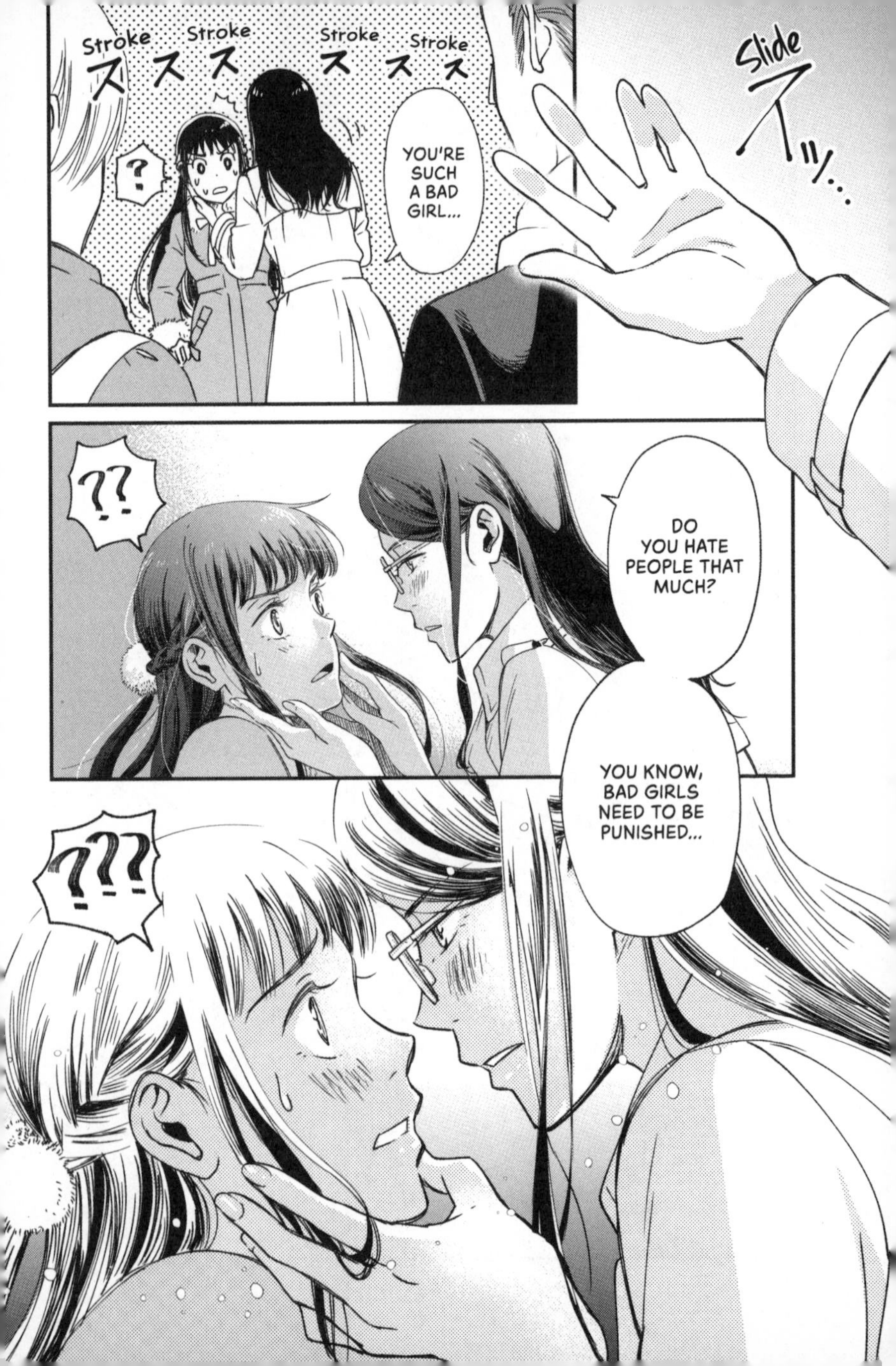

Slide
Stroke Stroke Stroke Stroke
YOU'RE SUCH A BAD GIRL...
?
DO YOU HATE PEOPLE THAT MUCH?
??
YOU KNOW, BAD GIRLS NEED TO BE PUNISHED...
???

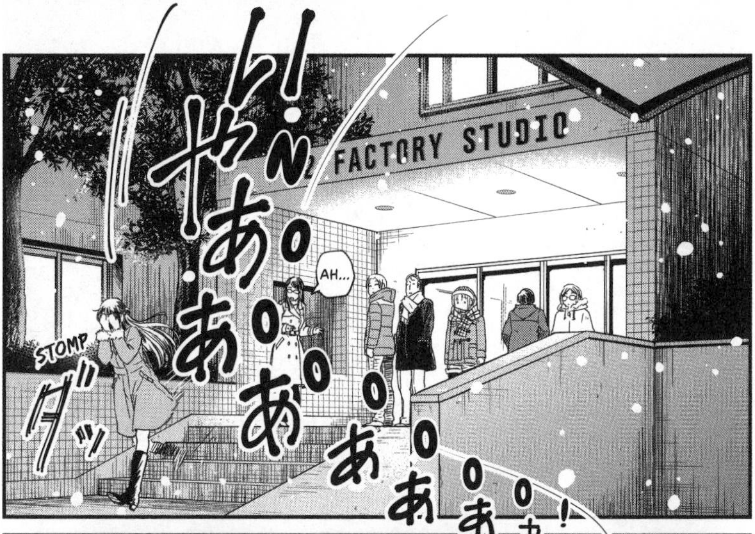
FACTORY STUDIO
AH...
STOMP
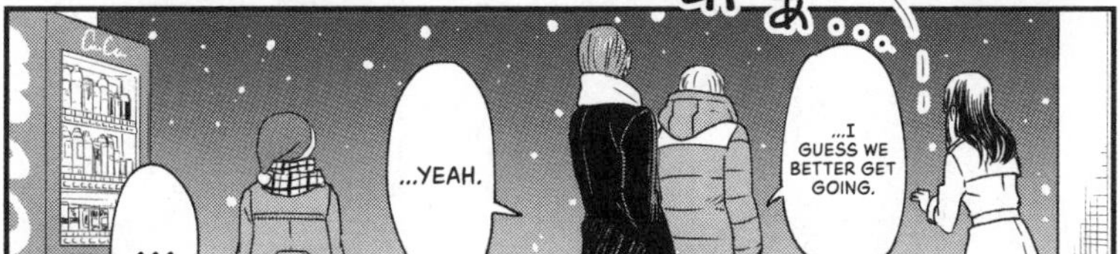
...I GUESS WE BETTER GET GOING.
...YEAH.
...
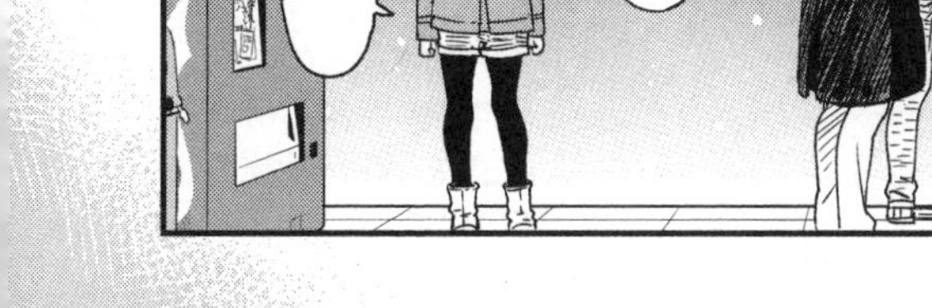

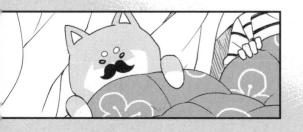

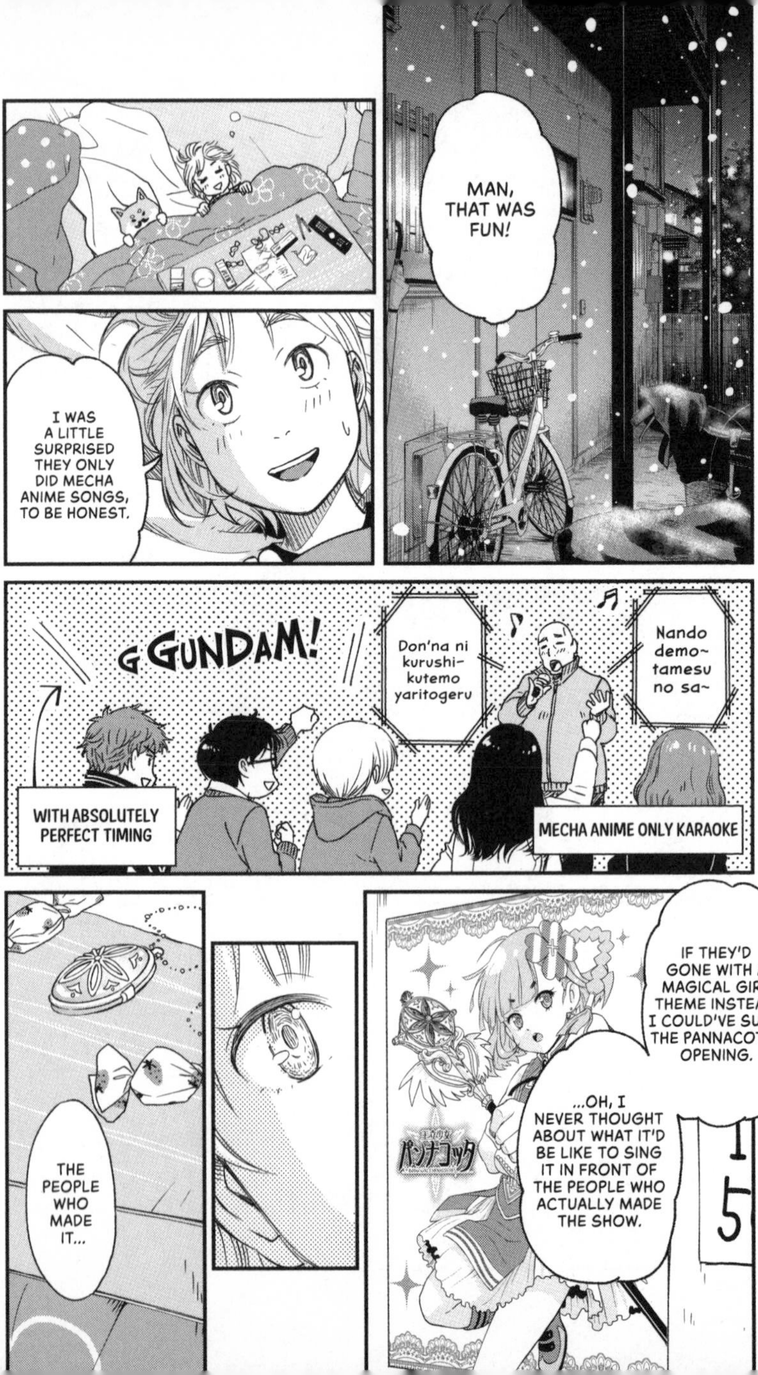

MAN, THAT WAS FUN!
I WAS A LITTLE SURPRISED THEY ONLY DID MECHA ANIME SONGS, TO BE HONEST.
Nando demo~ tamesu no sa~
MECHA ANIME ONLY KARAOKE
Don'na ni kurushi-kutemo yaritogeru
G GUNDAM!
WITH ABSOLUTELY PERFECT TIMING
IF THEY'D GONE WITH A MAGICAL GIRL THEME INSTEAD, I COULD'VE SUNG THE PANNACOTTA OPENING.
...OH, I NEVER THOUGHT ABOUT WHAT IT'D BE LIKE TO SING IT IN FRONT OF THE PEOPLE WHO ACTUALLY MADE THE SHOW.
パンナコッタ
THE PEOPLE WHO MADE IT...

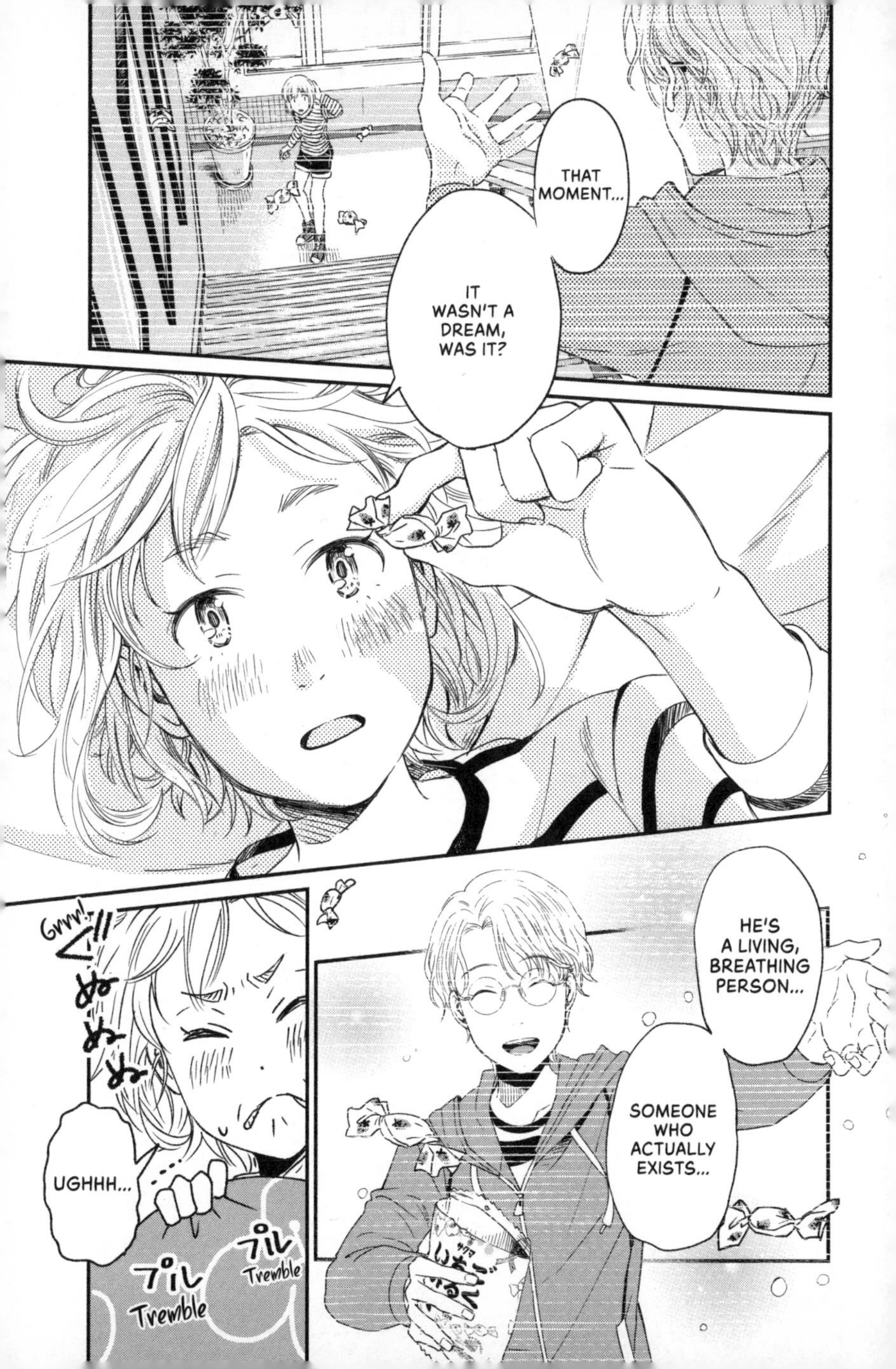
THAT MOMENT...
IT WASN'T A DREAM, WAS IT?
HE'S A LIVING, BREATHING PERSON...
SOMEONE WHO ACTUALLY EXISTS...
Grrr!
ぬぬぬぬ
UGHHH...
プル Tremble
プル Tremble

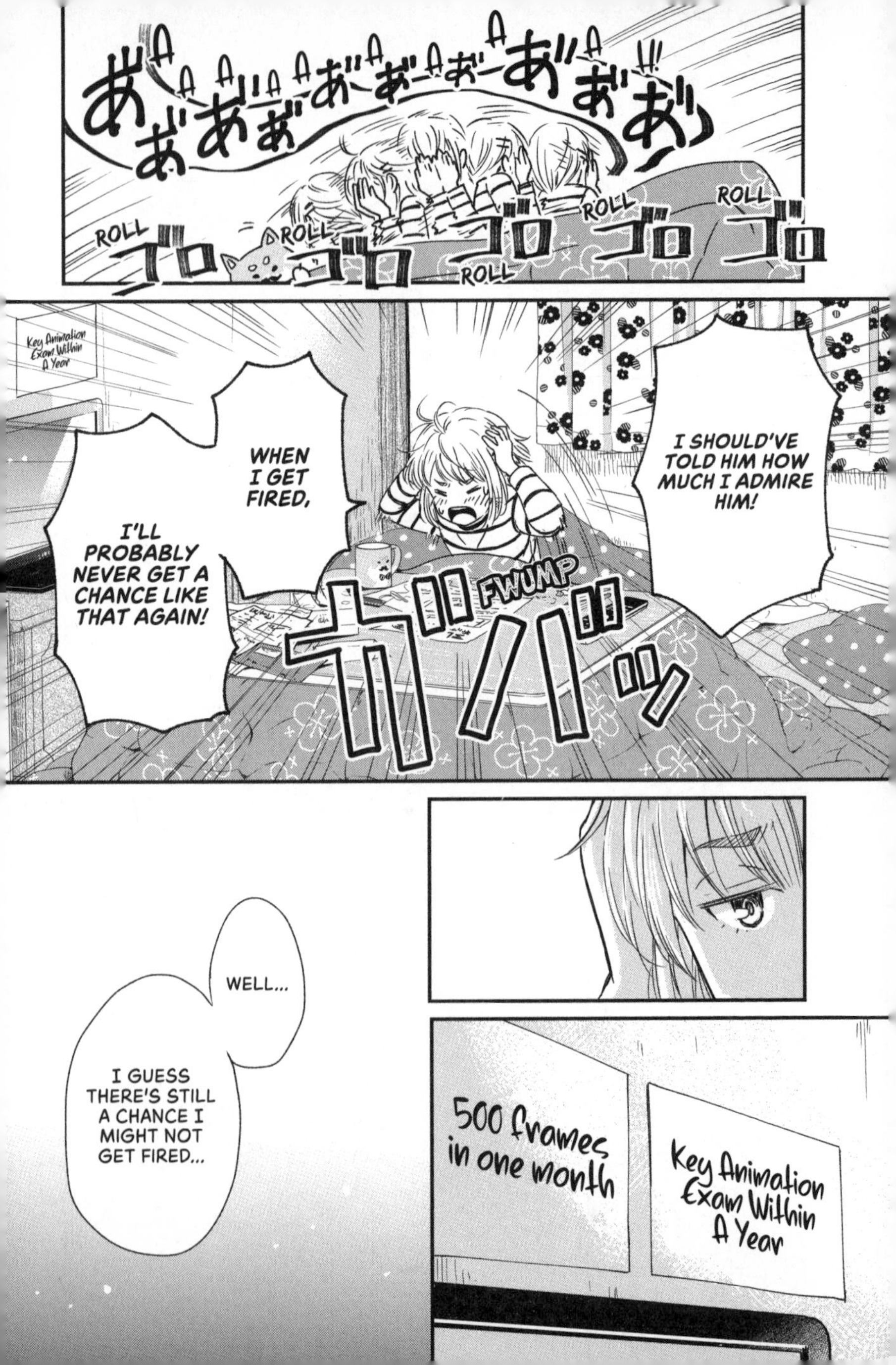

ROLL ゴロ
ROLL ゴロ
ROLL ゴロ
ROLL ゴロ
ROLL
I SHOULD'VE TOLD HIM HOW MUCH I ADMIRE HIM!
FWUMP ガバッ
WHEN I GET FIRED,
I'LL PROBABLY NEVER GET A CHANCE LIKE THAT AGAIN!
Key Animation Exam Within A Year
Key Animation Exam Within A Year
500 frames in one month
WELL...
I GUESS THERE'S STILL A CHANCE I MIGHT NOT GET FIRED...

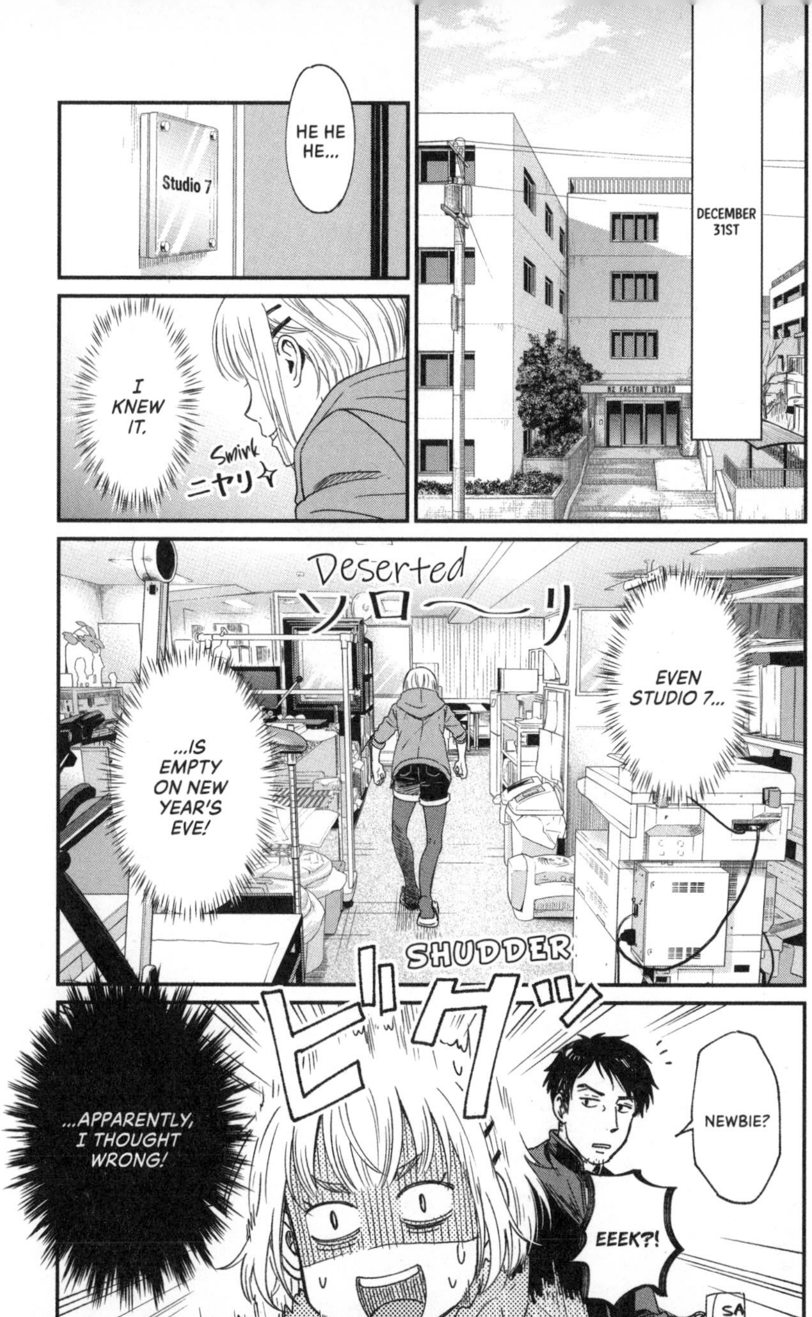
DECEMBER 31ST
92 FACTORY STUDIO
Studio 7
HE HE HE...
I KNEW IT.
Smirk
ニヤリ
Deserted
ソローーリ
EVEN STUDIO 7...
...IS EMPTY ON NEW YEAR'S EVE!
SHUDDER
NEWBIE?
EEEK?!
...APPARENTLY, I THOUGHT WRONG!

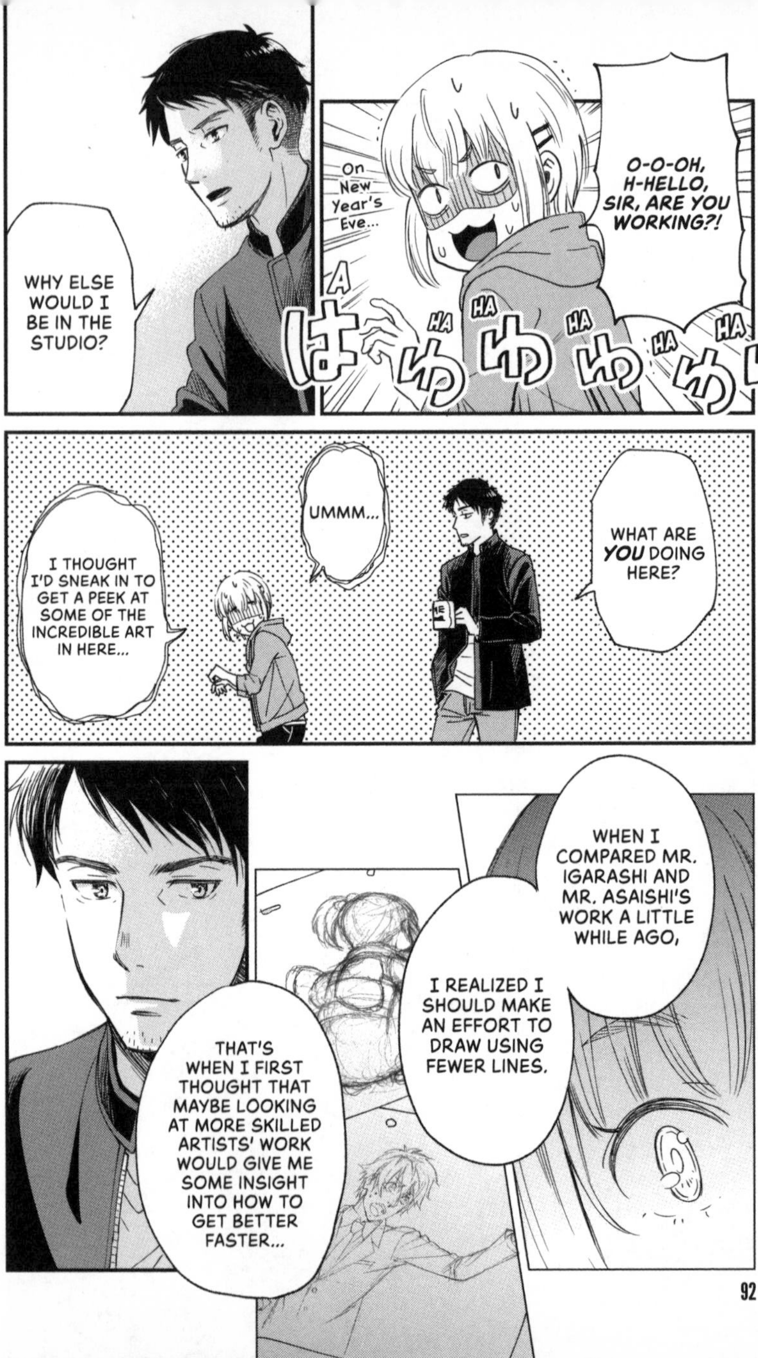
O-O-OH, H-HELLO, SIR, ARE YOU WORKING?!
On New Year's Eve...
はゆゆゆゆゆ
A HA HA HA HA HA
WHY ELSE WOULD I BE IN THE STUDIO?
WHAT ARE *YOU* DOING HERE?
UMMM...
I THOUGHT I'D SNEAK IN TO GET A PEEK AT SOME OF THE INCREDIBLE ART IN HERE...
WHEN I COMPARED MR. IGARASHI AND MR. ASAISHI'S WORK A LITTLE WHILE AGO,
I REALIZED I SHOULD MAKE AN EFFORT TO DRAW USING FEWER LINES.
THAT'S WHEN I FIRST THOUGHT THAT MAYBE LOOKING AT MORE SKILLED ARTISTS' WORK WOULD GIVE ME SOME INSIGHT INTO HOW TO GET BETTER FASTER...

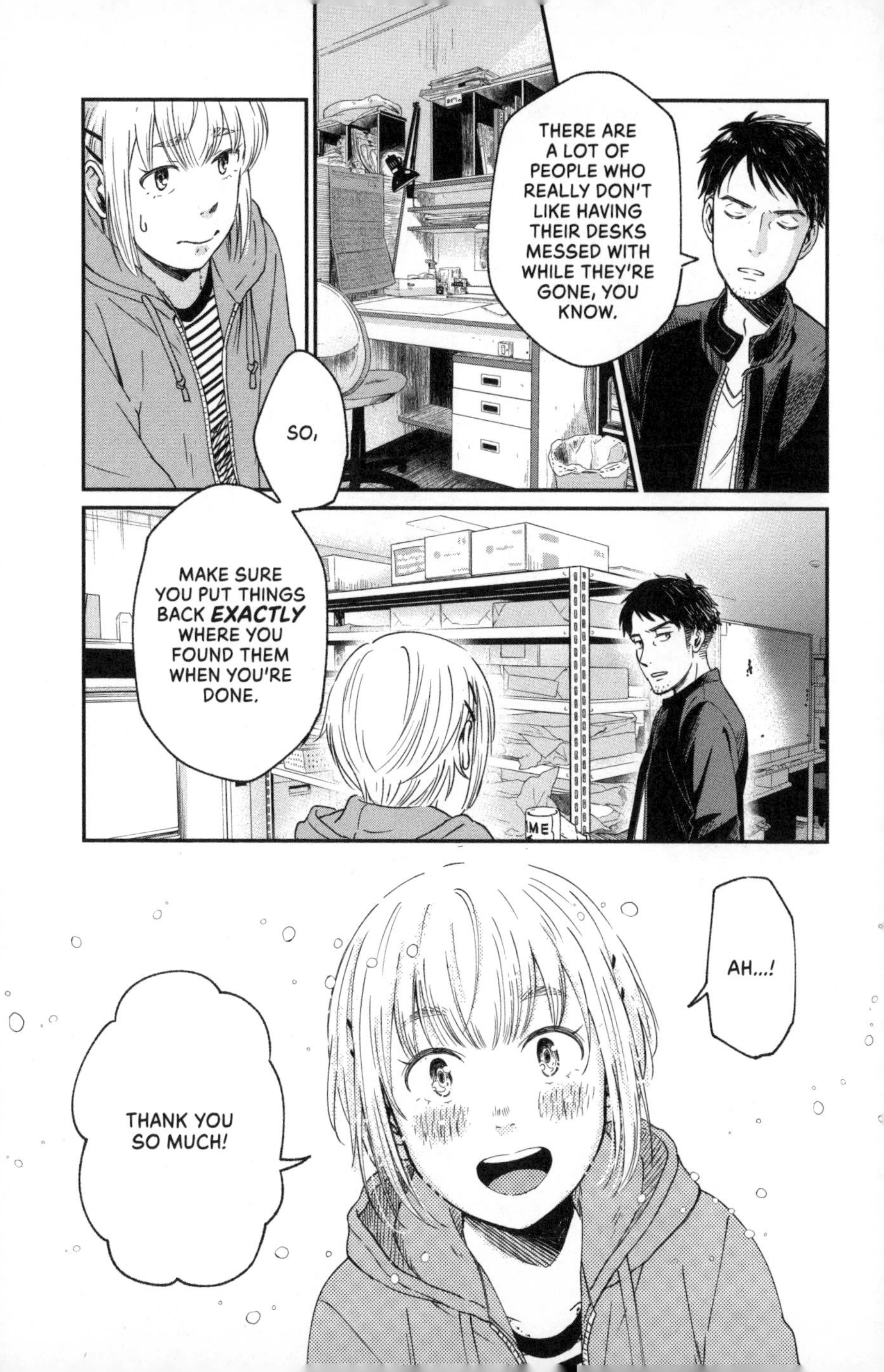
THERE ARE A LOT OF PEOPLE WHO REALLY DON'T LIKE HAVING THEIR DESKS MESSED WITH WHILE THEY'RE GONE, YOU KNOW.
SO,
MAKE SURE YOU PUT THINGS BACK **EXACTLY** WHERE YOU FOUND THEM WHEN YOU'RE DONE.
ME
AH...!
THANK YOU SO MUCH!

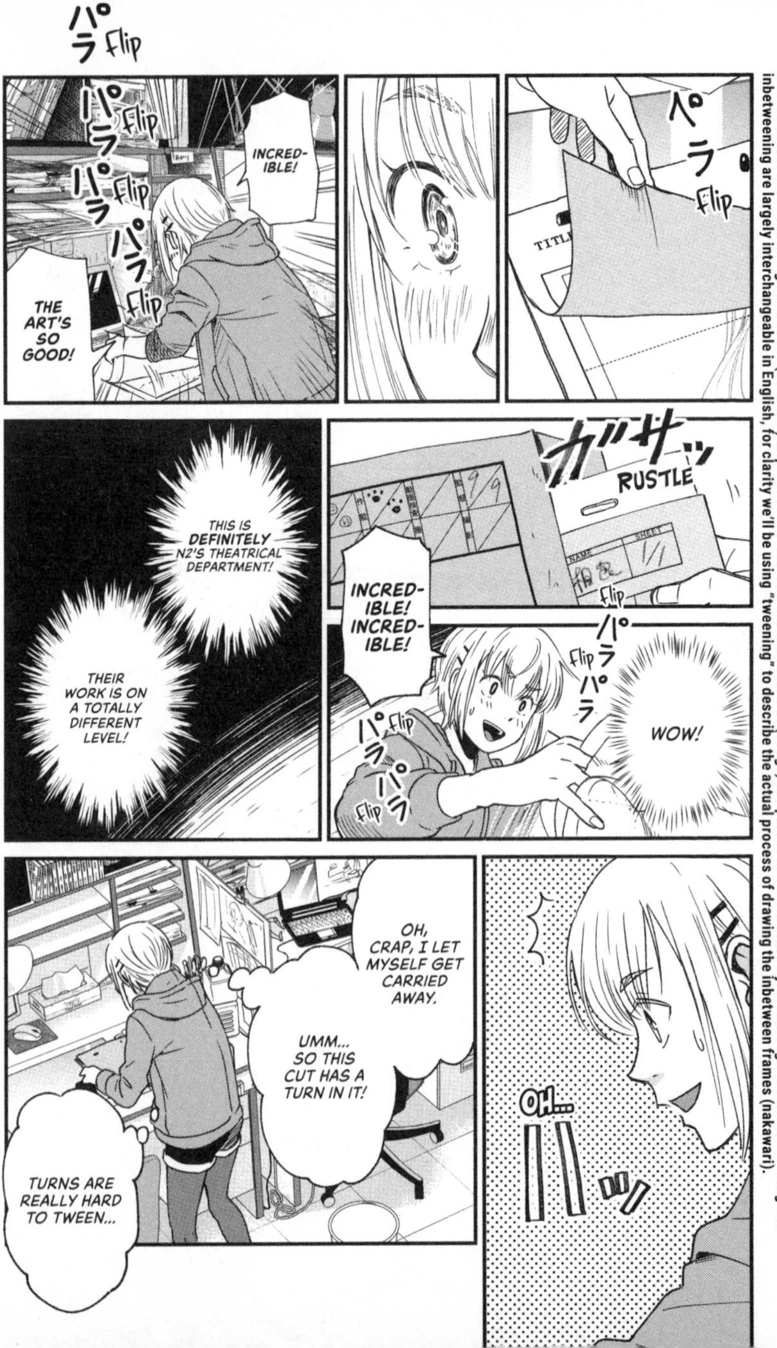
パラ Flip
パラ Flip
パラ Flip パラ Flip パラ Flip
INCREDIBLE!
THE ART'S SO GOOD!
ガサッ RUSTLE
NAME
SHEET
TITLE
INCREDIBLE! INCREDIBLE!
WOW!
Flip パラ Flip パラ
パラ Flip パラ Flip
THIS IS DEFINITELY N2'S THEATRICAL DEPARTMENT!
THEIR WORK IS ON A TOTALLY DIFFERENT LEVEL!
OH...
OH, CRAP, I LET MYSELF GET CARRIED AWAY.
UMM... SO THIS CUT HAS A TURN IN IT!
TURNS ARE REALLY HARD TO TWEEN...

Tweening (Nakawari): The process of adding frames in between keyframes, so the animation moves smoothly. In Japan, both tracing and cleaning the raw keyframes (genga) and the actual work of drawing inbetweens (nakawari) to produce the finalized animation frames (douga) are part of an inbetweener's job. Although the terms tweening and inbetweening are largely interchangeable in English, for clarity we'll be using "tweening" to describe the actual process of drawing the inbetween frames (nakawari).

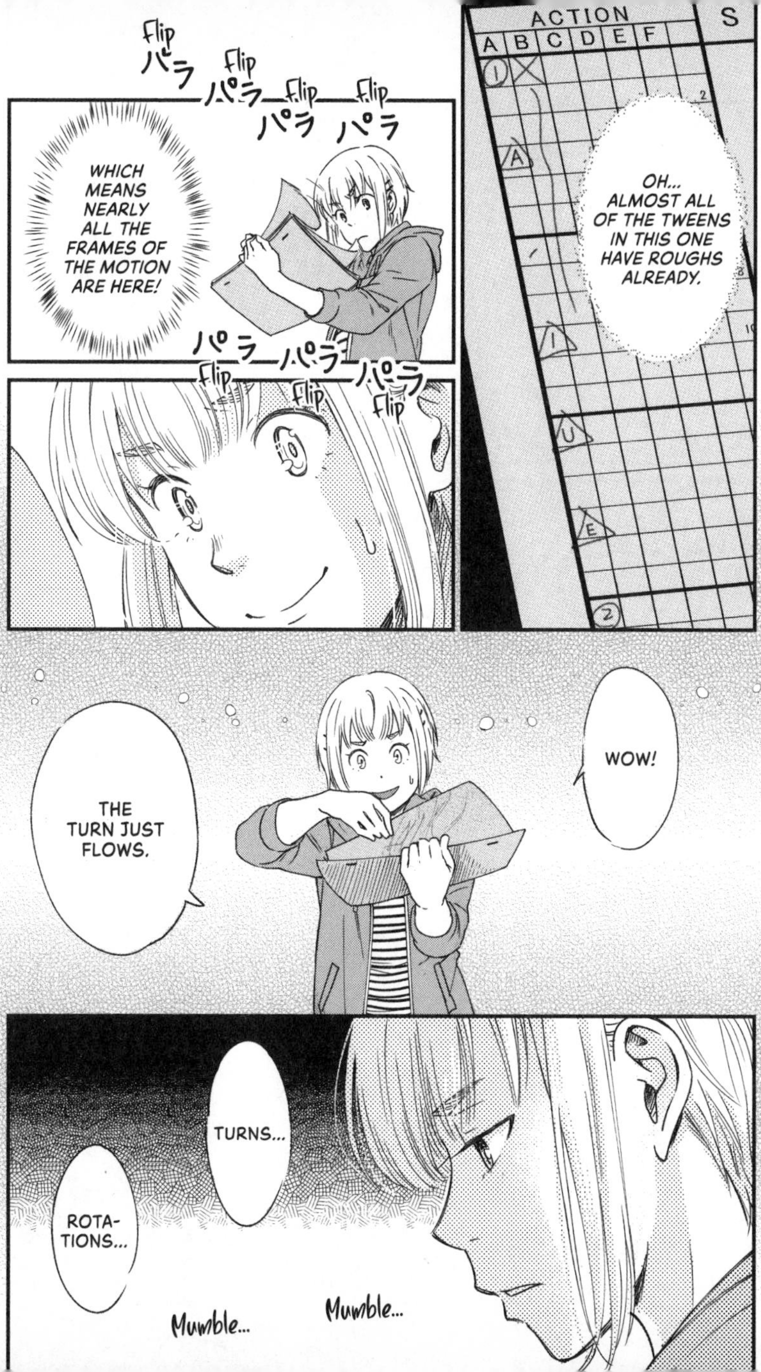

ACTION
S
A B C D E F
OH... ALMOST ALL OF THE TWEENS IN THIS ONE HAVE ROUGHS ALREADY.
Flip パラ Flip パラ Flip パラ Flip パラ
WHICH MEANS NEARLY ALL THE FRAMES OF THE MOTION ARE HERE!
パラ Flip パラ Flip パラ Flip
WOW!
THE TURN JUST FLOWS.
TURNS...
ROTA-TIONS...
Mumble...
Mumble...

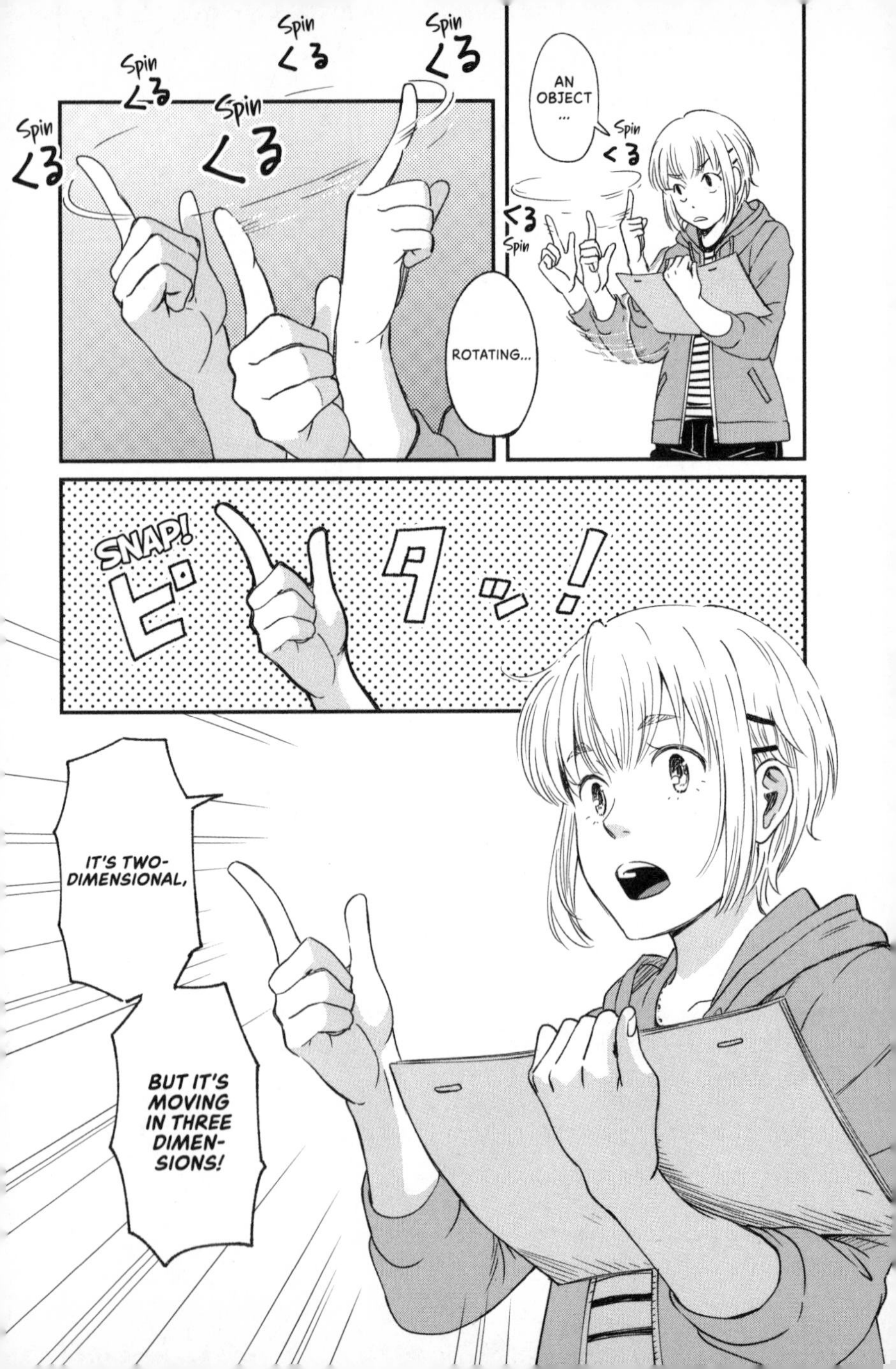
AN OBJECT ...
Spin くる
くる Spin
ROTATING...
Spin くる
Spin くる
Spin くる
Spin くる
Spin くる
SNAP! ピタッ!
IT'S TWO-DIMENSIONAL,
BUT IT'S MOVING IN THREE DIMENSIONS!

CHAPTER 19: BUILDING A FORTUNE MONEY CAN'T BUY

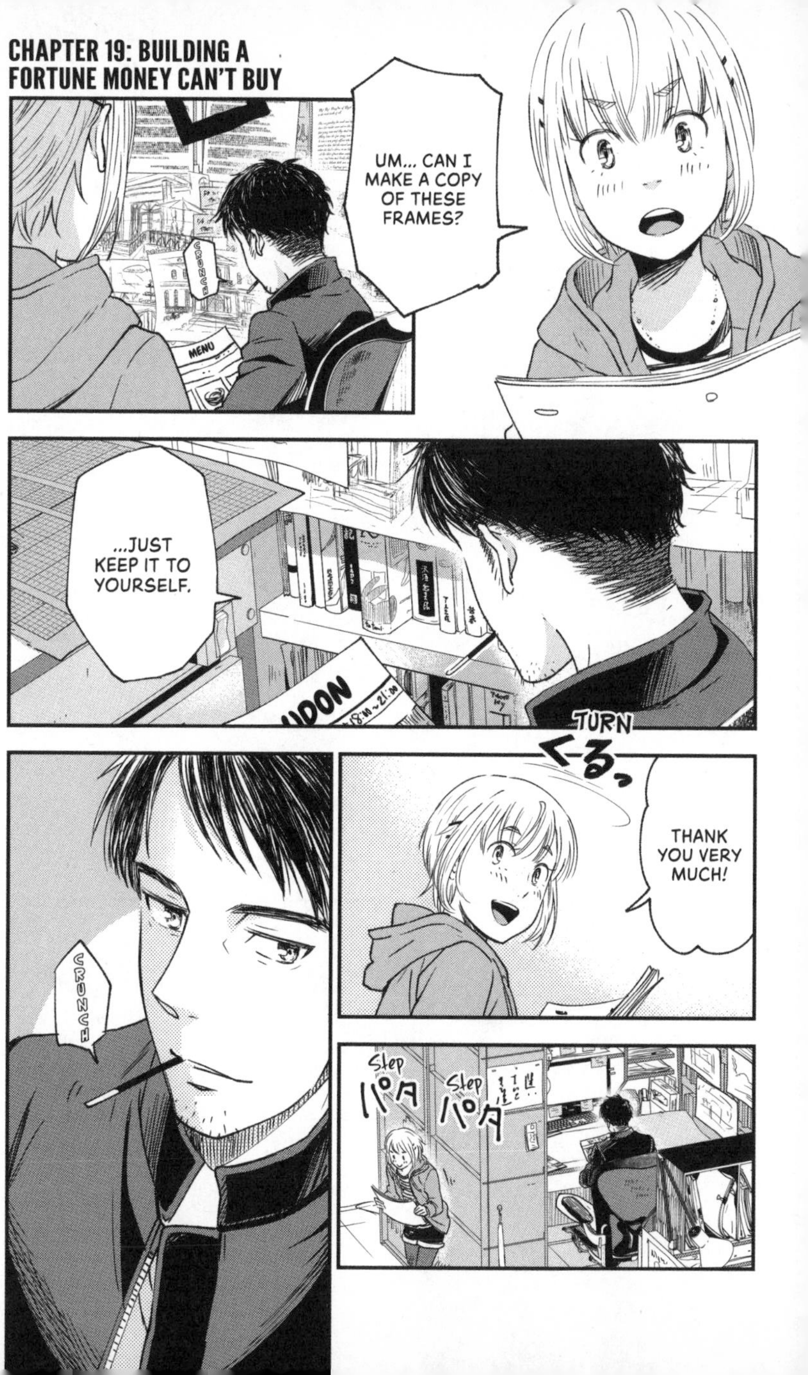
UM... CAN I MAKE A COPY OF THESE FRAMES?
CRUNCH
MENU
...JUST KEEP IT TO YOURSELF.
UDON
TURN
くるっ
THANK YOU VERY MUCH!
Step
パタ
Step
パタ
CRUNCH

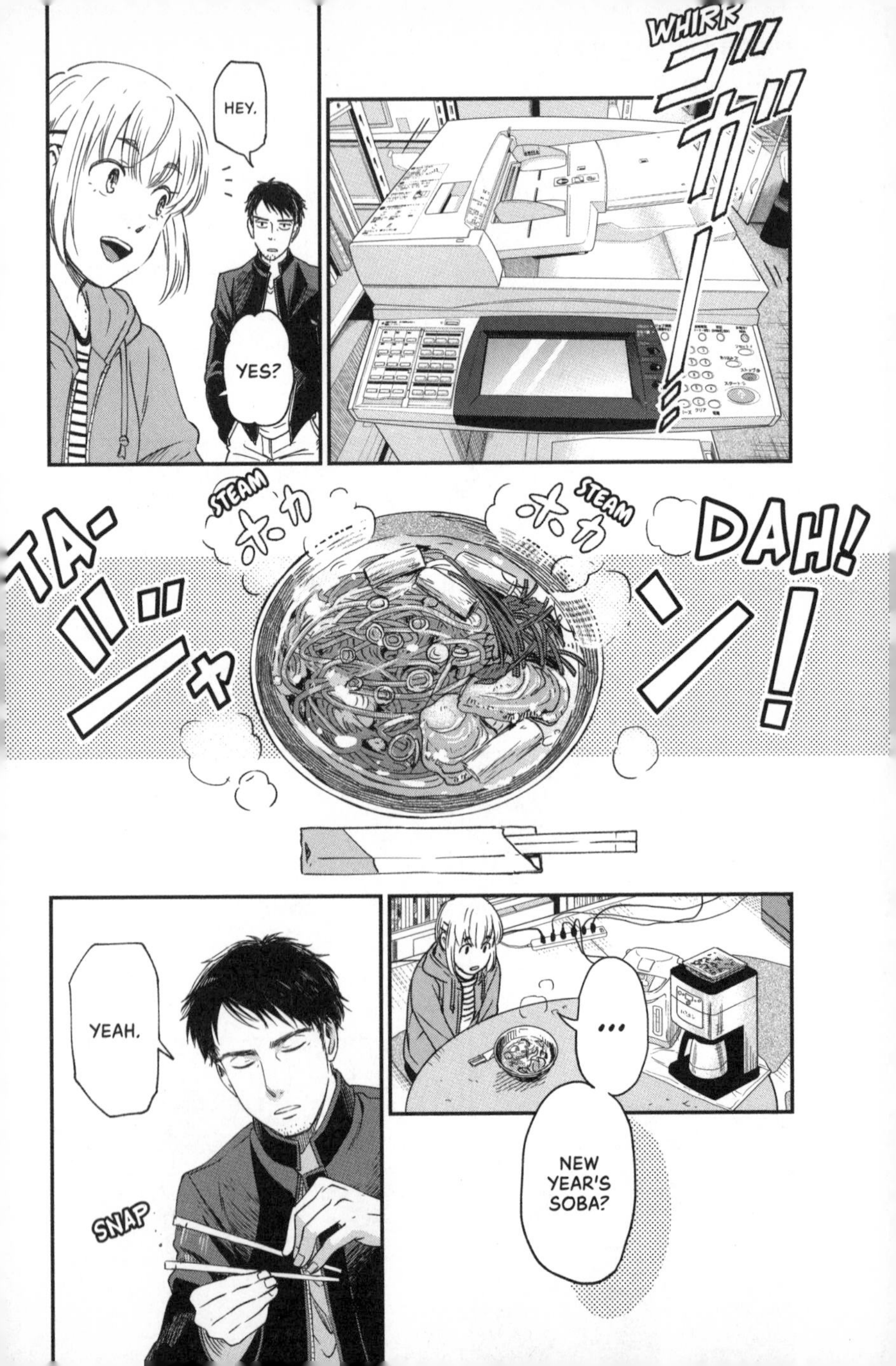
WHIRRK
ゴガー
HEY.
YES?
STEAM
ホカ
STEAM
ホカ
TA-DAH!
ジャーン!
...
NEW YEAR'S SOBA?
YEAH.
SNAP

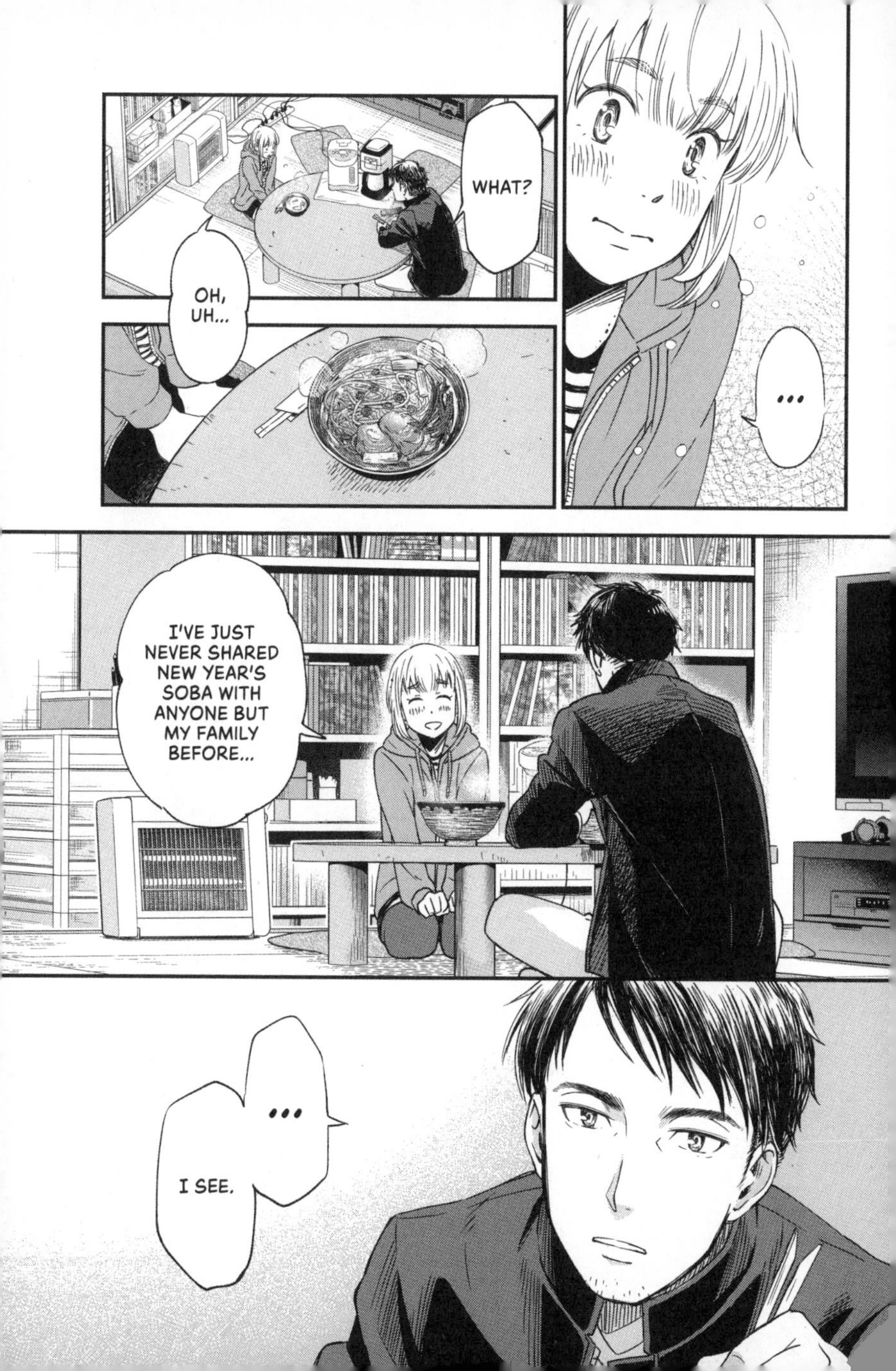
...
WHAT?
OH, UH...
I'VE JUST NEVER SHARED NEW YEAR'S SOBA WITH ANYONE BUT MY FAMILY BEFORE...
...
I SEE.

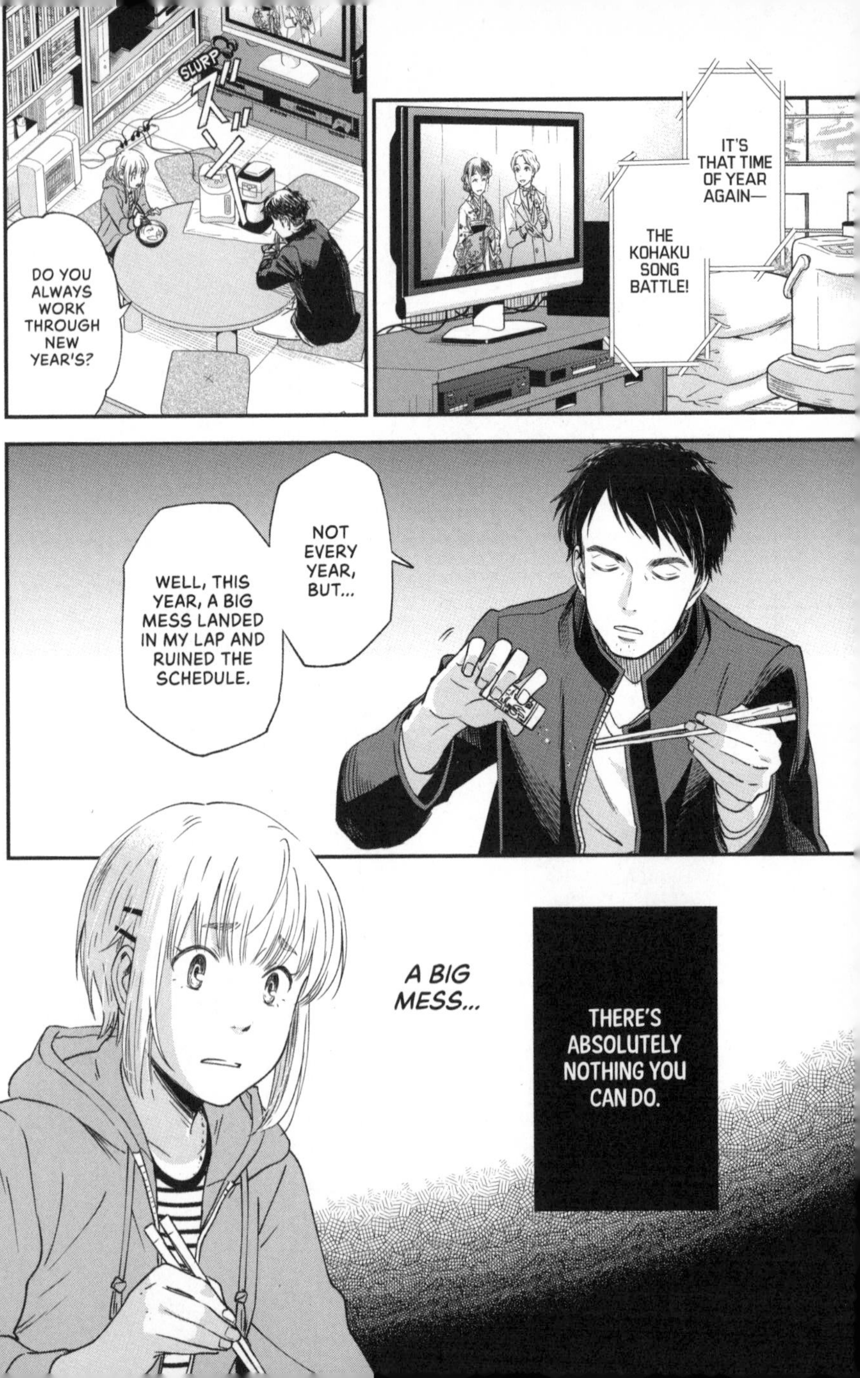
IT'S THAT TIME OF YEAR AGAIN—
THE KOHAKU SONG BATTLE!
SLURP
DO YOU ALWAYS WORK THROUGH NEW YEAR'S?
NOT EVERY YEAR, BUT...
WELL, THIS YEAR, A BIG MESS LANDED IN MY LAP AND RUINED THE SCHEDULE.
THERE'S ABSOLUTELY NOTHING YOU CAN DO.
A BIG MESS...

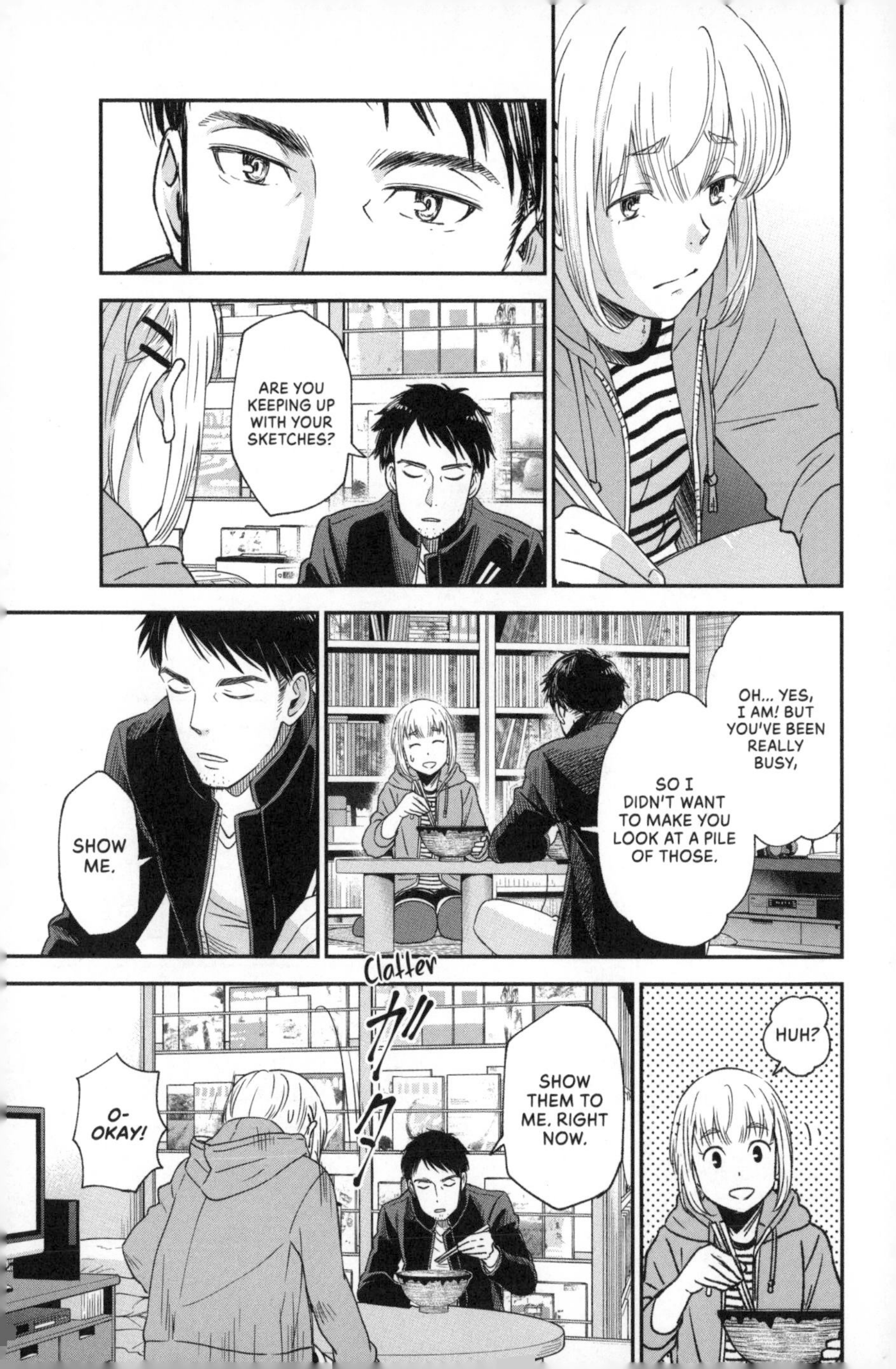
ARE YOU KEEPING UP WITH YOUR SKETCHES?
OH... YES, I AM! BUT YOU'VE BEEN REALLY BUSY,
SO I DIDN'T WANT TO MAKE YOU LOOK AT A PILE OF THOSE.
SHOW ME.
HUH?
SHOW THEM TO ME, RIGHT NOW.
Clatter
O-OKAY!

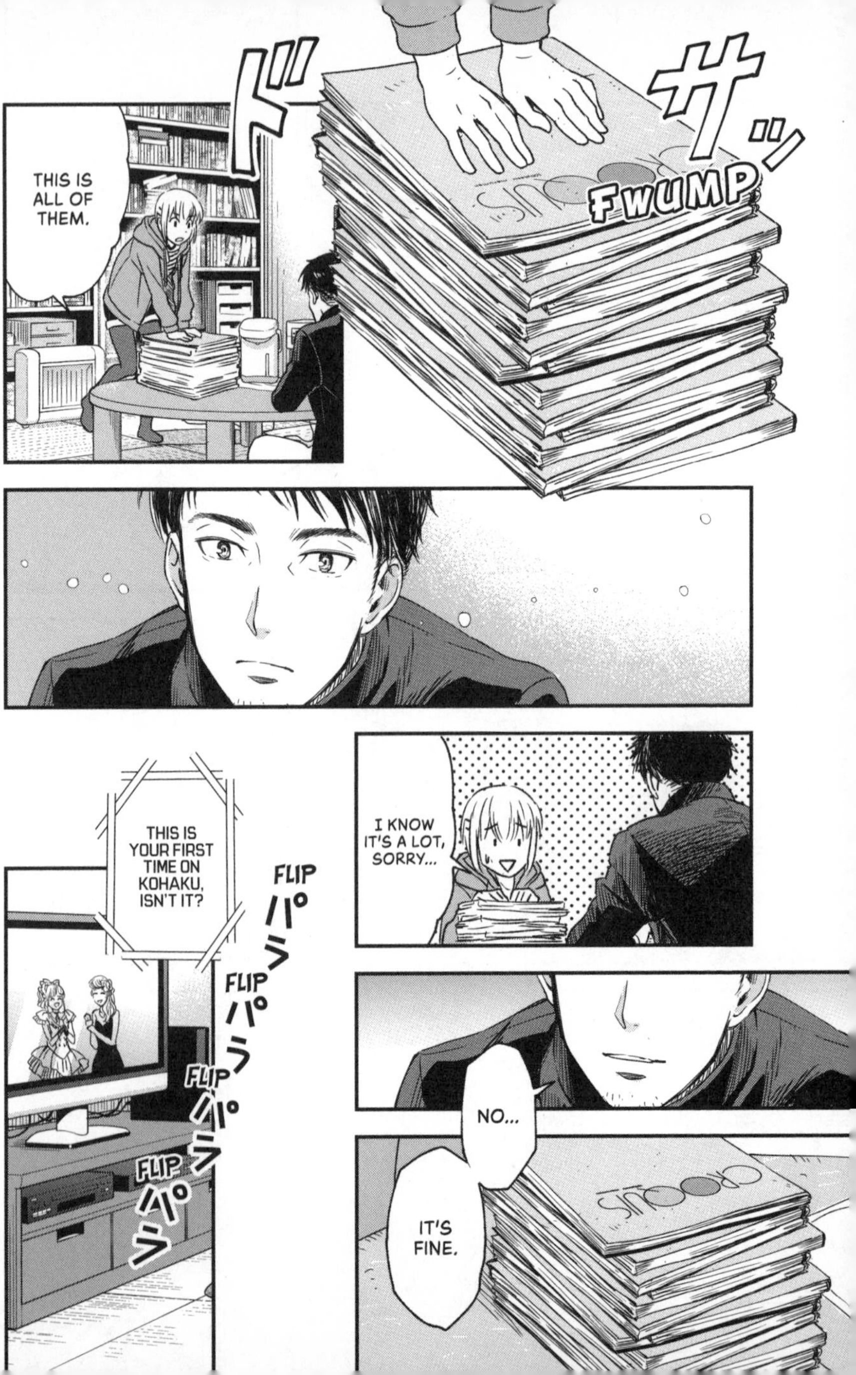
ド
ザッ
FWUMP
THIS IS ALL OF THEM.
I KNOW IT'S A LOT, SORRY...
NO...
IT'S FINE.
THIS IS YOUR FIRST TIME ON KOHAKU, ISN'T IT?
FLIP
パラ
FLIP
パラ
FLIP
パラ
FLIP
パラ

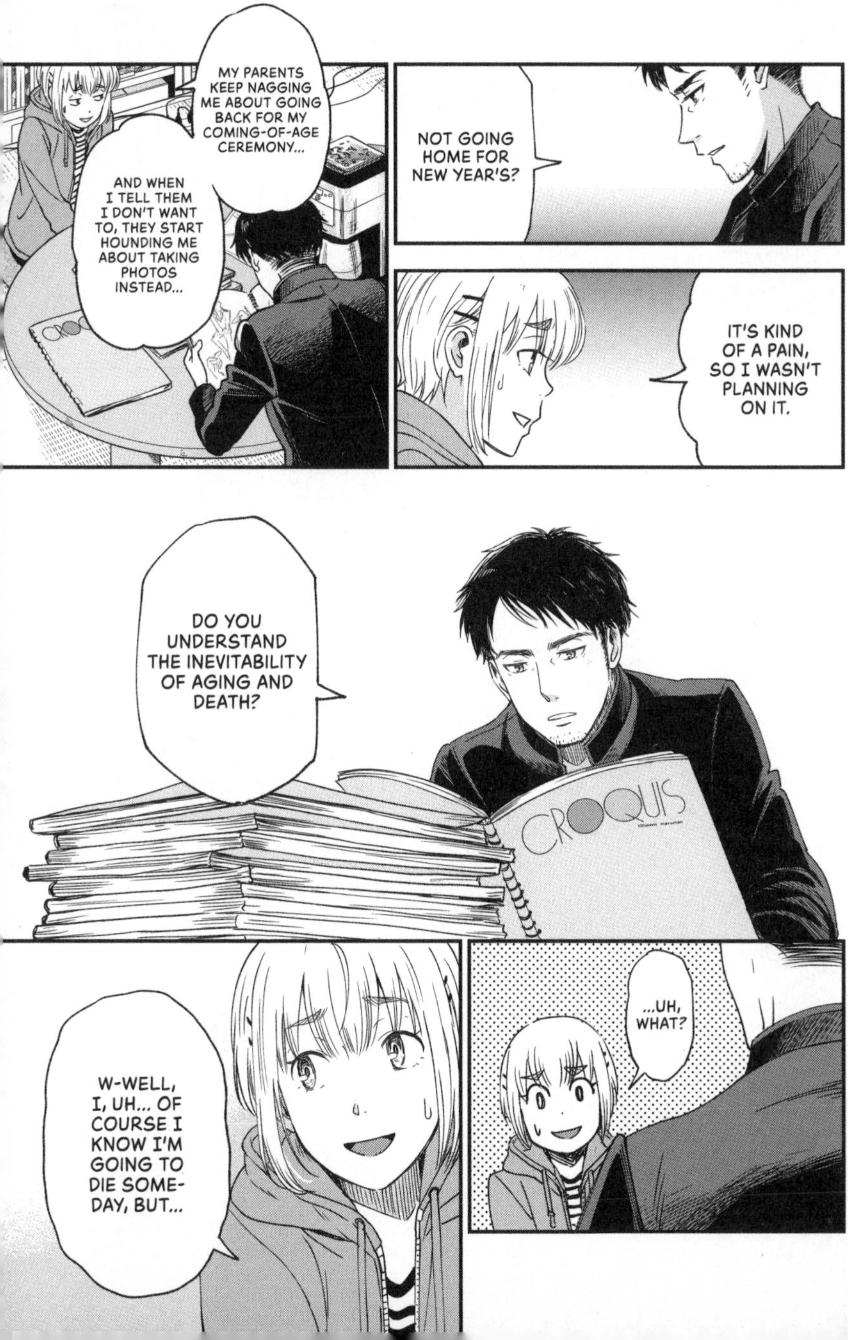
NOT GOING HOME FOR NEW YEAR'S?
IT'S KIND OF A PAIN, SO I WASN'T PLANNING ON IT.
MY PARENTS KEEP NAGGING ME ABOUT GOING BACK FOR MY COMING-OF-AGE CEREMONY...
AND WHEN I TELL THEM I DON'T WANT TO, THEY START HOUNDING ME ABOUT TAKING PHOTOS INSTEAD...
DO YOU UNDERSTAND THE INEVITABILITY OF AGING AND DEATH?
CROQUIS
...UH, WHAT?
W-WELL, I, UH... OF COURSE I KNOW I'M GOING TO DIE SOME-DAY, BUT...

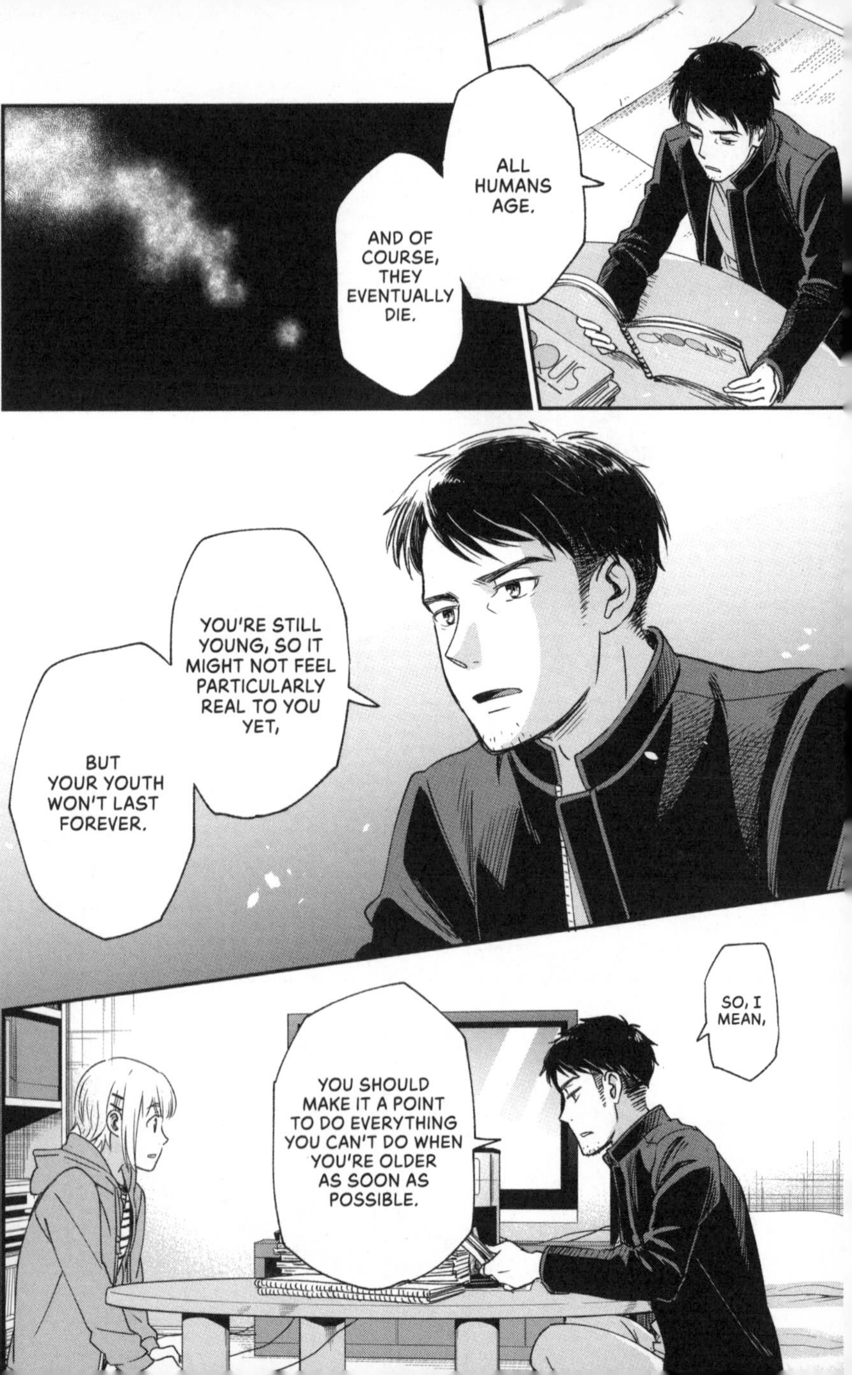
ALL HUMANS AGE.
AND OF COURSE, THEY EVENTUALLY DIE.
YOU'RE STILL YOUNG, SO IT MIGHT NOT FEEL PARTICULARLY REAL TO YOU YET,
BUT YOUR YOUTH WON'T LAST FOREVER.
SO, I MEAN,
YOU SHOULD MAKE IT A POINT TO DO EVERYTHING YOU CAN'T DO WHEN YOU'RE OLDER AS SOON AS POSSIBLE.

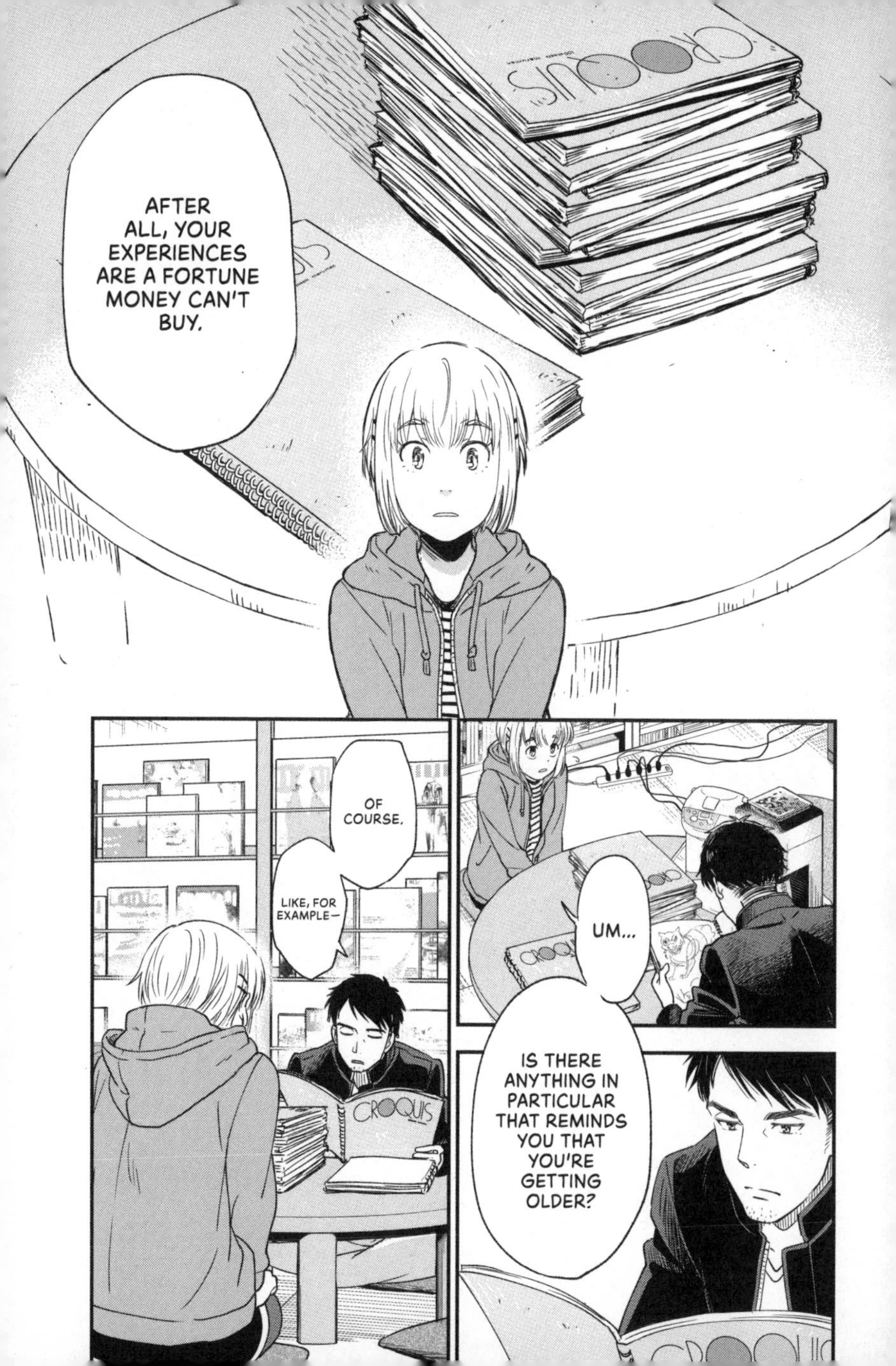
AFTER ALL, YOUR EXPERIENCES ARE A FORTUNE MONEY CAN'T BUY.
OF COURSE.
LIKE, FOR EXAMPLE—
UM...
IS THERE ANYTHING IN PARTICULAR THAT REMINDS YOU THAT YOU'RE GETTING OLDER?
CROQUIS

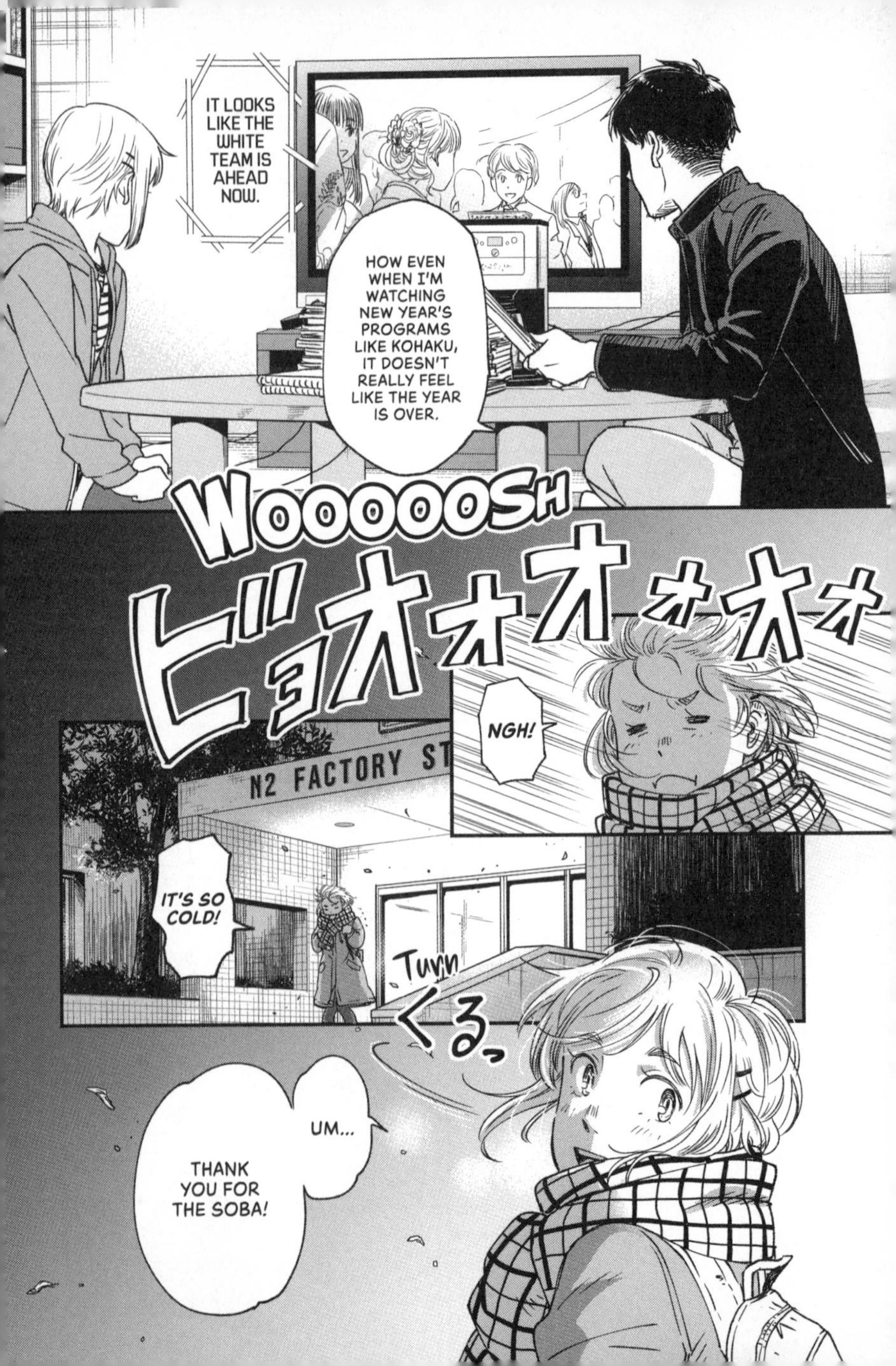

IT LOOKS LIKE THE WHITE TEAM IS AHEAD NOW.
HOW EVEN WHEN I'M WATCHING NEW YEAR'S PROGRAMS LIKE KOHAKU, IT DOESN'T REALLY FEEL LIKE THE YEAR IS OVER.
WOOOOOSH
ビョオォオォオォ
NGH!
N2 FACTORY ST
IT'S SO COLD!
Turn
くるっ
UM...
THANK YOU FOR THE SOBA!

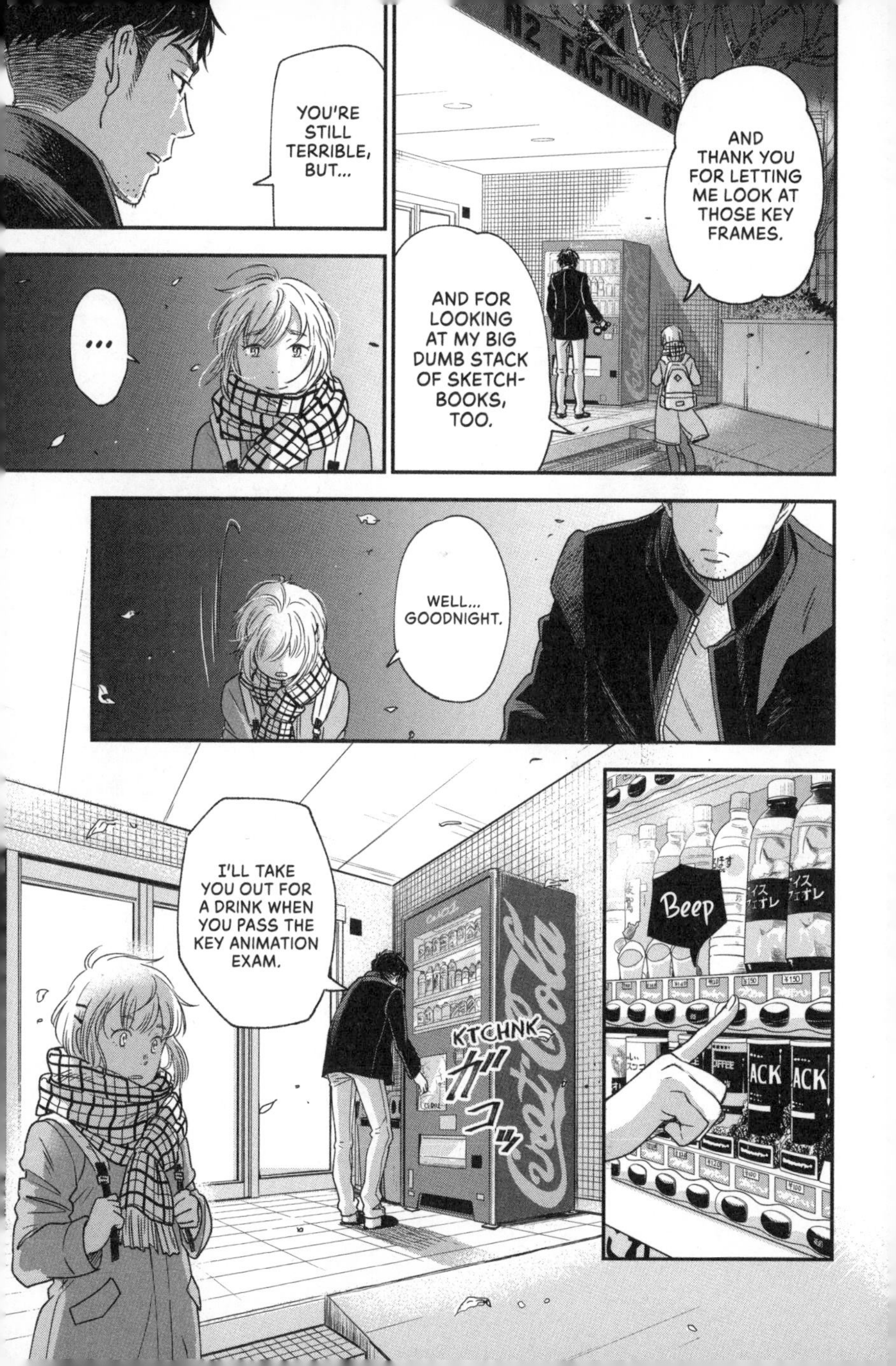
N2 FACTORY
AND THANK YOU FOR LETTING ME LOOK AT THOSE KEY FRAMES.
AND FOR LOOKING AT MY BIG DUMB STACK OF SKETCH-BOOKS, TOO.
YOU'RE STILL TERRIBLE, BUT...
...
WELL... GOODNIGHT.
Beep
I'LL TAKE YOU OUT FOR A DRINK WHEN YOU PASS THE KEY ANIMATION EXAM.
KTCHNK
ガコッ

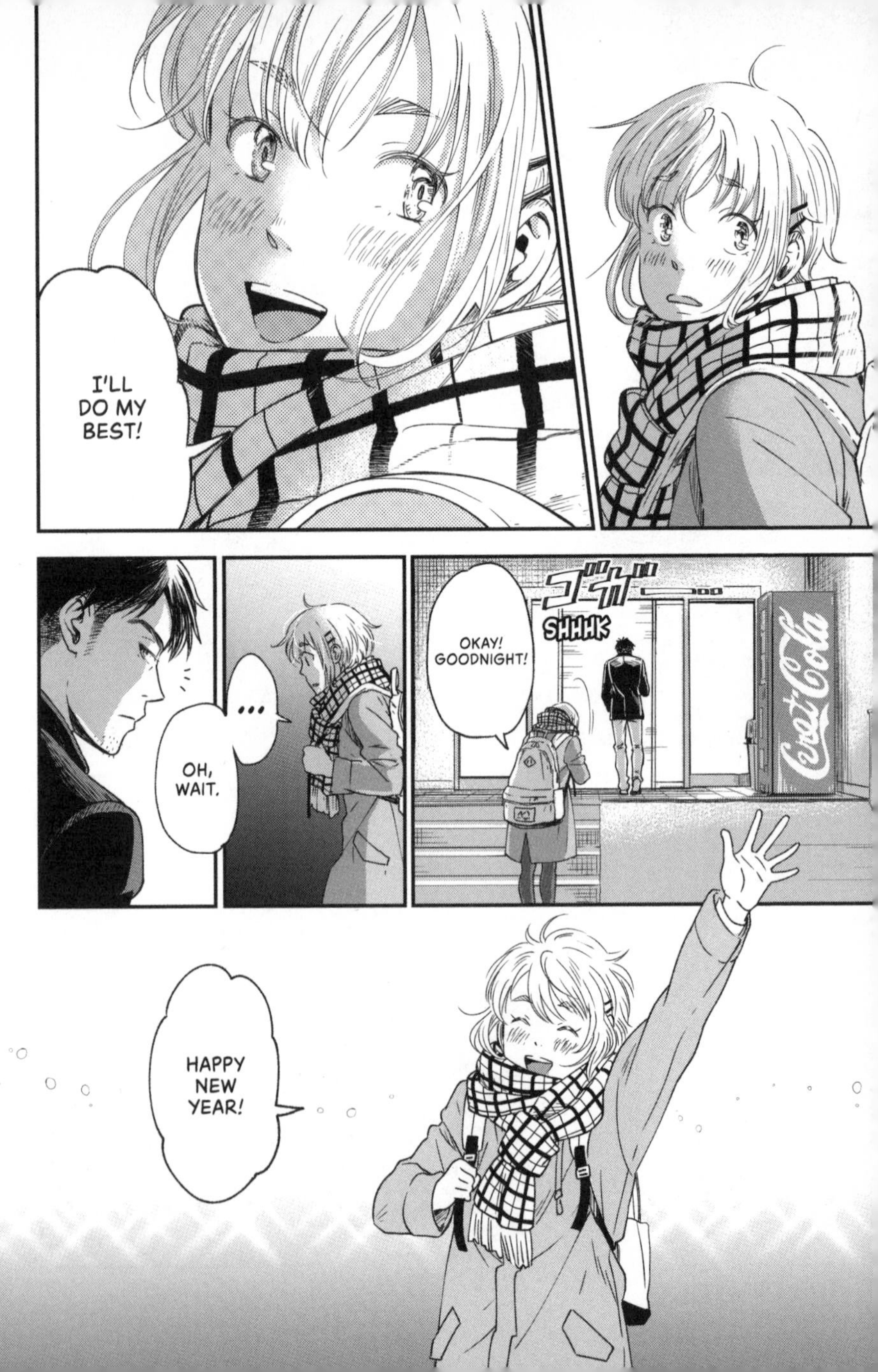
I'LL DO MY BEST!
OKAY! GOODNIGHT!
SHHHK
...
OH, WAIT.
HAPPY NEW YEAR!

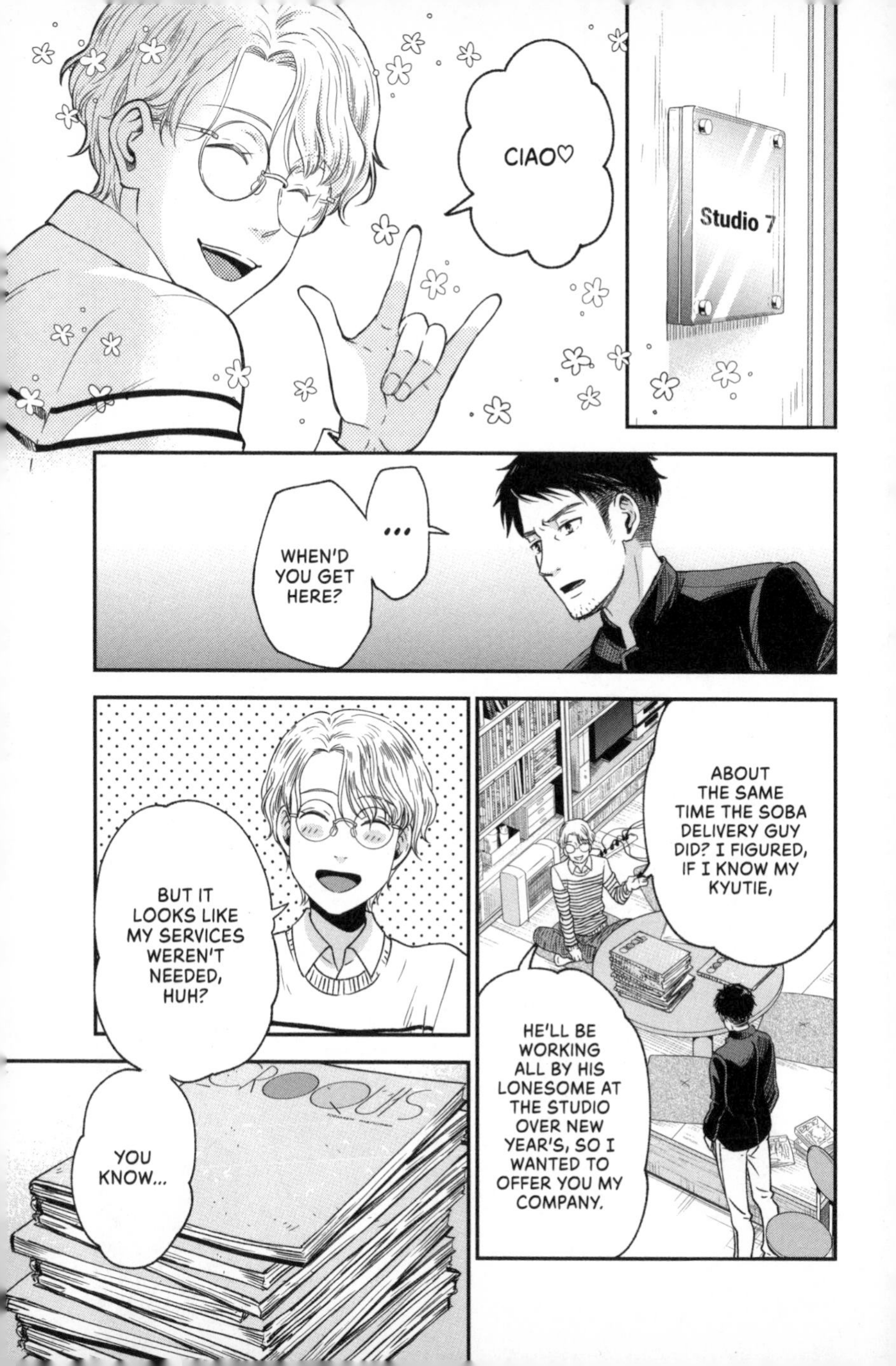
Studio 7
CIAO♡
...
WHEN'D YOU GET HERE?
ABOUT THE SAME TIME THE SOBA DELIVERY GUY DID? I FIGURED, IF I KNOW MY KYUTIE,
HE'LL BE WORKING ALL BY HIS LONESOME AT THE STUDIO OVER NEW YEAR'S, SO I WANTED TO OFFER YOU MY COMPANY.
BUT IT LOOKS LIKE MY SERVICES WEREN'T NEEDED, HUH?
YOU KNOW...

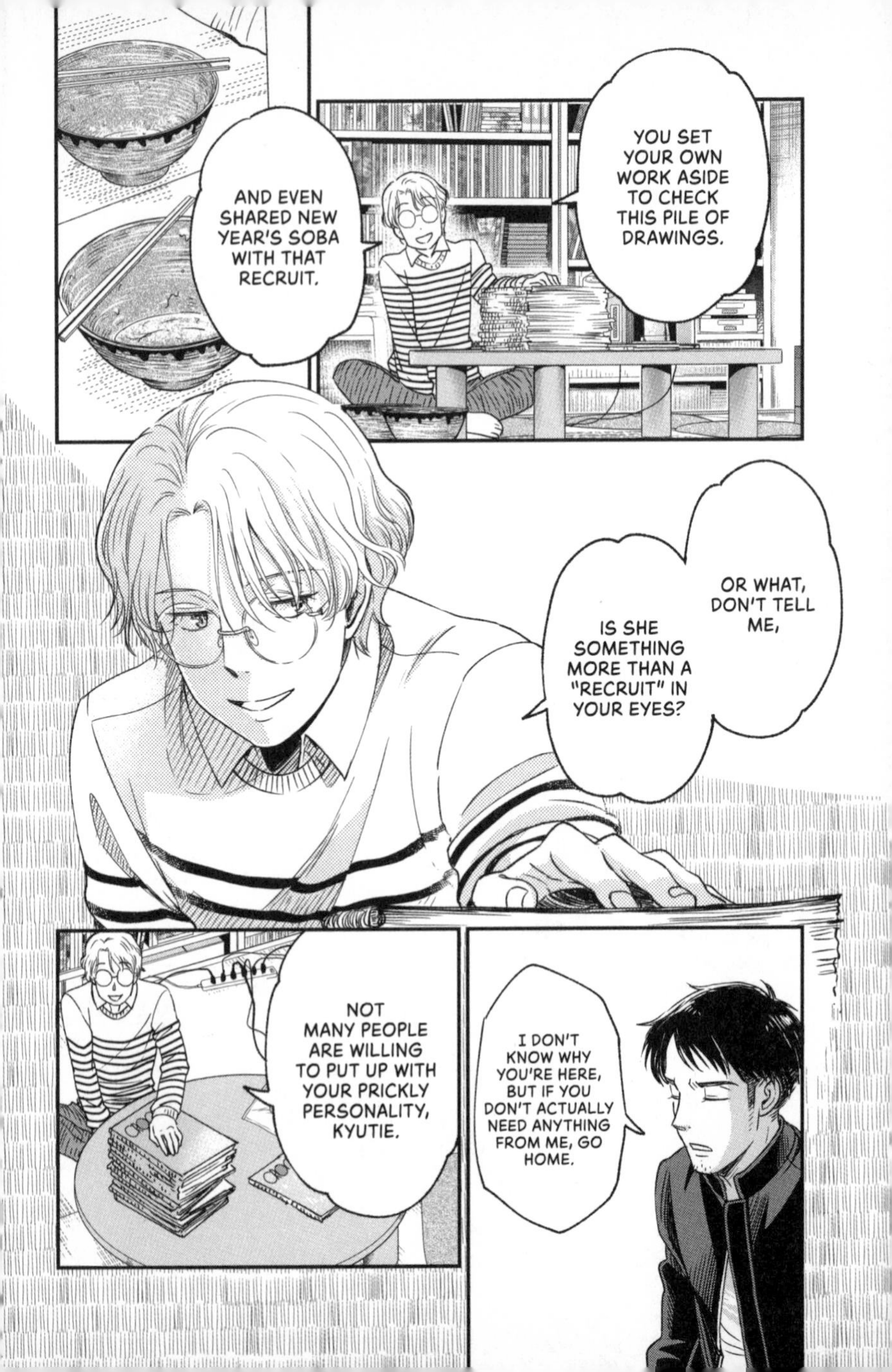
YOU SET YOUR OWN WORK ASIDE TO CHECK THIS PILE OF DRAWINGS.
AND EVEN SHARED NEW YEAR'S SOBA WITH THAT RECRUIT.
OR WHAT, DON'T TELL ME,
IS SHE SOMETHING MORE THAN A "RECRUIT" IN YOUR EYES?
I DON'T KNOW WHY YOU'RE HERE, BUT IF YOU DON'T ACTUALLY NEED ANYTHING FROM ME, GO HOME.
NOT MANY PEOPLE ARE WILLING TO PUT UP WITH YOUR PRICKLY PERSONALITY, KYUTIE.

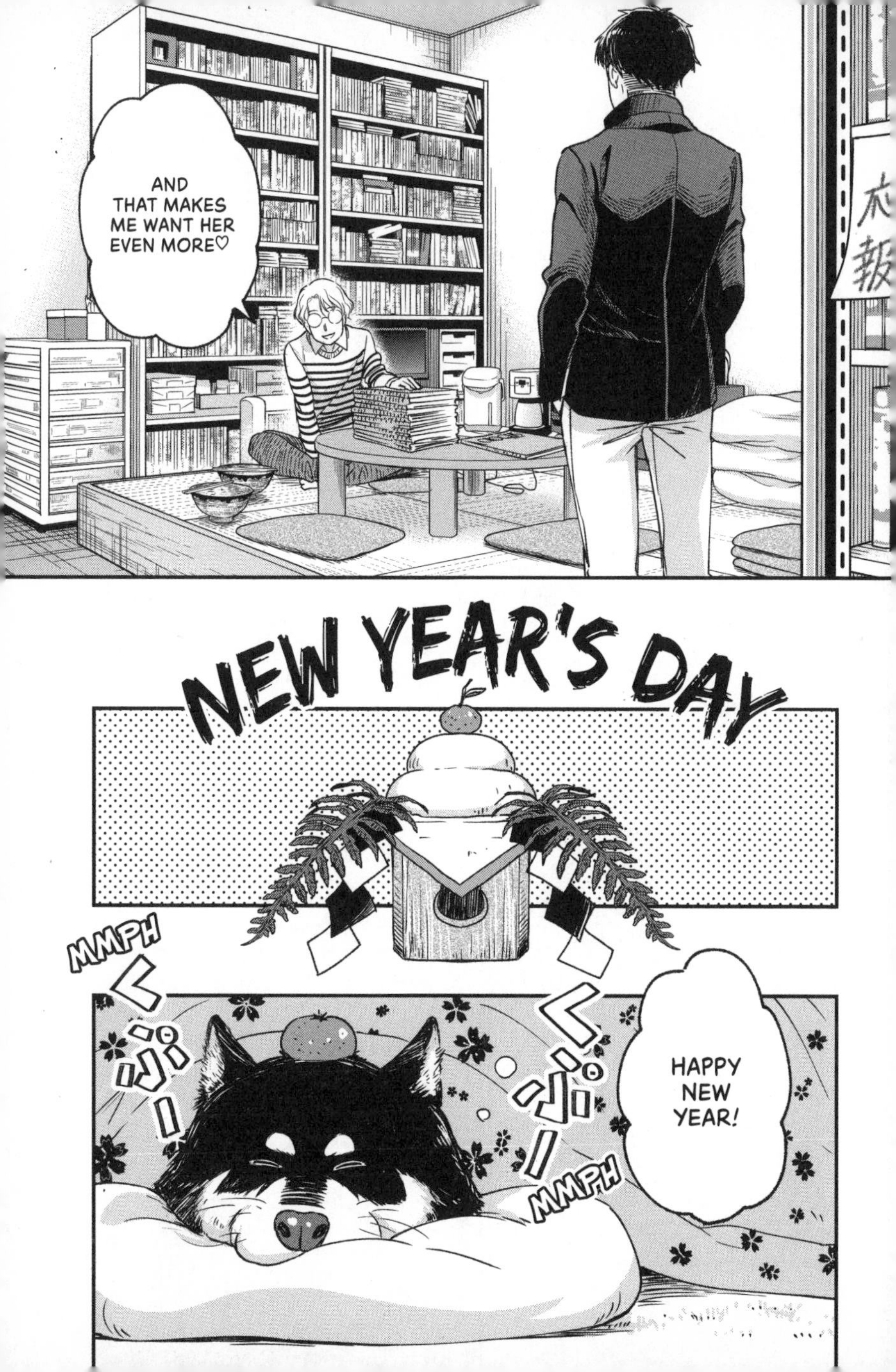
AND THAT MAKES ME WANT HER EVEN MORE♡
NEW YEAR'S DAY
HAPPY NEW YEAR!
MMPH
MMPH

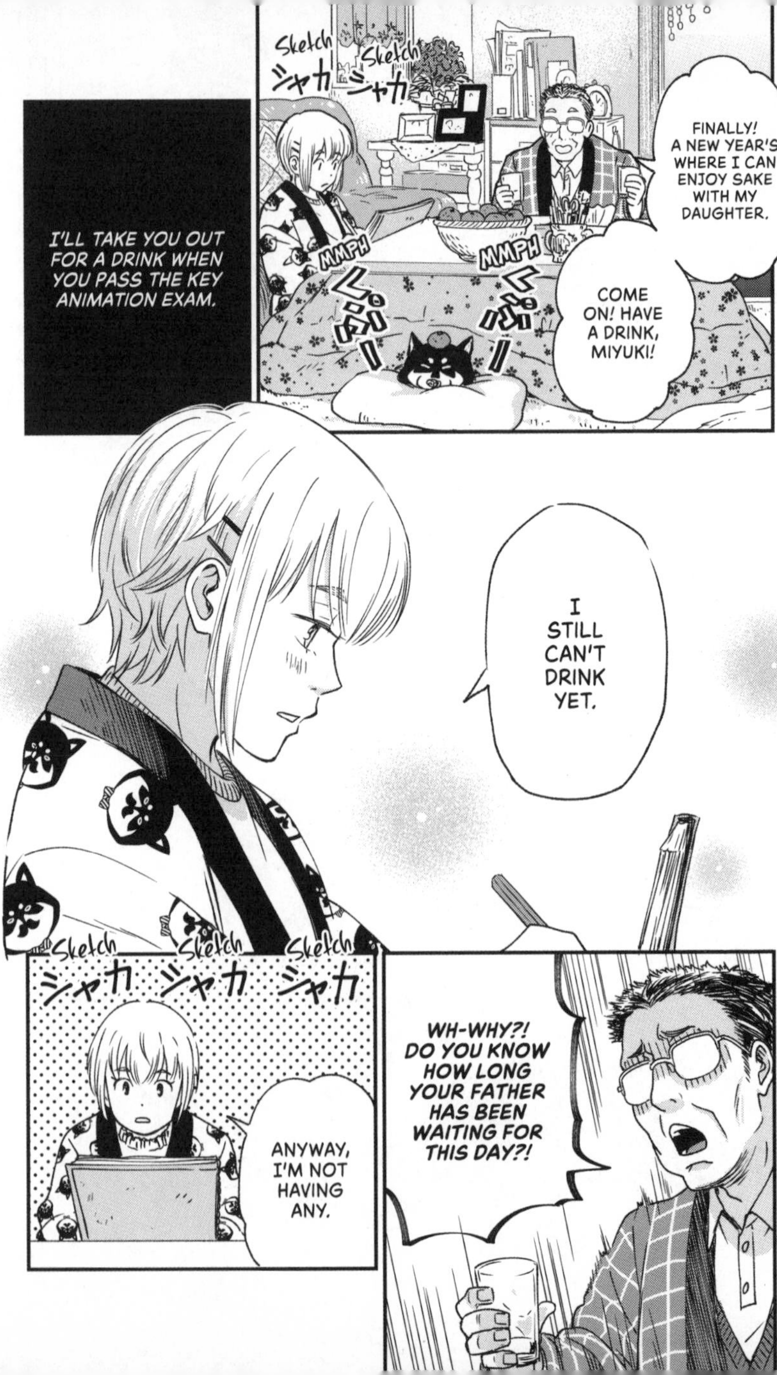
Sketch シャカ
Sketch シャカ
FINALLY! A NEW YEAR'S WHERE I CAN ENJOY SAKE WITH MY DAUGHTER.
COME ON! HAVE A DRINK, MIYUKI!
MMPH
MMPH
I'LL TAKE YOU OUT FOR A DRINK WHEN YOU PASS THE KEY ANIMATION EXAM.
I STILL CAN'T DRINK YET.
WH-WHY?! DO YOU KNOW HOW LONG YOUR FATHER HAS BEEN WAITING FOR THIS DAY?!
Sketch シャカ
Sketch シャカ
Sketch シャカ
ANYWAY, I'M NOT HAVING ANY.

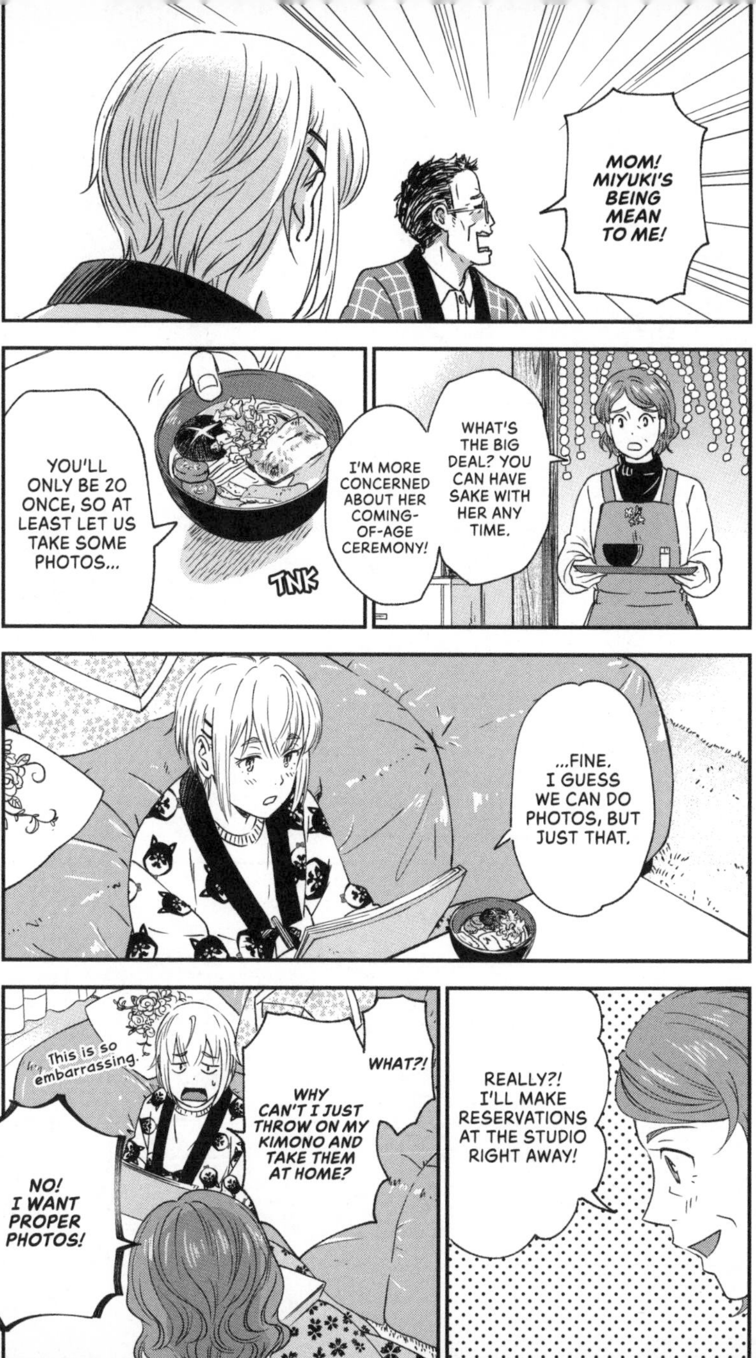
MOM! MIYUKI'S BEING MEAN TO ME!
WHAT'S THE BIG DEAL? YOU CAN HAVE SAKE WITH HER ANY TIME.
I'M MORE CONCERNED ABOUT HER COMING-OF-AGE CEREMONY!
YOU'LL ONLY BE 20 ONCE, SO AT LEAST LET US TAKE SOME PHOTOS...
TNK
...FINE. I GUESS WE CAN DO PHOTOS, BUT JUST THAT.
REALLY?! I'LL MAKE RESERVATIONS AT THE STUDIO RIGHT AWAY!
WHAT?!
WHY CAN'T I JUST THROW ON MY KIMONO AND TAKE THEM AT HOME?
This is so embarrassing.
NO! I WANT PROPER PHOTOS!

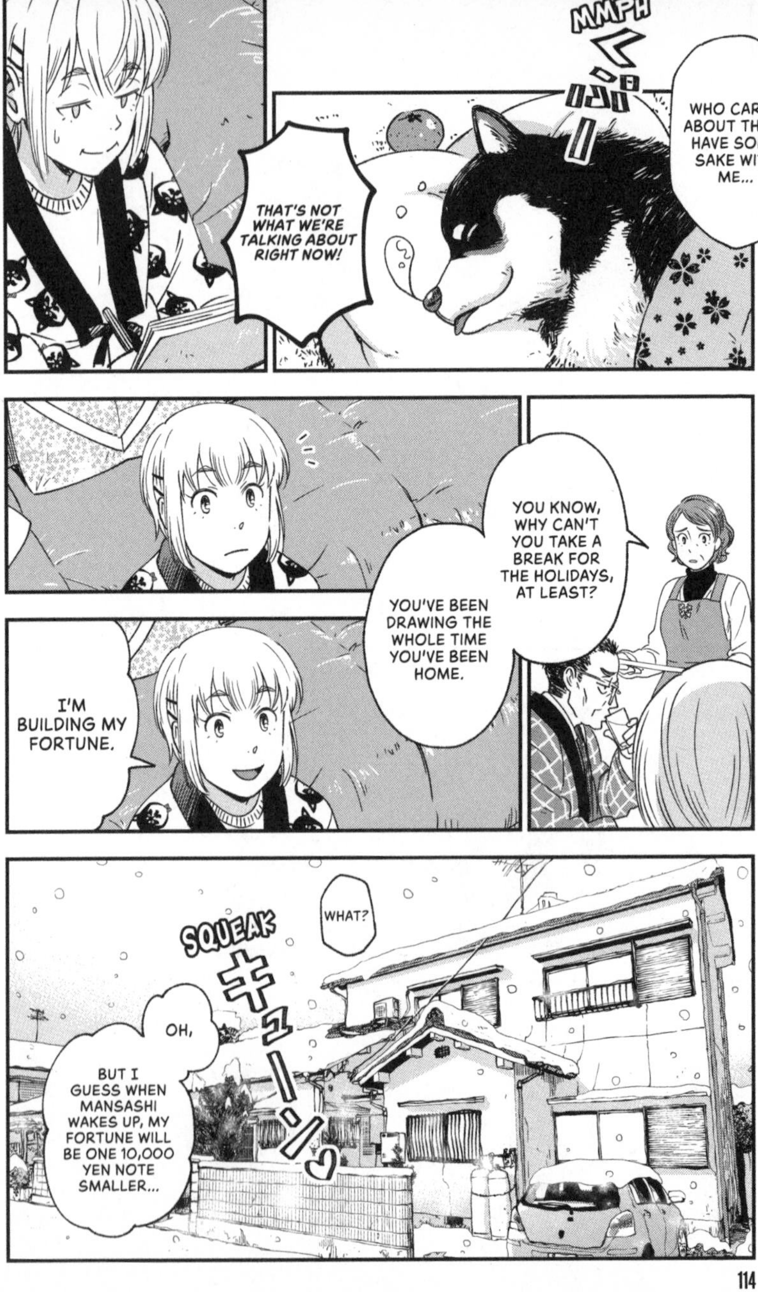
MMPH
WHO CARES ABOUT THAT? HAVE SOME SAKE WITH ME...
THAT'S NOT WHAT WE'RE TALKING ABOUT RIGHT NOW!
YOU KNOW, WHY CAN'T YOU TAKE A BREAK FOR THE HOLIDAYS, AT LEAST?
YOU'VE BEEN DRAWING THE WHOLE TIME YOU'VE BEEN HOME.
I'M BUILDING MY FORTUNE.
WHAT?
SQUEAK
OH,
BUT I GUESS WHEN MANSASHI WAKES UP, MY FORTUNE WILL BE ONE 10,000 YEN NOTE SMALLER...

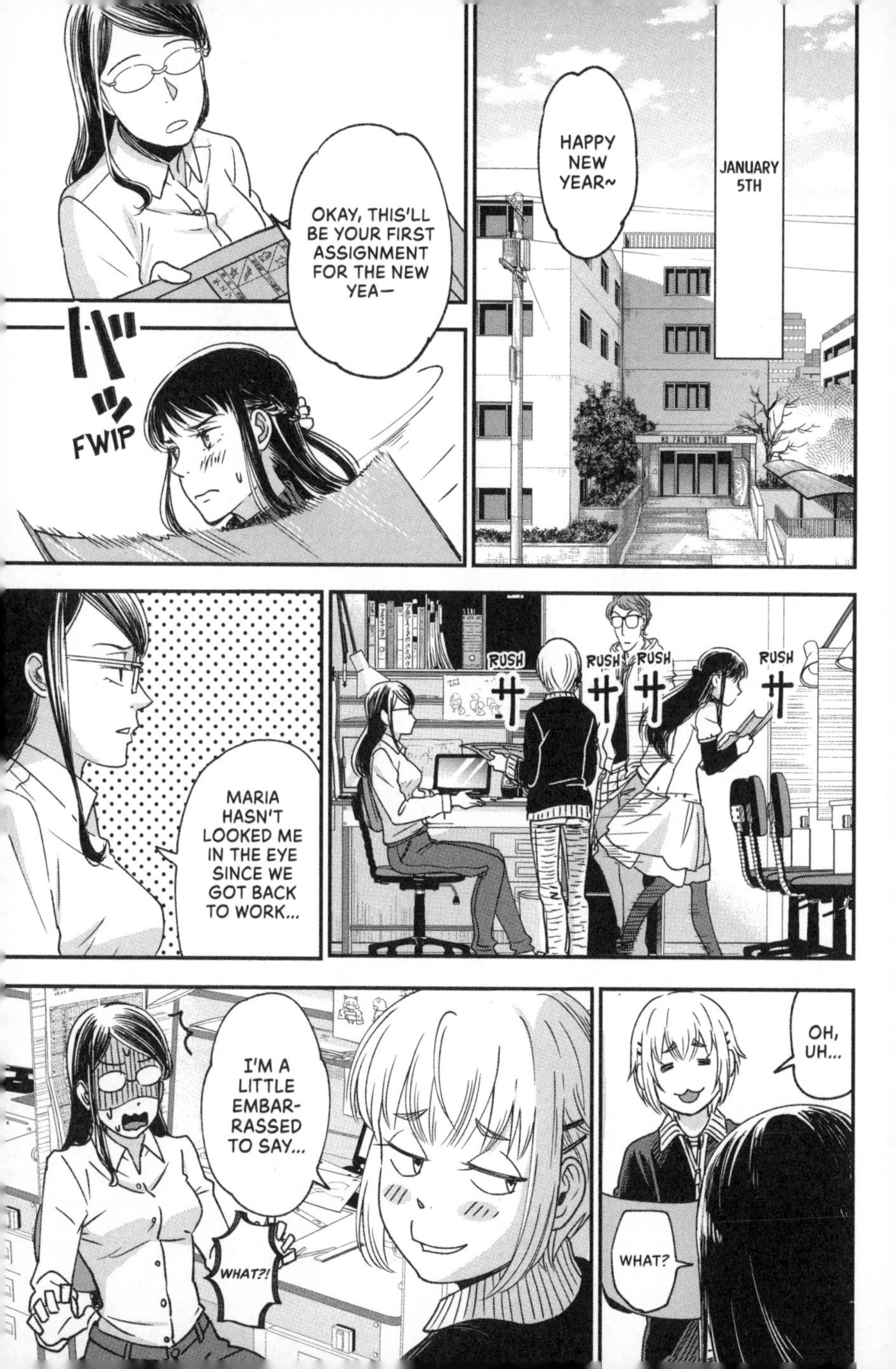
JANUARY 5TH
HAPPY NEW YEAR~
OKAY, THIS'LL BE YOUR FIRST ASSIGNMENT FOR THE NEW YEA—
バッ
FWIP
RUSH
RUSH
RUSH
RUSH
MARIA HASN'T LOOKED ME IN THE EYE SINCE WE GOT BACK TO WORK...
OH, UH...
WHAT?
I'M A LITTLE EMBAR-RASSED TO SAY...
WHAT?!

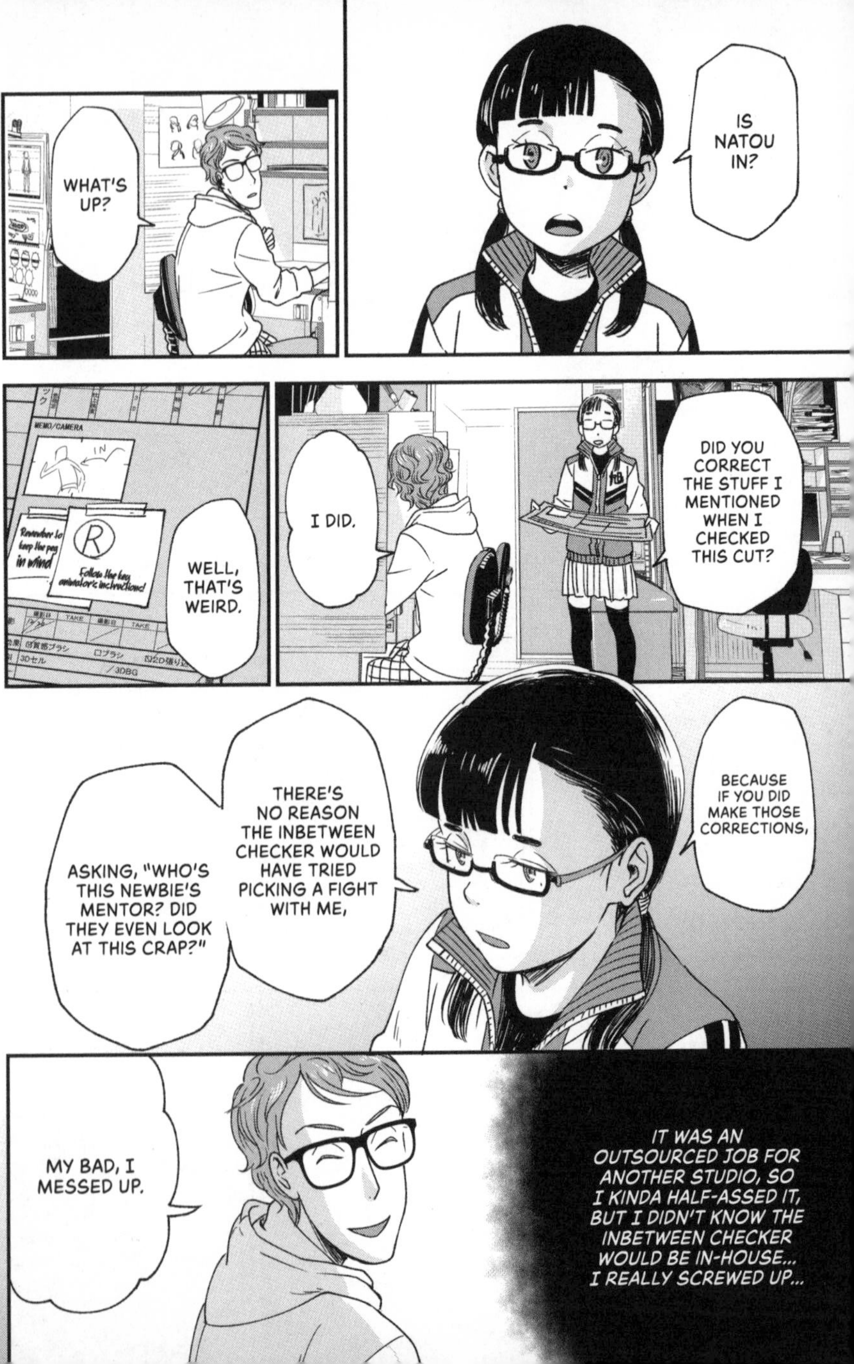
IS NATOU IN?
WHAT'S UP?
DID YOU CORRECT THE STUFF I MENTIONED WHEN I CHECKED THIS CUT?
I DID.
WELL, THAT'S WEIRD.
BECAUSE IF YOU DID MAKE THOSE CORRECTIONS,
THERE'S NO REASON THE INBETWEEN CHECKER WOULD HAVE TRIED PICKING A FIGHT WITH ME,
ASKING, "WHO'S THIS NEWBIE'S MENTOR? DID THEY EVEN LOOK AT THIS CRAP?"
IT WAS AN OUTSOURCED JOB FOR ANOTHER STUDIO, SO I KINDA HALF-ASSED IT, BUT I DIDN'T KNOW THE INBETWEEN CHECKER WOULD BE IN-HOUSE... I REALLY SCREWED UP...
MY BAD, I MESSED UP.

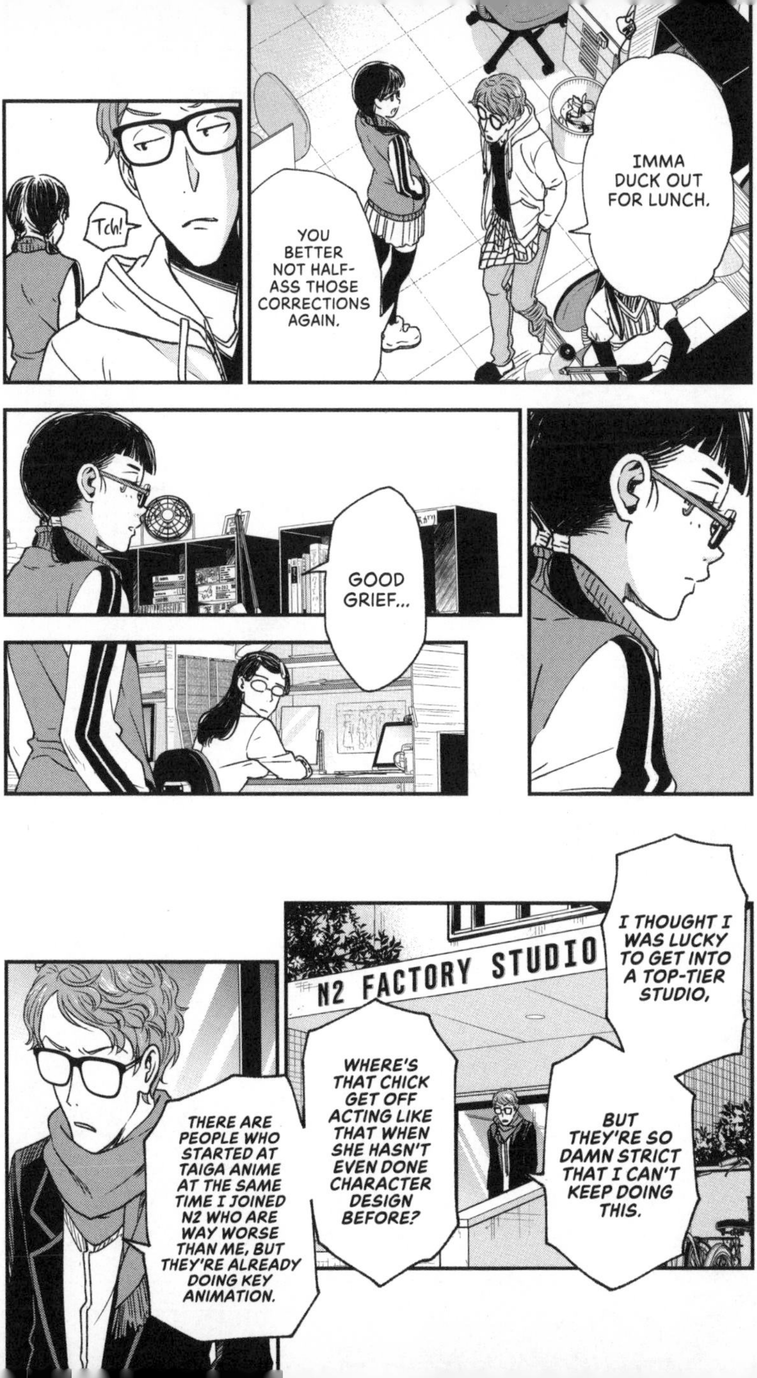
IMMA DUCK OUT FOR LUNCH.
YOU BETTER NOT HALF-ASS THOSE CORRECTIONS AGAIN.
Tch!
GOOD GRIEF...
N2 FACTORY STUDIO
I THOUGHT I WAS LUCKY TO GET INTO A TOP-TIER STUDIO,
BUT THEY'RE SO DAMN STRICT THAT I CAN'T KEEP DOING THIS.
WHERE'S THAT CHICK GET OFF ACTING LIKE THAT WHEN SHE HASN'T EVEN DONE CHARACTER DESIGN BEFORE?
THERE ARE PEOPLE WHO STARTED AT TAIGA ANIME AT THE SAME TIME I JOINED N2 WHO ARE WAY WORSE THAN ME, BUT THEY'RE ALREADY DOING KEY ANIMATION.

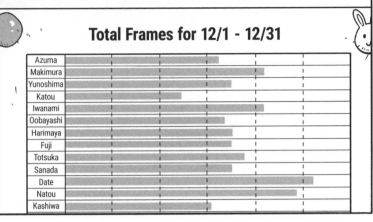

Total Frames for 12/1 - 12/31

Azuma							
Makimura							
Yunoshima							
Katou							
Iwanami							
Oobayashi							
Harimaya							
Fuji							
Totsuka							
Sanada							
Date							
Natou							
Kashiwa							

HE DOESN'T TAKE HIS TIME WITH CORRECTIONS AND HALF-ASSES IT WHEN IT'S OUTSIDE WORK.

YOU DON'T USUALLY SEE A NEWBIE WHO TAKES ALL THEIR VACATION AND OTHER DAYS OFF EARLY GETTING SO CLOSE TO 500 FRAMES A MONTH.

I THOUGHT SOMETHING WAS WEIRD.

I GUESS THAT MAKES SENSE.

ANY NEWBIE CAPABLE OF DRAWING 500 GOOD FRAMES IN A MONTH HAS TO BE A CUT ABOVE THE REST.

Date

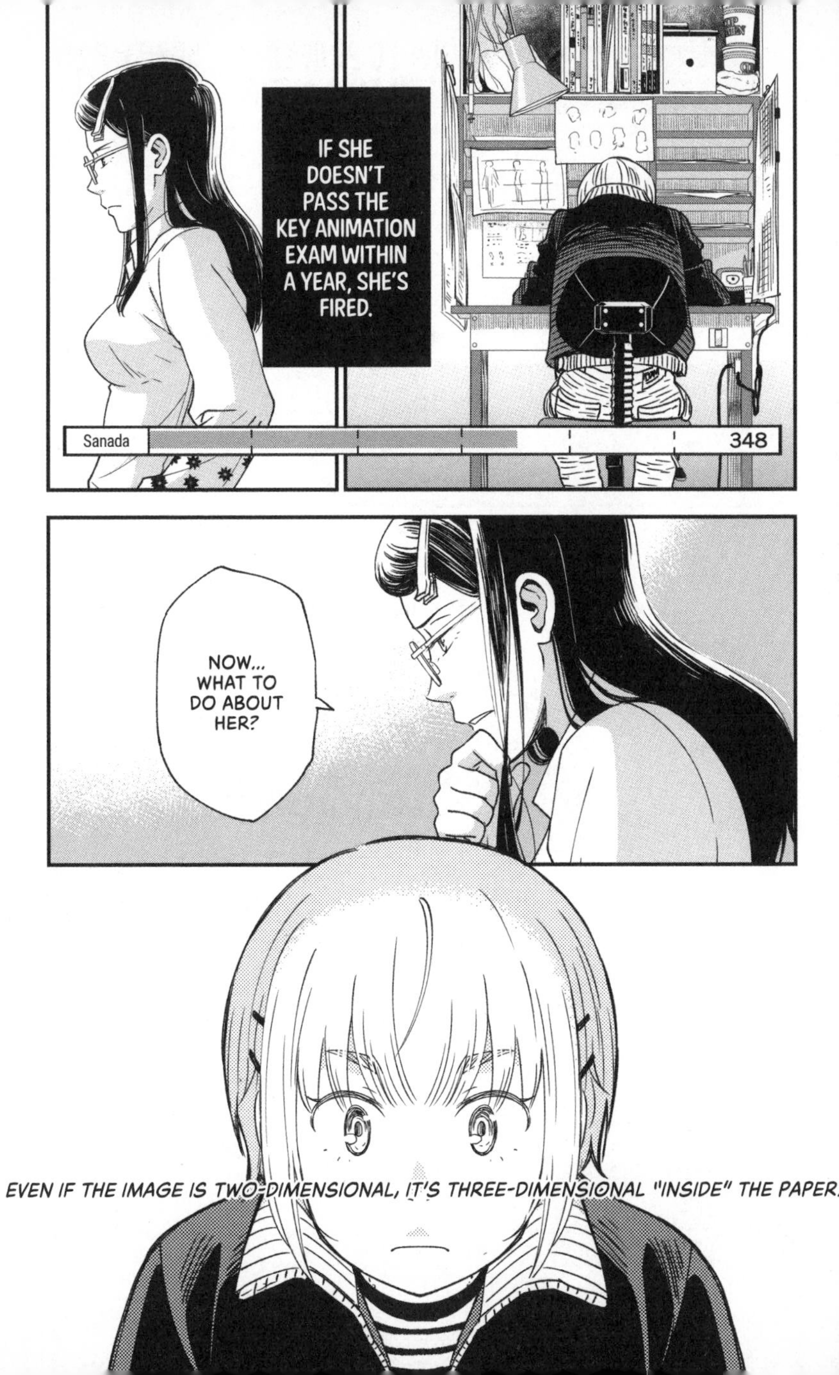
IF SHE DOESN'T PASS THE KEY ANIMATION EXAM WITHIN A YEAR, SHE'S FIRED.
Sanada
348
NOW... WHAT TO DO ABOUT HER?
EVEN IF THE IMAGE IS TWO-DIMENSIONAL, IT'S THREE-DIMENSIONAL "INSIDE" THE PAPER.

frames off the pegs and shifting them to find the point of greatest commonality, then using that as a reference to draw the midpoint of those frames as a tween.

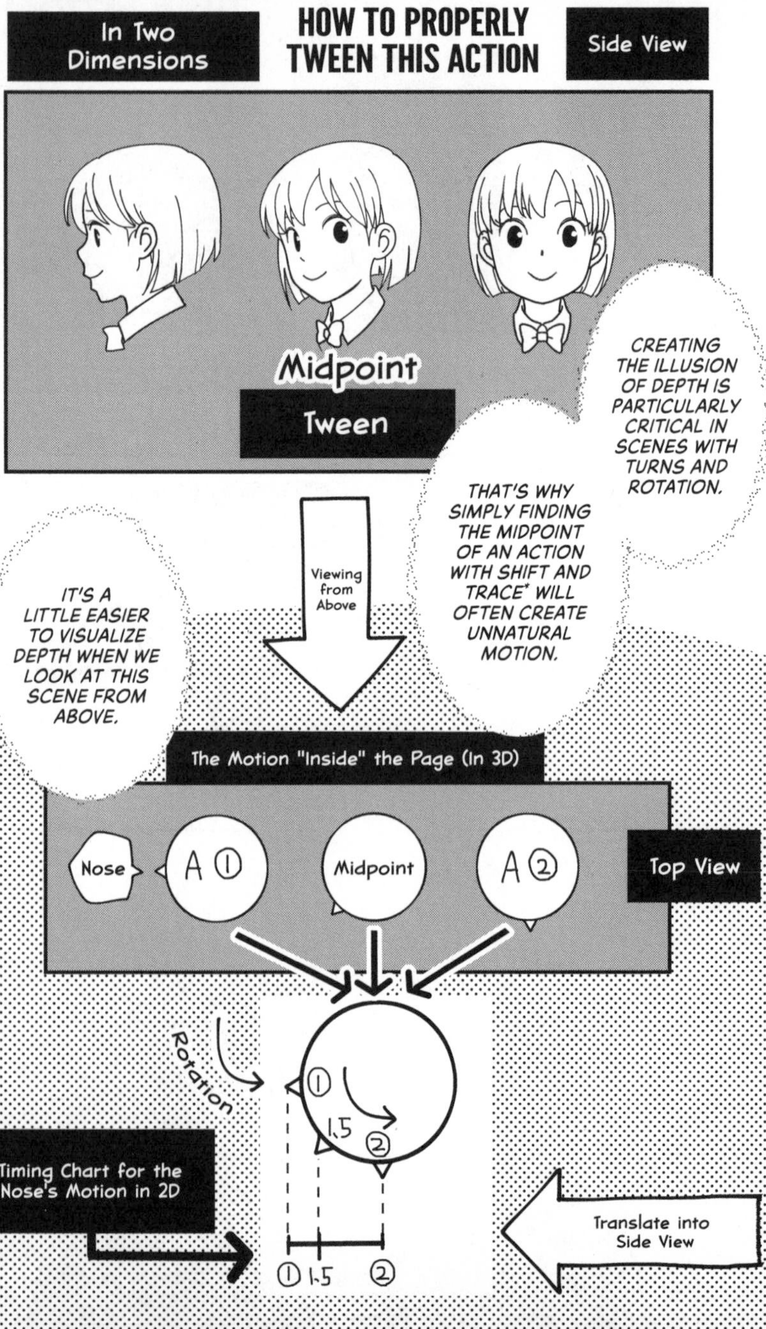

HOW TO PROPERLY TWEEN THIS ACTION
In Two Dimensions
Side View
Midpoint
Tween
CREATING THE ILLUSION OF DEPTH IS PARTICULARLY CRITICAL IN SCENES WITH TURNS AND ROTATION.
THAT'S WHY SIMPLY FINDING THE MIDPOINT OF AN ACTION WITH SHIFT AND TRACE* WILL OFTEN CREATE UNNATURAL MOTION.
IT'S A LITTLE EASIER TO VISUALIZE DEPTH WHEN WE LOOK AT THIS SCENE FROM ABOVE.
Viewing from Above
The Motion "Inside" the Page (In 3D)
Top View
Nose
A ①
Midpoint
A ②
Rotation
①
1.5
②
Timing Chart for the Nose's Motion in 2D
Translate into Side View
① 1.5 ②

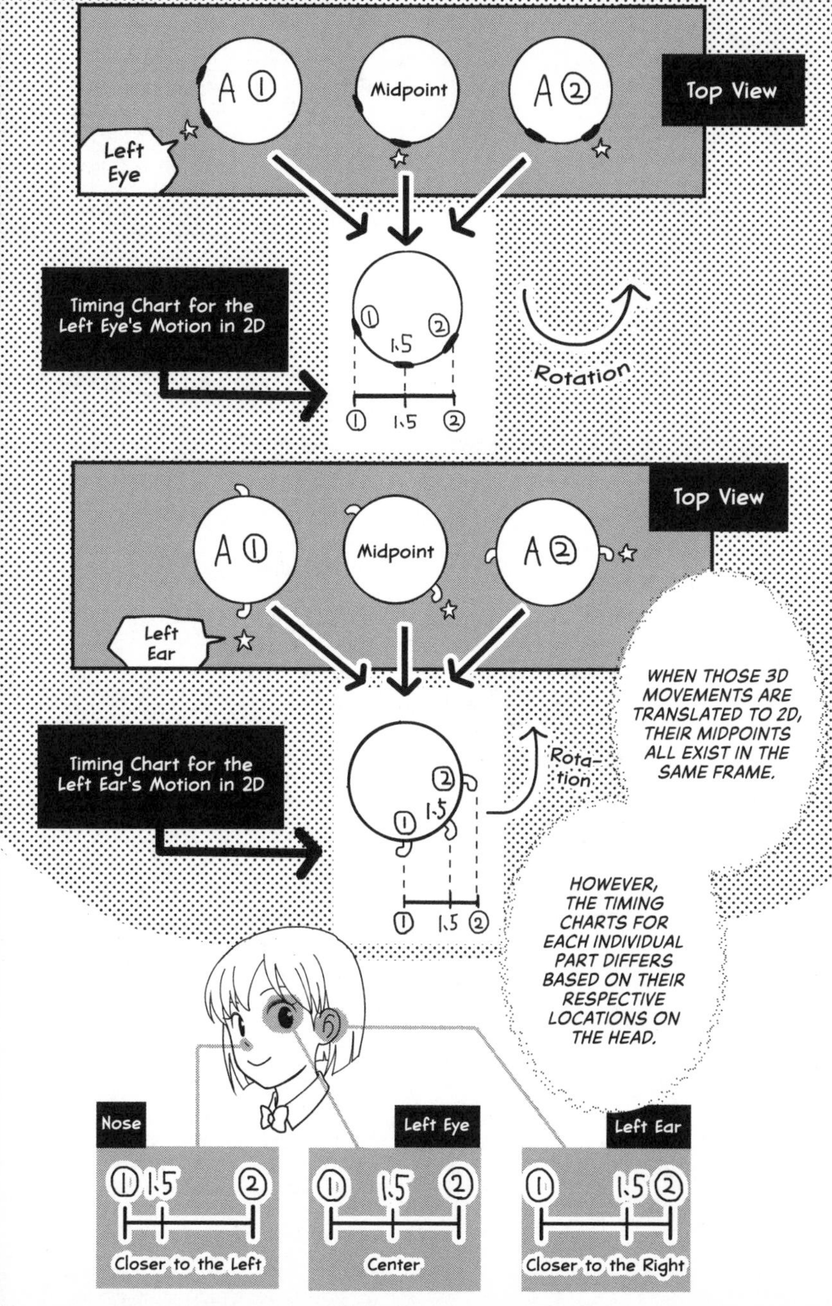

Top View
A ①
Midpoint
A ②
Left Eye
Timing Chart for the Left Eye's Motion in 2D
① ② 1.5
① 1.5 ②
Rotation
Top View
A ①
Midpoint
A ②
Left Ear
Timing Chart for the Left Ear's Motion in 2D
② 1.5 ①
① 1.5 ②
Rota-tion
WHEN THOSE 3D MOVEMENTS ARE TRANSLATED TO 2D, THEIR MIDPOINTS ALL EXIST IN THE SAME FRAME.
HOWEVER, THE TIMING CHARTS FOR EACH INDIVIDUAL PART DIFFERS BASED ON THEIR RESPECTIVE LOCATIONS ON THE HEAD.
Nose
① 1.5 ②
Closer to the Left
Left Eye
① 1.5 ②
Center
Left Ear
① 1.5 ②
Closer to the Right

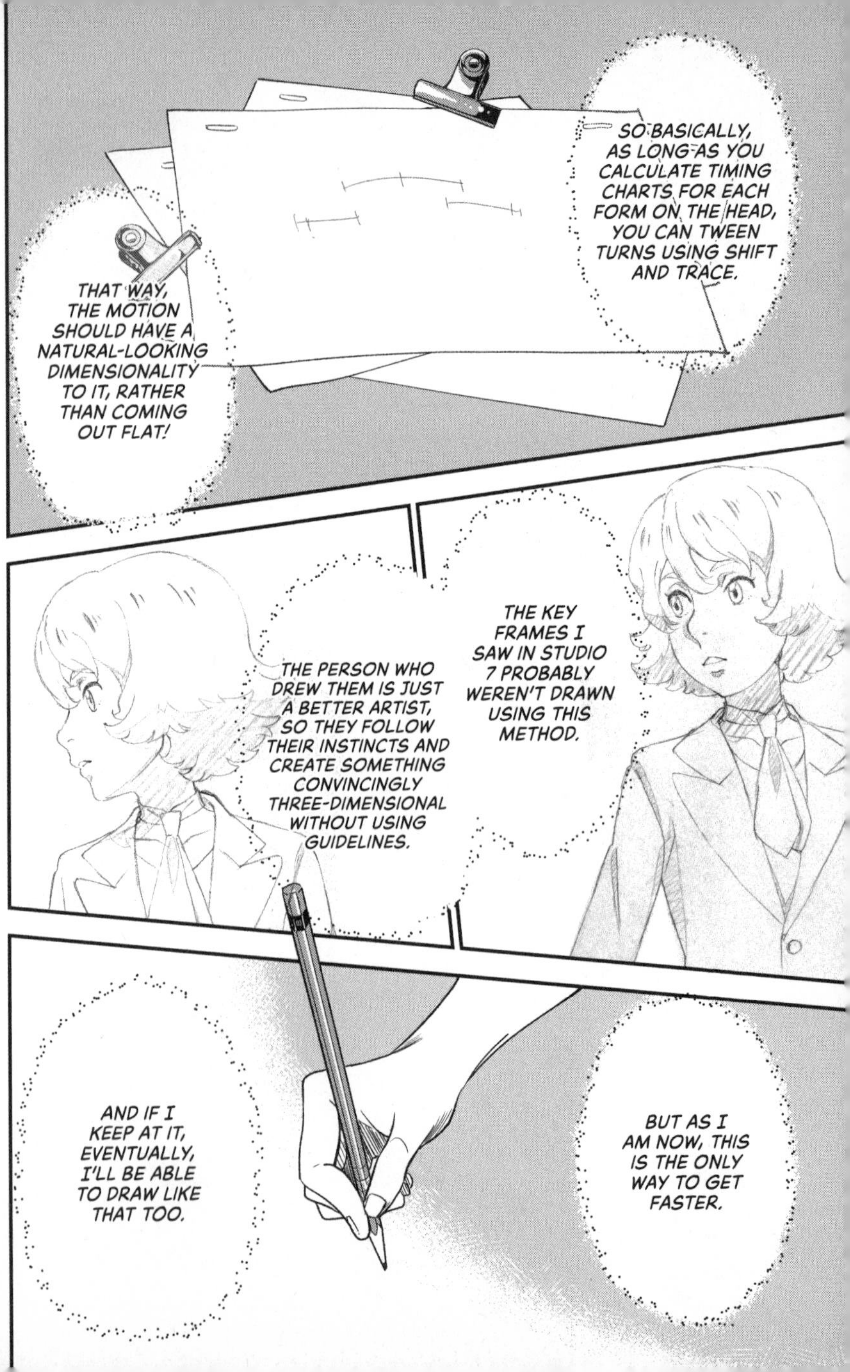
SO BASICALLY, AS LONG AS YOU CALCULATE TIMING CHARTS FOR EACH FORM ON THE HEAD, YOU CAN TWEEN TURNS USING SHIFT AND TRACE.
THAT WAY, THE MOTION SHOULD HAVE A NATURAL-LOOKING DIMENSIONALITY TO IT, RATHER THAN COMING OUT FLAT!
THE KEY FRAMES I SAW IN STUDIO 7 PROBABLY WEREN'T DRAWN USING THIS METHOD.
THE PERSON WHO DREW THEM IS JUST A BETTER ARTIST, SO THEY FOLLOW THEIR INSTINCTS AND CREATE SOMETHING CONVINCINGLY THREE-DIMENSIONAL WITHOUT USING GUIDELINES.
BUT AS I AM NOW, THIS IS THE ONLY WAY TO GET FASTER.
AND IF I KEEP AT IT, EVENTUALLY, I'LL BE ABLE TO DRAW LIKE THAT TOO.

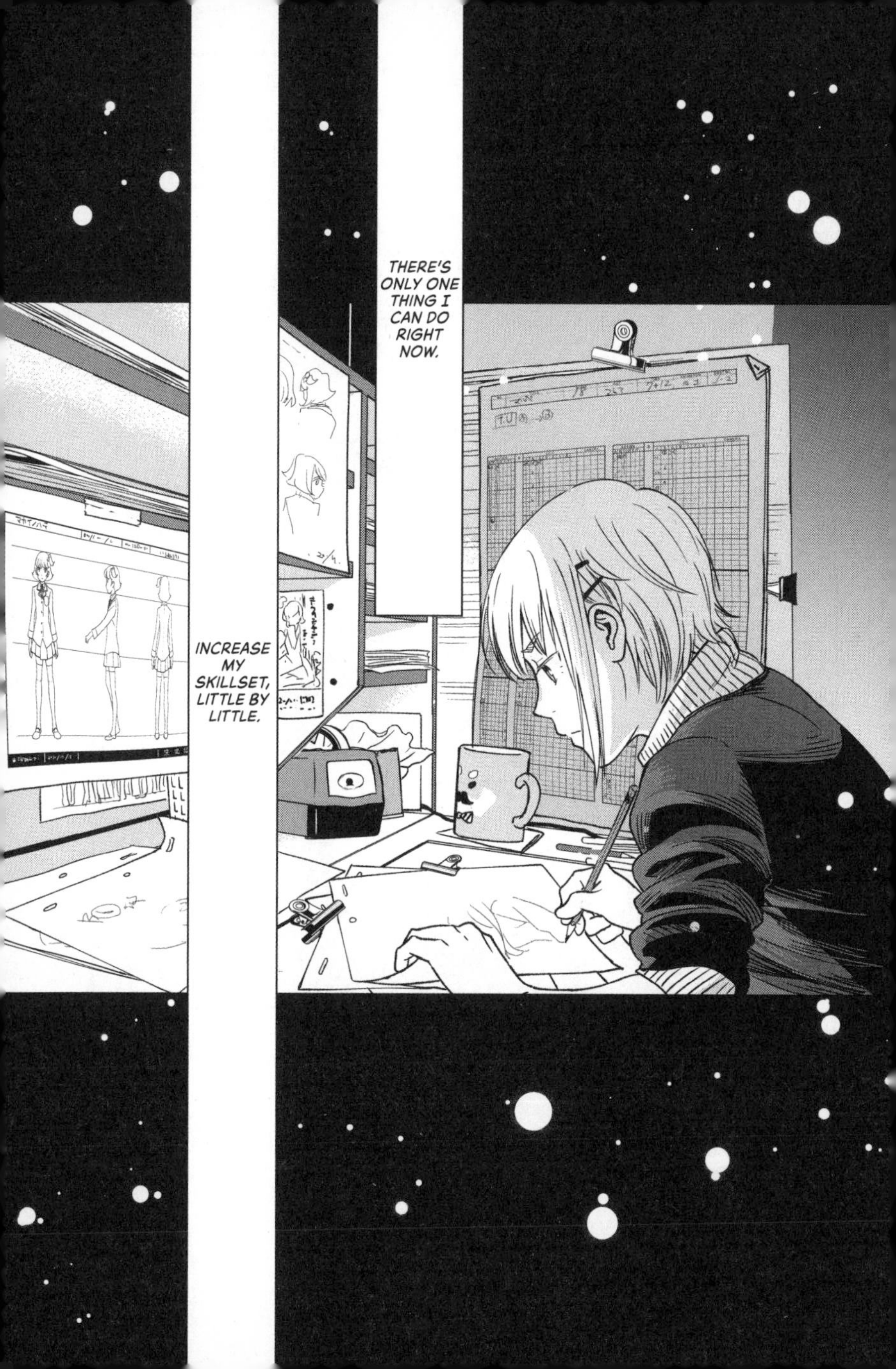
THERE'S ONLY ONE THING I CAN DO RIGHT NOW.
INCREASE MY SKILLSET, LITTLE BY LITTLE.

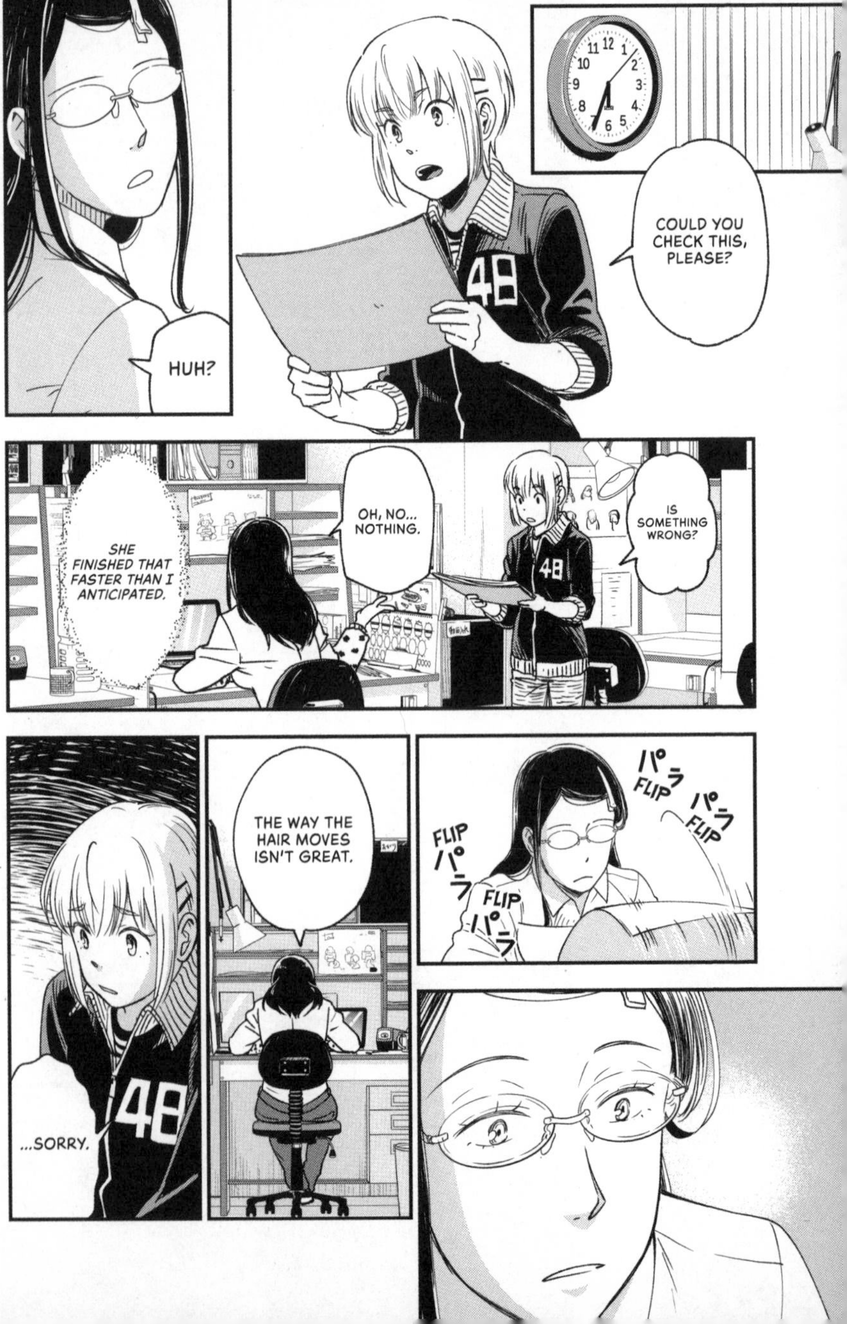
COULD YOU CHECK THIS, PLEASE?
HUH?
IS SOMETHING WRONG?
OH, NO... NOTHING.
SHE FINISHED THAT FASTER THAN I ANTICIPATED.
パラ FLIP
パラ FLIP
パラ FLIP
パラ FLIP
THE WAY THE HAIR MOVES ISN'T GREAT.
...SORRY.

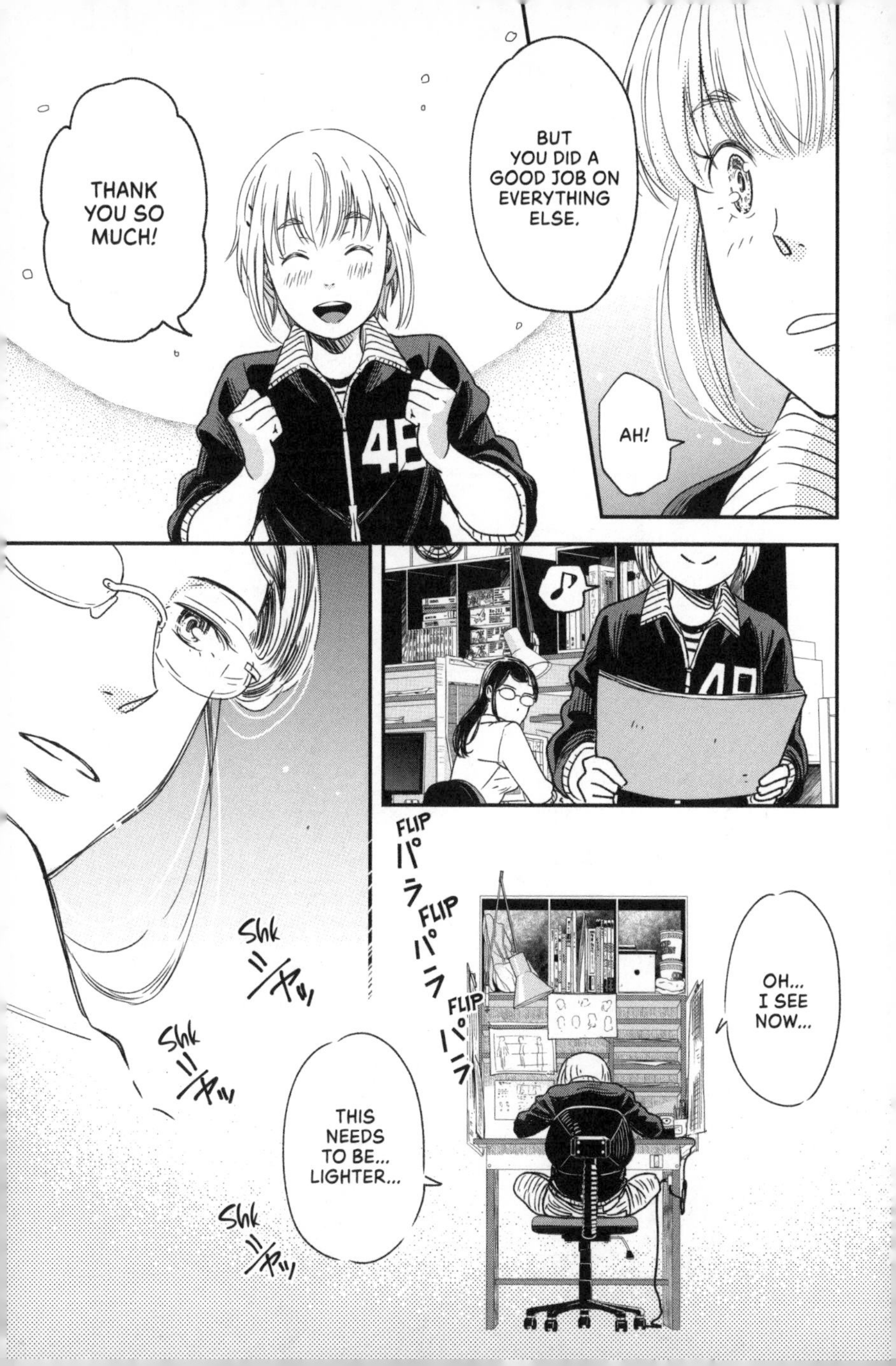
BUT YOU DID A GOOD JOB ON EVERYTHING ELSE.
AH!
THANK YOU SO MUCH!
♪
FLIP パラ
FLIP パラ
FLIP パラ
OH... I SEE NOW...
THIS NEEDS TO BE... LIGHTER...
Shk シャッ
Shk シャッ
Shk シャッ

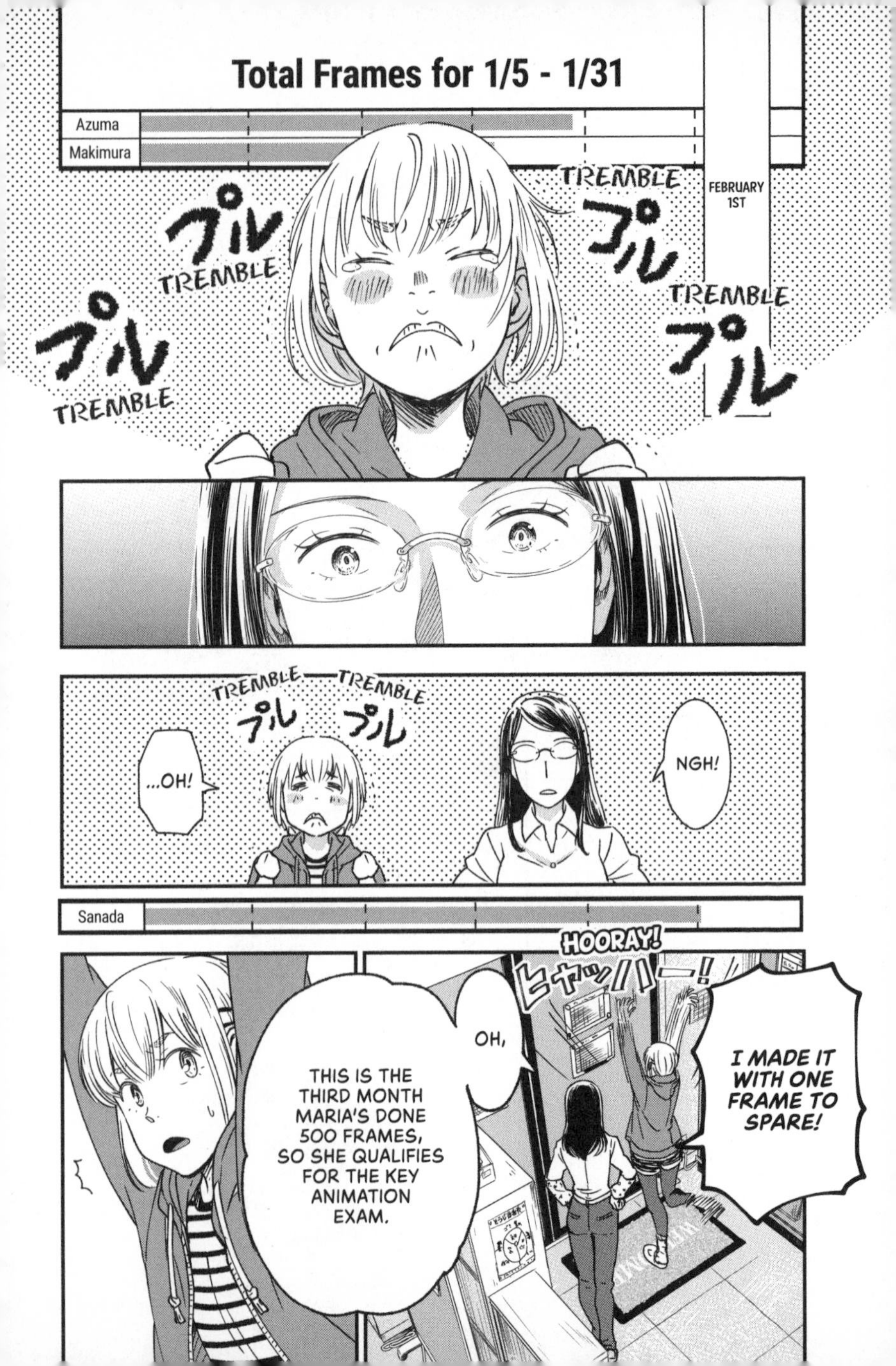
Total Frames for 1/5 - 1/31
Azuma
Makimura
FEBRUARY 1ST
プル
TREMBLE
プル
TREMBLE
プル
TREMBLE
プル
TREMBLE
プル
TREMBLE
プル
TREMBLE
NGH!
...OH!
Sanada
ヒャッハー!
HOORAY!
I MADE IT WITH ONE FRAME TO SPARE!
OH,
THIS IS THE THIRD MONTH MARIA'S DONE 500 FRAMES, SO SHE QUALIFIES FOR THE KEY ANIMATION EXAM.

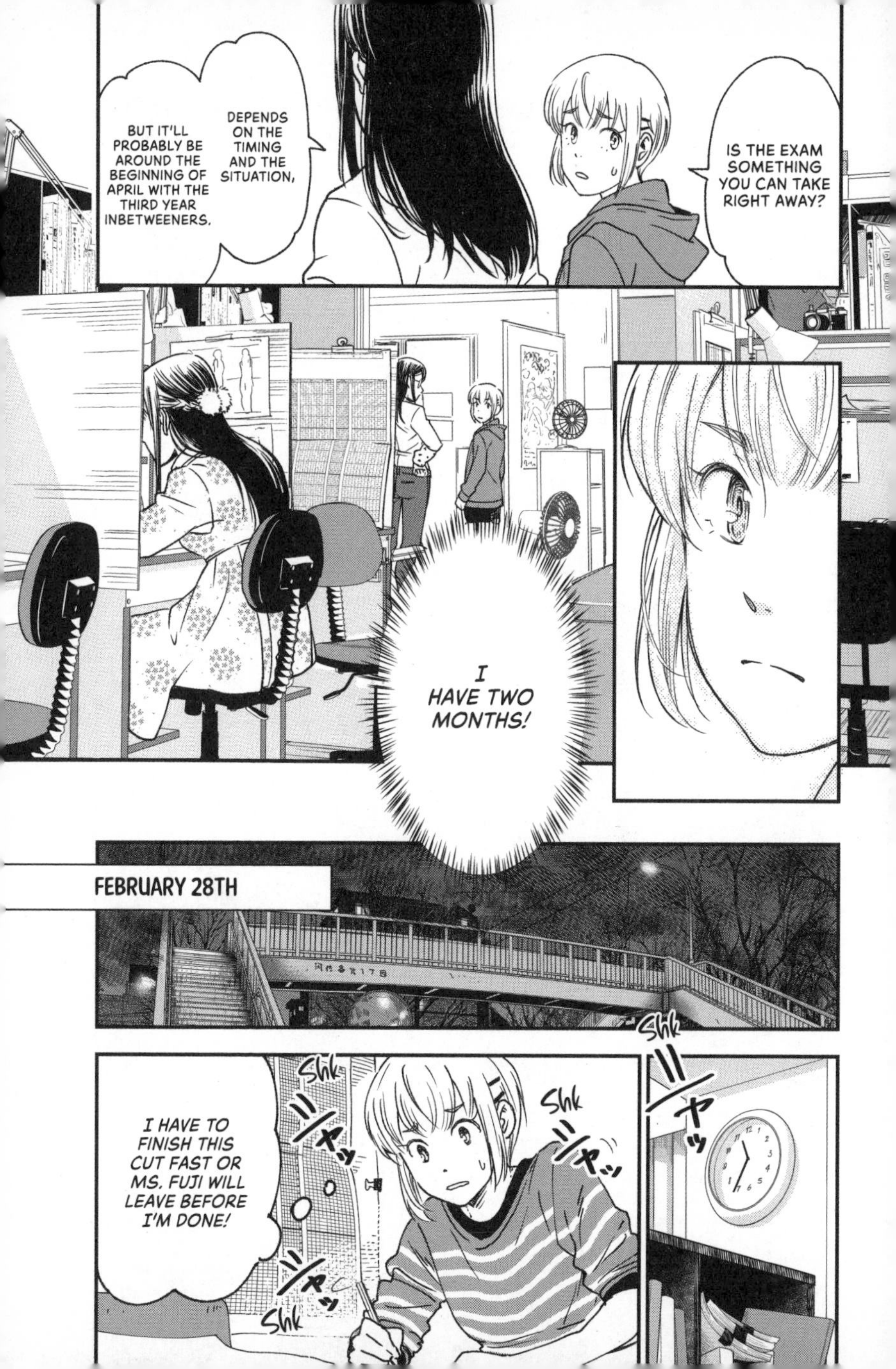
IS THE EXAM SOMETHING YOU CAN TAKE RIGHT AWAY?
DEPENDS ON THE TIMING AND THE SITUATION,
BUT IT'LL PROBABLY BE AROUND THE BEGINNING OF APRIL WITH THE THIRD YEAR INBETWEENERS.
I HAVE TWO MONTHS!
FEBRUARY 28TH
Shk
Shk
Shk
Shk
I HAVE TO FINISH THIS CUT FAST OR MS. FUJI WILL LEAVE BEFORE I'M DONE!

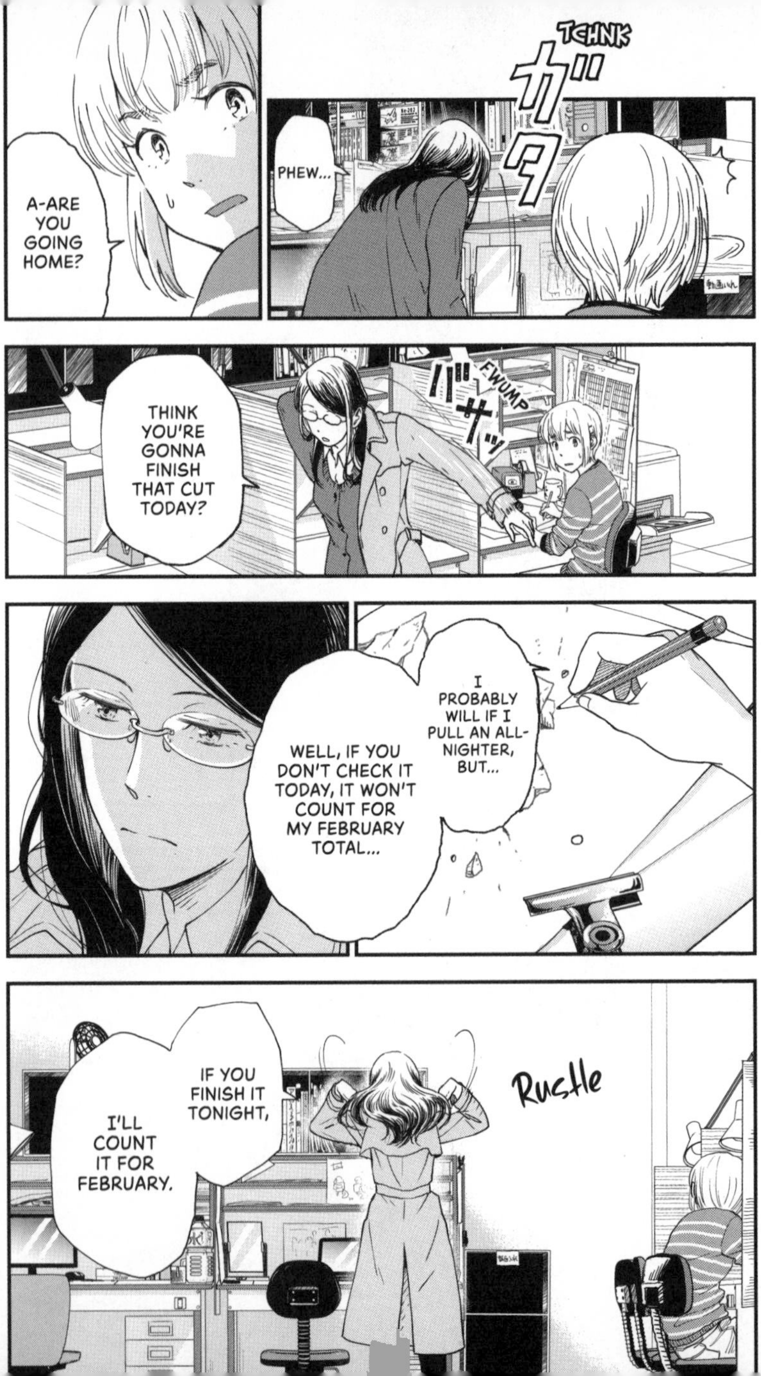
TCHNK
ガタ
PHEW...
A-ARE YOU GOING HOME?
FWUMP
バサッ
THINK YOU'RE GONNA FINISH THAT CUT TODAY?
I PROBABLY WILL IF I PULL AN ALL-NIGHTER, BUT...
WELL, IF YOU DON'T CHECK IT TODAY, IT WON'T COUNT FOR MY FEBRUARY TOTAL...
Rustle
IF YOU FINISH IT TONIGHT,
I'LL COUNT IT FOR FEBRUARY.

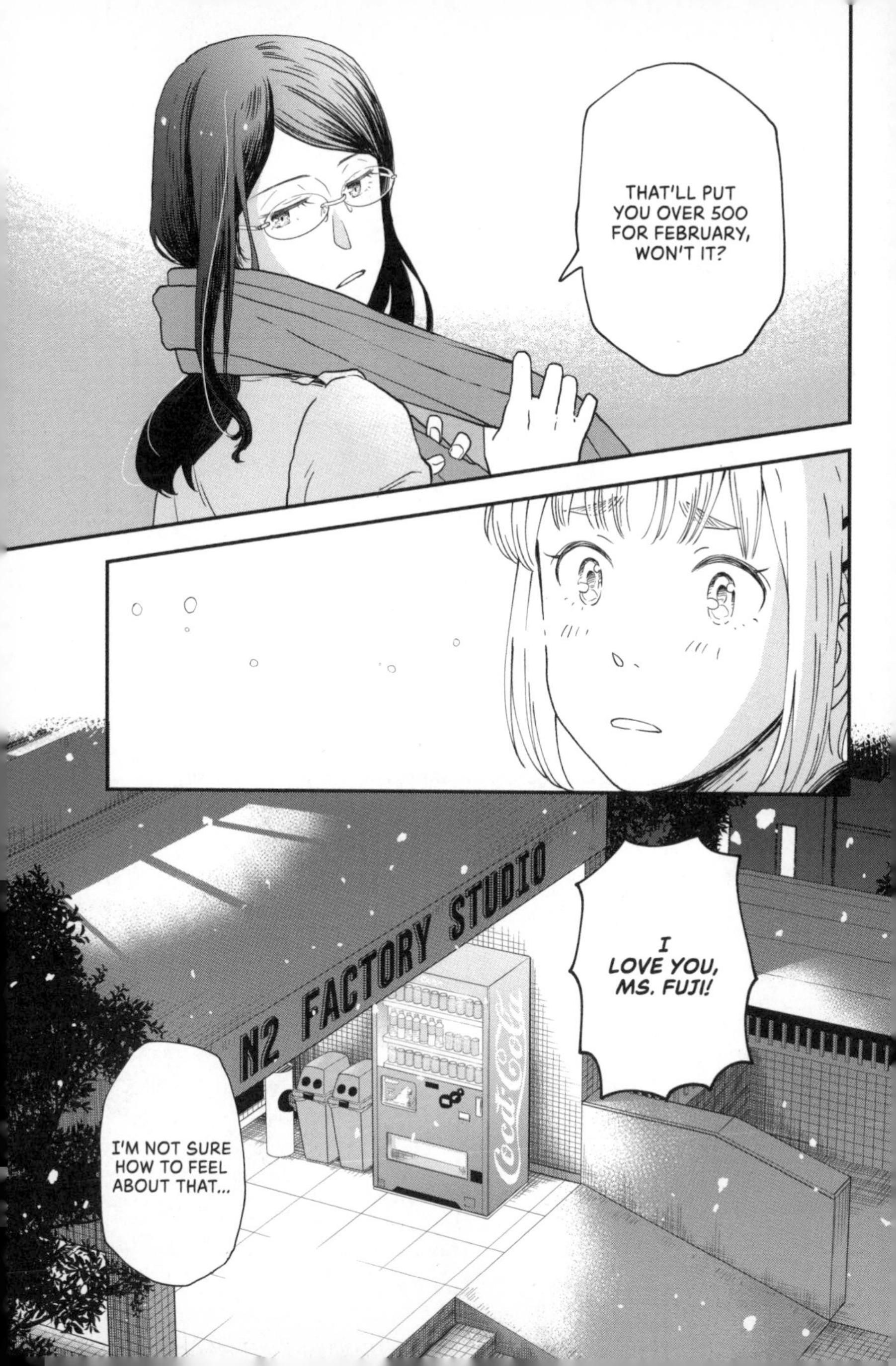
THAT'LL PUT YOU OVER 500 FOR FEBRUARY, WON'T IT?
I LOVE YOU, MS. FUJI!
N2 FACTORY STUDIO
I'M NOT SURE HOW TO FEEL ABOUT THAT...

Total Frames for 2/1 - 2/28

		MARCH 1ST	56
Azuma			:05
Makimura			
Yunoshima			
Sanada			513

THANK YOU SO MUCH.

I WOULDN'T HAVE MADE IT IF YOU DIDN'T CUT ME SOME SLACK.

I DIDN'T DO ANYTHING.

YOU PUT IN THE HARD WORK TO GET YOUR NUMBERS UP, YUKIMURA.

Title **Karisome**

HERE. THIS IS YOUR NEXT CUT.

OKAY!

SIGH...

パラ パラ パラ
Flip Flip Flip

AH!

THIS IS A REALLY HEAVY* CUT!

Flip パラ パラ

*One that's going to take a really long time

130

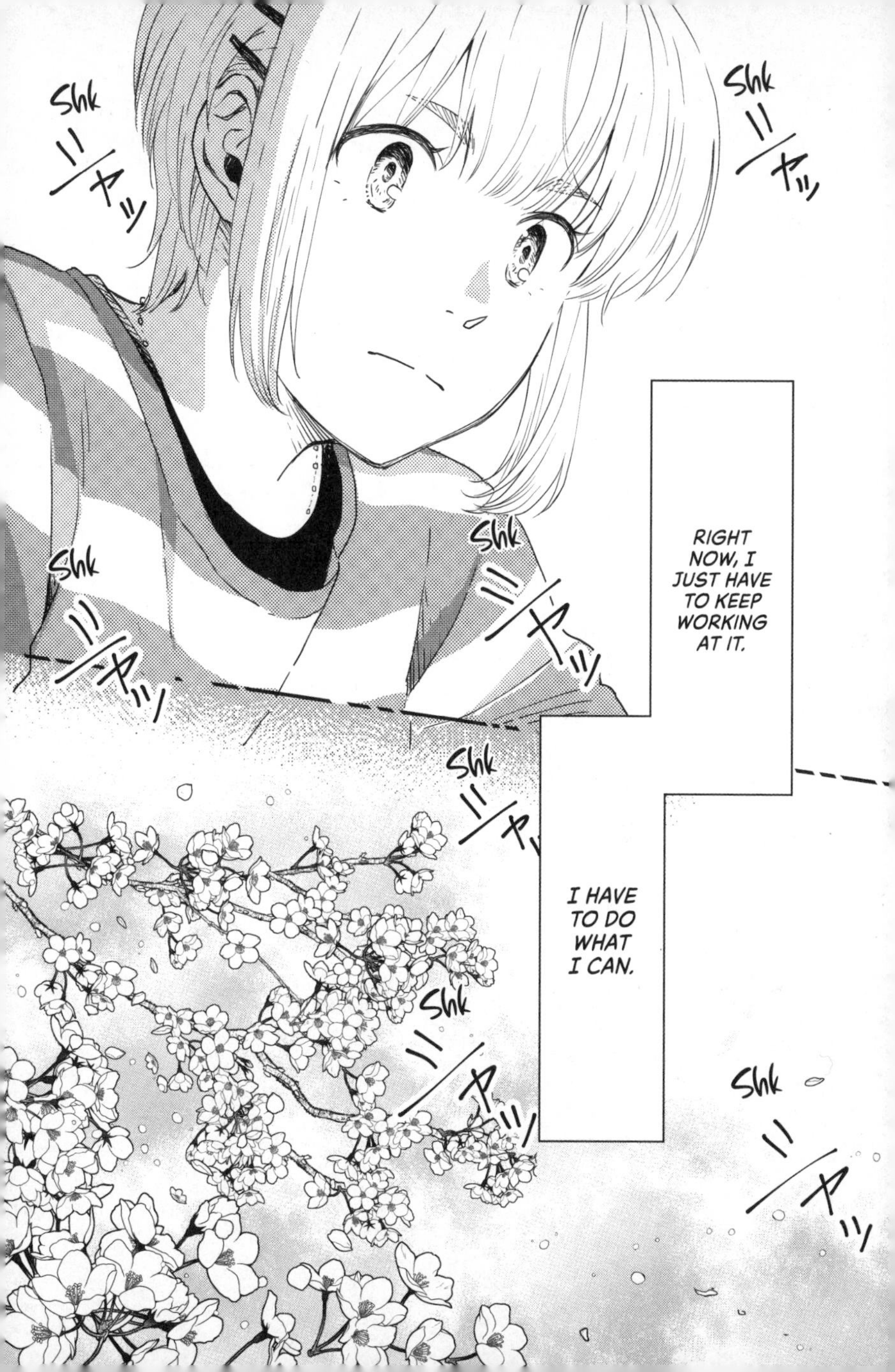
Shk
Shk
Shk
Shk
RIGHT NOW, I JUST HAVE TO KEEP WORKING AT IT.
I HAVE TO DO WHAT I CAN.
Shk
Shk
Shk

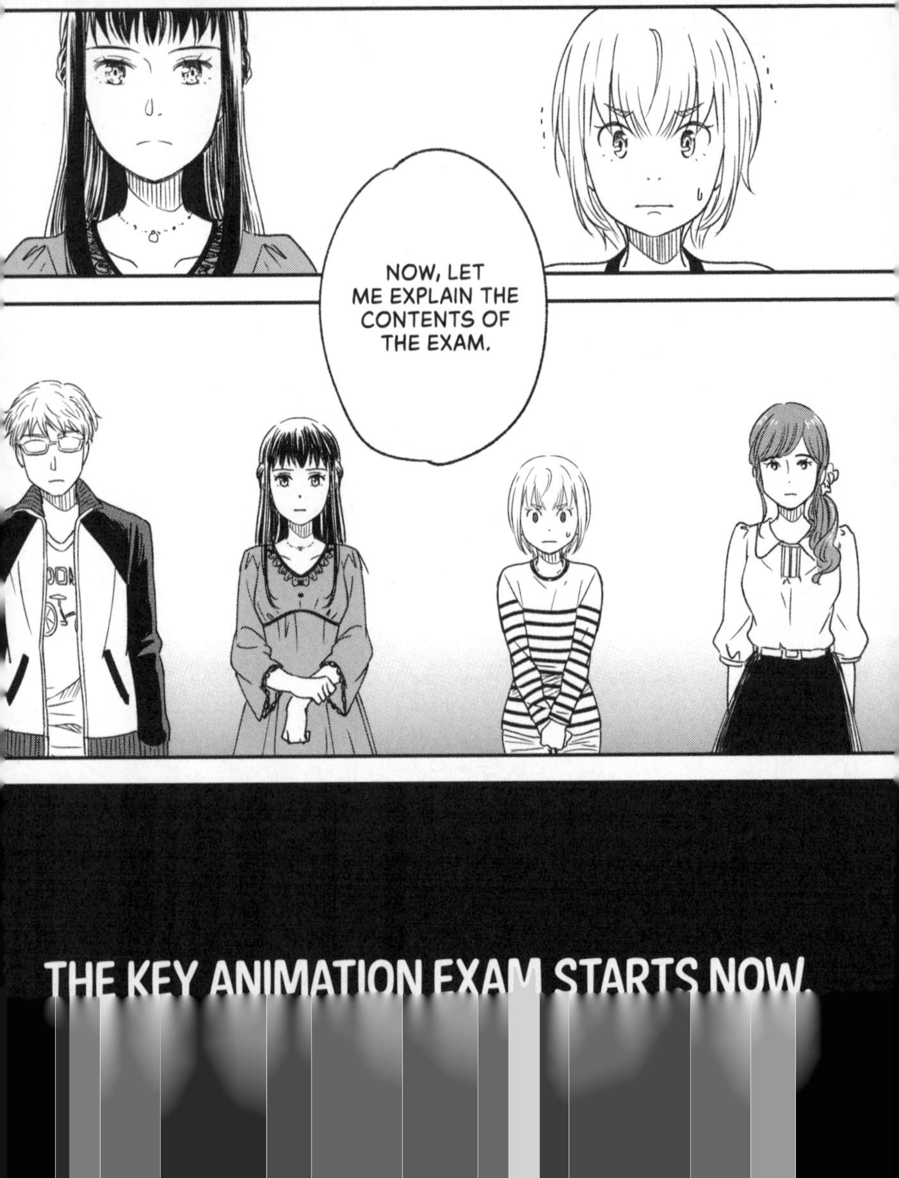
NOW, LET ME EXPLAIN THE CONTENTS OF THE EXAM.
THE KEY ANIMATION EXAM STARTS NOW.

CHAPTER 20: THE FRUITS OF YOUR LABOR

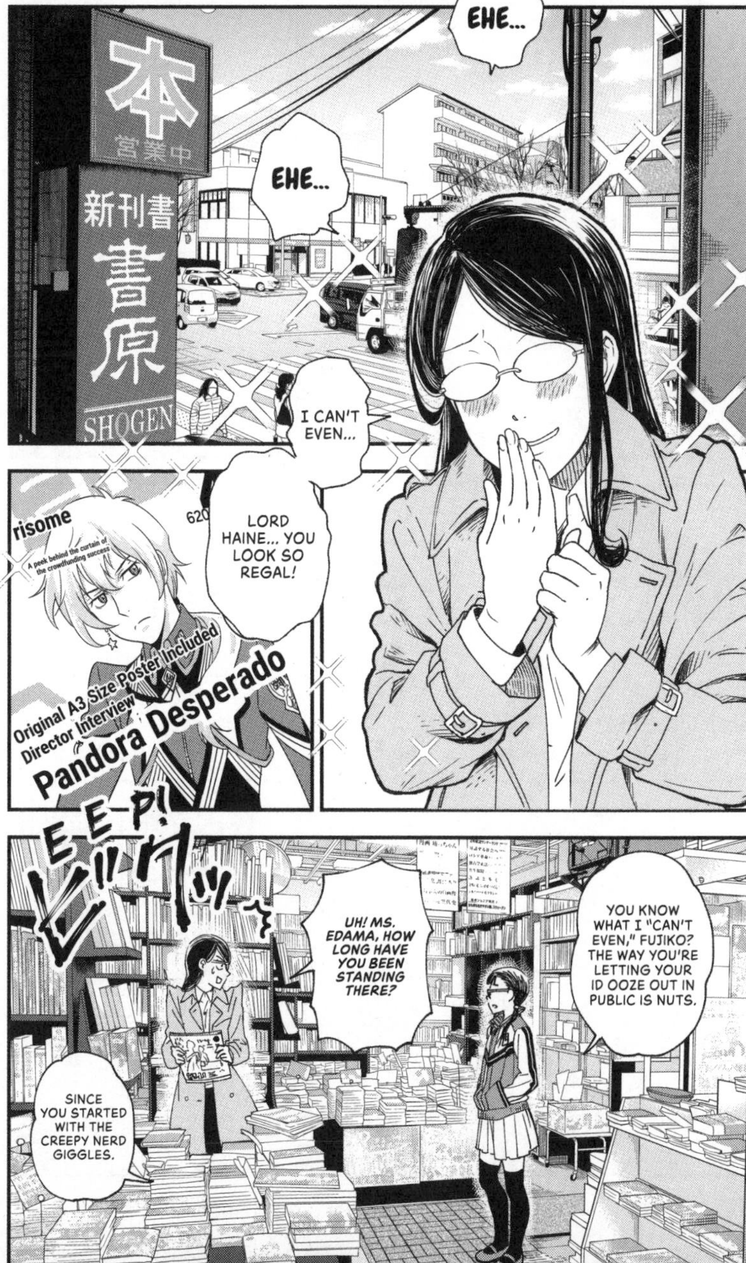
EHE...
EHE...
本
営業中
新刊書
書原
SHOGEN
I CAN'T EVEN...
LORD HAINE... YOU LOOK SO REGAL!
risome
620
A peek behind the curtain of the crowdfunding success
Original A3 Size Poster Included
Director Interview
Pandora Desperado
EEP!
YOU KNOW WHAT I "CAN'T EVEN," FUJIKO? THE WAY YOU'RE LETTING YOUR ID OOZE OUT IN PUBLIC IS NUTS.
UH! MS. EDAMA, HOW LONG HAVE YOU BEEN STANDING THERE?
SINCE YOU STARTED WITH THE CREEPY NERD GIGGLES.

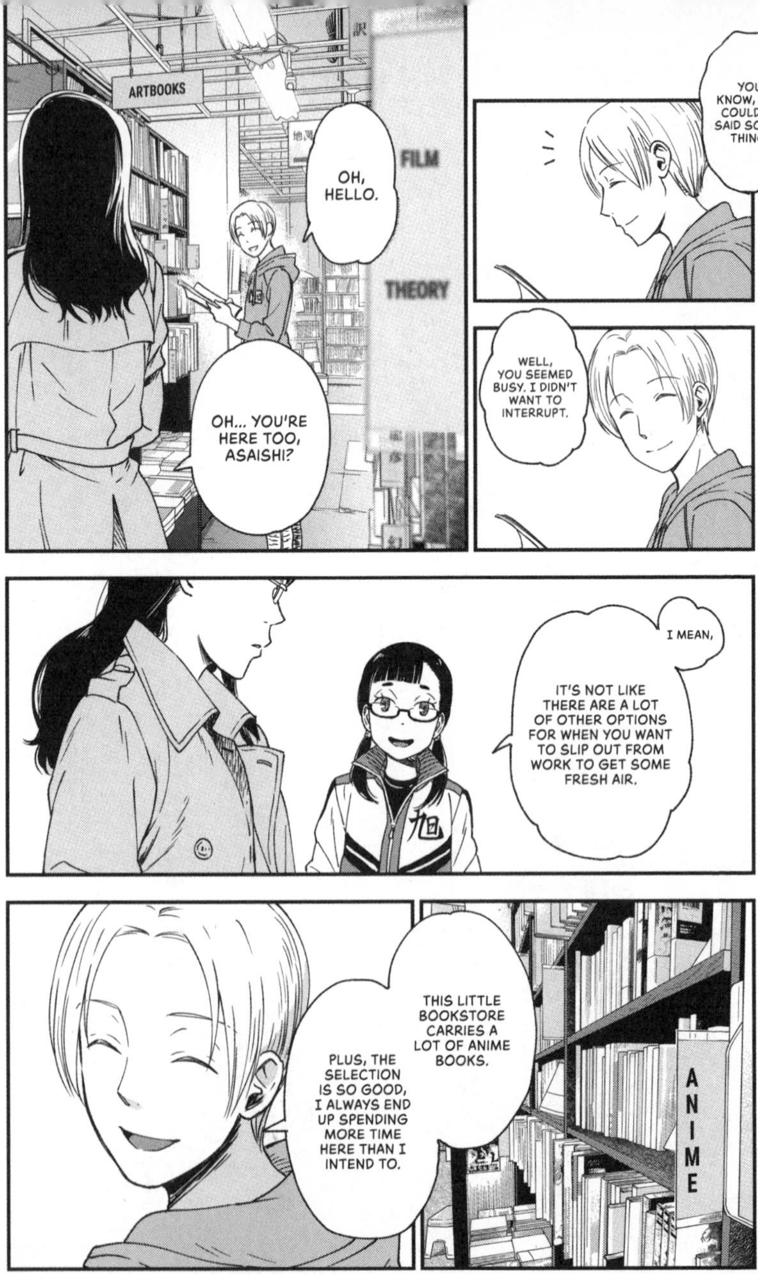
YOU KNOW, YOU COULD'VE SAID SOME-THING.
WELL, YOU SEEMED BUSY. I DIDN'T WANT TO INTERRUPT.
ARTBOOKS
FILM
THEORY
OH, HELLO.
OH... YOU'RE HERE TOO, ASAISHI?
I MEAN,
IT'S NOT LIKE THERE ARE A LOT OF OTHER OPTIONS FOR WHEN YOU WANT TO SLIP OUT FROM WORK TO GET SOME FRESH AIR.
ANIME
THIS LITTLE BOOKSTORE CARRIES A LOT OF ANIME BOOKS.
PLUS, THE SELECTION IS SO GOOD, I ALWAYS END UP SPENDING MORE TIME HERE THAN I INTEND TO.

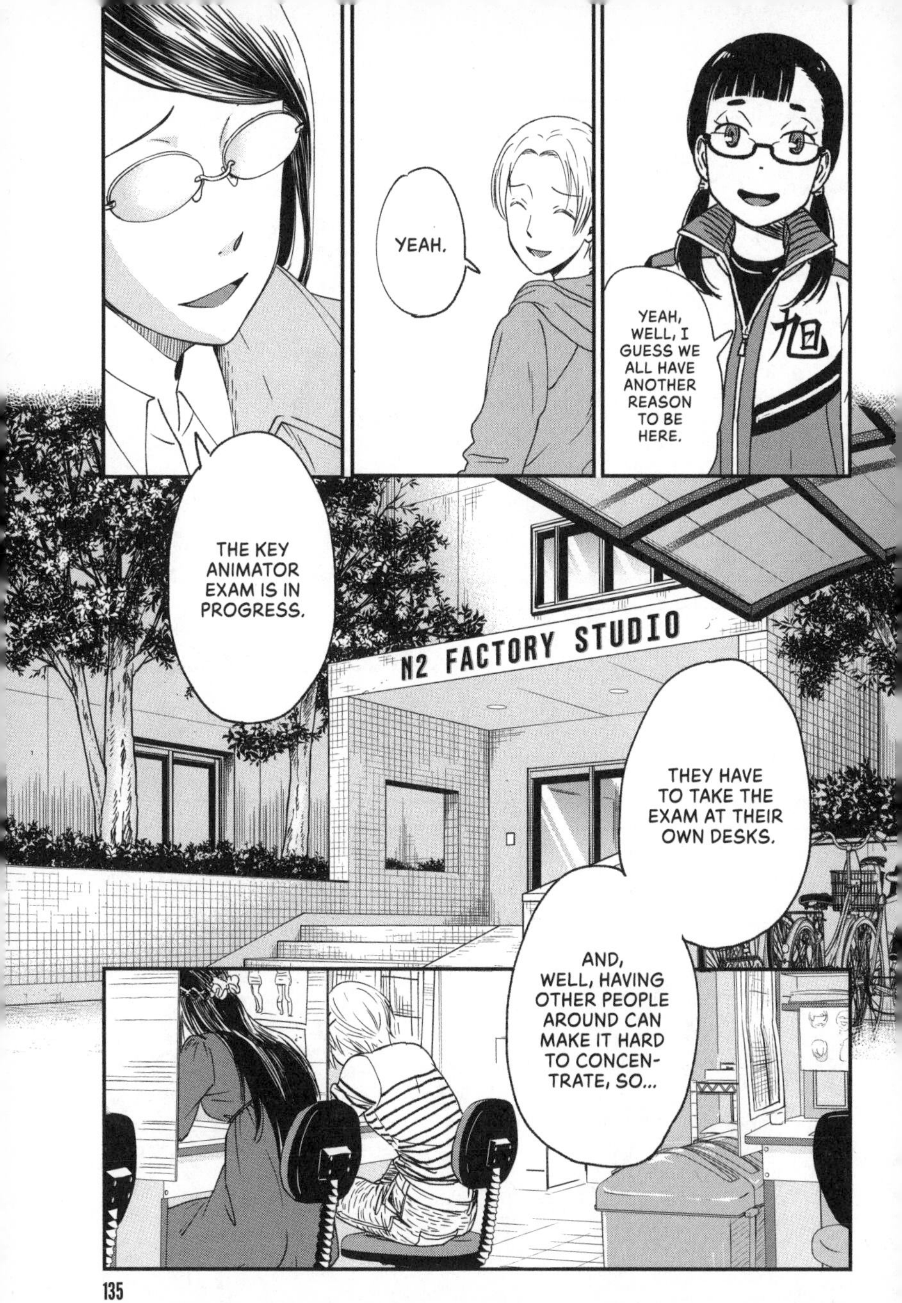
YEAH, WELL, I GUESS WE ALL HAVE ANOTHER REASON TO BE HERE.
YEAH.
THE KEY ANIMATOR EXAM IS IN PROGRESS.
N2 FACTORY STUDIO
THEY HAVE TO TAKE THE EXAM AT THEIR OWN DESKS.
AND, WELL, HAVING OTHER PEOPLE AROUND CAN MAKE IT HARD TO CONCEN-TRATE, SO...

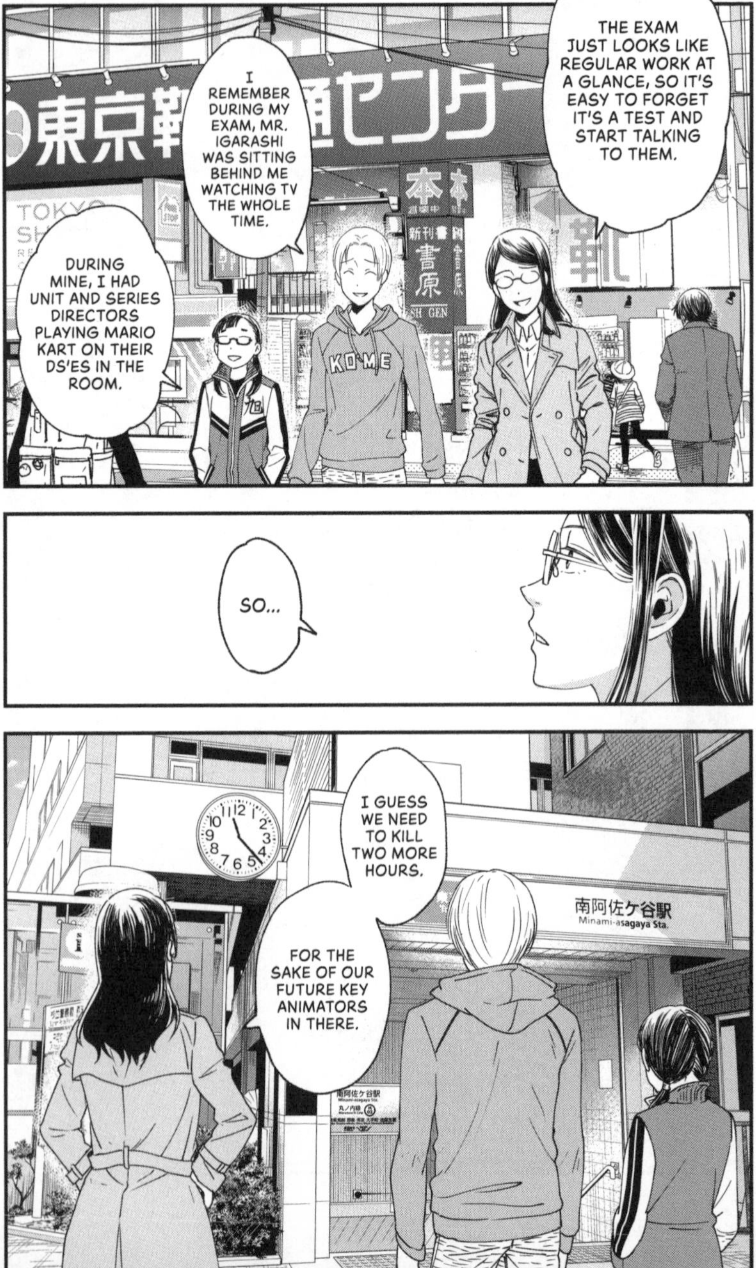
THE EXAM JUST LOOKS LIKE REGULAR WORK AT A GLANCE, SO IT'S EASY TO FORGET IT'S A TEST AND START TALKING TO THEM.
I REMEMBER DURING MY EXAM, MR. IGARASHI WAS SITTING BEHIND ME WATCHING TV THE WHOLE TIME.
DURING MINE, I HAD UNIT AND SERIES DIRECTORS PLAYING MARIO KART ON THEIR DS'ES IN THE ROOM.
KOME
SO...
I GUESS WE NEED TO KILL TWO MORE HOURS.
FOR THE SAKE OF OUR FUTURE KEY ANIMATORS IN THERE.
南阿佐ケ谷駅
Minami-asagaya Sta.

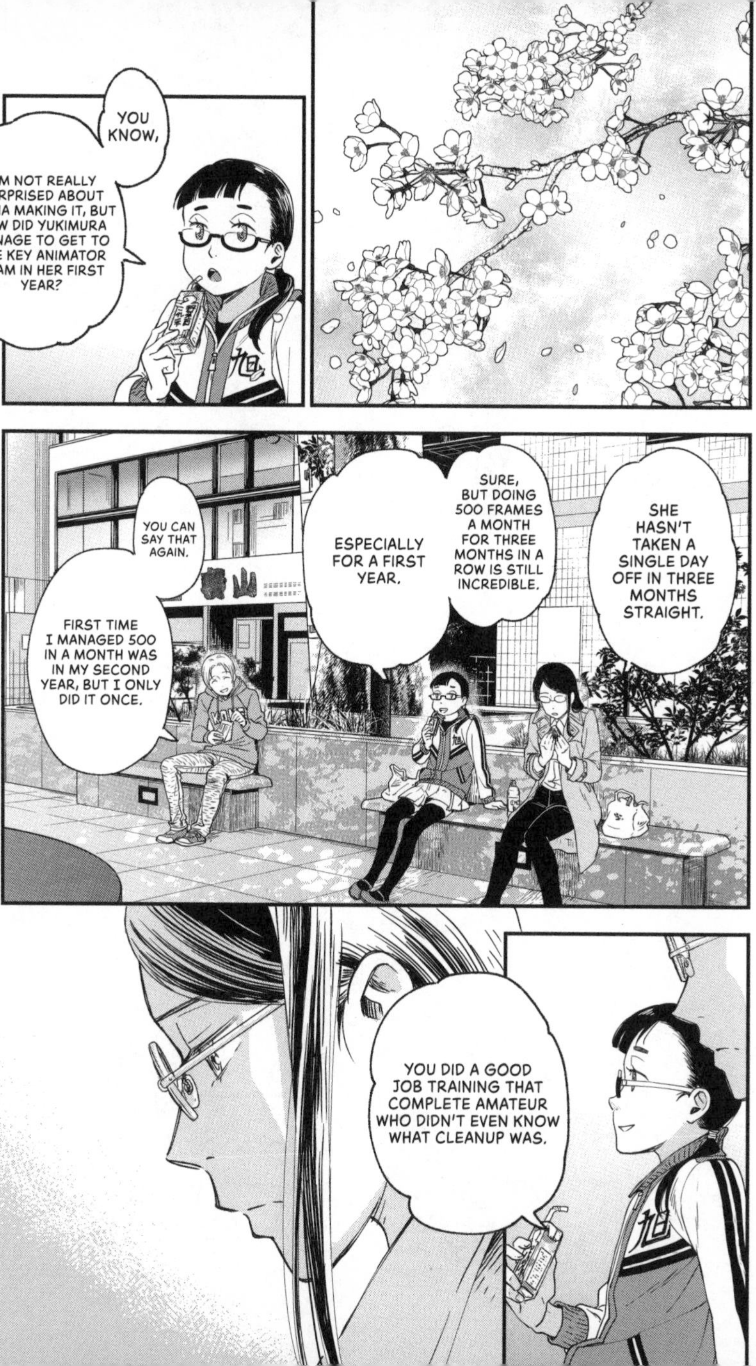
YOU KNOW,
I'M NOT REALLY SURPRISED ABOUT MARIA MAKING IT, BUT HOW DID YUKIMURA MANAGE TO GET TO THE KEY ANIMATOR EXAM IN HER FIRST YEAR?
SHE HASN'T TAKEN A SINGLE DAY OFF IN THREE MONTHS STRAIGHT.
SURE, BUT DOING 500 FRAMES A MONTH FOR THREE MONTHS IN A ROW IS STILL INCREDIBLE.
ESPECIALLY FOR A FIRST YEAR.
YOU CAN SAY THAT AGAIN.
FIRST TIME I MANAGED 500 IN A MONTH WAS IN MY SECOND YEAR, BUT I ONLY DID IT ONCE.
YOU DID A GOOD JOB TRAINING THAT COMPLETE AMATEUR WHO DIDN'T EVEN KNOW WHAT CLEANUP WAS.

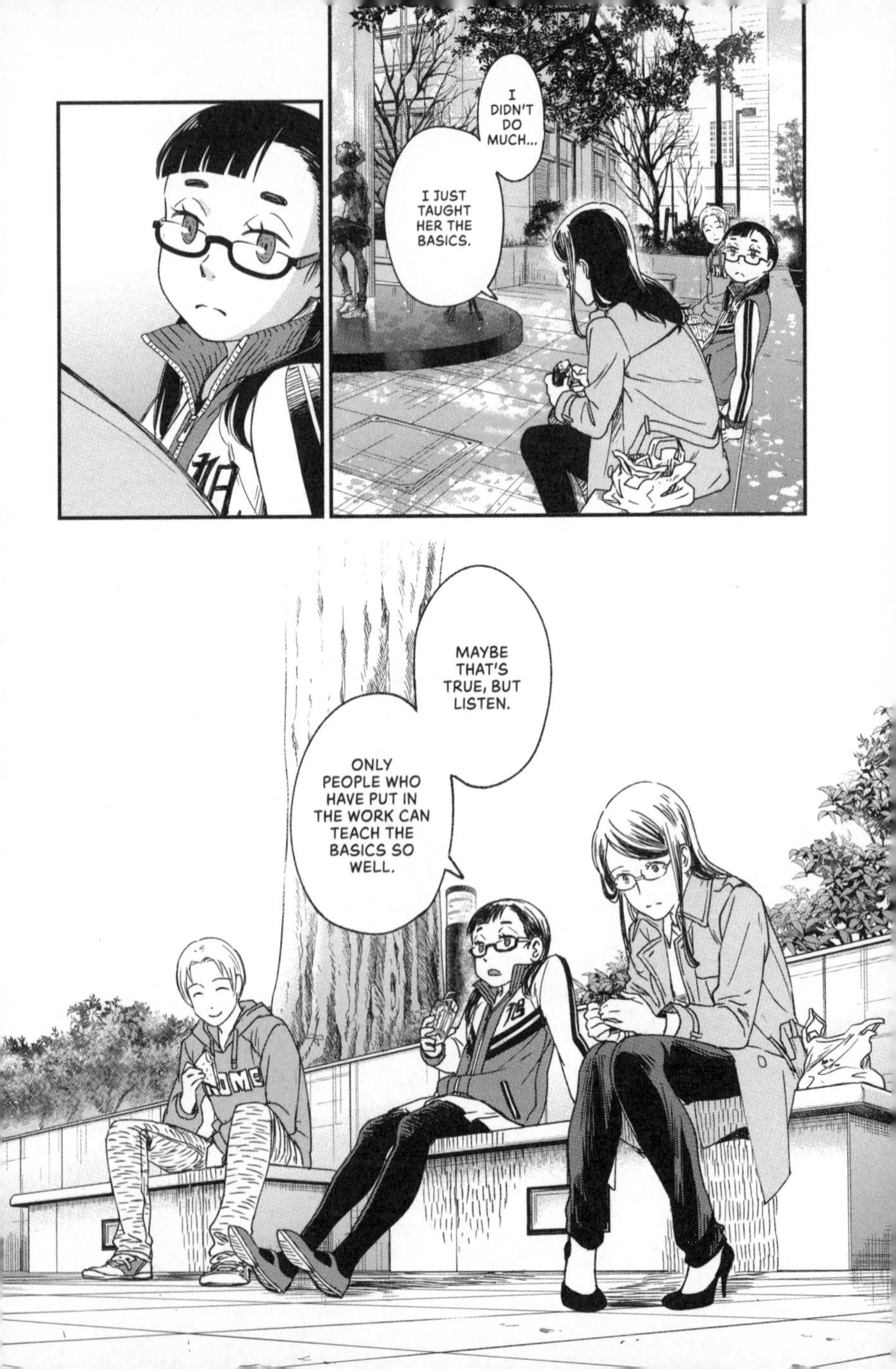
I DIDN'T DO MUCH...
I JUST TAUGHT HER THE BASICS.
MAYBE THAT'S TRUE, BUT LISTEN.
ONLY PEOPLE WHO HAVE PUT IN THE WORK CAN TEACH THE BASICS SO WELL.

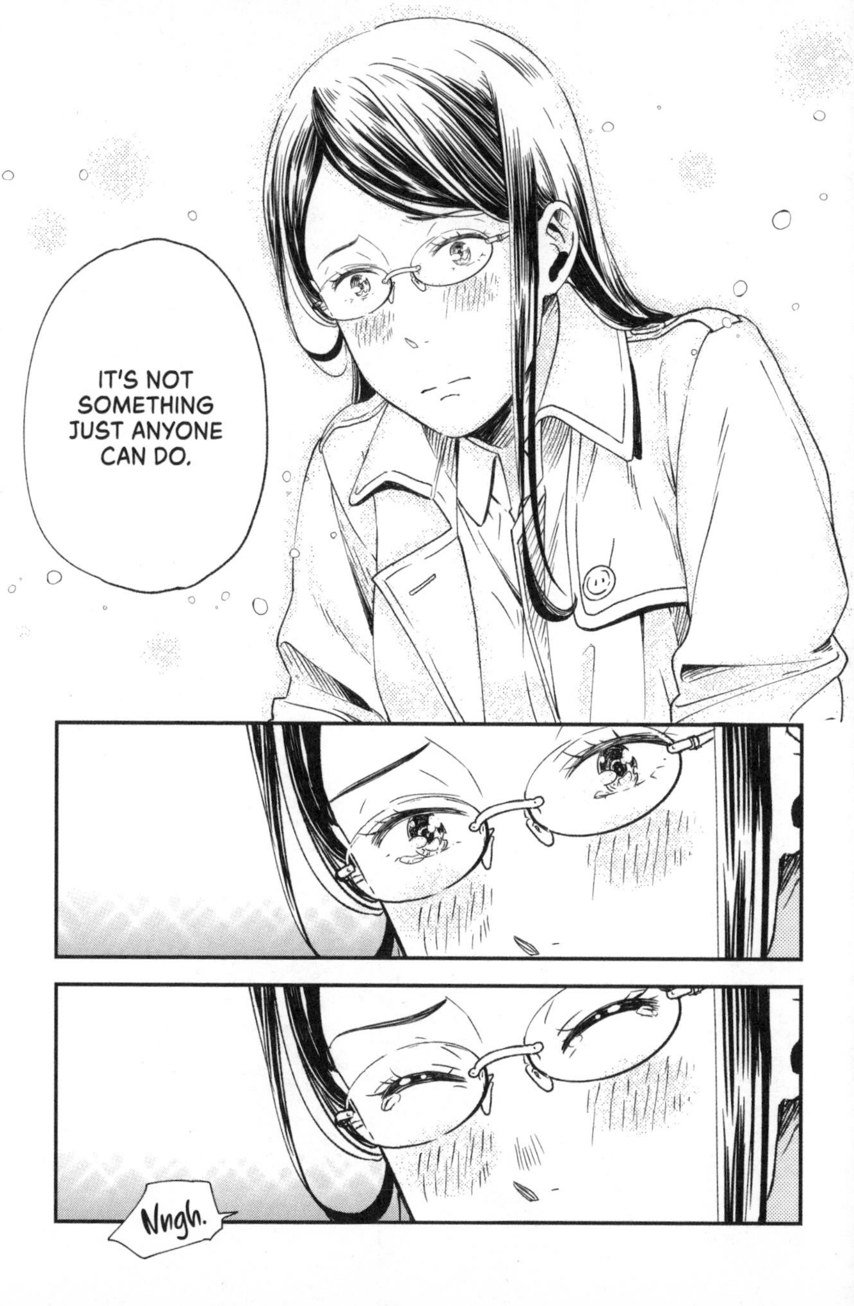
IT'S NOT SOMETHING JUST ANYONE CAN DO.
Nngh.

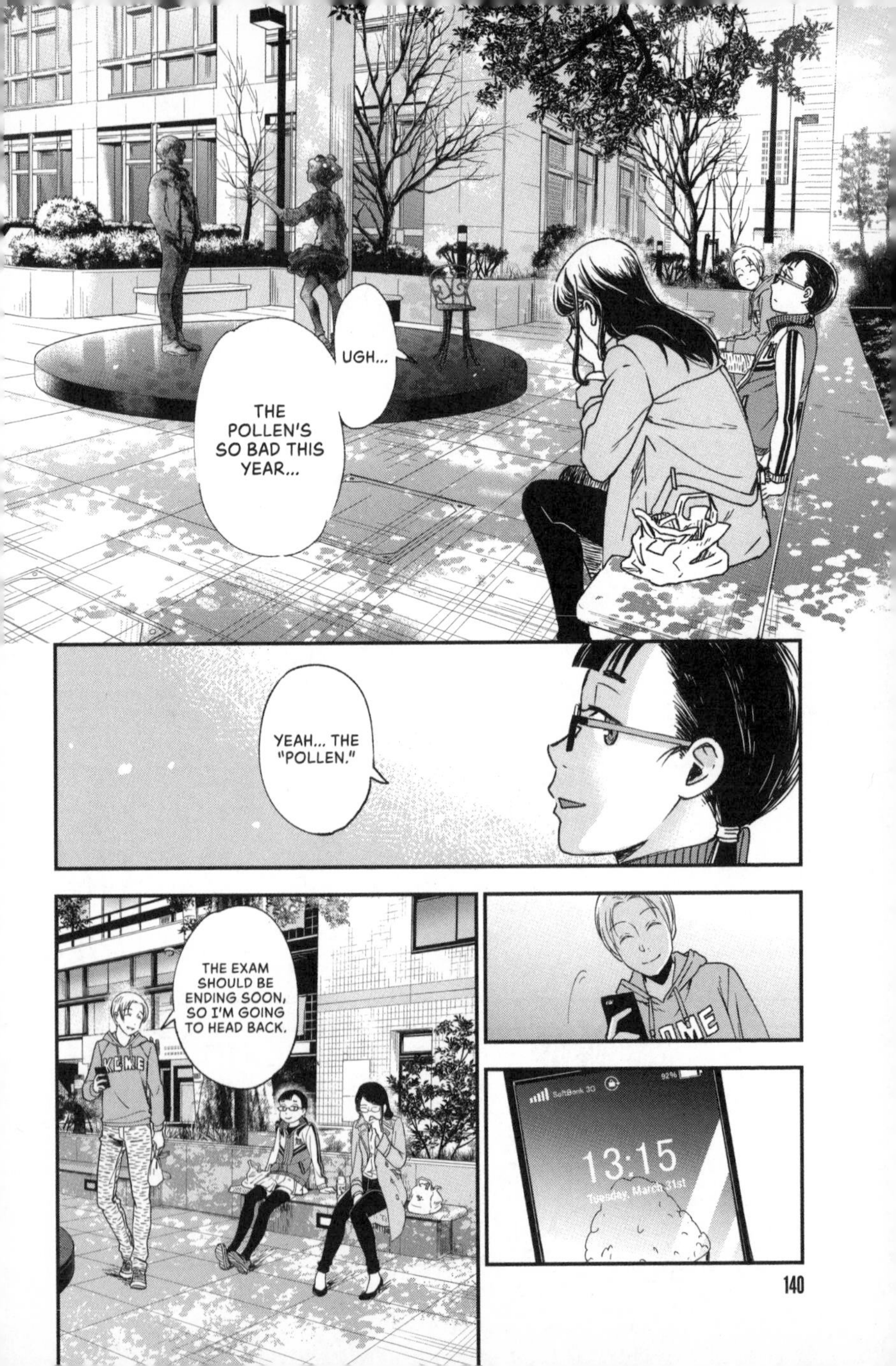
UGH...
THE POLLEN'S SO BAD THIS YEAR...
YEAH... THE "POLLEN."
SoftBank 3G
92%
13:15
Tuesday, March 31st
THE EXAM SHOULD BE ENDING SOON, SO I'M GOING TO HEAD BACK.

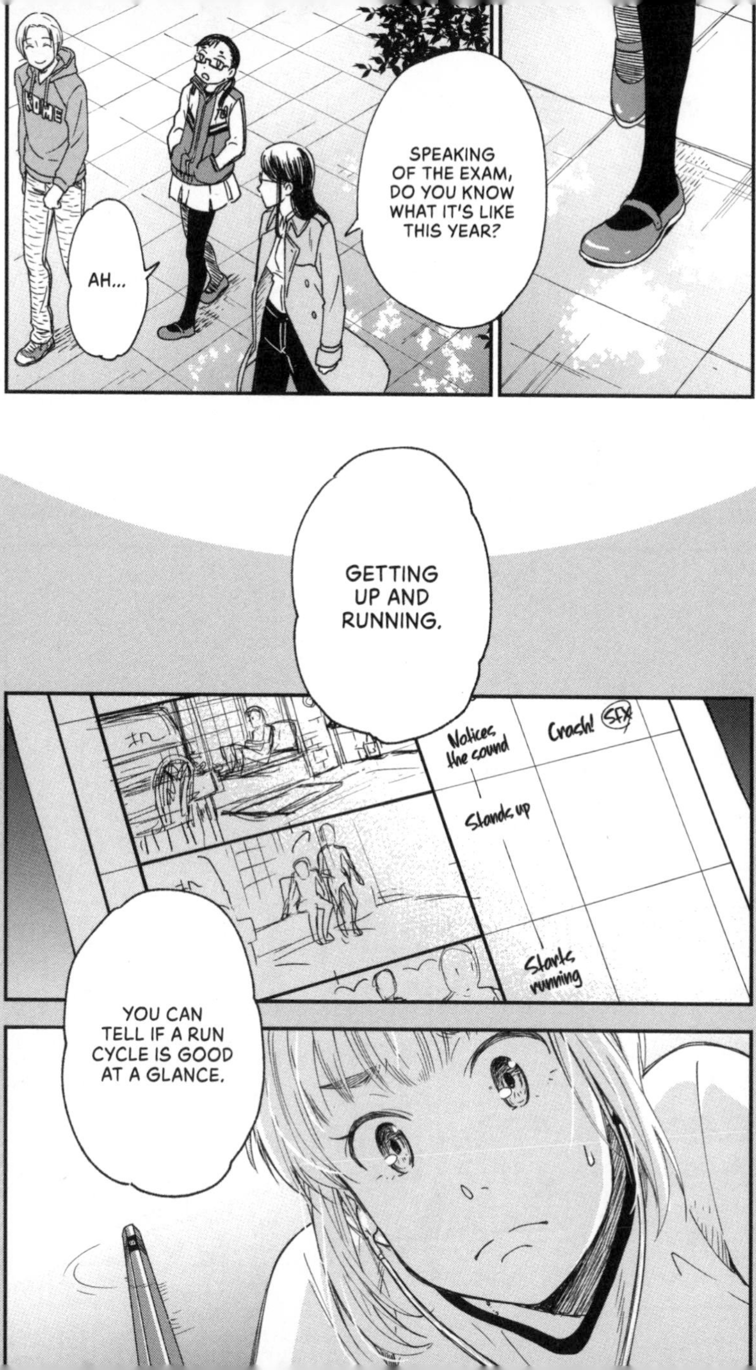
SPEAKING OF THE EXAM, DO YOU KNOW WHAT IT'S LIKE THIS YEAR?
AH...
GETTING UP AND RUNNING.
Crash! SFX
Notices the sound
Stands up
Starts running
YOU CAN TELL IF A RUN CYCLE IS GOOD AT A GLANCE.

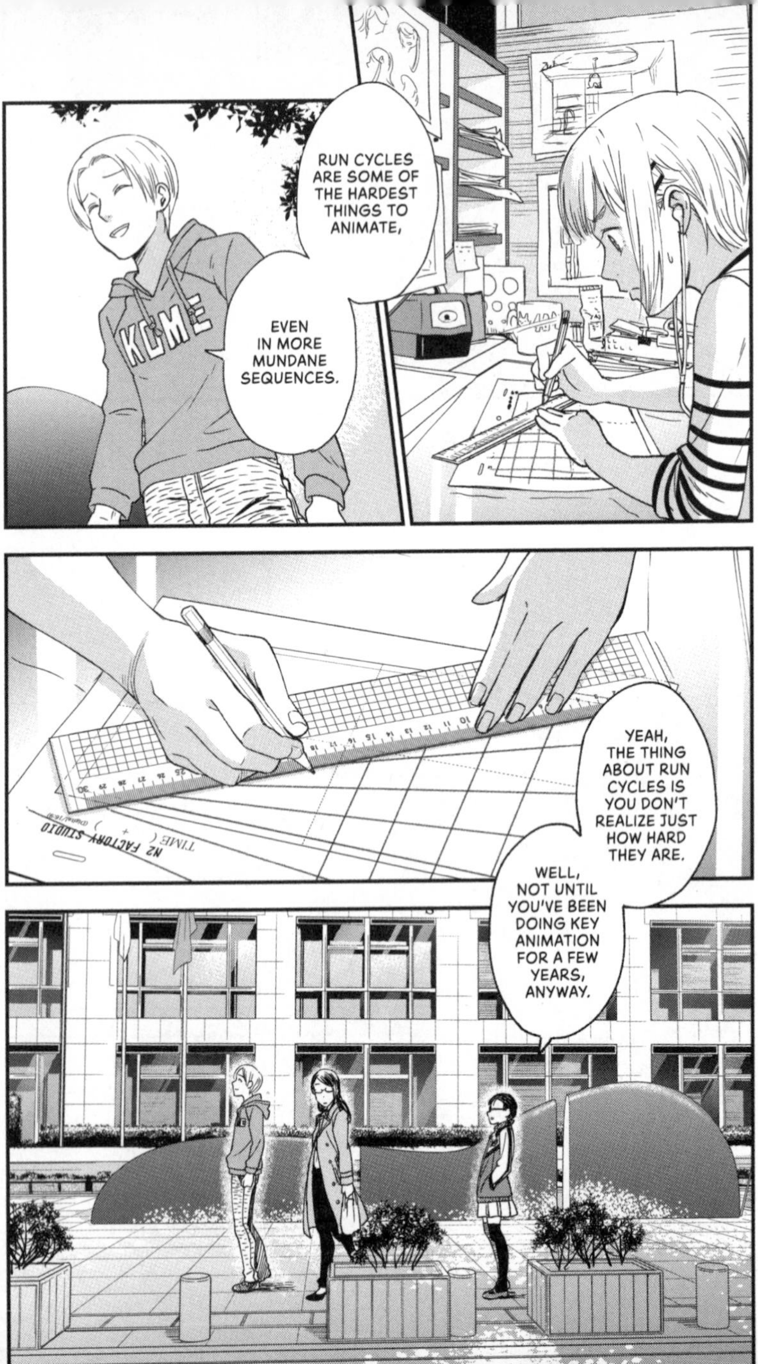
RUN CYCLES ARE SOME OF THE HARDEST THINGS TO ANIMATE,
EVEN IN MORE MUNDANE SEQUENCES.
KOME
YEAH, THE THING ABOUT RUN CYCLES IS YOU DON'T REALIZE JUST HOW HARD THEY ARE.
WELL, NOT UNTIL YOU'VE BEEN DOING KEY ANIMATION FOR A FEW YEARS, ANYWAY.

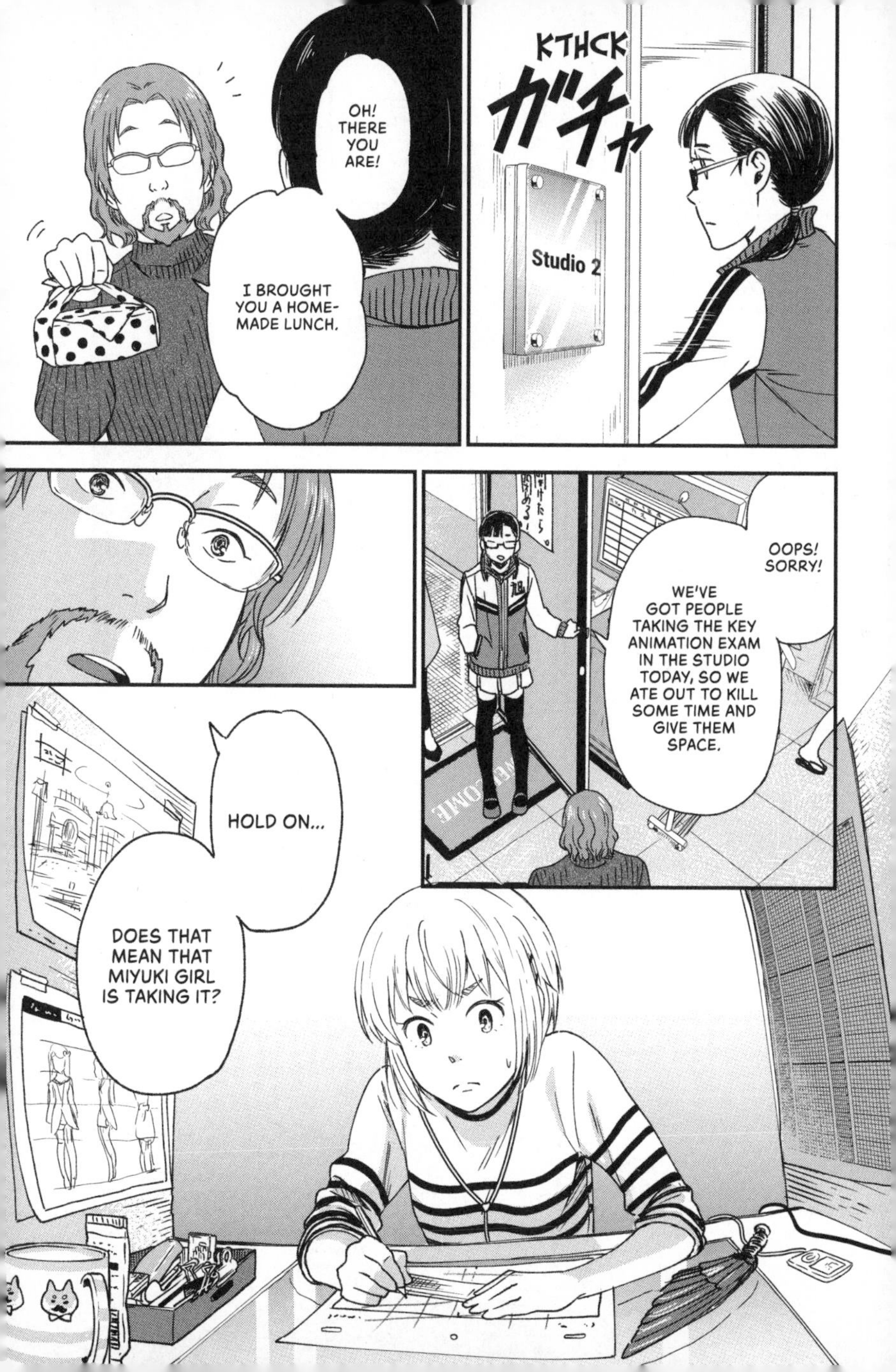
KTHCK
ガチャ
Studio 2
OH! THERE YOU ARE!
I BROUGHT YOU A HOME-MADE LUNCH.
OOPS! SORRY!
WE'VE GOT PEOPLE TAKING THE KEY ANIMATION EXAM IN THE STUDIO TODAY, SO WE ATE OUT TO KILL SOME TIME AND GIVE THEM SPACE.
HOLD ON...
DOES THAT MEAN THAT MIYUKI GIRL IS TAKING IT?

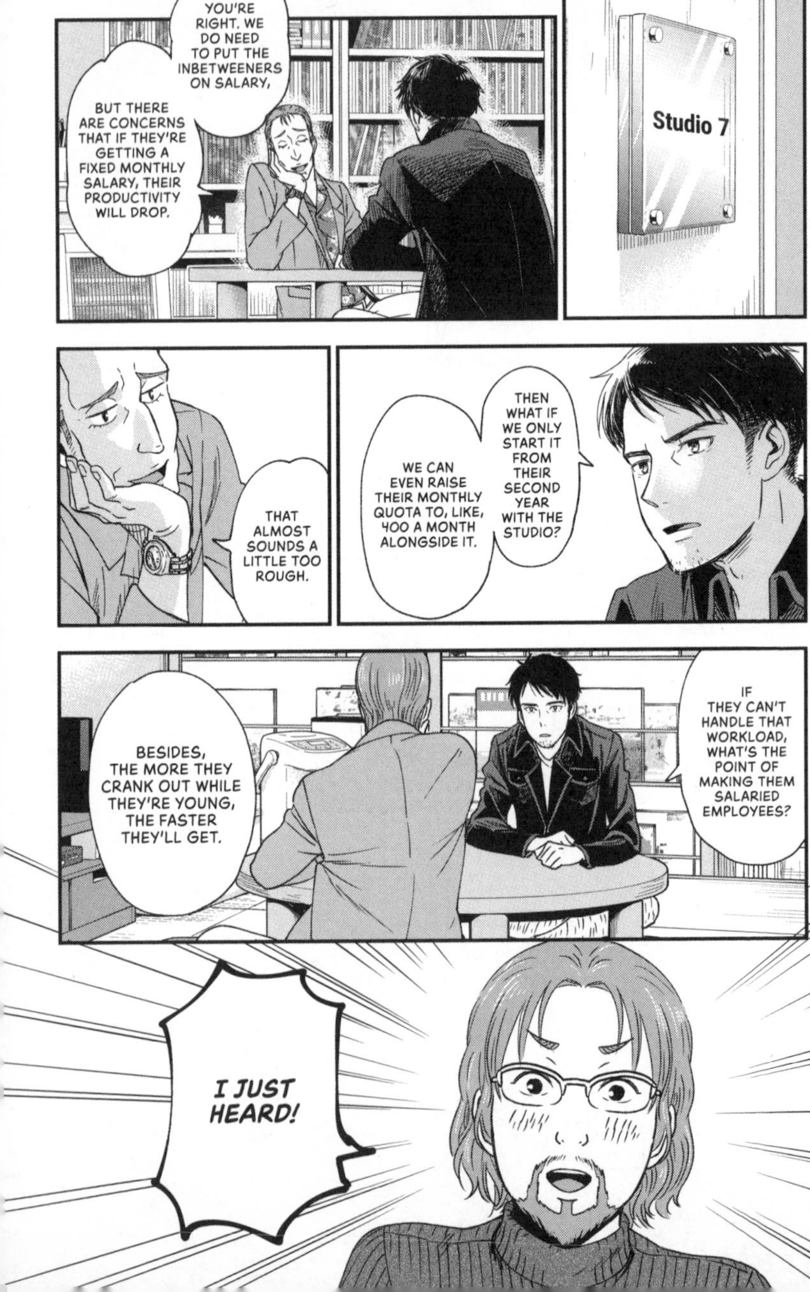
Studio 7
YOU'RE RIGHT. WE DO NEED TO PUT THE INBETWEENERS ON SALARY,
BUT THERE ARE CONCERNS THAT IF THEY'RE GETTING A FIXED MONTHLY SALARY, THEIR PRODUCTIVITY WILL DROP.
THEN WHAT IF WE ONLY START IT FROM THEIR SECOND YEAR WITH THE STUDIO?
WE CAN EVEN RAISE THEIR MONTHLY QUOTA TO, LIKE, 400 A MONTH ALONGSIDE IT.
THAT ALMOST SOUNDS A LITTLE TOO ROUGH.
IF THEY CAN'T HANDLE THAT WORKLOAD, WHAT'S THE POINT OF MAKING THEM SALARIED EMPLOYEES?
BESIDES, THE MORE THEY CRANK OUT WHILE THEY'RE YOUNG, THE FASTER THEY'LL GET.
I JUST HEARD!

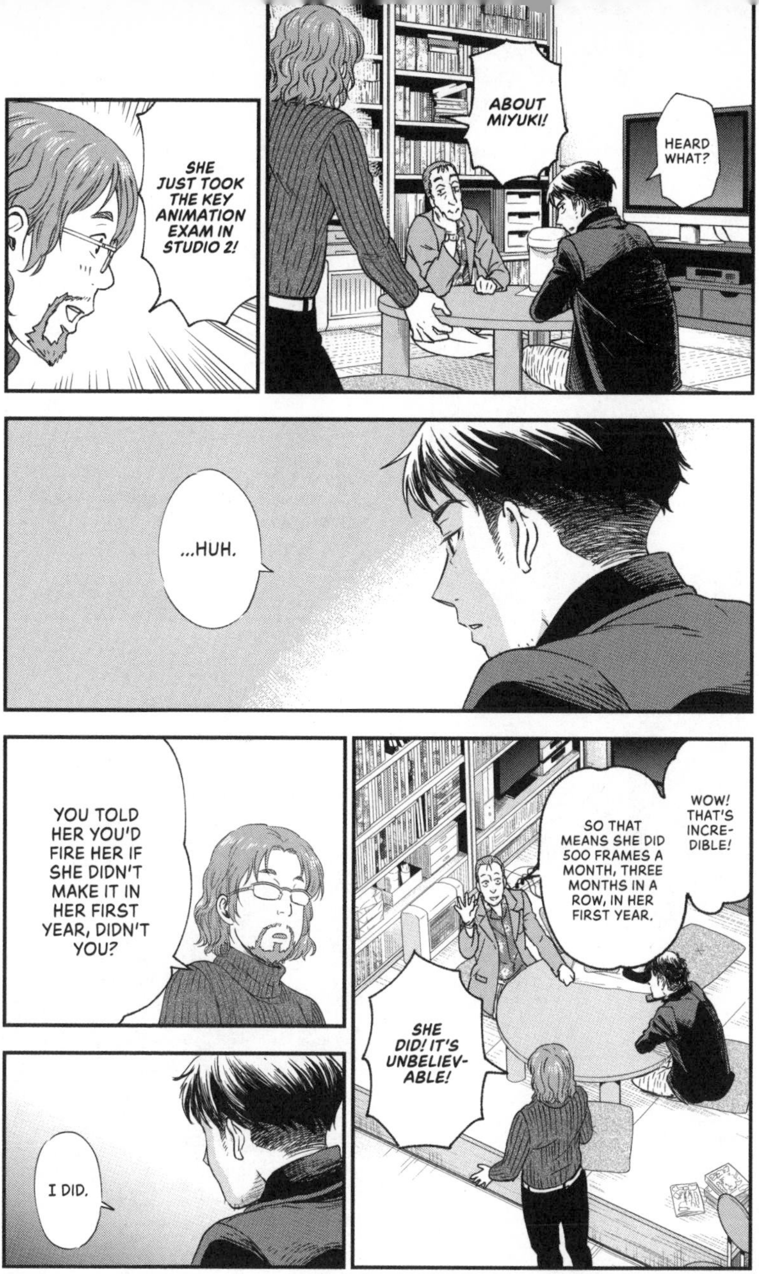
HEARD WHAT?
ABOUT MIYUKI!
SHE JUST TOOK THE KEY ANIMATION EXAM IN STUDIO 2!
...HUH.
WOW! THAT'S INCRE-DIBLE!
SO THAT MEANS SHE DID 500 FRAMES A MONTH, THREE MONTHS IN A ROW, IN HER FIRST YEAR.
SHE DID! IT'S UNBELIEV-ABLE!
YOU TOLD HER YOU'D FIRE HER IF SHE DIDN'T MAKE IT IN HER FIRST YEAR, DIDN'T YOU?
I DID.

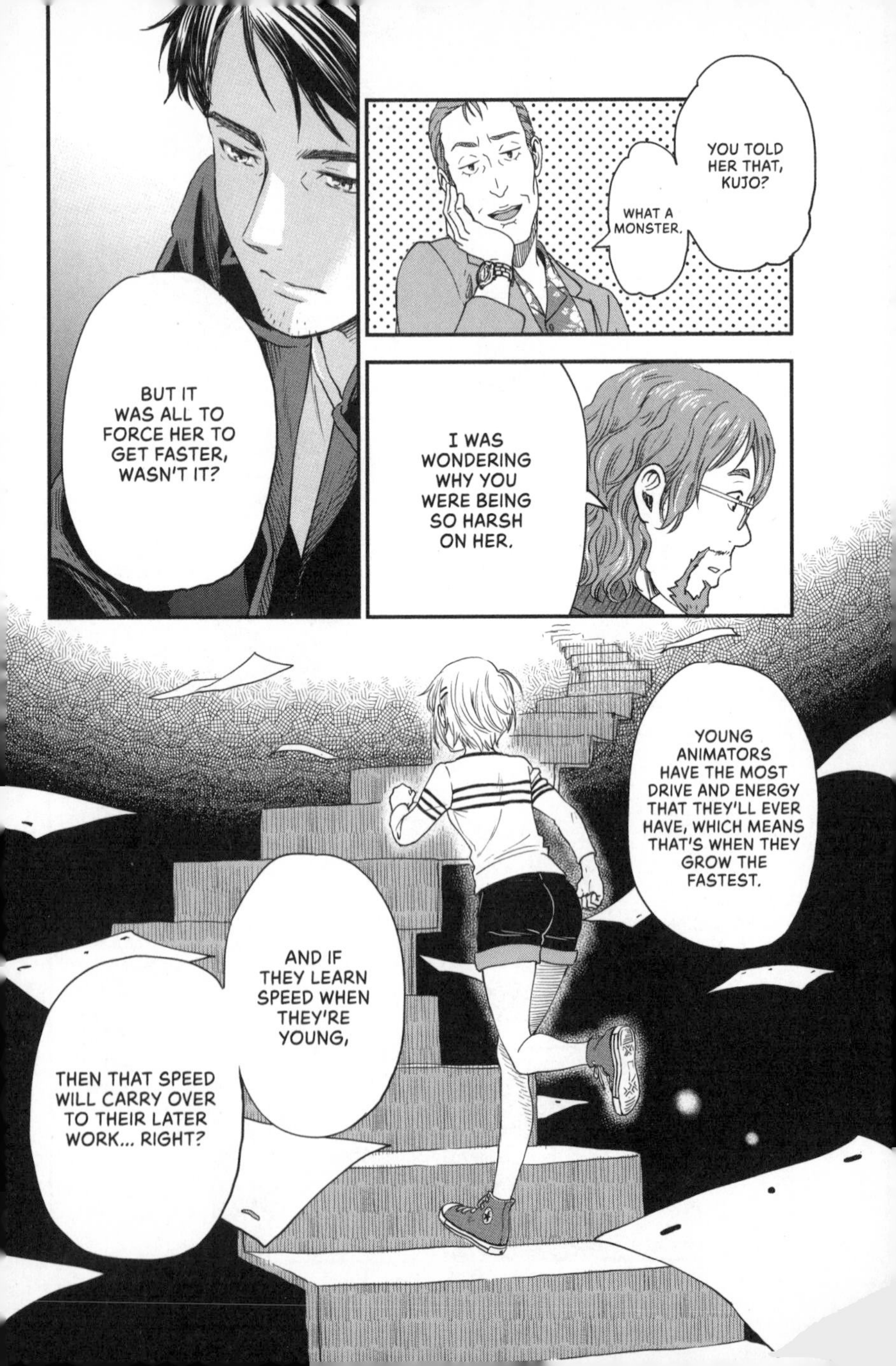
YOU TOLD HER THAT, KUJO?
WHAT A MONSTER.
I WAS WONDERING WHY YOU WERE BEING SO HARSH ON HER.
BUT IT WAS ALL TO FORCE HER TO GET FASTER, WASN'T IT?
YOUNG ANIMATORS HAVE THE MOST DRIVE AND ENERGY THAT THEY'LL EVER HAVE, WHICH MEANS THAT'S WHEN THEY GROW THE FASTEST.
AND IF THEY LEARN SPEED WHEN THEY'RE YOUNG,
THEN THAT SPEED WILL CARRY OVER TO THEIR LATER WORK... RIGHT?

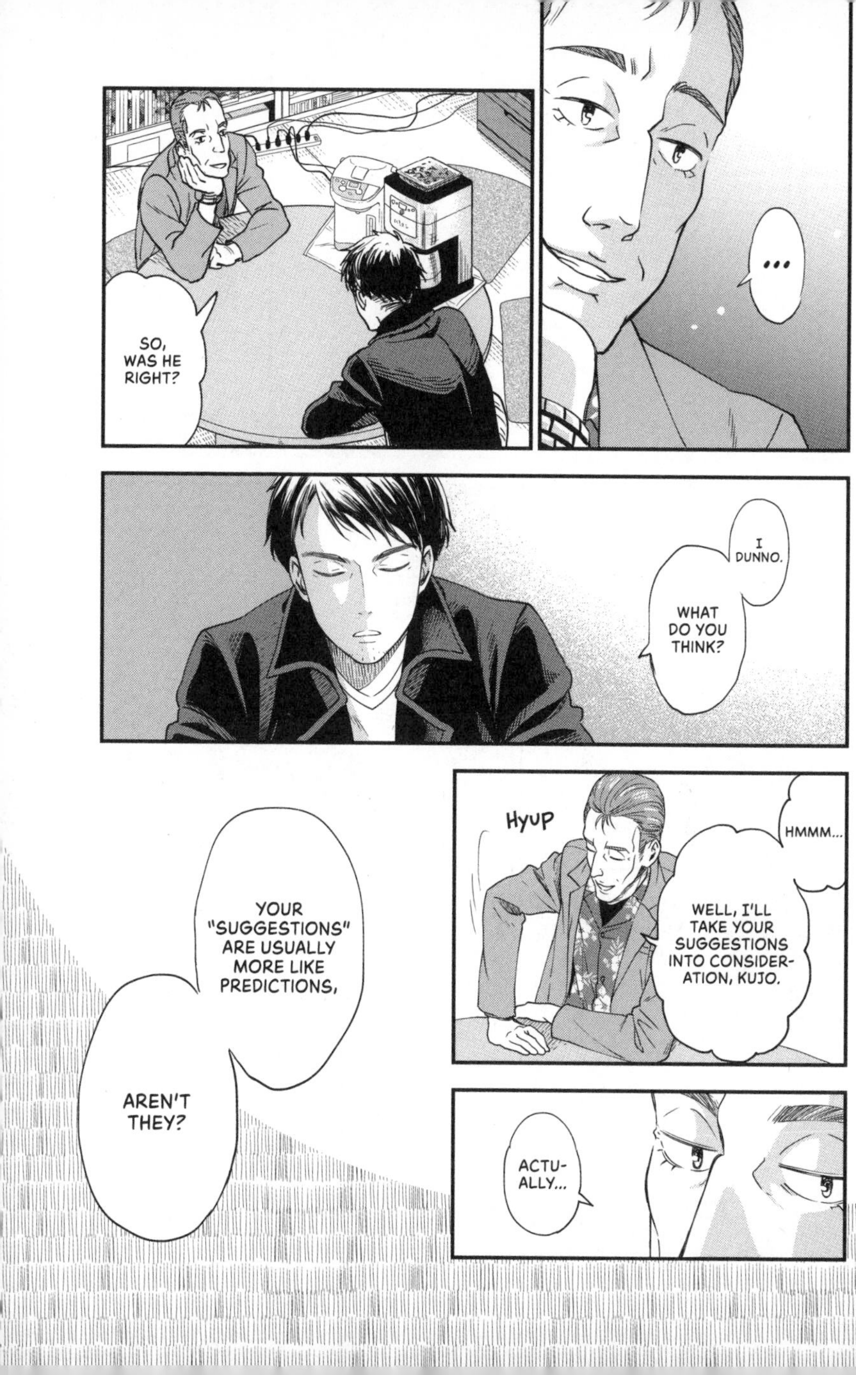
...
SO, WAS HE RIGHT?
I DUNNO.
WHAT DO YOU THINK?
HMMM...
Hyup
WELL, I'LL TAKE YOUR SUGGESTIONS INTO CONSIDERATION, KUJO.
ACTUALLY...
YOUR "SUGGESTIONS" ARE USUALLY MORE LIKE PREDICTIONS,
AREN'T THEY?

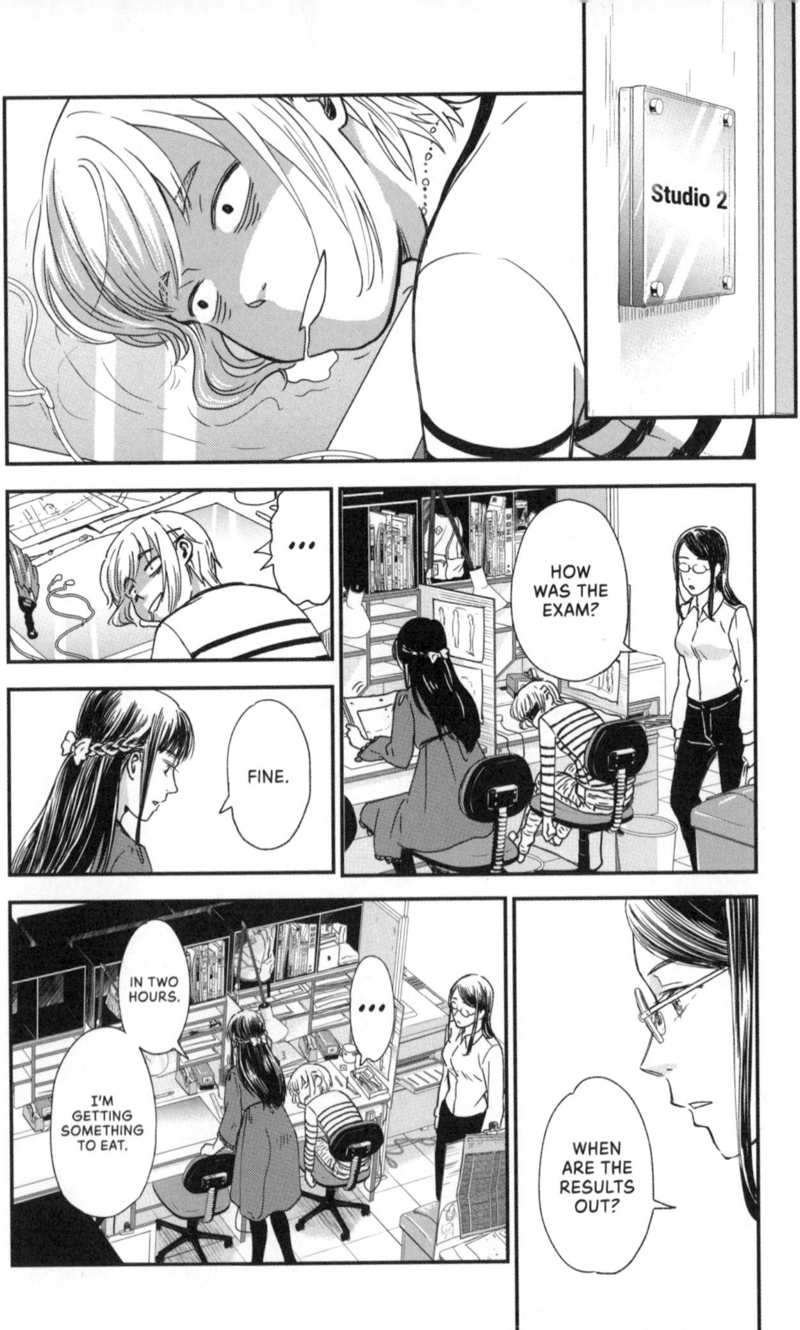
Studio 2
HOW WAS THE EXAM?
...
FINE.
WHEN ARE THE RESULTS OUT?
IN TWO HOURS.
...
I'M GETTING SOMETHING TO EAT.

KTCHK

HAVE FUN.

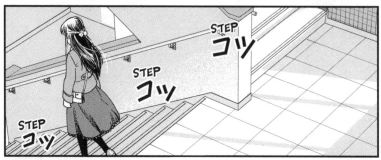

STEP
コツ

STEP
コツ

STEP
コツ

N2 FACTORY STUDIO

ピ

タ

PAUSE

Coca Cola

SQUEEZE

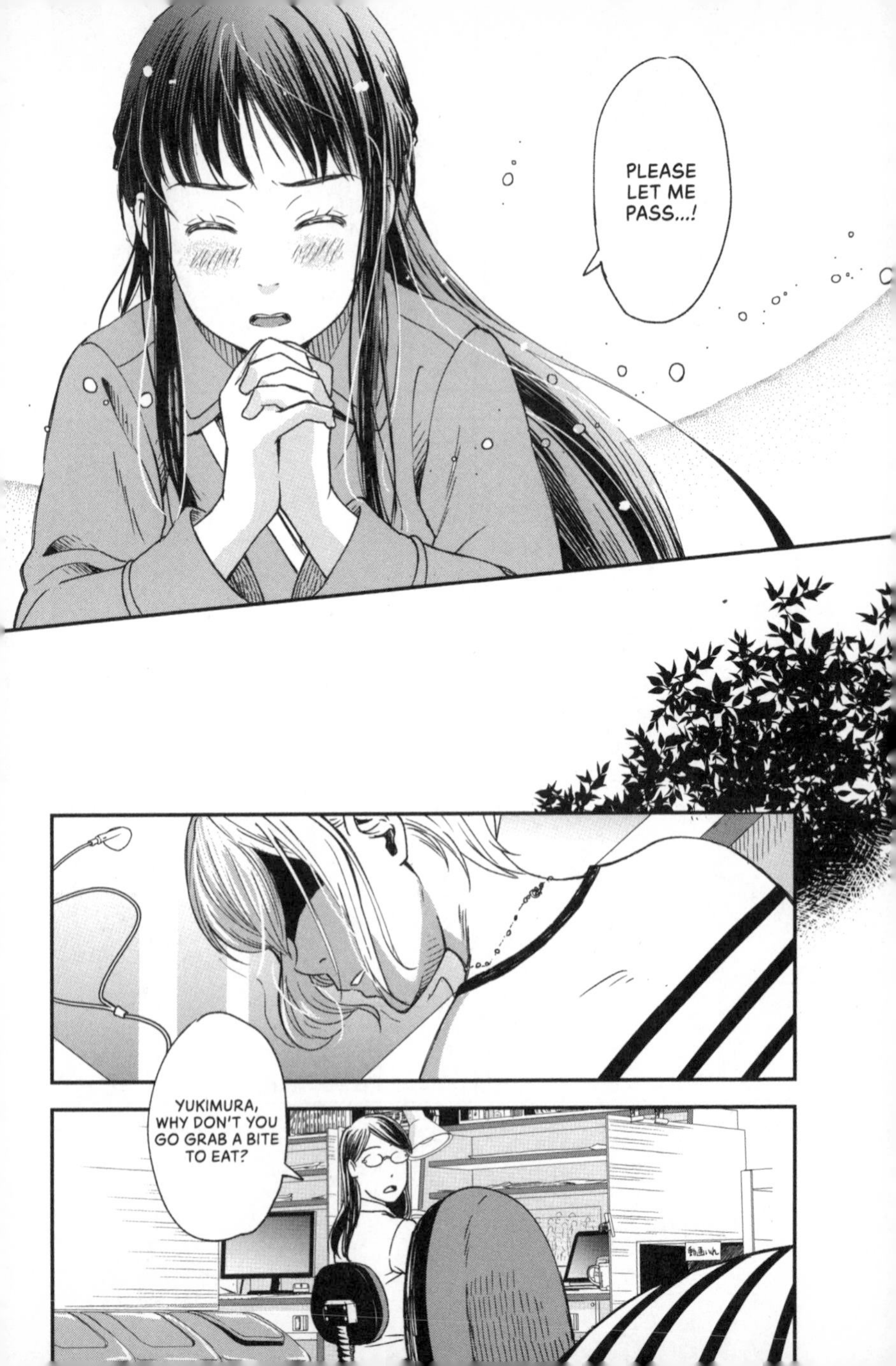
PLEASE LET ME PASS...!
YUKIMURA, WHY DON'T YOU GO GRAB A BITE TO EAT?

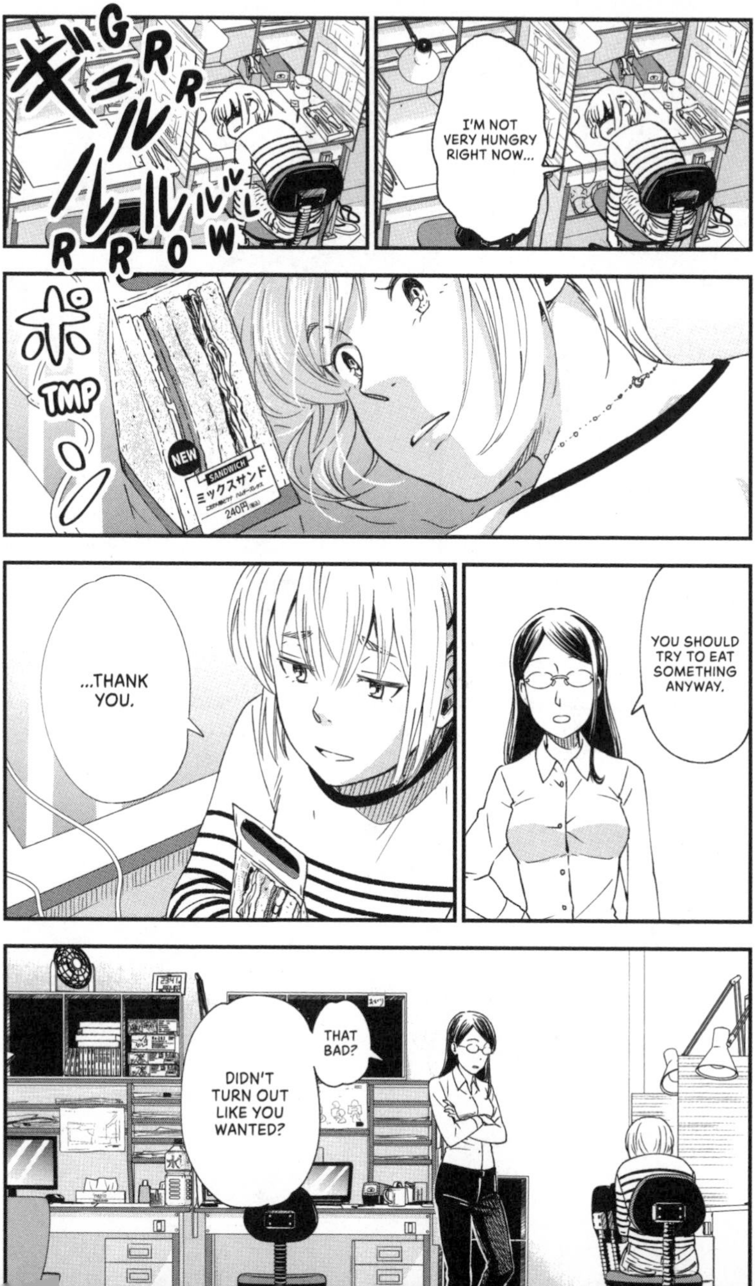

I'M NOT VERY HUNGRY RIGHT NOW...
ギュルルルルル
GRRRRROWL
ポ
TMP
NEW
SANDWICH
ミックスサンド
240円
YOU SHOULD TRY TO EAT SOMETHING ANYWAY.
...THANK YOU.
THAT BAD?
DIDN'T TURN OUT LIKE YOU WANTED?

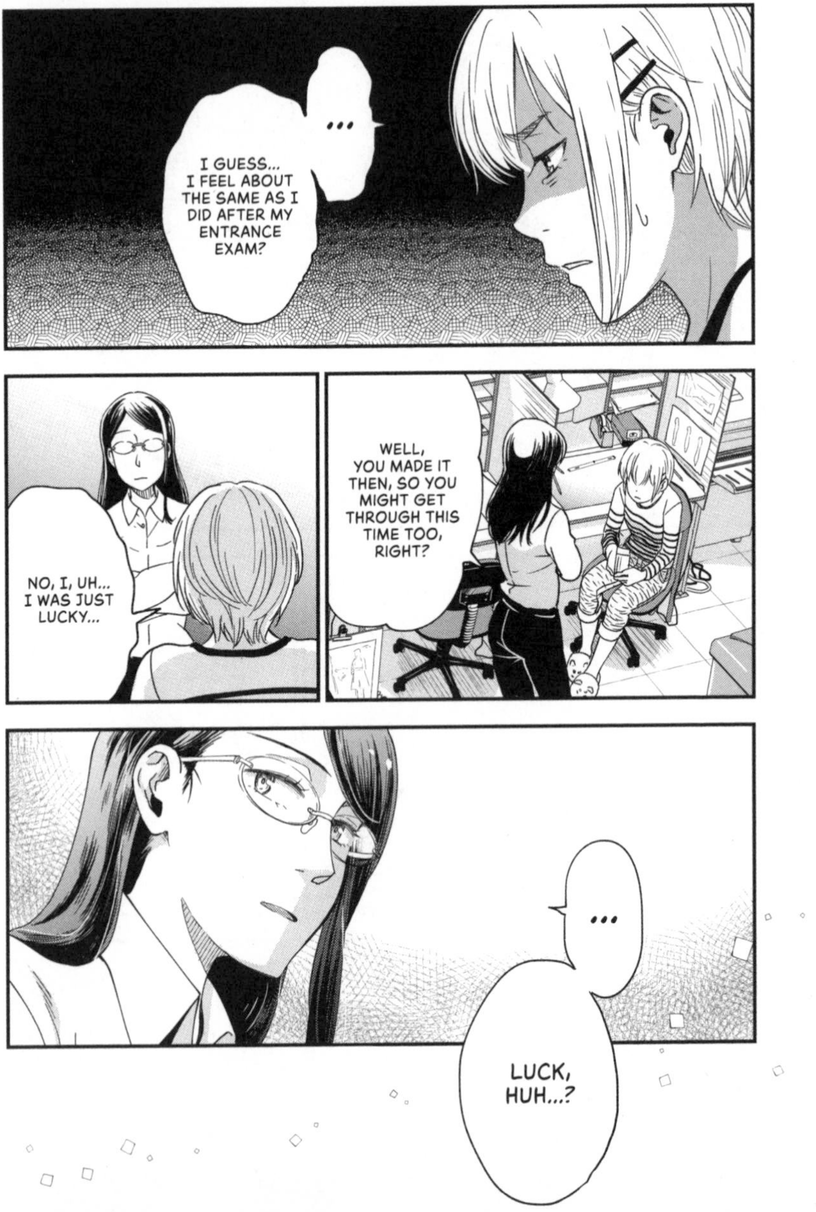
...
I GUESS... I FEEL ABOUT THE SAME AS I DID AFTER MY ENTRANCE EXAM?
WELL, YOU MADE IT THEN, SO YOU MIGHT GET THROUGH THIS TIME TOO, RIGHT?
NO, I, UH... I WAS JUST LUCKY...
...
LUCK, HUH...?

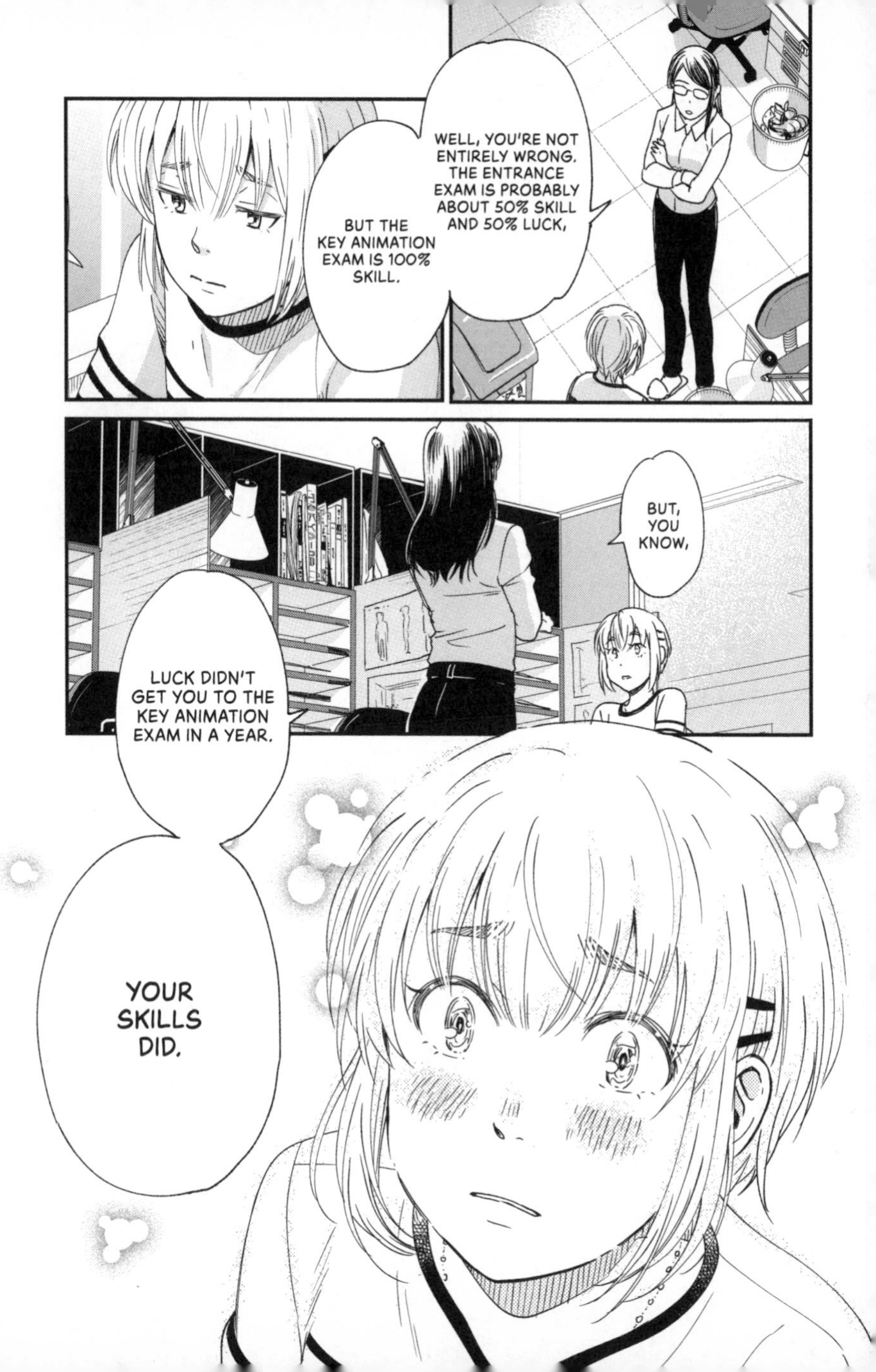
WELL, YOU'RE NOT ENTIRELY WRONG. THE ENTRANCE EXAM IS PROBABLY ABOUT 50% SKILL AND 50% LUCK,
BUT THE KEY ANIMATION EXAM IS 100% SKILL.
BUT, YOU KNOW,
LUCK DIDN'T GET YOU TO THE KEY ANIMATION EXAM IN A YEAR.
YOUR SKILLS DID.

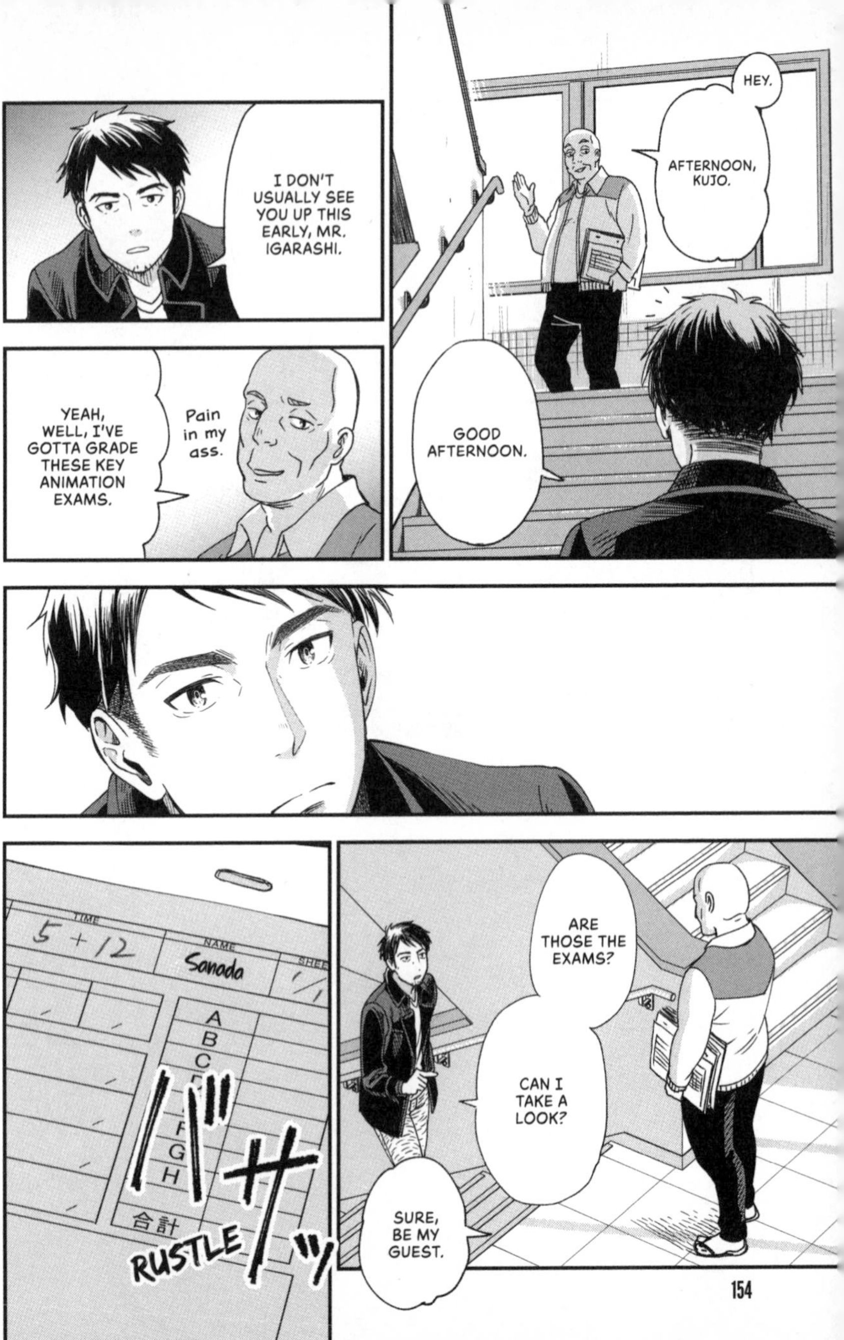

HEY.
AFTERNOON, KUJO.
GOOD AFTERNOON.
I DON'T USUALLY SEE YOU UP THIS EARLY, MR. IGARASHI.
Pain in my ass.
YEAH, WELL, I'VE GOTTA GRADE THESE KEY ANIMATION EXAMS.
ARE THOSE THE EXAMS?
CAN I TAKE A LOOK?
SURE, BE MY GUEST.
TIME
5 + 12
NAME
Sanada
A
B
C
G
H
合計
RUSTLE

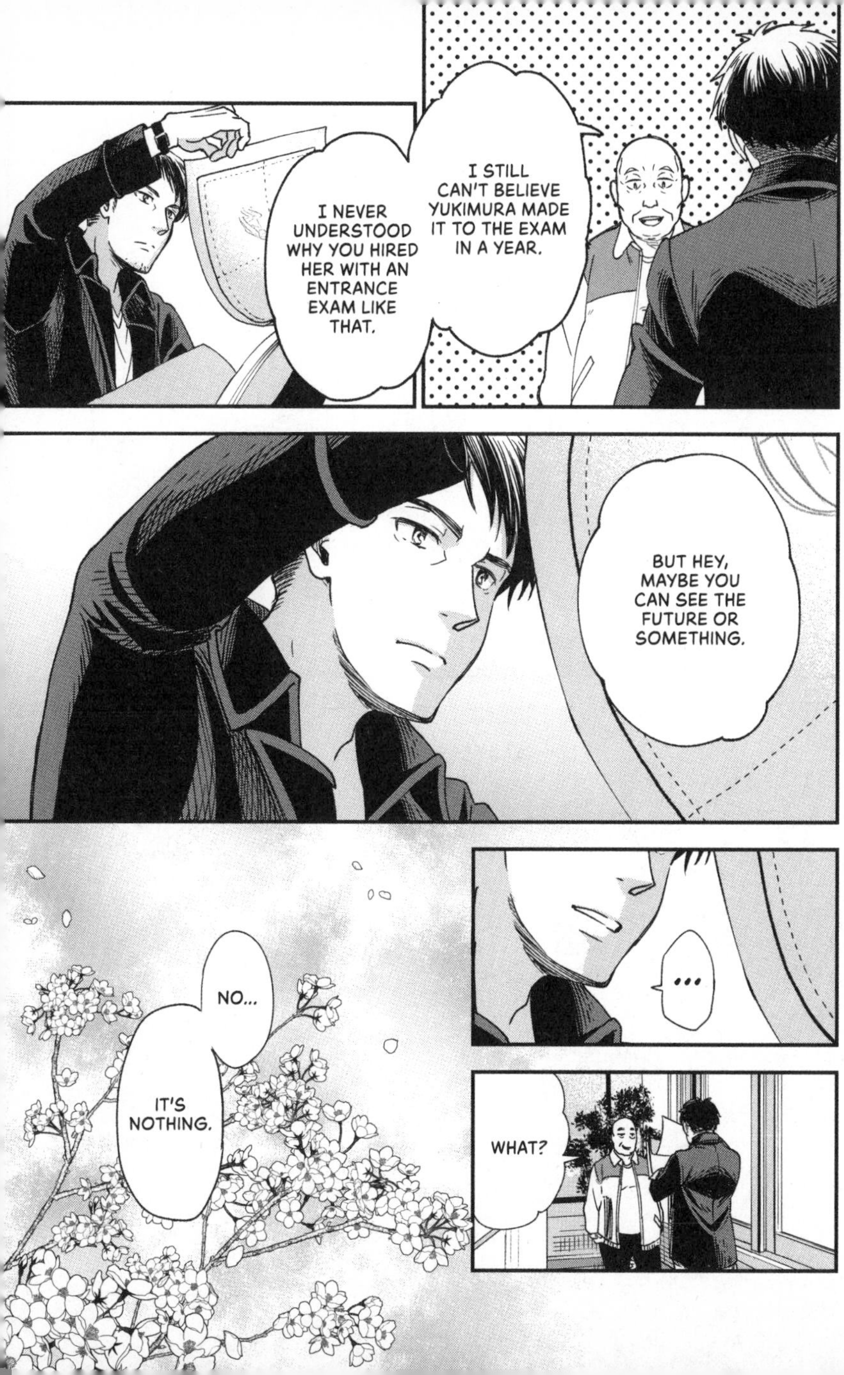
I STILL CAN'T BELIEVE YUKIMURA MADE IT TO THE EXAM IN A YEAR.
I NEVER UNDERSTOOD WHY YOU HIRED HER WITH AN ENTRANCE EXAM LIKE THAT.
BUT HEY, MAYBE YOU CAN SEE THE FUTURE OR SOMETHING.
...
WHAT?
NO...
IT'S NOTHING.

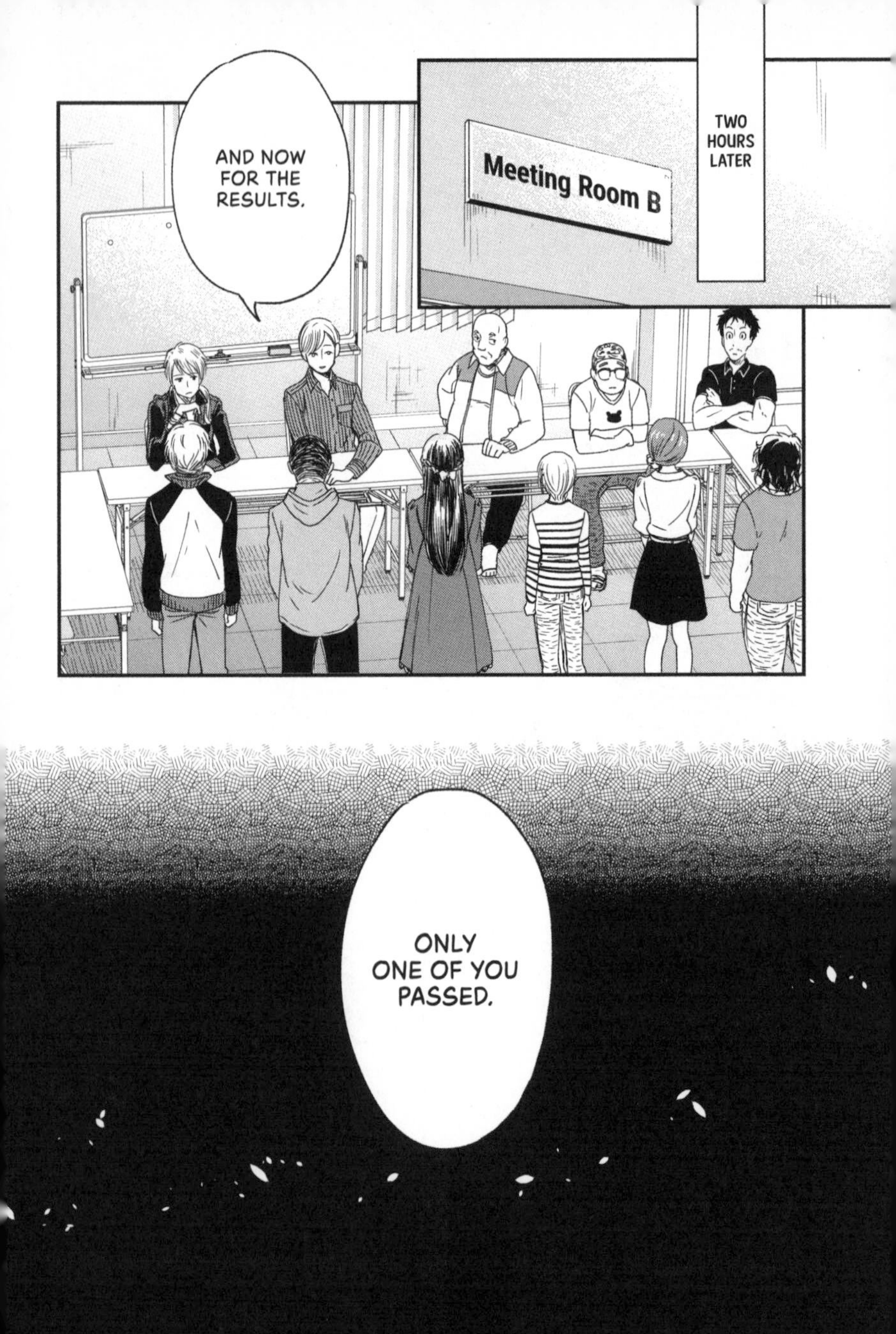
TWO HOURS LATER
Meeting Room B
AND NOW FOR THE RESULTS.
ONLY ONE OF YOU PASSED.

CHAPTER 21: WHERE DID THAT SMILE GO?

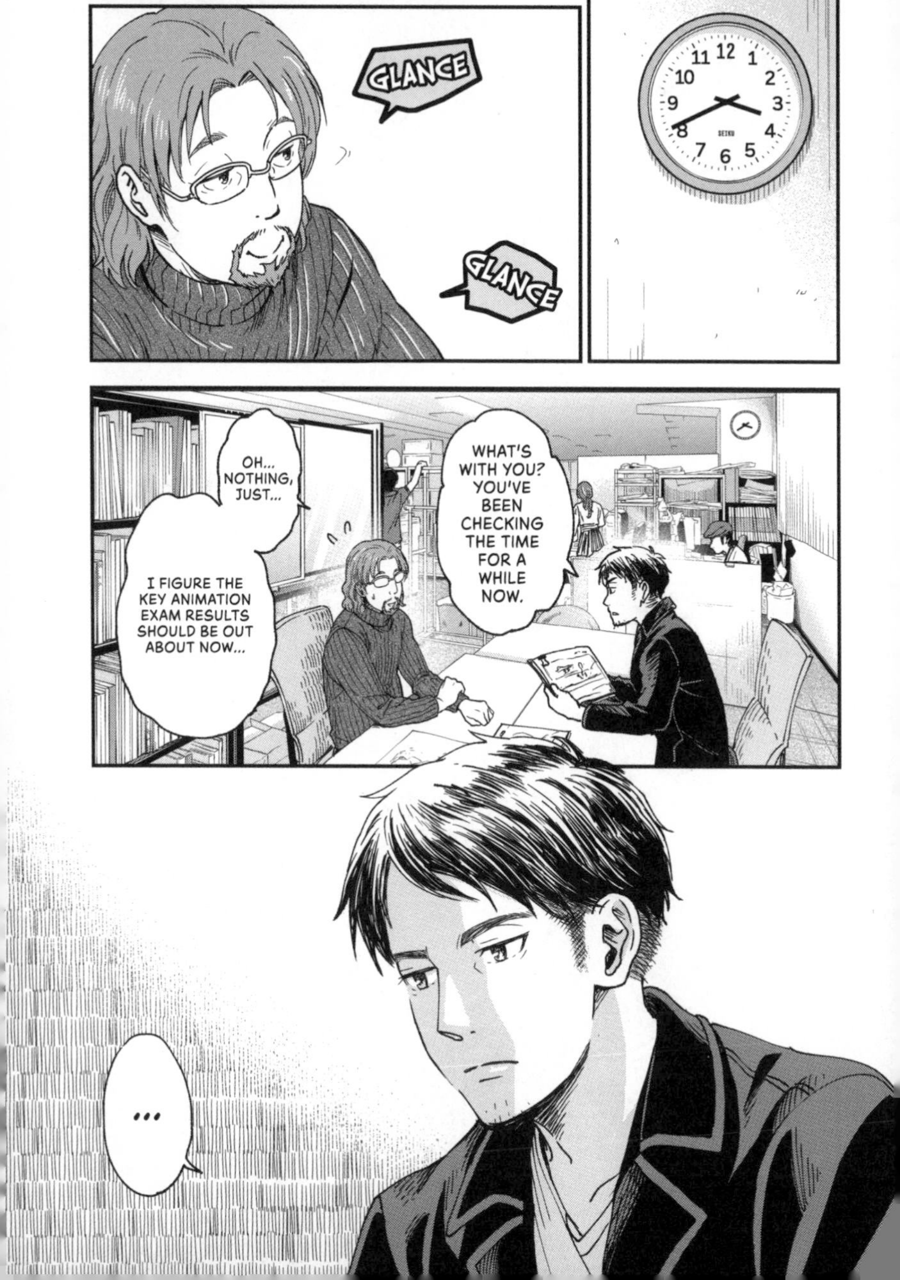
GLANCE
GLANCE
WHAT'S WITH YOU? YOU'VE BEEN CHECKING THE TIME FOR A WHILE NOW.
OH... NOTHING, JUST...
I FIGURE THE KEY ANIMATION EXAM RESULTS SHOULD BE OUT ABOUT NOW...
...

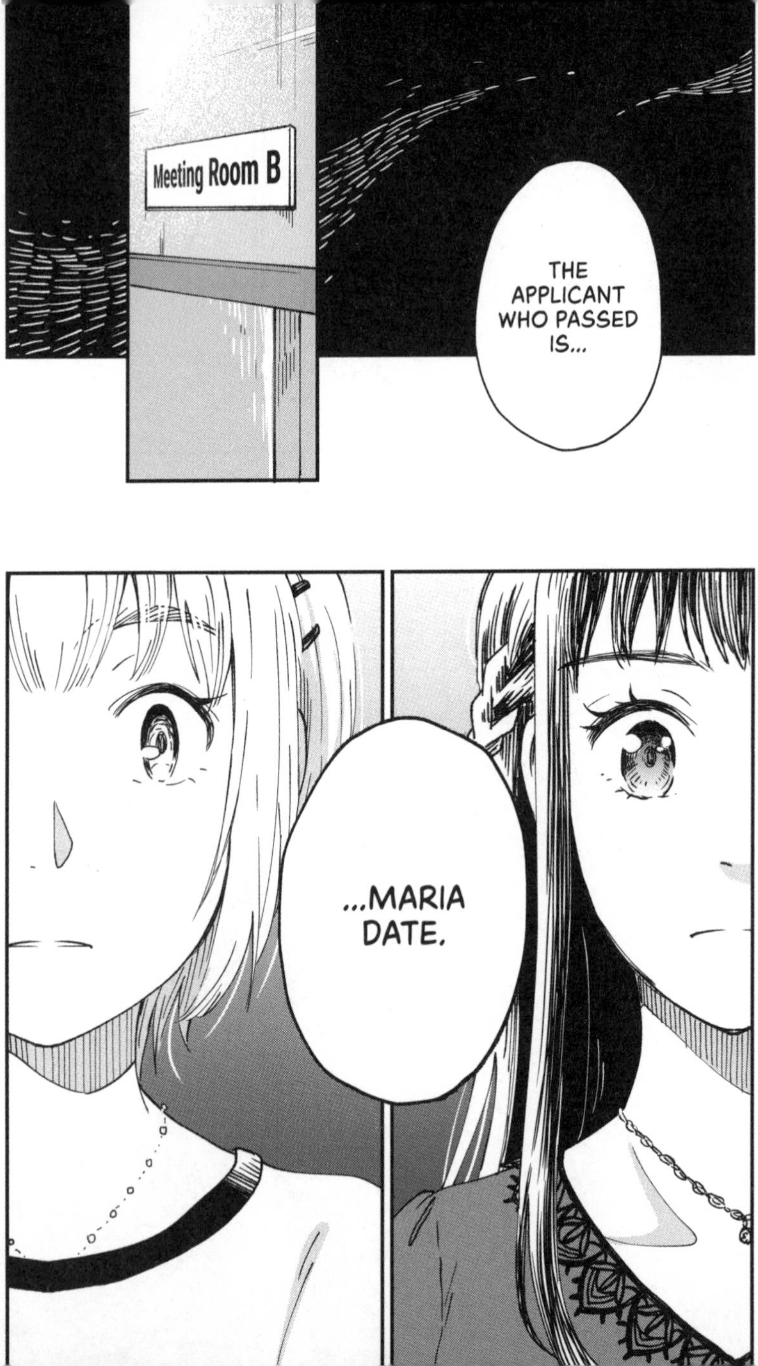
Meeting Room B
THE APPLICANT WHO PASSED IS...
...MARIA DATE.

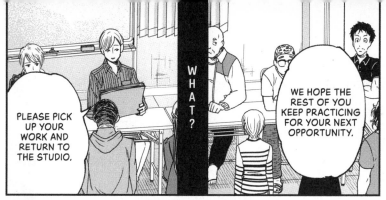

WE HOPE THE REST OF YOU KEEP PRACTICING FOR YOUR NEXT OPPORTUNITY.
WHAT?
PLEASE PICK UP YOUR WORK AND RETURN TO THE STUDIO.
MS. DATE.
Congratulations.
MR. TANAKA.
MS. FUJIWARA.
MR. KASAKI.
MR. HAMADERA.
I...
MS. SANADA.

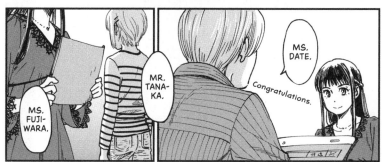

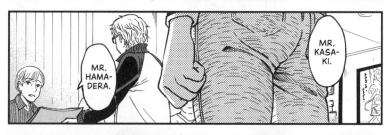

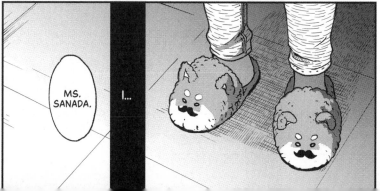

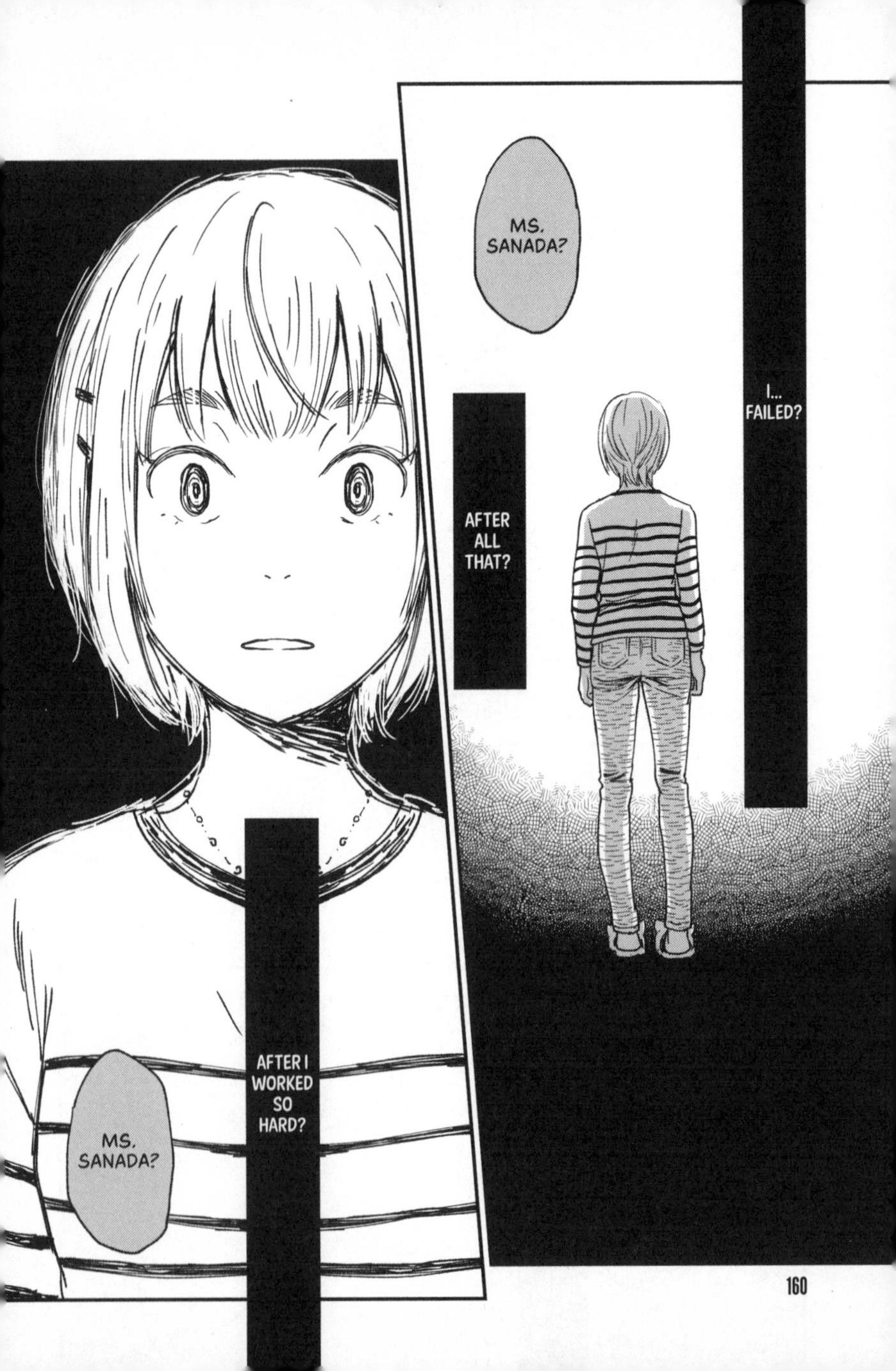
I... FAILED?
MS. SANADA?
AFTER ALL THAT?
AFTER I WORKED SO HARD?
MS. SANADA?

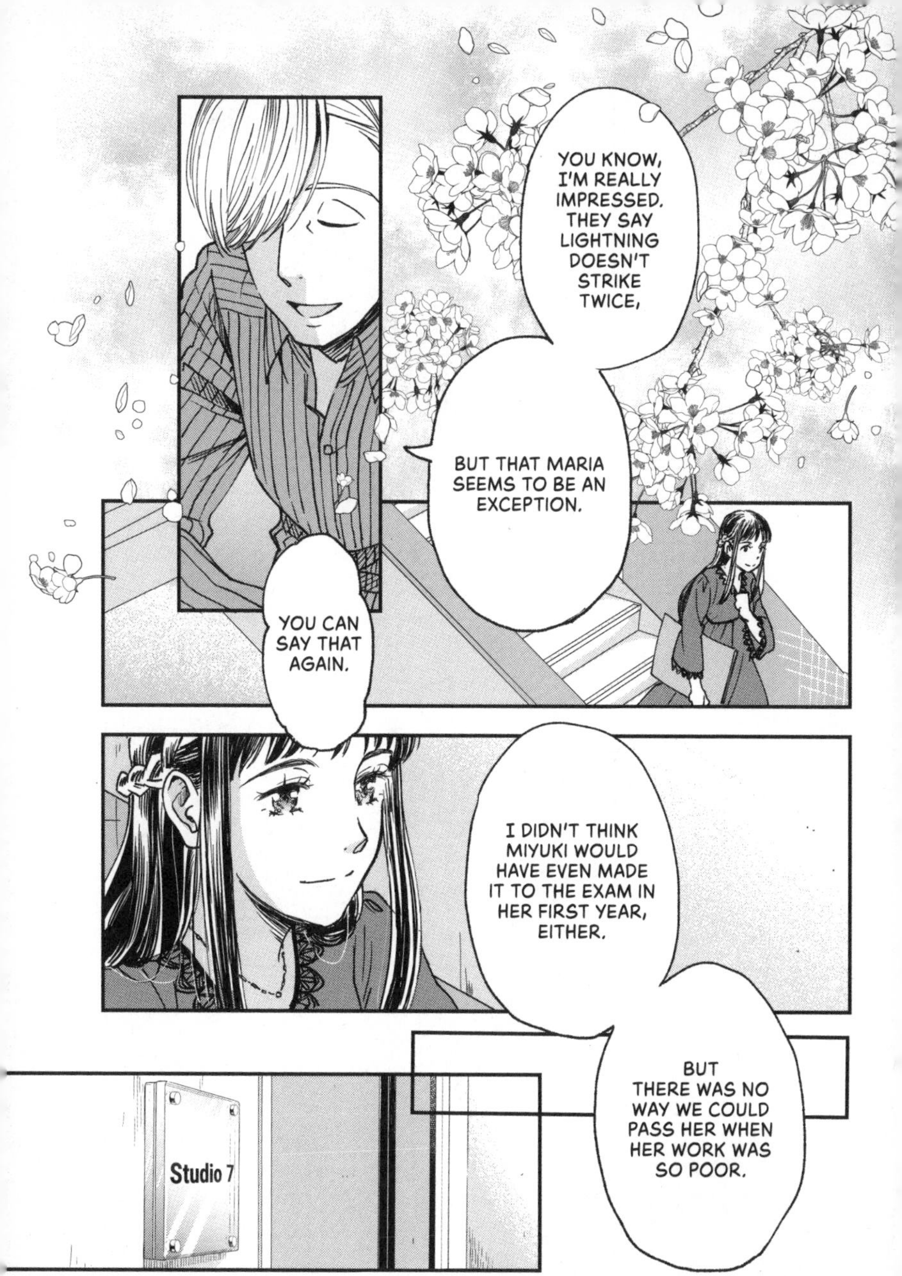
YOU KNOW, I'M REALLY IMPRESSED. THEY SAY LIGHTNING DOESN'T STRIKE TWICE,
BUT THAT MARIA SEEMS TO BE AN EXCEPTION.
YOU CAN SAY THAT AGAIN.
I DIDN'T THINK MIYUKI WOULD HAVE EVEN MADE IT TO THE EXAM IN HER FIRST YEAR, EITHER.
BUT THERE WAS NO WAY WE COULD PASS HER WHEN HER WORK WAS SO POOR.
Studio 7

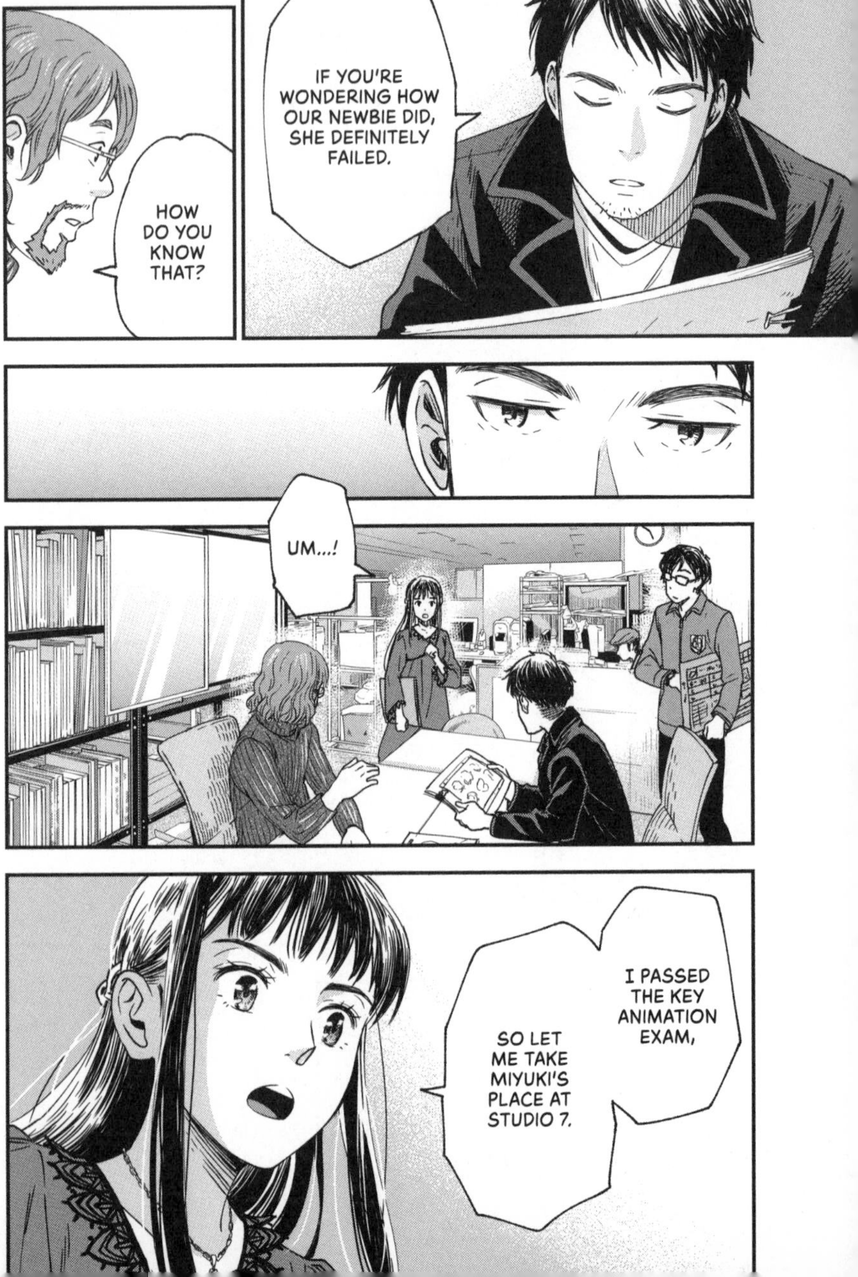
IF YOU'RE WONDERING HOW OUR NEWBIE DID, SHE DEFINITELY FAILED.
HOW DO YOU KNOW THAT?
UM...!
I PASSED THE KEY ANIMATION EXAM,
SO LET ME TAKE MIYUKI'S PLACE AT STUDIO 7.

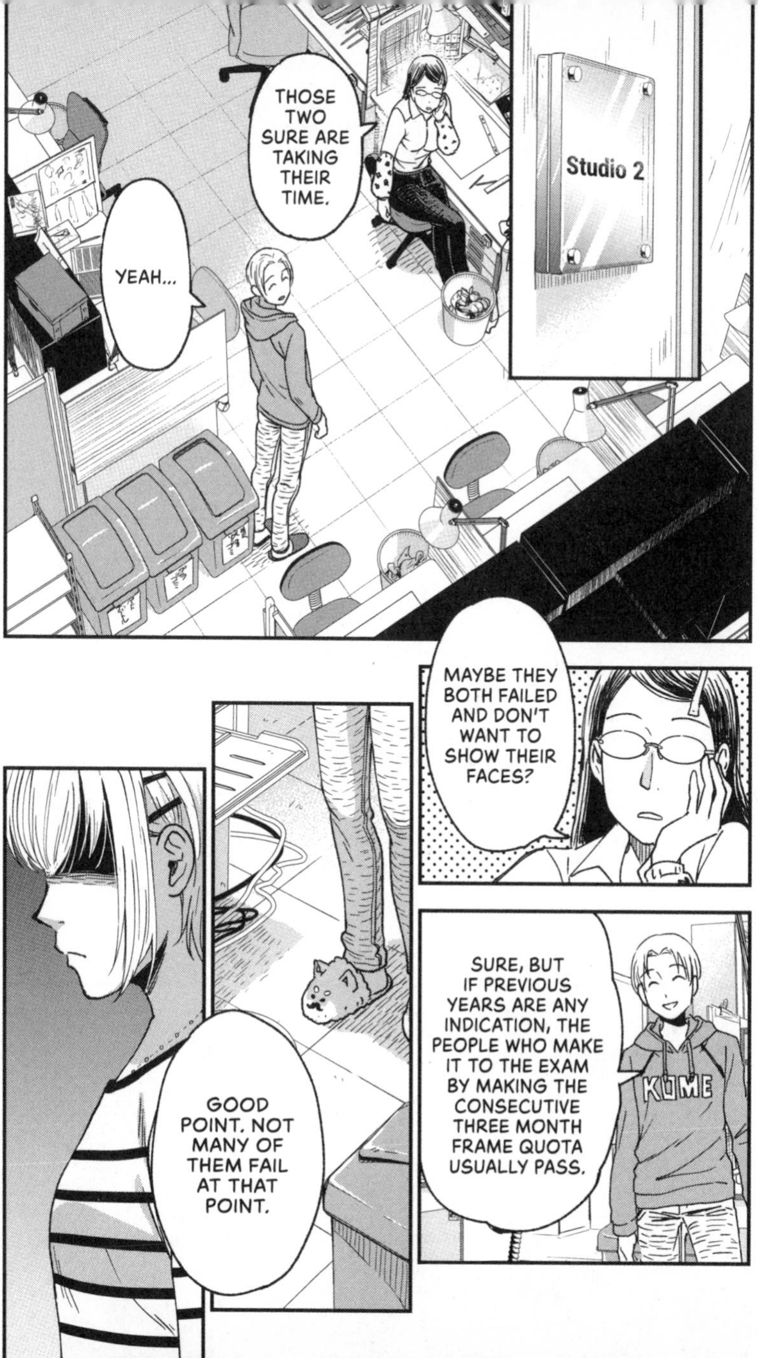
Studio 2
THOSE TWO SURE ARE TAKING THEIR TIME.
YEAH...
MAYBE THEY BOTH FAILED AND DON'T WANT TO SHOW THEIR FACES?
SURE, BUT IF PREVIOUS YEARS ARE ANY INDICATION, THE PEOPLE WHO MAKE IT TO THE EXAM BY MAKING THE CONSECUTIVE THREE MONTH FRAME QUOTA USUALLY PASS.
KOME
GOOD POINT. NOT MANY OF THEM FAIL AT THAT POINT.

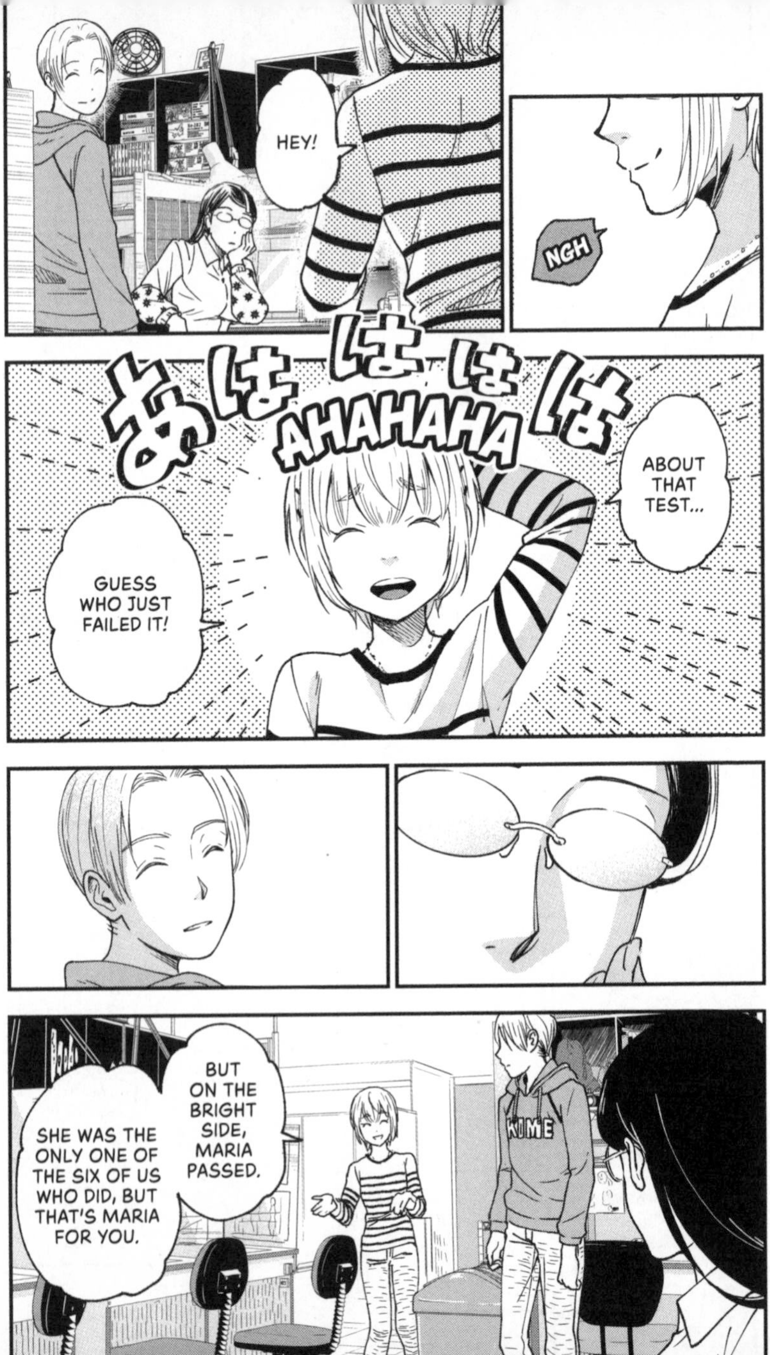

NGH
HEY!
ABOUT THAT TEST...
あははは AHAHAHA
GUESS WHO JUST FAILED IT!
KIME
BUT ON THE BRIGHT SIDE, MARIA PASSED.
SHE WAS THE ONLY ONE OF THE SIX OF US WHO DID, BUT THAT'S MARIA FOR YOU.

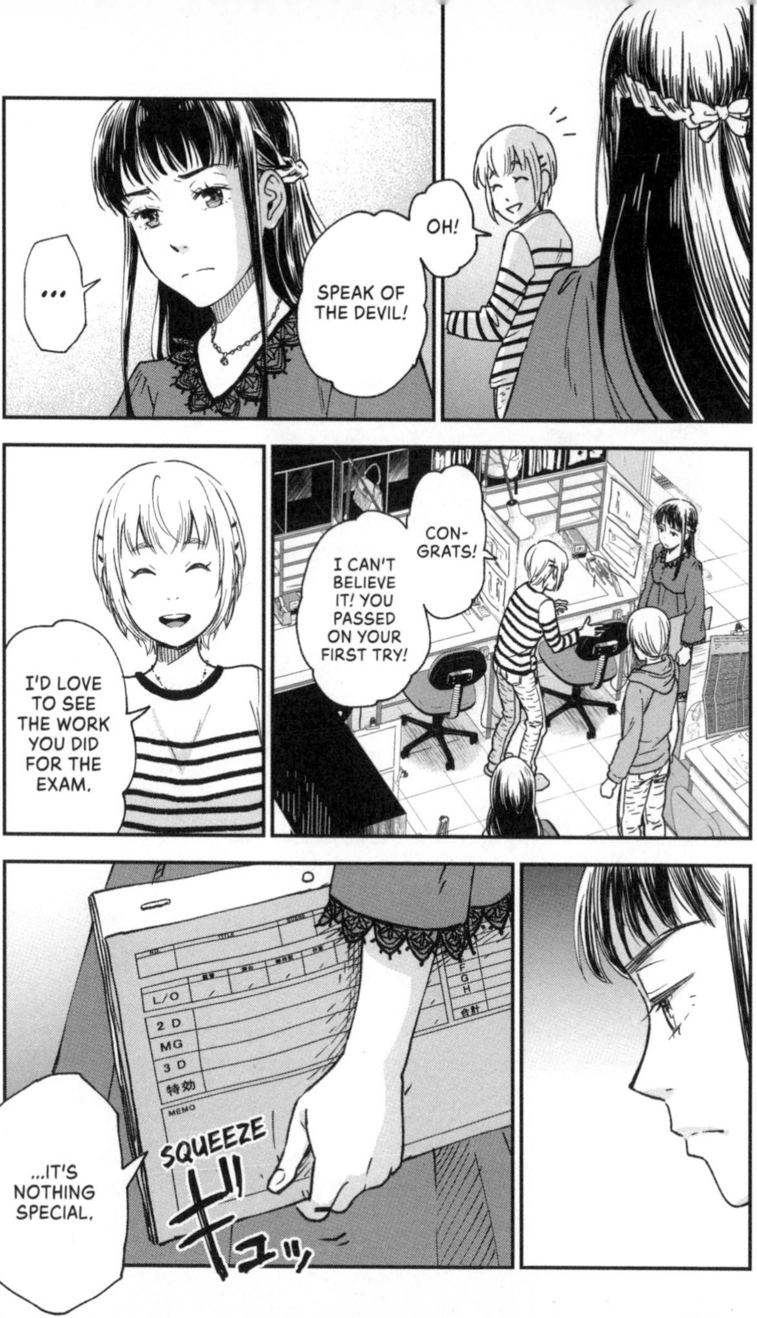
OH!
SPEAK OF THE DEVIL!
...
CON-GRATS!
I CAN'T BELIEVE IT! YOU PASSED ON YOUR FIRST TRY!
I'D LOVE TO SEE THE WORK YOU DID FOR THE EXAM.
SQUEEZE
...IT'S NOTHING SPECIAL.

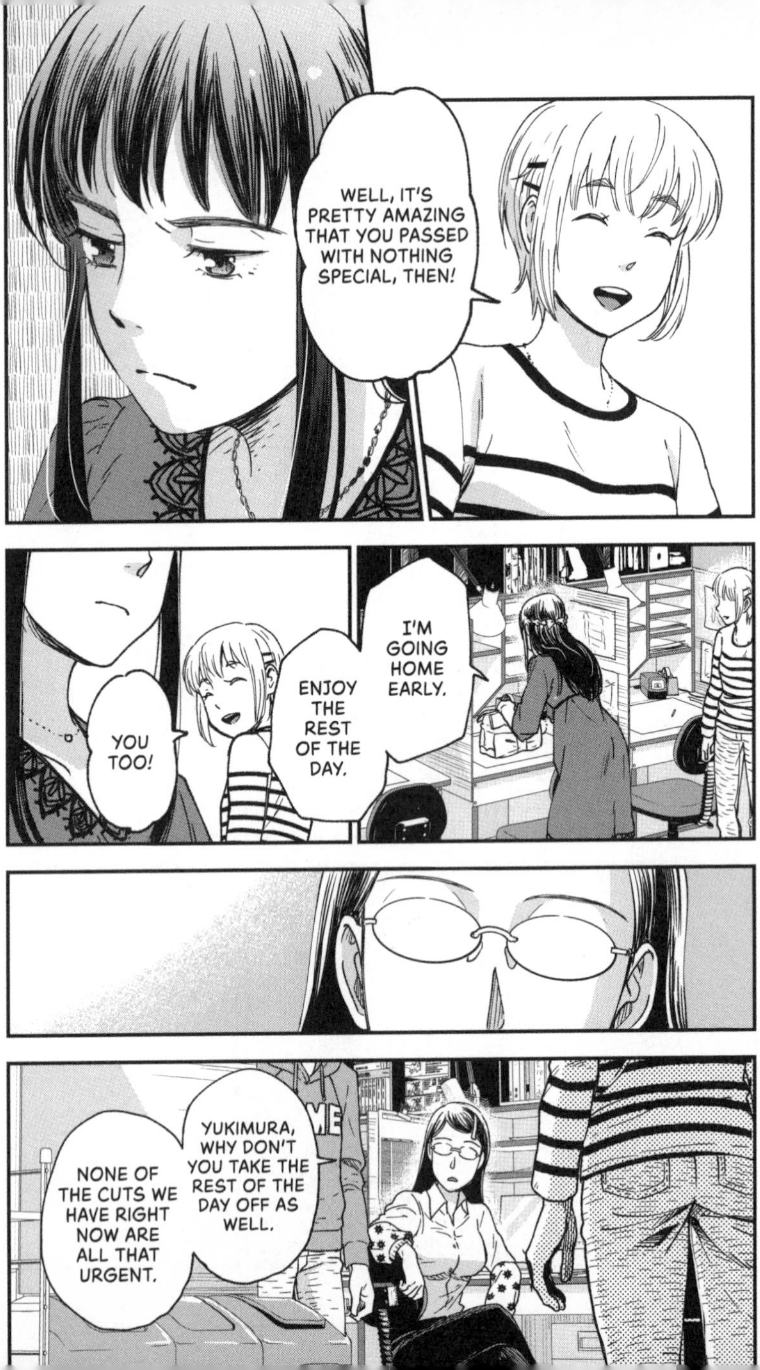
WELL, IT'S PRETTY AMAZING THAT YOU PASSED WITH NOTHING SPECIAL, THEN!
I'M GOING HOME EARLY.
ENJOY THE REST OF THE DAY.
YOU TOO!
YUKIMURA, WHY DON'T YOU TAKE THE REST OF THE DAY OFF AS WELL.
NONE OF THE CUTS WE HAVE RIGHT NOW ARE ALL THAT URGENT.

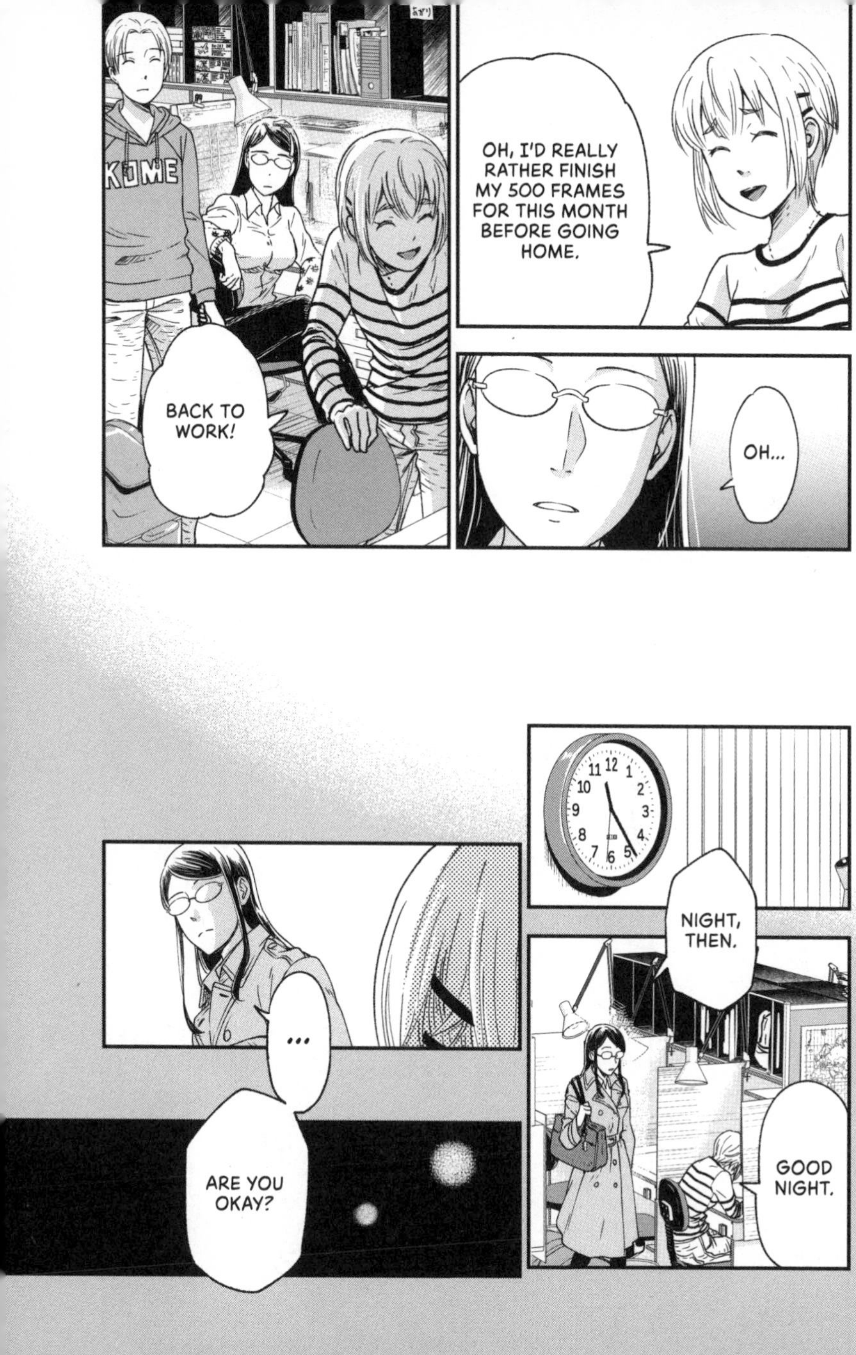
OH, I'D REALLY RATHER FINISH MY 500 FRAMES FOR THIS MONTH BEFORE GOING HOME.
OH...
BACK TO WORK!
NIGHT, THEN.
GOOD NIGHT.
...
ARE YOU OKAY?

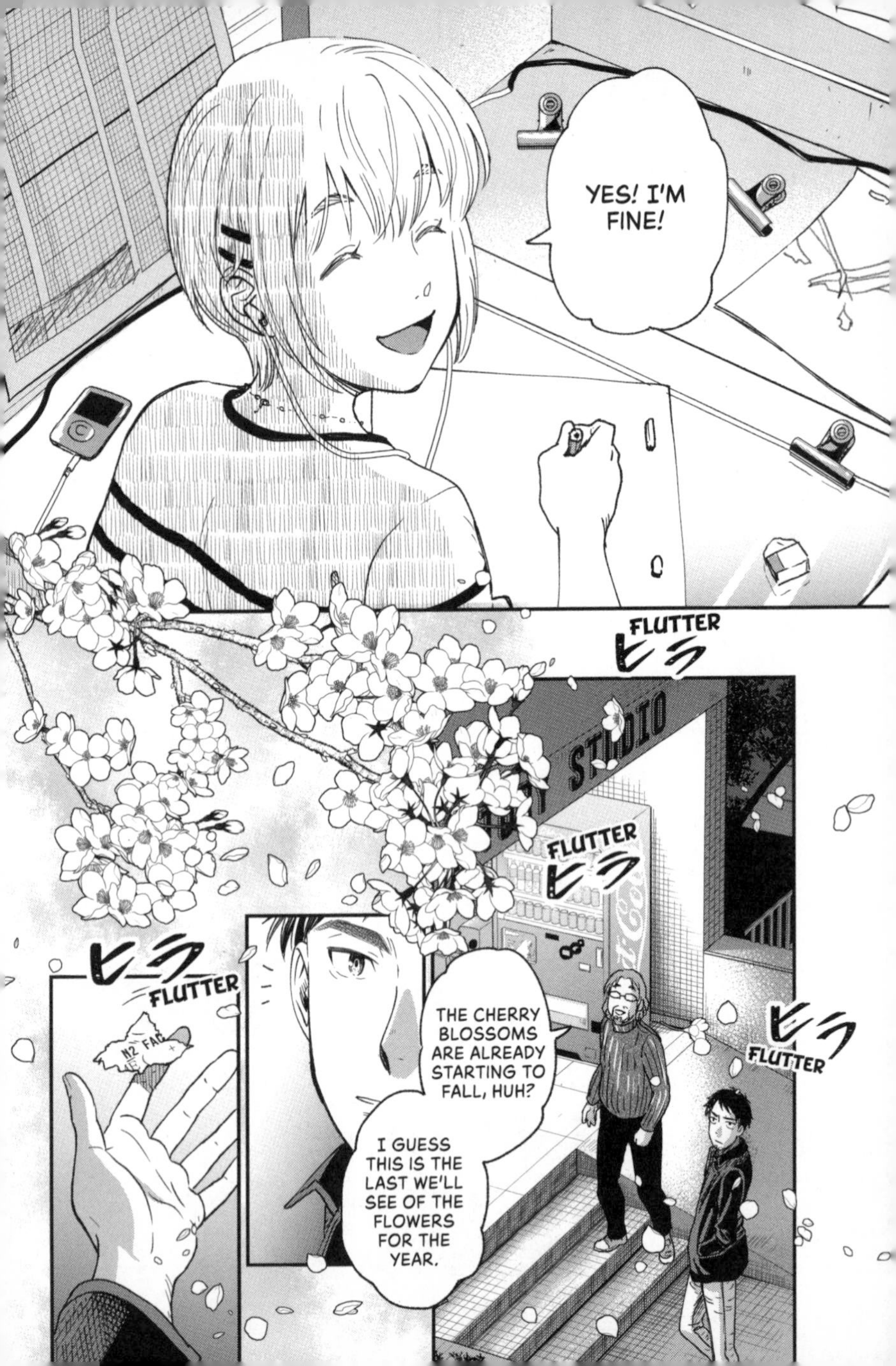
YES! I'M FINE!
ヒラ FLUTTER
ヒラ FLUTTER
ヒラ FLUTTER
THE CHERRY BLOSSOMS ARE ALREADY STARTING TO FALL, HUH?
I GUESS THIS IS THE LAST WE'LL SEE OF THE FLOWERS FOR THE YEAR.
ヒラ FLUTTER

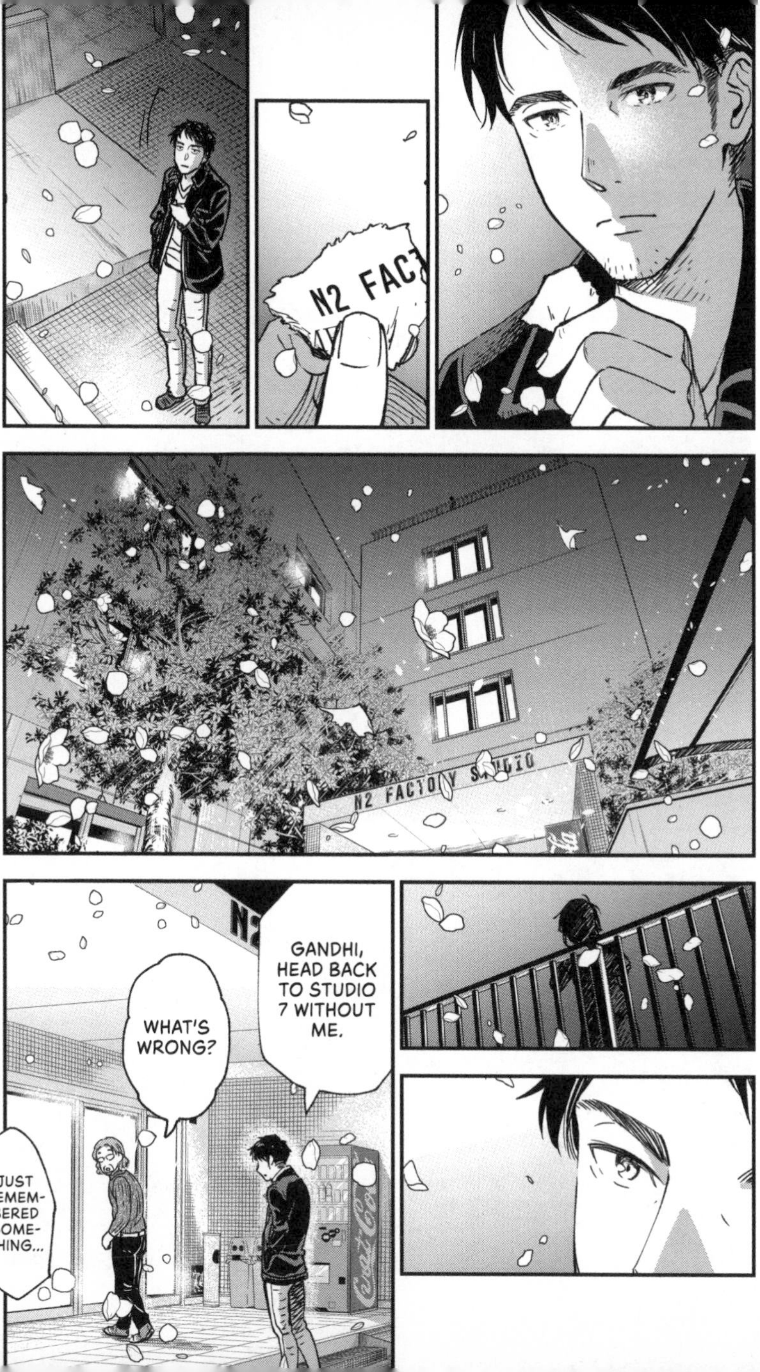
N2 FACT
GANDHI, HEAD BACK TO STUDIO 7 WITHOUT ME.
WHAT'S WRONG?
JUST REMEMBERED SOMETHING...

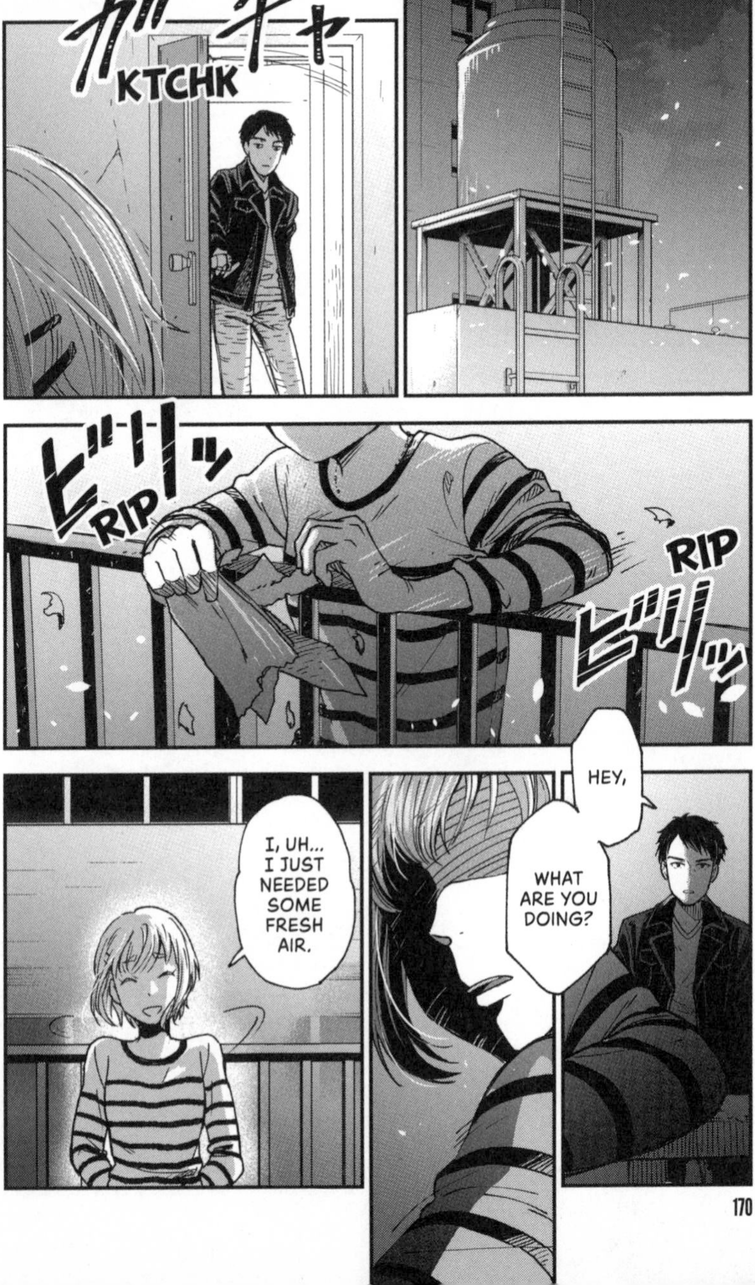
ガチャ
KTCHK
ビリッ
RIP
ビリッ
RIP
HEY,
WHAT ARE YOU DOING?
I, UH... I JUST NEEDED SOME FRESH AIR.

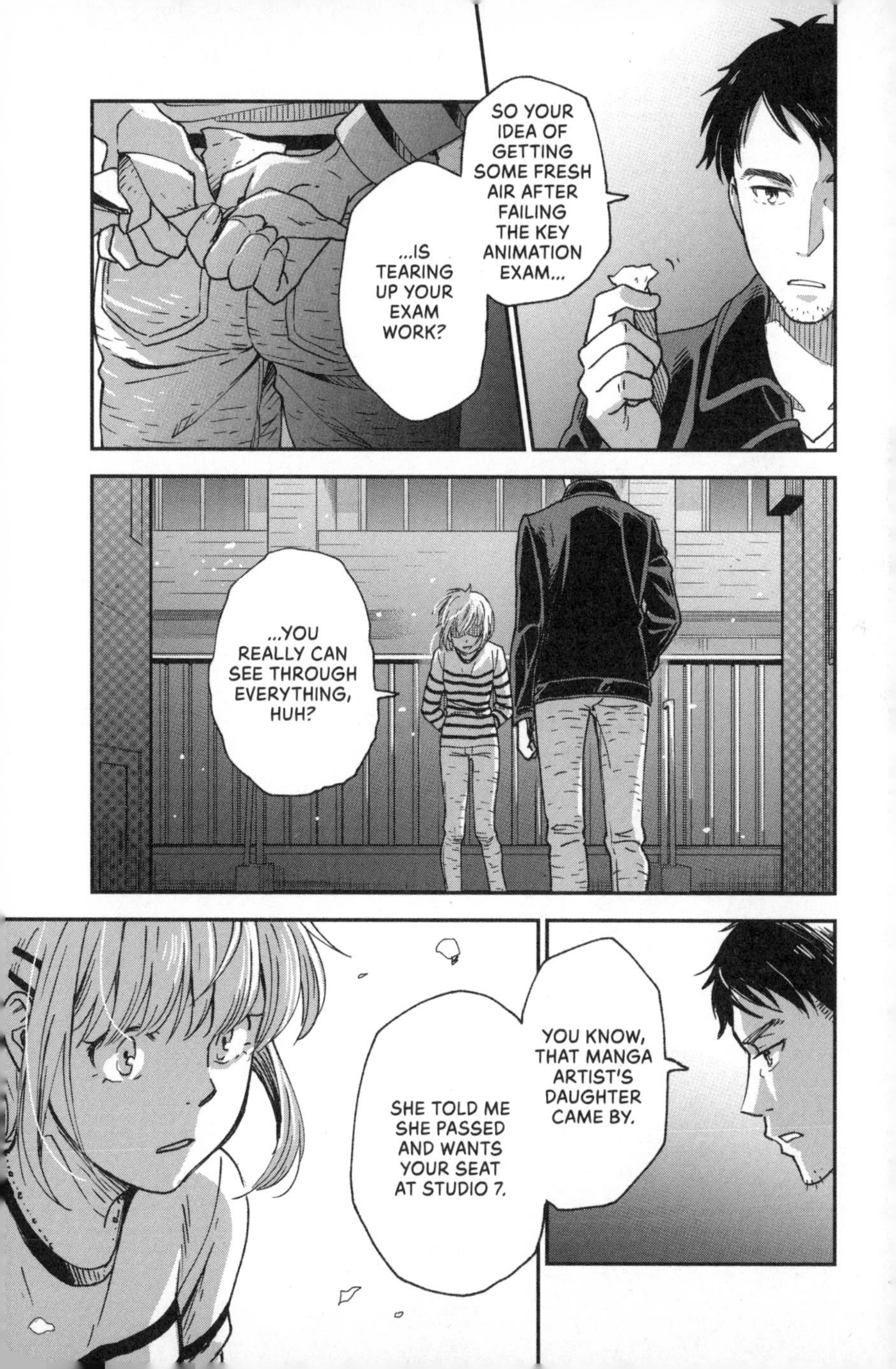
SO YOUR IDEA OF GETTING SOME FRESH AIR AFTER FAILING THE KEY ANIMATION EXAM...
...IS TEARING UP YOUR EXAM WORK?
...YOU REALLY CAN SEE THROUGH EVERYTHING, HUH?
YOU KNOW, THAT MANGA ARTIST'S DAUGHTER CAME BY.
SHE TOLD ME SHE PASSED AND WANTS YOUR SEAT AT STUDIO 7.

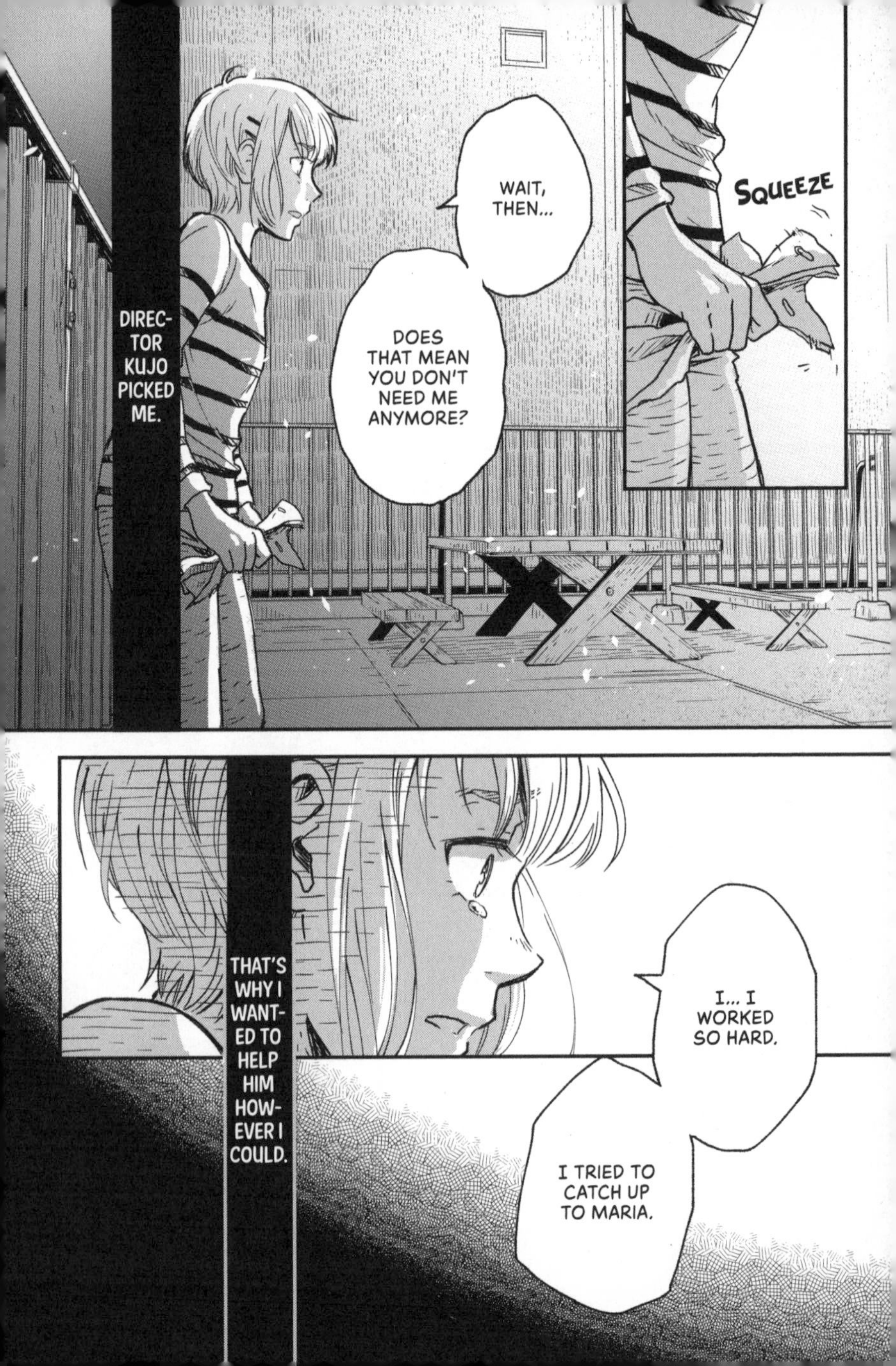
SQUEEZE
WAIT, THEN...
DOES THAT MEAN YOU DON'T NEED ME ANYMORE?
DIRECTOR KUJO PICKED ME.
I... I WORKED SO HARD.
I TRIED TO CATCH UP TO MARIA.
THAT'S WHY I WANTED TO HELP HIM HOWEVER I COULD.

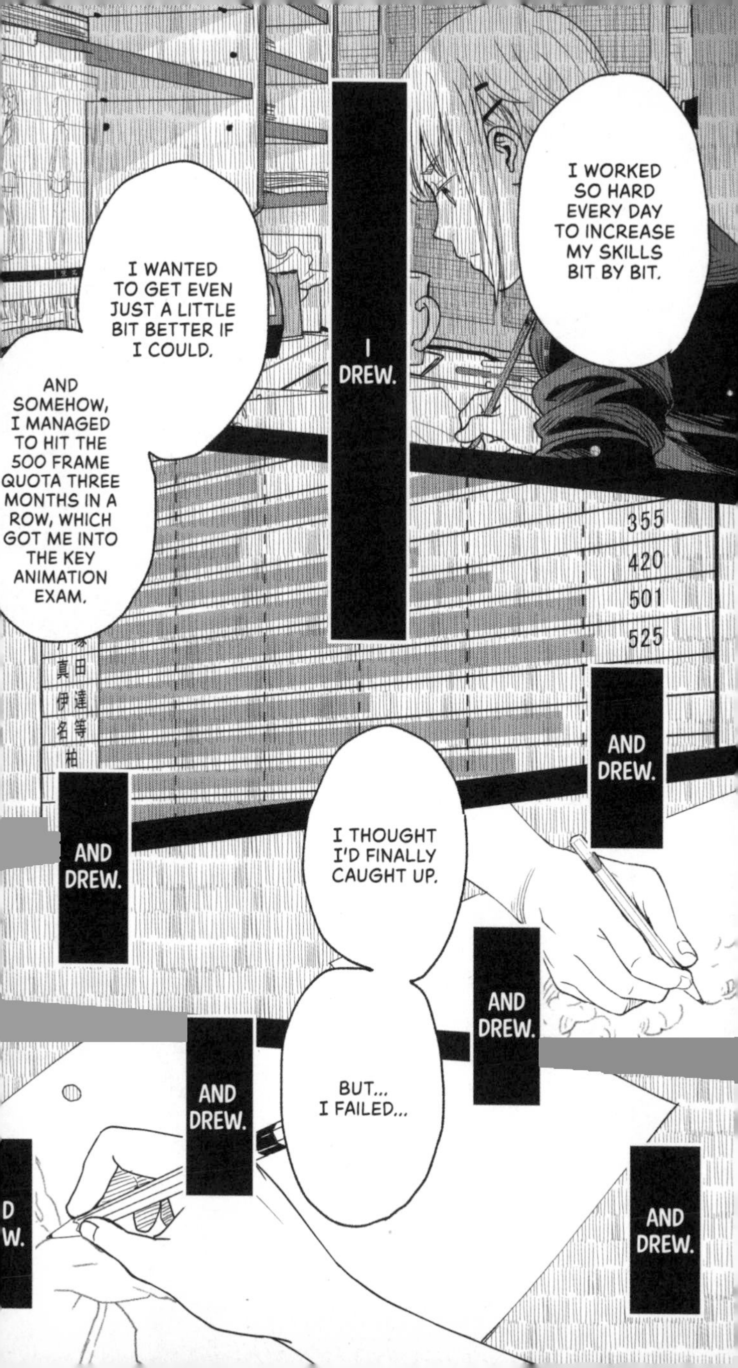
I WORKED SO HARD EVERY DAY TO INCREASE MY SKILLS BIT BY BIT.
I DREW.
I WANTED TO GET EVEN JUST A LITTLE BIT BETTER IF I COULD.
AND SOMEHOW, I MANAGED TO HIT THE 500 FRAME QUOTA THREE MONTHS IN A ROW, WHICH GOT ME INTO THE KEY ANIMATION EXAM.
355
420
501
525
真田
伊達
AND DREW.
I THOUGHT I'D FINALLY CAUGHT UP.
AND DREW.
AND DREW.
AND DREW.
BUT... I FAILED...
AND DREW.

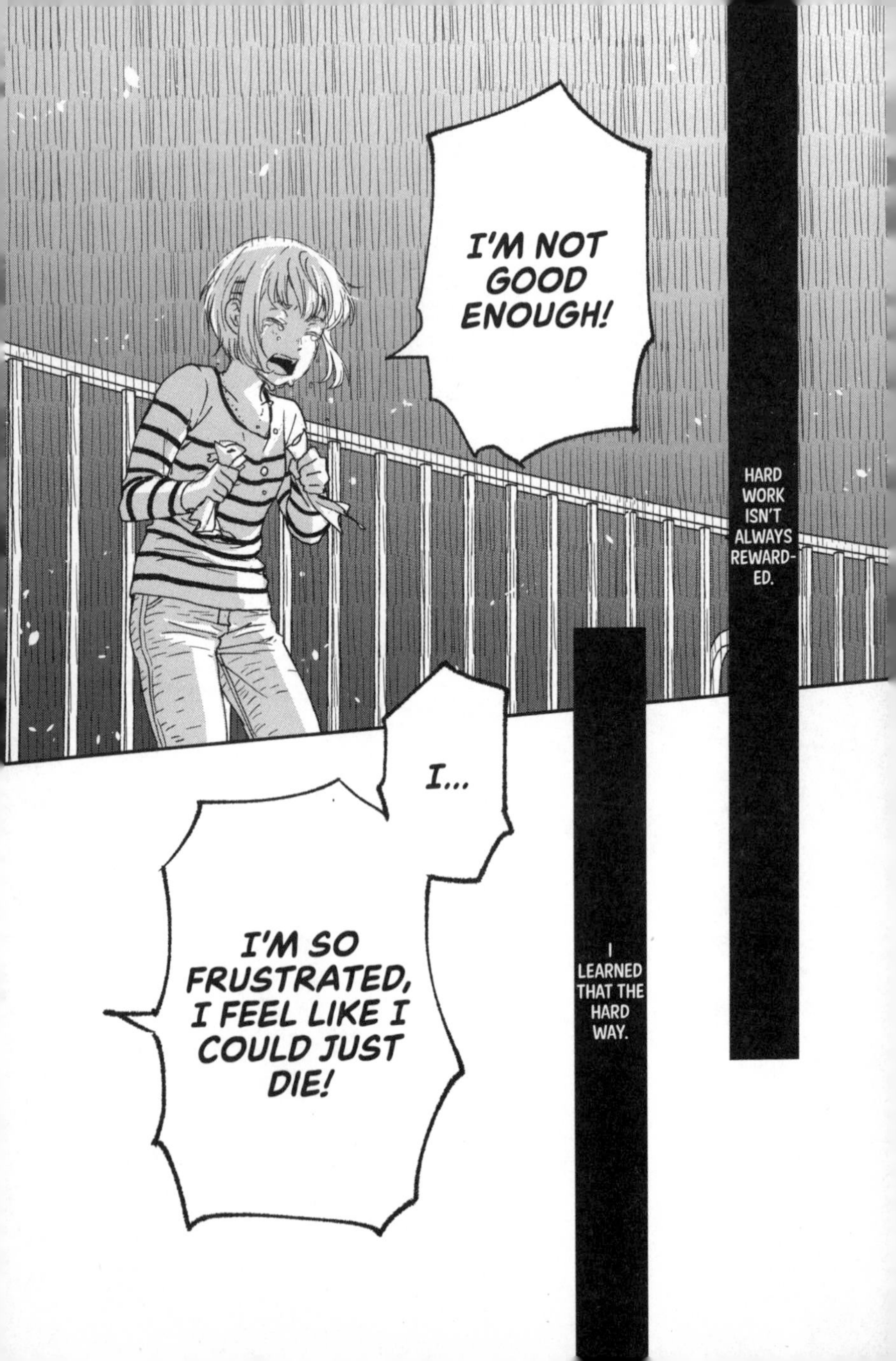
I'M NOT GOOD ENOUGH!
HARD WORK ISN'T ALWAYS REWARD-ED.
I...
I LEARNED THAT THE HARD WAY.
I'M SO FRUSTRATED, I FEEL LIKE I COULD JUST DIE!

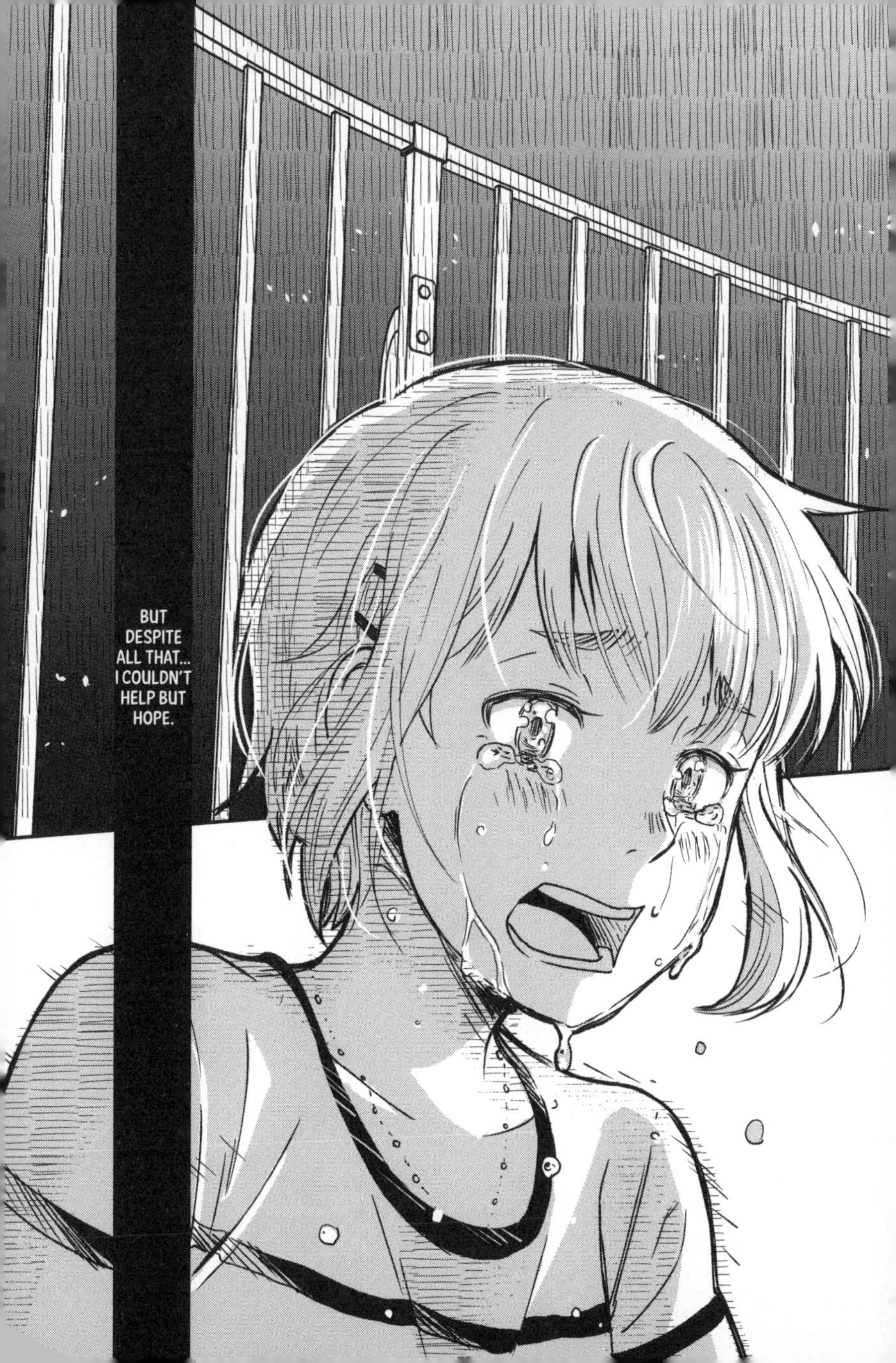
BUT DESPITE ALL THAT... I COULDN'T HELP BUT HOPE.

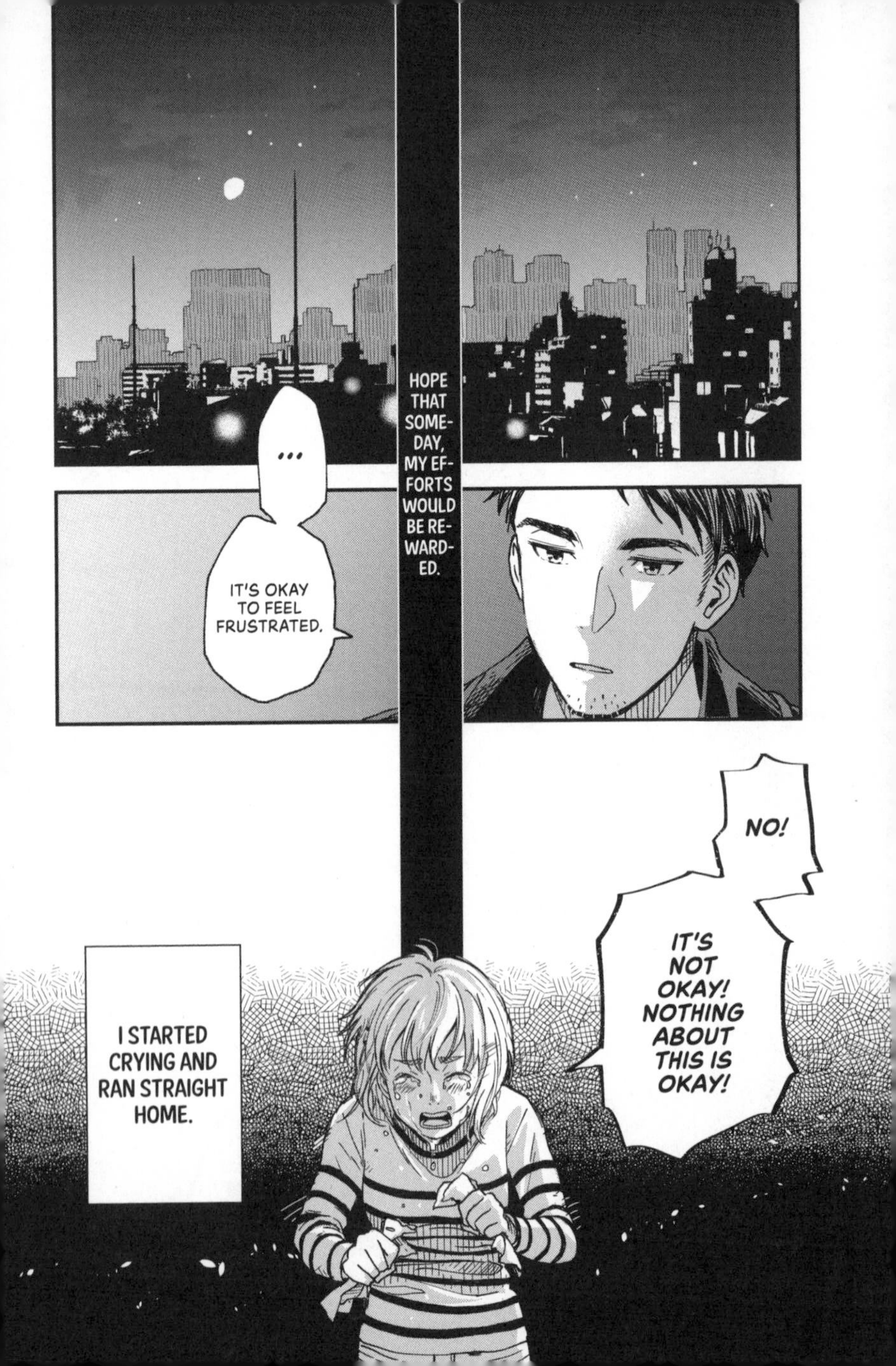
HOPE THAT SOMEDAY, MY EFFORTS WOULD BE REWARDED.
...
IT'S OKAY TO FEEL FRUSTRATED.
NO!
IT'S NOT OKAY! NOTHING ABOUT THIS IS OKAY!
I STARTED CRYING AND RAN STRAIGHT HOME.

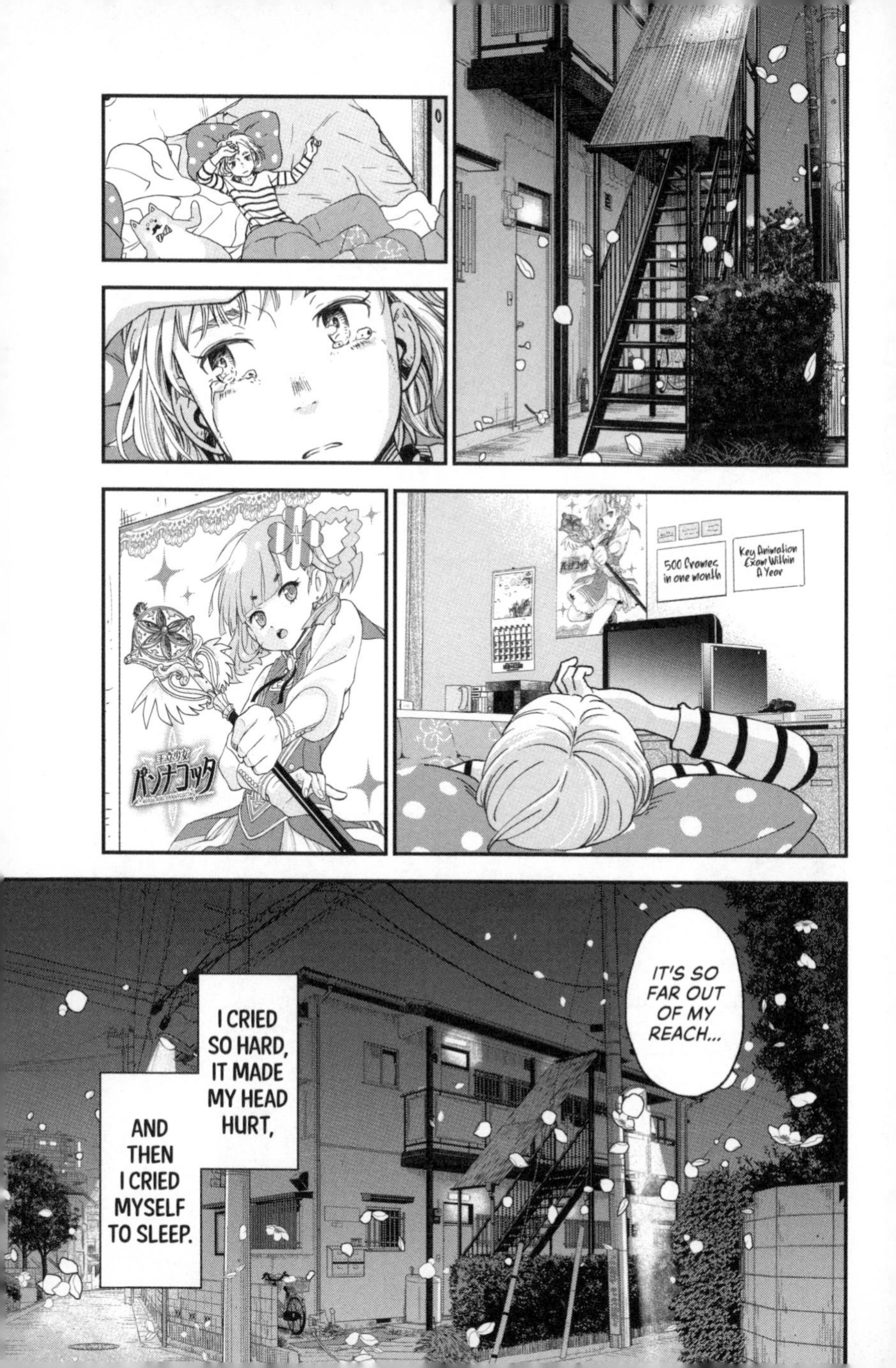
Key Animation Exam Within A Year
500 frames in one month
パンナコッタ
IT'S SO FAR OUT OF MY REACH...
I CRIED SO HARD, IT MADE MY HEAD HURT,
AND THEN I CRIED MYSELF TO SLEEP.

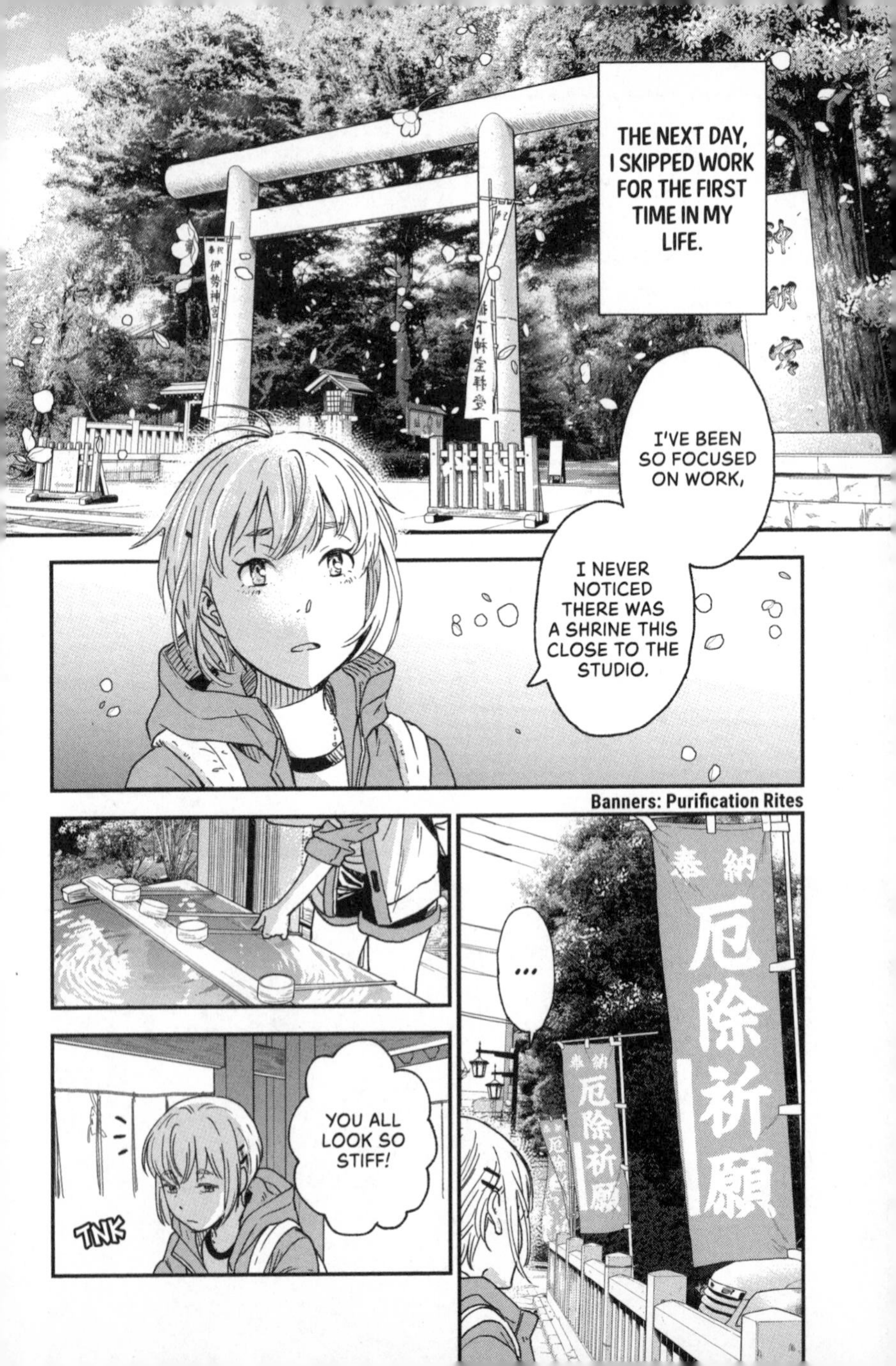
THE NEXT DAY, I SKIPPED WORK FOR THE FIRST TIME IN MY LIFE.
I'VE BEEN SO FOCUSED ON WORK,
I NEVER NOTICED THERE WAS A SHRINE THIS CLOSE TO THE STUDIO.
Banners: Purification Rites
奉納
厄除祈願
...
YOU ALL LOOK SO STIFF!
TNK

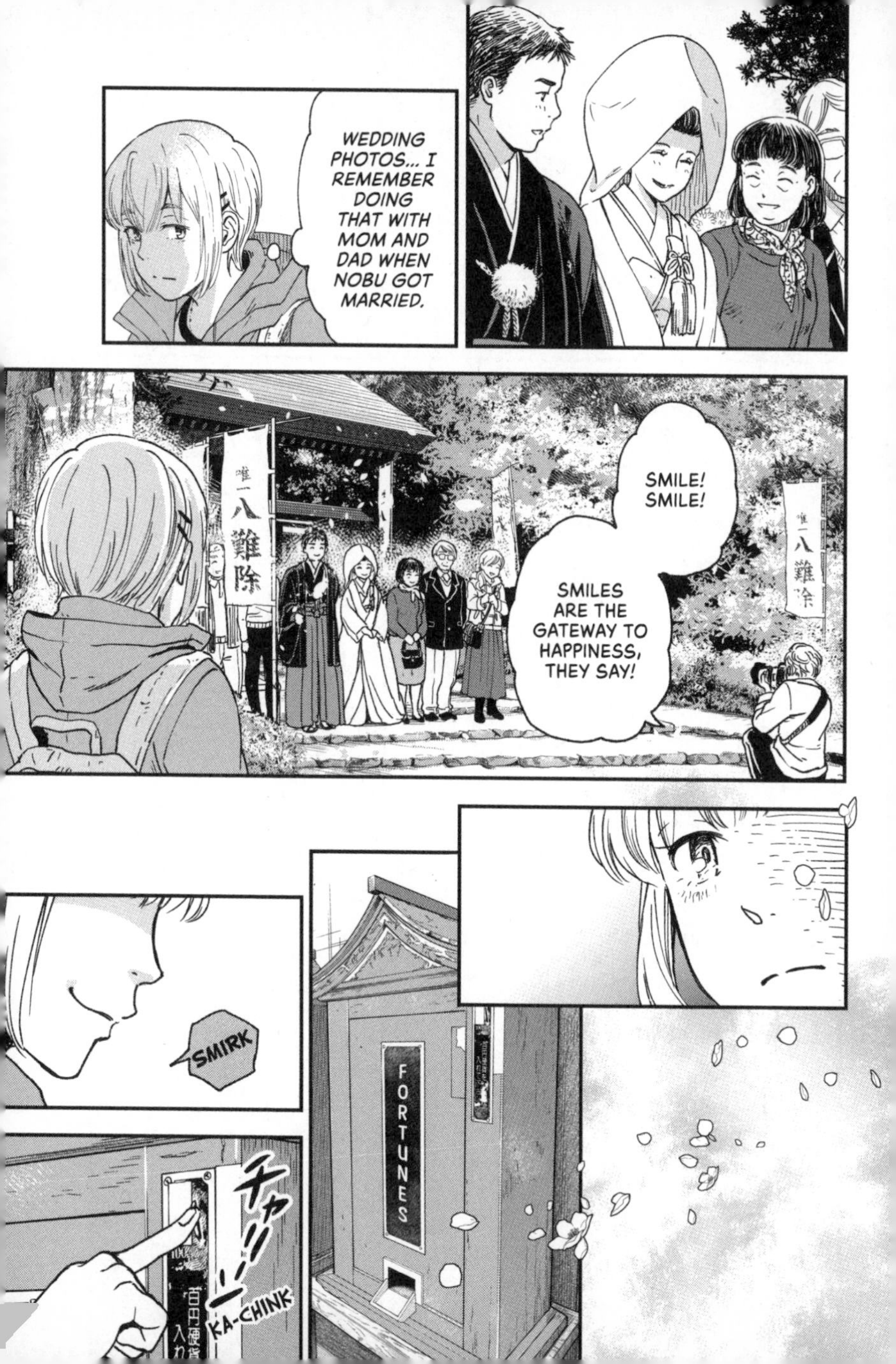
WEDDING PHOTOS... I REMEMBER DOING THAT WITH MOM AND DAD WHEN NOBU GOT MARRIED.
唯一八難除
SMILE! SMILE!
SMILES ARE THE GATEWAY TO HAPPINESS, THEY SAY!
唯一八難除
SMIRK
FORTUNES
チャリーン
KA-CHINK

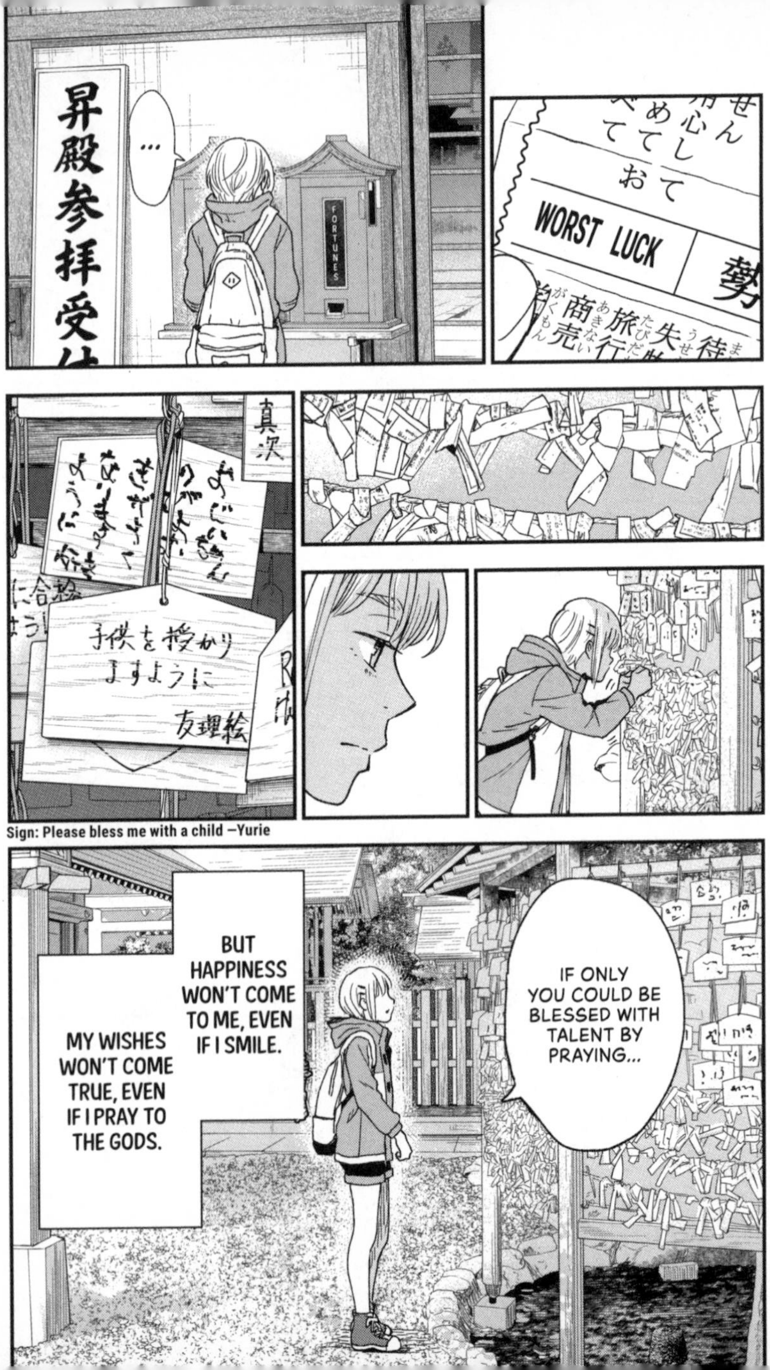
WORST LUCK
昇殿参拝受付
FORTUNES
...
子供を授かりますように
友理絵
IF ONLY YOU COULD BE BLESSED WITH TALENT BY PRAYING...
MY WISHES WON'T COME TRUE, EVEN IF I PRAY TO THE GODS.
BUT HAPPINESS WON'T COME TO ME, EVEN IF I SMILE.
Sign: Please bless me with a child —Yurie

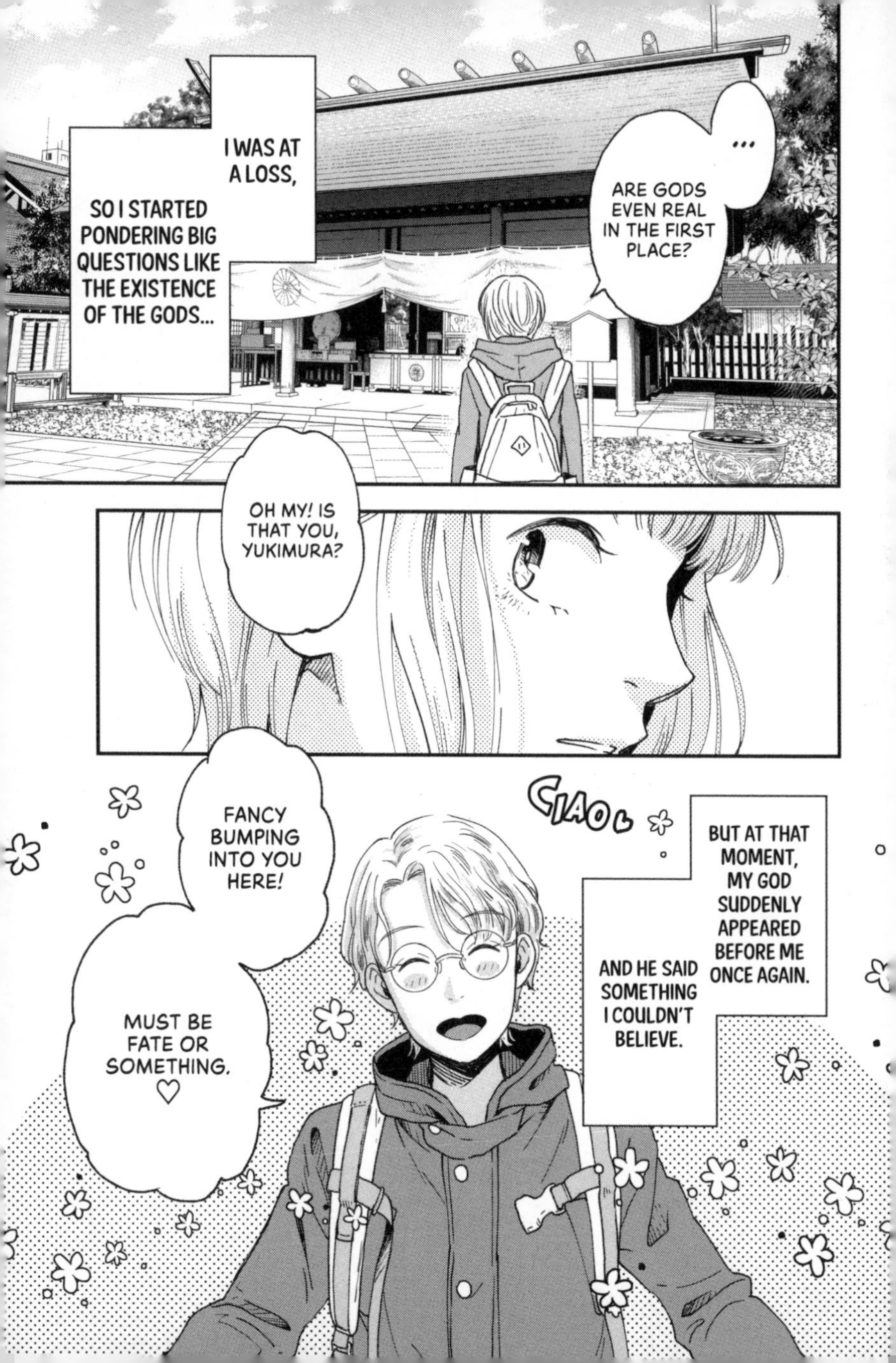
I WAS AT A LOSS,
SO I STARTED PONDERING BIG QUESTIONS LIKE THE EXISTENCE OF THE GODS...
...
ARE GODS EVEN REAL IN THE FIRST PLACE?
OH MY! IS THAT YOU, YUKIMURA?
FANCY BUMPING INTO YOU HERE!
MUST BE FATE OR SOMETHING. ♡
CIAO
BUT AT THAT MOMENT, MY GOD SUDDENLY APPEARED BEFORE ME ONCE AGAIN.
AND HE SAID SOMETHING I COULDN'T BELIEVE.

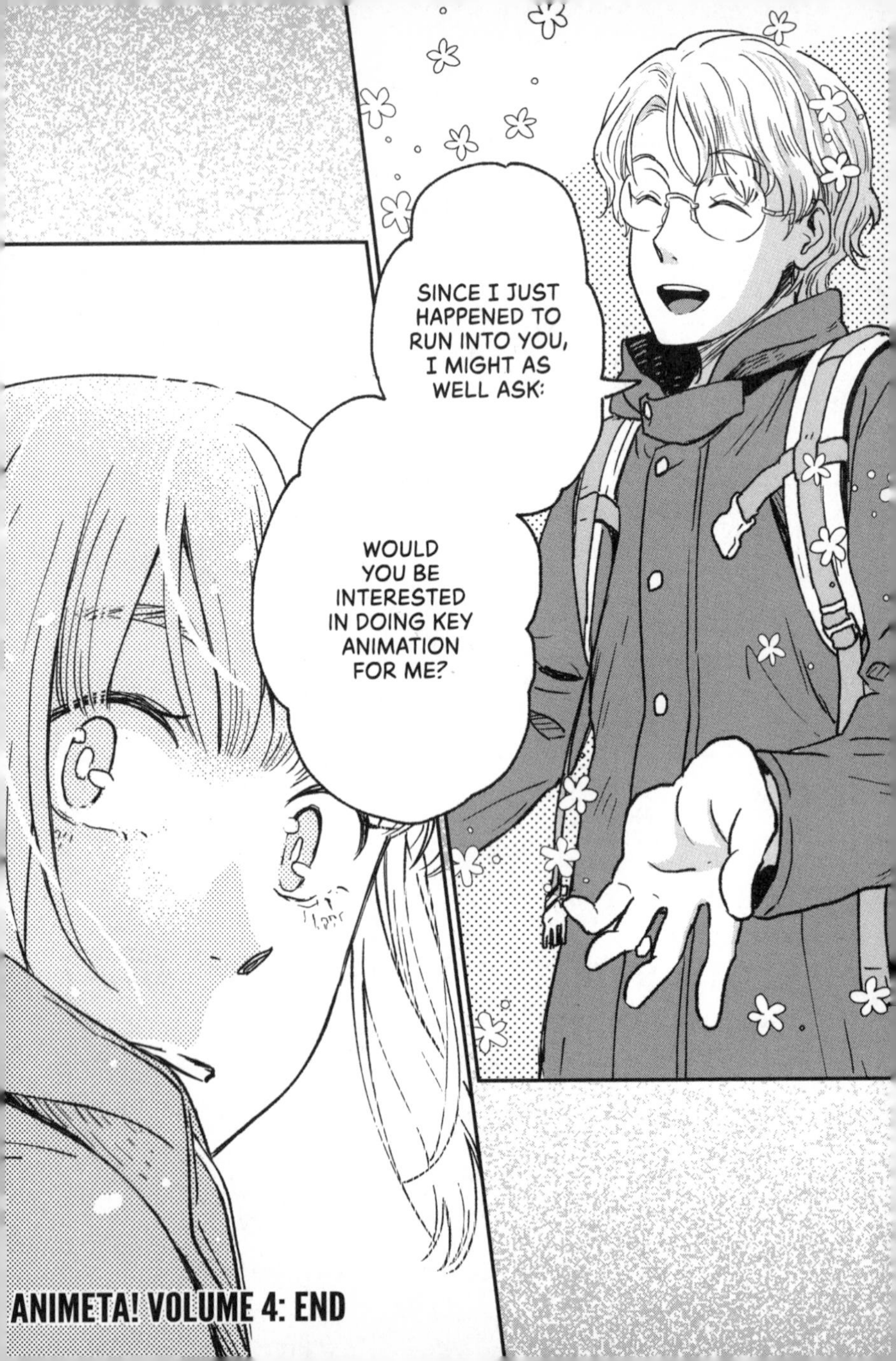
SINCE I JUST HAPPENED TO RUN INTO YOU, I MIGHT AS WELL ASK:
WOULD YOU BE INTERESTED IN DOING KEY ANIMATION FOR ME?

ANIMETA! VOLUME 4: END

A Special Bonus Chat with Animation Director Kenji Kamiyama and Yaso Hanamura

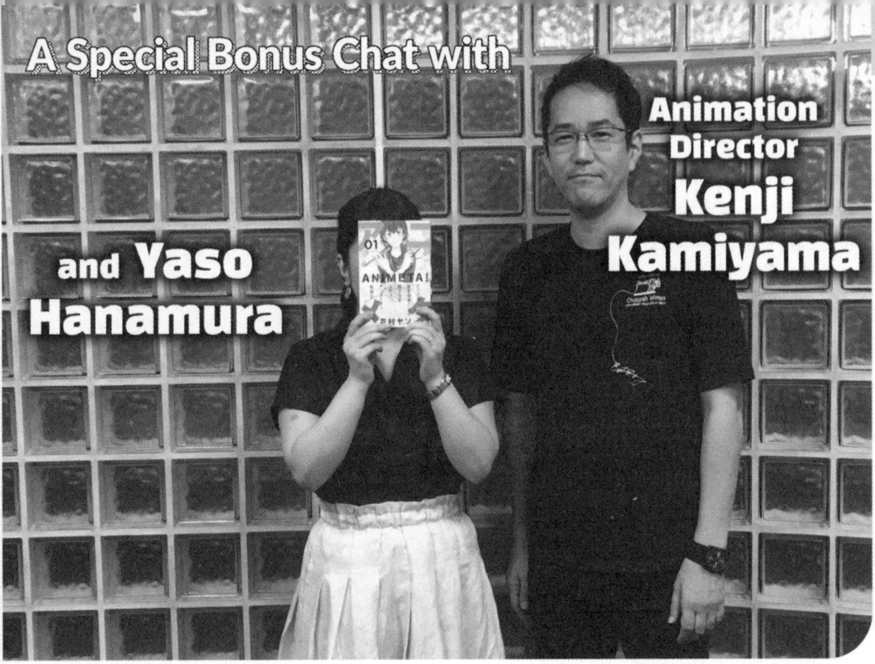

Yaso Hanamura, who used her experiences as an animator to create her currently running series ***Animeta!***, and Kenji Kamiyama, who was Hanamura's boss when she was working as an animator at Production I.G., sit down for a chat about the current conditions in the industry and to reminisce about old times to celebrate the release of volume 4.

HANAMURA: When volume one was about to go on sale, I asked him for a comment for the obi, and he snapped back at me saying it was too soon for that! Then he made a promise that if I made it to volume four, he'd sit down for a little chat like this. That got me motivated to give it a shot and, well, now we're here thanks to that, I guess...

KAMIYAMA: You finally made it to volume four... (laughs)

HANAMURA: I had to take a lot of breaks, so it took a while in the end. This was my first time drawing manga, too. I finally understand what a hard job it is...

KAMIYAMA: Anime is a group effort where the job is typically to polish existing source material, so it's quite different.

HANAMURA: I always think back to that awful face you used to make when you were drawing storyboards. I feel like I kind of get it now. Now I get how hard that is! I mean, storyboarding is pretty much a solo effort for you, isn't it? Like it was during *GitS: S.A.C.*[1] at least.

KAMIYAMA: I think it might have been at the time.

HANAMURA: I always thought it looked like really hard work, but now that I'm in a position where I have to create a story completely from scratch, I understand that it's even tougher than I imagined. It made me wonder how much pressure was on you back in the day. With manga, it's all on me, but you have tons of people depending on you in anime production. What's that like?

KAMIYAMA: I didn't feel much pressure, really, but I do think the difficulty of the job is slightly different from making manga, since you can't just make the thing on your own terms and have to consider the other people you're working with. That said, while it wasn't original work exactly, I spent significantly more time correcting other people's drawings.

HANAMURA: I was working at Studio 9 on *GitS: S.A.C.* while Mamoru Oshii's *Innocence*[2] was in production and we kept losing staff to *Innocence.*

KAMIYAMA: We were definitely short staffed when you were here. People would always say that the quality of the little staff we did have was garbage, but I think they were much better than people we've been getting lately.

HANAMURA: So you think so too, huh? You hear this a lot, but it really does feel like the industry is failing these days...

<u>THE GOOD OLD DAYS OF STUDIO 9</u>

KAMIYAMA: You started out in the *Jin-Roh* room, didn't you?

HANAMURA: I did. Studio 3 made *Jin-Roh*[3] and even after production wrapped, people kept calling it the "*Jin-Roh* room". It was a studio with a strange power balance where all the key animators were incredible and all the inbetweeners were mediocre.

KAMIYAMA: We'd lost our inbetweeners who could draw movie-quality tweens, so we'd actually hired quite a few before you joined. But when you only have freelance animators at a studio, it makes it difficult for the inbetweeners to learn anything, so that's why we brought in genius inbetween checker, Ms. Mita.

HANAMURA: She was my mentor, and I modeled *Animeta!*'s Fuji after her.

KAMIYAMA: She was an extraordinarily good teacher.

HANAMURA: Even though she was super scary. (laughs) I remember back then she'd order me to draw all the way out to 1cm outside the frame, and I figured it'd be fine as long as I went out a little bit, but when I stopped at 5mm, an eraser came flying at my head and I'd hear her shout "you're 5mm short!". (laughs) Fuji is way nicer than she was. I saw her throw cut envelopes at other inbetween checkers and call their work garbage too... She really was strict when it came to inbetweening.

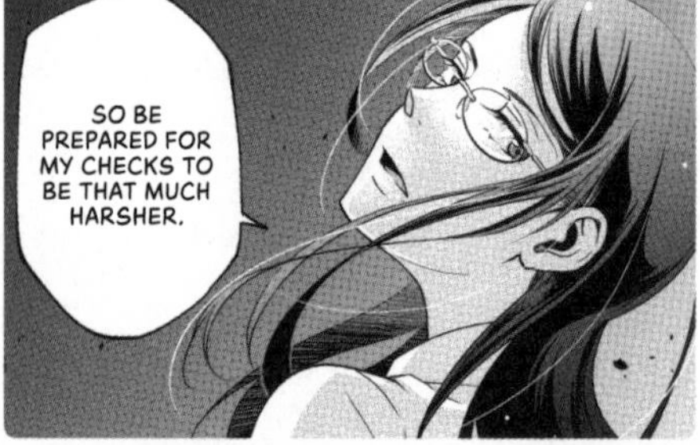
SO BE PREPARED FOR MY CHECKS TO BE THAT MUCH HARSHER.

The terror my real mentor inspired can't even compare.

KAMIYAMA: Well, the core quality of a production rests on the inbetween checker's shoulders. No matter how incredible the keyframes might be, if the inbetweens turn them into wiggly mush, it's all over. So in that respect, it worked out because I.G. has top-notch inbetween checkers. It's much harder to do when inbetweening is outsourced, but when the inbetweeners are in-house, the checker can be uncompromising and keep demanding work be redone until it's fully up to standard. Of course, this led to people saying things like it's impossible to make a living as an inbetweener at I.G....

HANAMURA: I was so poor back then. I might actually be worse off now, though... I wish there was just a little something more, like some kind of assistance for the first two years at least or something.

THE QUALITY OF A PRODUCTION RESTS ON THE INBWETWEEN CHECKER'S SHOULDERS

KAMIYAMA: Conversations about the industry are quick to turn to how poor the pay and working conditions are, but young actors just starting out have it pretty tough too.

HANAMURA: Manga's not much better either, unfortunately. (laughs) Maybe this is what happens when you try to make a living off any sort of artistic talent...

KAMIYAMA: We have studios in the anime industry, so the idea of exploiting workers' passion often comes up, but if you really take a close look at how people in the industry actually work, they tend to function more like independent contractors. And if you look at manga artists and actors and the like, their success in their field typically translates into personal success, but that's absolutely not the case when it comes to anime. I guess since what you're drawing is largely determined from the start with anime, you're not creating as much as manga artists or actors do, so maybe it's just inevitable. You can blame it on the anime industry being fundamentally exploitative, but there is no singular evil mastermind behind it all or anything.

HANAMURA: People like to blame the sponsors, but you can always turn it around and point to how low the production costs are to begin with...

KAMIYAMA: A big part of that is this unwillingness to deviate from the way things were done in the past—"you used to be able to do it for this much!" or "you used to be able to produce that quality for this price!" they say. And honestly, it's a really hard attitude to change.

HANAMURA: Plus, the sheer number of series being produced now is a problem in and of itself.

KAMIYAMA: Studios started taking on more work because they couldn't survive, but even if the number of series in production was reduced, it's unlikely that it would mean a proportional increase in money invested in the remaining productions. I don't know if we'll ever be able to go back.

HANAMURA: That's part of why there's a shortage of animators, huh?

KAMIYAMA: Supposedly, there are about 3,000 working animators in Japan. There must be more manga artists than that.

HANAMURA: There are web manga now, but even if you only go by the titles on store shelves, I think there definitely must be more.

KAMIYAMA: Sounds like you made the right choice becoming a manga artist, then. (laughs)

HANAMURA: Go me! (laughs)

AS DARK AS THE ANIME INDUSTRY MIGHT BE, THERE IS NO EVIL MASTERMIND

HANAMURA: When I was a key animator, you actually told me that I was more suited to drawing manga. I thought you said it because I sucked at key animation. (laughs) But I was earning a little extra money from one-off illustrations[4], and I was getting a lot more praise for that work, so I started to think I might just not be very good at drawing moving pictures.

KAMIYAMA: Not to mention the fact that it always took you longer to accept things than other people. Anime's a pretty brutal and unfair industry, after all, so I always thought you'd burn out from getting hung up on small things. (laughs)

HANAMURA: Well, I've always had a stubborn personality.

KAMIYAMA: And that's why I thought you were better suited to something independent like manga.

HANAMURA: Yeah, now everything's my responsibility.

KAMIYAMA: There's a sort of unfair quality to anime where it's a creative job, but you're not really expressing your own point of view. Of course, figuring out how to navigate that is also part of what makes anime interesting. But, as I said, this is why I thought you were probably better suited to making manga. That's not to say you're an entirely uncooperative person or anything, though.

HANAMURA: I got along with everyone, thank you very much! (laughs) Though, when I first started at Studio 3, the production runner in charge of collecting inbetweens didn't think very highly of the job, and that pissed me off. I'd just about gotten the job of inbetweener down when Studio 9 was formed to produce *GitS: S.A.C.* And thankfully, I was asked to join the studio because an inbetweener would be useful. Back then, switching sub-studios was pretty much unheard of. It was something of an unspoken rule that once you were in, you'd stick with that studio until the end. So in a way, I felt like an exception within an exception. The thing about Studio 9 was that it was filled with freelancers who were all in high-level main credit roles like series/film directors, unit directors, and animation directors. There were no regular old key animators, but there was me, a lone inbetweener. I felt rather out of place. (laughs)

KAMIYAMA: Well, we were still glad to have you. You may not have been an inbetween checker, but when we were short on time, you always fixed things on short notice.

HANAMURA: We had a lot of situations where things were so down to the wire that every second mattered, huh? Not to mention that as an inbetweener, even if I was only being asked to correct a single frame of someone else's work, I would get paid, so financially it was good for me. I'd get the ridiculously difficult sequences to work on so they wouldn't have to be outsourced, but I'd also get priority on the easiest ones to help keep my wages up. Normally, inbetweeners don't get to choose what they work on, so I was really lucky to be in Studio 9. You don't often get the chance to participate in a sub-studio's founding, either.

KAMIYAMA: A freshly founded studio has a really unique energy to it, doesn't it?

HANAMURA: Everyone was so young. You were around 37 at the time, about the same age as I am now. I finally understand how incredible of an accomplishment it was to be making what you were at that age. There's no way I could ever do something like that.

KAMIYAMA: Well, I was working twenty-four hour days at times back then, too. (laughs)

HANAMURA: I always wondered when you slept. It was scary that you were just skin and bones even when you went out drinking late at night. But you didn't drink, so you'd always get pineapple juice. (laughs)

MAYBE YOU'RE BETTER SUITED TO MANGA THAN ANIME?

HANAMURA: Do you remember going to the hot springs with everyone?

KAMIYAMA: Yeah. We were so busy, but we did have some free time. It feels like you have a lot more free time when you're young.

HANAMURA: I think it's just because when you're working that hard, you have a hard time getting to sleep. (laughs) I could never manage it now. I wish I could sleep twelve hours a night, and if I don't get at least eight, I can't draw.

KAMIYAMA: I had this sudden desire to eat soba, so I decided to go to the Shuzenji hot springs, but I didn't want to go alone, so I gathered a bunch of people from the studio...

HANAMURA: I still have pictures from that trip. (laughs) The leather jacket Batou wears in the first season of *GitS: S.A.C.* was based on the one you wore.

KAMIYAMA: What an honor... Man, I really was thin back then.

HANAMURA: You were a twig! And you look like you're fun to be around in this one, but back at the studio, you always had this look in your eyes like you were ready to kill someone. (laughs)

KAMIYAMA: You were so young!

HANAMURA: Of course I was! I mean, I was what, 23 back then? Man, that was over ten years ago...

KAMIYAMA: You look like the kinda person who's fresh out of the boonies, though.

HANAMURA: Rude! But you're not wrong. I really didn't have any fashion sense. I mean, I went straight into animation instead of going to college and I was a total loser nerd to boot. Though, I don't think any animators back then came to work looking particularly put together.

KAMIYAMA: Was everyone this thin? You really must not have been eating much. (laughs)

HANAMURA: I was the only really young person in Studio 9, so everyone else would treat me to meals, which was a real problem. At one point, I decided to go on a diet and was only eating plain tofu. You happened to see me doing it and concluded that I must've been just that broke and were so concerned, you dragged me out for some barbecue. I went out drinking with everyone plenty of times too, and even though it was hard because of the financial end of things, it was so much fun!

A rare shot from February 2003.

BOTH ANIME AND MANGA ARE A SORT OF PRIMARY INDUSTRY

HANAMURA: So, while I felt like my time in the industry was tough, I ultimately had fun and learned a lot... But honestly, it feels like that's not a very common experience anymore.

KAMIYAMA: Yeah, it does kind of feel like we're teetering on the edge of the anime industry collapsing.

HANAMURA: I feel like you see people talking about how we need to train inbetweeners every once in a while these days, though.

KAMIYAMA: I think that'd be pretty difficult, considering we've basically stopped doing that. Not to mention, there isn't really anyone to train in the first place... Apparently, there's a similar issue facing the automotive industry right now. Enrollment in technical schools for mechanics is at near zero, and there are concerns about a critical shortage of trained mechanics in the coming years. That's another advantage manga has, because it's an individual effort.

HANAMURA: Once I started working on *Animeta!*, I felt like I couldn't possibly handle any more work, and then you told me that I should be planning at least two other projects at the same time. And I was just like, "like hell I should!". (laughs) I think we just have a fundamental difference in work capacity, if you can manage to plan other projects while working on an original one of your own.

KAMIYAMA: Well, it's not like I have to do it all myself.

HANAMURA: I think memory's a big factor, honestly. Like being able to remember people's faces after you've only met them once. I think that's a helpful talent. Most of the artists I know who I've asked have good memories, so I'm pretty confident there's a correlation there. And you always had such a memory for details in movies when we'd talk about them. Like, did you remember all that after just one viewing?

KAMIYAMA: I didn't exactly have the time to watch things more than once back then.

HANAMURA: You would always explain scenes and plots from movies to me in great detail, but it was always really interesting. I'd inevitably go to see one of the films you'd mentioned because they sounded fascinating, but more than a few times I ended up feeling like your explanations were more interesting than the actual film. I guess that just goes to show how good you are at setting a scene. You'd be like, "Well, if I'd written Armageddon, it'd be more like Ar-ME-geddon". (laughs) Have you ever thought about directing a Hollywood movie?

KAMIYAMA: I don't think I ever considered making anything but anime. I get the sense that a lot of people from my generation didn't really give much thought to going international. I guess part of it was that the Japanese market was just that strong back then. That's not so much the case now, though. It feels like there's this looming sense of dread about losing people.

HANAMURA: There are fewer kids now too, huh?

KAMIYAMA: Isn't that an issue with manga as well?

HANAMURA: There are a lot of series you can read for free now, but honestly, I just feel thankful that a lot of people still buy books.

KAMIYAMA: Manga hasn't really gone up in price either, has it? When I started buying manga in elementary school, individual volumes were about 380 yen, but it's almost forty years later and the price hasn't even doubled. Pork buns, on the other hand, have tripled in price. (laughs)

HANAMURA: Anime's in the same boat. Why is it that even though the quality of the content of anime and manga keeps improving, the price stays the same?